Jack C. Richards & Chuck Sandy

Passages
Third Edition

Teacher's Edition **2**

CAMBRIDGE
UNIVERSITY PRESS

CAMBRIDGE
UNIVERSITY PRESS

32 Avenue of the Americas, New York, NY 10013-2473, USA

Cambridge University Press is part of the University of Cambridge.

It furthers the University's mission by disseminating knowledge in the pursuit of education, learning and research at the highest international levels of excellence.

www.cambridge.org
Information on this title: www.cambridge.org/9781107627666

© Cambridge University Press 2015

This publication is in copyright. Subject to statutory exception and to the provisions of relevant collective licensing agreements, no reproduction of any part may take place without the written permission of Cambridge University Press.

First published 1998
Second edition 2008

Printed in Hong Kong, China, by Golden Cup Printing Company Limited

A catalog record for this publication is available from the British Library.

ISBN 978-1-107-62707-9 Student's Book 2
ISBN 978-1-107-62714-7 Student's Book 2A
ISBN 978-1-107-62715-4 Student's Book 2B
ISBN 978-1-107-62726-0 Workbook 2
ISBN 978-1-107-62734-5 Workbook 2A
ISBN 978-1-107-62780-2 Workbook 2B
ISBN 978-1-107-62766-6 Teacher's Edition 2 with Assessment Audio CD/CD-ROM
ISBN 978-1-107-62749-9 Class Audio 2 CDs
ISBN 978-1-107-62773-4 Full Contact 2
ISBN 978-1-107-62774-1 Full Contact 2A
ISBN 978-1-107-62777-2 Full Contact 2B
ISBN 978-1-107-62764-2 DVD 2
ISBN 978-1-107-68650-2 Presentation Plus 2

Additional resources for this publication at www.cambridge.org/passages

It is normally necessary for written permission for copying to be obtained in advance from a publisher. The worksheets and language summaries at the back of this book are designed to be copied and distributed in class. The normal requirements are waived here and it is not necessary to write to Cambridge University Press for permission for an individual teacher to make copies for use within his or her own classroom. Only those pages that carry the wording "© Cambridge University Press" may be copied.

Cambridge University Press has no responsibility for the persistence or accuracy of URLs for external or third-party Internet Web sites referred to in this publication and does not guarantee that any content on such Web sites is, or will remain, accurate or appropriate. Information regarding prices, travel timetables, and other factual information given in this work is correct at the time of first printing but Cambridge University Press does not guarantee the accuracy of such information thereafter.

Teacher's Edition art direction, book design, layout services, and photo research: Q2A / Bill Smith
Assessment materials design and layout services: Cenveo Publisher Services / Nesbitt Graphics, Inc.
Assessment materials audio production: John Marshall Media

Contents

Introduction

Plan of Student's Book 2 iv
Authors' acknowledgments viii
A letter from the authors ix
The new edition x
Core series components xi
Student's Book overview xii
Workbook overview xvi
Online Workbook overview xvii
Teacher's Edition overview xviii
Video Program overview xx
Presentation Plus overview xxii
Placement Test Program overview xxiii
Teacher Support Site overview xxiv
Introduction to the CEFR xxv

Teaching notes

1 Relationships T-2
2 Clothes and appearance T-10
3 Science and technology T-18
Units 1–3 Communication review T-26
4 Superstitions and beliefs T-28
5 Movies and television T-36
6 Musicians and music T-44
Units 4–6 Communication review T-52
7 Changing times T-54
8 Consumer culture T-62
9 Nature T-70
Units 7–9 Communication review T-78
10 Language T-80
11 Exceptional people T-88
12 Business matters T-96
Units 10–12 Communication review T-104

Grammar Plus 106

Vocabulary Plus 130

Additional resources

Grammar Plus answer key T-142
Vocabulary Plus answer key T-148
Language summaries T-152
Student's Book audio scripts T-164
Workbook answer key T-178
Video activity worksheets T-190
Video notes T-214
Video scripts T-238
Student's Book credits 250
Video activity worksheets credits 251

iii

Plan of **BOOK 2**

	FUNCTIONS	GRAMMAR	VOCABULARY
UNIT 1 Relationships pages 2–9			
A The best of friends B Make new friends, but keep the old . . .	■ Defining and describing friendship ■ Expressing opinions ■ Disagreeing politely ■ Stating preferences ■ Sharing advice about friendship	■ Phrasal verbs ■ Gerund and infinitive constructions	■ Adjectives and verbs to describe friendship ■ re- verbs
UNIT 2 Clothes and appearance pages 10–17			
A The way we dress B How we appear to others	■ Discussing approaches to fashion ■ Describing style and trends ■ Expressing opinions about clothing ■ Talking about first impressions ■ Describing outward appearance	■ Review of verb patterns ■ Cleft sentences with *what*	■ Adjectives to describe style ■ Adjectives to describe outward appearance
UNIT 3 Science and technology pages 18–25			
A Good science, bad science B Technology and you	■ Talking about scientific advances ■ Analyzing the effects of science and technology ■ Expressing caution and confidence ■ Describing technology troubles	■ Indefinite and definite articles ■ *-ing* clauses	■ Adjectives to discuss technology-related issues ■ Collocations to express different attitudes
UNITS 1–3 Communication review pages 26–27			
UNIT 4 Superstitions and beliefs pages 28–35			
A Superstitions B Believe it or not	■ Talking about personal beliefs ■ Comparing beliefs ■ Reporting what other people believe ■ Expressing opinions	■ Reporting clauses ■ Reporting clauses in the passive	■ Expressions with *luck* ■ Adjectives to describe truth and fabrication
UNIT 5 Movies and television pages 36–43			
A Movies B Television	■ Discussing movie trends ■ Expressing your attitude about trends ■ Discussing movie genre aspects and preferences ■ Discussing TV show preferences ■ Explaining the popularity of TV shows	■ Sentence adverbs ■ *Such . . . that* and *so . . . that*	■ Adjectives to describe movies ■ Types of TV programs
UNIT 6 Musicians and music pages 44–51			
A A world of music B Getting your big break	■ Sharing views on music ■ Expressing preferences ■ Comparing and contrasting ■ Defining success	■ Double comparatives ■ *Will* and *would* for habits and general truths	■ Collocations to describe music ■ Idioms used in the entertainment industry
UNITS 4–6 Communication review pages 52–53			

iv Introduction

SPEAKING	LISTENING	WRITING	READING
- Talking about what friends should have in common - Talking about the best way to meet people - Discussing ways to maintain friendships	- A talk about differences between friendships among men and friendships among women - A young woman describes a chance encounter	- Developing a thesis statement - Writing a composition with paragraphs supporting a thesis statement	- "How Social Media 'Friends' Translate into Real-life Friendships": Does social media encourage people to connect in real life?
- Discussing different opinions on fashion - Discussing how first impressions are formed - Discussing tips for making a good first impression - Discussing how people respond to appearance	- Three people describe their taste in fashion - Three people explain what is important for them when forming an impression	- Writing a composition about a personal belief - Giving examples to support a thesis statement	- "Overcoming a Bad First Impression": How to change a bad first impression
- Discussing the positive effects and negative consequences of technology and science - Discussing your feelings about new technology - Taking a survey about your relationship with technology	- A reporter and technology editor talk about the impact of driverless car technology - A comedian talks about difficulties he has had with technology	- Identifying essential information for a summary of a text - Writing a summary of an article	- "I Took My Kids Offline": A mother bans all technology at home for six months
- Describing superstitions from your country or culture - Discussing superstitions - Taking a survey about luck - Telling stories - Discussing hoaxes and why people create them	- Three people give explanations for some superstitions - Two people discuss a journalistic hoax	- Restating the thesis in the last paragraph - Writing a composition about superstitions	- "Do Good Luck Charms Really Work in Competitions?": The effectiveness of superstitious rituals in sports
- Talking about movie trends - Talking about the results of a survey on movie genre preferences - Discussing aspects of different movie genres - Discussing what makes a TV show popular - Discussing and presenting an idea for a new TV show	- Four people describe what makes some movie genres effective - TV network employees brainstorm and present ideas for new TV shows	- Identifying essential information for a movie review - Writing a movie review	- "*One Day on Earth*: A Time Capsule of Our Lives": A movie shot in every country of the world on the same day
- Talking about personal tastes in music - Talking about styles of music - Discussing the role of music in different contexts - Discussing advice for success	- Two people share their opinions on different types of music - A young woman gives her friend advice on his music career	- Writing a compare-and-contrast essay - Describing similarities and differences	- "On the Trail of Sixto Rodriguez": Searching for a musician who was famous and didn't know it

	FUNCTIONS	GRAMMAR	VOCABULARY

UNIT 7 Changing times pages 54–61

A Lifestyles in transition **B** A change for the better	- Discussing changes in lifestyles - Analyzing how changes affect different people - Discussing attitudes toward change	- Optional and required relative pronouns - *As if*, *as though*, *as*, *the way*, and *like*	- Prefixes to create antonyms - Collocations with *change*

UNIT 8 Consumer culture pages 62–69

A What's new on the market? **B** Consumer awareness	- Talking about bargain shopping - Comparing shopping preferences - Comparing shopping experiences - Stating reasons - Giving and asking for advice - Discussing effective advertising	- Placement of direct and indirect objects - Verbs in the subjunctive	- Expressions to discuss shopping - Marketing strategies

UNIT 9 Nature pages 70–77

A Animals in our lives **B** In touch with nature	- Discussing the role of animals - Talking about specific and undetermined time and location - Talking about categories and features of animals - Expressing opinions about animals - Discussing careers in nature	- *Whenever* and *wherever* contrasted with *when* and *where* - Noun clauses with *whoever* and *whatever*	- Physical features of animals - Nature-related idioms

UNITS 7–9 Communication review pages 78–79

UNIT 10 Language pages 80–87

A Communication skills **B** Natural language	- Talking about effective communicators - Comparing attitudes toward public speaking - Talking about language - Discussing correct language use	- Overview of passives - Subject-verb agreement with quantifiers	- Discourse markers - Idioms related to the use of language

UNIT 11 Exceptional people pages 88–95

A High achievers **B** People we admire	- Talking about people who have had an impact - Describing values - Organizing events chronologically - Describing the qualities of a good role model	- Compound adjectives - Superlative compound adjectives	- Compound adjectives related to the body - Phrasal verbs

UNIT 12 Business matters pages 96–103

A Entrepreneurs **B** The new worker	- Talking about successful entrepreneurs - Talking about hypothetical situations - Comparing and contrasting personal preferences - Expressing values and preferences in work and business	- Subject-verb inversion in conditional sentences - Adverb clauses of condition	- Prepositions following *work* - Expressions related to success in the workplace

UNITS 10–12 Communication review pages 104–105

GRAMMAR PLUS: Additional grammar practice and explanation pages 106–129

VOCABULARY PLUS: Additional vocabulary practice pages 130–141

SPEAKING	LISTENING	WRITING	READING
- Discussing trends - Talking about personal changes - Talking about the results of a survey on coping with change	- A corporate executive speaks about the attitudes of different generations in the workplace - Two people talk about a volunteer program	- Writing about a personal experience - Providing background information and giving details	- "Leaving the Rat Race for the Simple Life": Reflections on a major change in lifestyle
- Talking about the best ways to shop for different items - Discussing compulsive shopping - Discussing the ethics of undercover marketing strategies	- Two people talk about their shopping preferences - Three radio advertisements	- Supporting an opinion - Writing a composition using details and examples to support an opinion about shopping	- "Word-of-Mouth Marketing": Testing the power of word-of-mouth as a marketing strategy
- Discussing the ethics of using animals in different fields - Discussing a survey on ethics associated with animals - Discussing ways of being in touch with nature	- News reports on animals that help people - The manager of an eco-resort describes its features to a reporter	- Organizing information into clear categories - Writing a classification essay	- "A Summer Job that's a Walk in the Park": The daily tasks of a park ranger fellow in New York City
- Discussing the qualities of effective communicators - Discussing a survey on public speaking - Discussing opinions about language issues - Talking about "text speak" and its appropriateness - Role-playing different ways of speaking	- An expert gives advice on how to make effective presentations - Three one-sided conversations	- Persuasive writing - Supporting a position - Arguing against the opposing position	- "Slang Abroad": Different varieties of English
- Discussing people who have had an impact on the world - Discussing the qualities and values of exceptional people - Discussing quotations from high achievers - Talking about heroic behavior in everyday life	- A motivational speaker talks about the qualities of high achievers - Two people talk about others who have made a difference in their lives	- Organizing information in chronological order - Writing a biographical profile	- "Ann Cotton, Social Entrepreneur": Advice from a successful NGO executive
- Discussing successful companies - Discussing job advertisements - Discussing a survey on ideal working conditions - Analyzing the qualities of the ideal job - Discussing the qualities of a successful worker	- Two people discuss unsuccessful business ventures - Three people talk about workshops they attended	- Understanding the parts of a formal letter - Writing a formal letter	- "The Value of Difference": Individual differences in the workplace

Authors' acknowledgments

A great number of people contributed to the development of *Passages Third Edition*. Particular thanks are owed to the following reviewers and institutions, as their insights and suggestions have helped define the content and format of the third edition:

Paulo A. Machado, Rio de Janeiro, Brazil; Simone C. Wanguestel, Niterói, Brazil; Athiná Arcadinos Leite, **ACBEU**, Salvador, Brazil; Lauren Osowski, **Adult Learning Center**, Nashua, NH, USA; Brenda Victoria, **AIF System**, Santiago, Dominican Republic; Alicia Mitchell-Boncquet, **ALPS Language School**, Seattle, WA, USA; Scott C. Welsh, **Arizona State University**, Tempe, AZ, USA; Silvia Corrêa, **Associação Alumni**, São Paulo, Brazil; Henrick Oprea, **Atlantic Idiomas**, Brasília, Brazil; Márcia Lima, **B.A. English School**, Goiânia, Brazil; Carlos Andrés Mejía Gómez, **BNC Centro Colombo Americano Pereira**, Pereira, Colombia; Tanja Jakimoska, **Brava Training**, Rio de Janeiro, Brazil; Paulo Henrique Gomes de Abreu, **Britannia International English**, Rio de Janeiro, Brazil; Gema Kuri Rodríguez, **Business & English**, Puebla, Mexico; Isabela Villas Boas, **Casa Thomas Jefferson**, Brasília, Brazil; Inara Lúcia Castillo Couto, **CEL-LEP**, São Paulo, Brazil; Ana Cristina Hebling Meira, **Centro Cultural Brasil-Estados Unidos**, Campinas, Brazil; Juliana Costa da Silva, **Centro de Cultura Anglo Americana**, Rio de Janeiro, Brazil; Heriberto Díaz Vázquez, **Centro de Investigación y Docencia Económicas**, Mexico City, Mexico; D. L. Dorantes-Salas, **Centro de Investigaciones Biológicas del Noroeste**, La Paz, Mexico; Elizabeth Carolina Llatas Castillo, **Centro Peruano Americano El Cultural**, Trujillo-La Libertad, Peru; Márcia M. A. de Brito, **Chance Language Center**, Rio de Janeiro, Brazil; Rosalinda Heredia, **Colegio Motolinia**, San Juan del Río, Mexico; Maria Regina Pereira Filgueiras, **College Language Center**, Londrina, Brazil; Lino Mendoza Rodriguez, **Compummunicate**, Izúcar de Matamoros, Mexico; Maria Lucia Sciamarelli, **Cultura Inglesa**, Campinas, Brazil; Elisabete Thess, **Cultura Inglesa**, Petrópolis, Brazil; Catarina M. B. Pontes Kruppa, **Cultura Inglesa**, São Paulo, Brazil; Sheila Lima, **Curso Oxford**, Rio de Janeiro, Brazil; Elaine Florencio, Beth Vasconcelos, **English House Corporate**, Rio de Janeiro, Brazil; Vasti Rodrigues e Silva, **Fox Idiomas**, Rio de Janeiro, Brazil; Ricardo Ramos Miguel Cézar, Walter Júnior Ribeiro Silva, **Friends Language Center**, Itapaci, Brazil; Márcia Maria Pedrosa Sá Freire de Souza, **IBEU**, Rio de Janeiro, Brazil; Jerusa Rafael, **IBEUV**, Vitória, Brazil; Lilianne de Souza Oliveira, **ICBEU**, Manaus, Brazil; Liviane Santana Paulino de Carvalho, **ICBEU**, São Luís, Brazil; Manuel Marrufo Vásquez, **iempac Instituto de Enseñanza del Idioma Ingles**, Tequila, Mexico; Nora Aquino, **Instituto de Ciencias y Humanidades Tabasco**, Villahermosa, Mexico; Andrea Grimaldo, **Instituto Laurens**, Monterrey, Mexico; Cenk Aykut, Staci Jenkins, Kristen Okada, **Interactive College of Technology**, Chamblee, GA, USA; Imeen Manahan-Vasquez, Zuania Serrano, **Interactive Learning Systems**, Pasadena, TX, USA; Nicholas J. Jackson, **Jackson English School**, Uruapan, Mexico; Marc L. Cummings, **Jefferson Community and Technical College**, Louisville, KY, USA; Solange Nery Veloso, **Nery e Filho Idiomas**, Rio de Janeiro, Brazil; Tomas Sparano Martins, **Phil Young's English School**, Curitiba, Brazil; Paulo Cezar Lira Torres, **PRIME Language Center**, Vitória, Brazil; Angie Vasconcellos, **Robin English School**, Petrópolis, Brazil; Barbara Raifsnider, **San Diego Community College District**, San Diego, CA, USA; James Drury de Matos Fonseca, **SENAC**, Fortaleza, Brazil; Manoel Fialho da Silva Neto, **SENAC**, Recife, Brazil; Marilyn Ponder, **Tecnológico de Monterrey**, Irapuato, Mexico; Linda M. Holden, **The College of Lake County**, Grayslake, IL, USA; Janaína da Silva Cardoso, **UERJ**, Rio de Janeiro, Brazil; Gustavo Reges Ferreira, Sandlei Moraes de Oliveira, **UFES**, Vitória, Brazil; Nancy Alarcón Mendoza, **UNAM, Facultad de Estudios Superiores Zaragoza**, Mexico City, Mexico; Rosa Awilda López Fernández, **UNAPEC**, Santo Domingo, Dominican Republic; Vera Lúcia Ratide, **Unilínguas**, São Leopoldo, Brazil; Elsa Yolanda Cruz Maldonado, **Universidad Autónoma de Chiapas**, Tapachula, Mexico; Deida Perea, **Universidad Autónoma de Ciudad Juárez**, Ciudad Juárez, Mexico; Gabriela Ladrón de Guevara de León, **Universidad Autónoma de la Ciudad de México**, Mexico City, Mexico; Juan Manuel Ardila Prada, **Universidad Autónoma de Occidente**, Cali, Colombia; Lizzete G. Acosta Cruz, **Universidad Autónoma de Zacatecas**, Fresnillo, Mexico; Ary Guel, Fausto Noriega, Areli Martínez Suaste, **Universidad Autónoma de Zacatecas**, Zacatecas, Mexico; Gabriela Cortés Sánchez, **Universidad Autónoma Metropolitana Azcapotzalco**, Mexico City, Mexico; Secundino Isabeles Flores, Guillermo Guadalupe Duran Garcia, Maria Magdalena Cass Zubiria, **Universidad de Colima**, Colima, Mexico; Alejandro Rodríguez Sánchez, **Universidad del Golfo de México Norte**, Orizaba, Mexico; Fabiola Meneses Argüello, **Universidad La Salle Cancún**, Cancún, Mexico; Claudia Isabel Fierro Castillo, **Universidad Politécnica de Chiapas**, Tuxtla Gutierrez, Mexico; Eduardo Aguirre Rodríguez, M.A. Carolina Labastida Villa, **Universidad Politécnica de Quintana Roo**, Cancún, Mexico; Gabriela de Jesús Aubry González, **Universidad TecMilenio Campus Veracruz**, Boca del Rio, Mexico; Frank Ramírez Marín, **Universidad Veracruzana**, Boca del Río, Mexico.

Additional thanks are owed to Alex Tilbury for revising the Self-assessment charts, Paul MacIntyre for revising the Grammar Plus section, and Karen Kawaguchi for writing the Vocabulary Plus section.

A letter from the authors

Dear teachers and colleagues,

Together with Cambridge University Press, we have always been committed to ensuring that the *Passages* series continues to provide you and your students with the best possible teaching and learning resources. Accordingly, we always seek ways to add new tools and support to the course to make sure it not only reflects the best practices in language teaching, but also provides your students with the means to take their English to a whole new level.

Here are some of the things you can look forward to in the third edition:

- a fresh **new design**, **new images**, and **new and updated content** to reflect contemporary English usage

- more vocabulary support and practice with the new **Vocabulary Plus** section in the back of the Student's Book and the interactive **Online Vocabulary Accelerator**

- a new **Video Program** and accompanying **Video Activity Worksheets** to reinforce target language through compelling, real-world videos linked to unit topics

- a revised **Teacher's Edition**, now with an **Assessment Audio CD/CD-ROM** that features both ready-to-print and customizable quizzes and tests

- **new digital** resources to support teaching and enhance learning inside and outside of the classroom, including an **Online Workbook** and **Presentation Plus**, lesson planning and classroom presentation software

In addition, all the features that have made *Passages* one of the most successful English courses for upper-level students continue to be the hallmarks of the third edition:

- the same **trusted methodology** and proven approach
- relevant **thought-provoking, real-life content**
- **flexibility** for use in any teaching situation

We look forward to introducing you to the third edition of *Passages*.

With best wishes and warmest regards,

Jack C. Richards & Chuck Sandy

The new edition

Passages Third Edition is a fully revised edition of one of the most successful upper-level series for adult and young adult learners of English.

Based on the feedback from teachers and students from all over the world, the course has been thoroughly updated to ensure that it remains the innovative series that has successfully taken students to higher levels of achievement. There is new content in every unit, additional vocabulary practice, new readings drawn from authentic sources, and multiple opportunities for students to develop advanced writing, speaking, and listening skills.

What's new

Content – Virtually all of the readings are new, and many other sections are new or have been updated.

Vocabulary Plus – This new section in the back of the Student's Book provides additional vocabulary practice that students can do in class or as homework.

Communication Reviews – The statements in the Self-assessment charts are now aligned with the Common European Framework of Reference, allowing students to more effectively assess their ability to communicate.

Online Vocabulary Accelerator - This new powerful online learning tool will help increase the speed and ease of acquiring *Passages* vocabulary.

Online Workbook – The online version of the Workbook also includes extra video and listening comprehension activities.

Video Program – This all-new program includes short videos in a variety of real-life genres to reinforce and extend the language taught in each unit. Each video is supported by a photocopiable Video Activity Worksheet and teaching notes.

Presentation Plus – This powerful lesson planning and classroom presentation software conveniently combines the Student's Book, Workbook, Video Activity Worksheets, Class Audio, and Video Program into a single interactive component to help keep students engaged and focused.

Assessment Audio CD / CD-ROM – Oral and written quizzes for each unit, as well as progress tests, are available both as ready-to-print and customizable files. The audio program, audio scripts, and answer keys are also included on the disc.

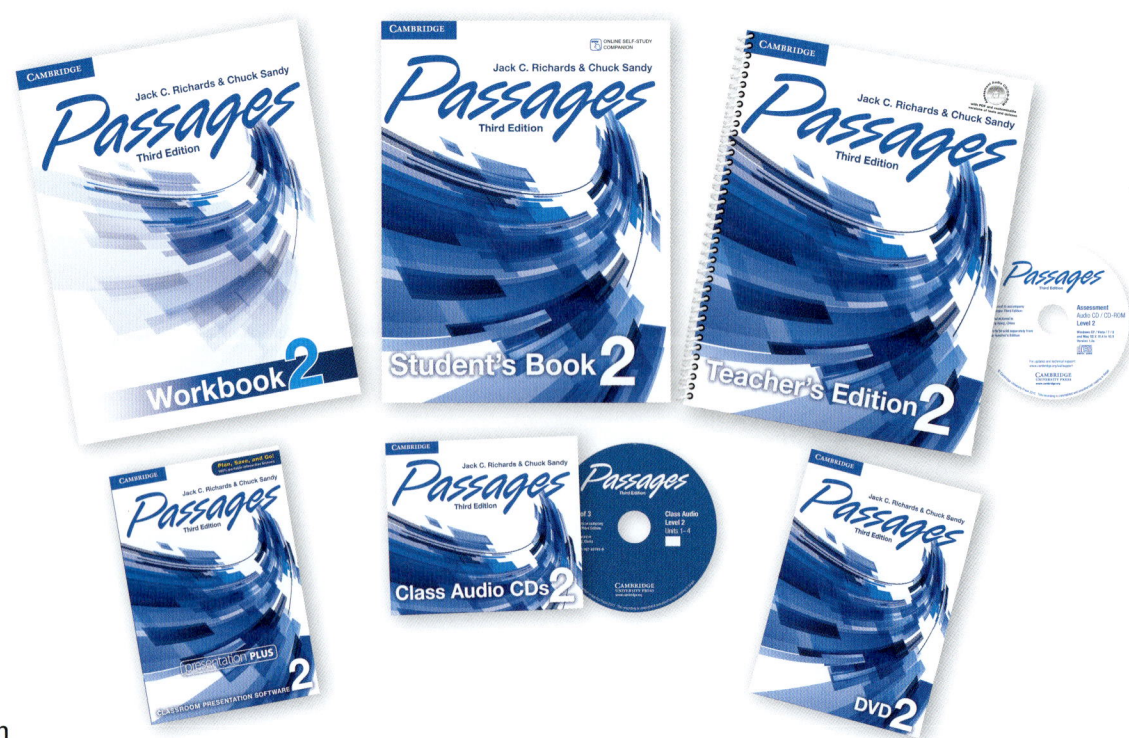

Core series components

Passages Third Edition has several tools that are designed to help you and your students take English to a whole new level. Here is a list of the program's core components.

COMPONENT	DESCRIPTION
Student's Book	The Student's Book is intended for classroom use and contains 12 eight-page units, 4 two-page review units, and extra grammar and vocabulary practice sections.
	It also provides access to extra interactive vocabulary practice with the *Passages Online Vocabulary Accelerator*.
Class Audio CDs	The Class Audio CDs are intended for classroom use. The CDs provide audio for all the listening sections in the Student's Book.
Teacher's Edition with NEW! Assessment Audio CD / CD-ROM	The interleaved Teacher's Edition with Assessment Audio CD/CD-ROM includes: • Page-by-page teaching notes with step-by-step lesson plans • Audio scripts and answer keys for the Student's Book, Workbook, and DVD • Language summaries of the new vocabulary and expressions in each unit • Photocopiable Video Activity Worksheets and video teaching notes • A complete assessment program, including oral and written quizzes, as well as progress tests, in both ready-to-print PDF and customizable Microsoft Word formats
Workbook	The Workbook's six-page units can be used in class or for homework. Each unit provides students with additional grammar, vocabulary, writing, and reading practice.
NEW! Online Workbook	The Online Workbook is an interactive version of the print workbook, optimized for online practice. It also includes extra video and listening comprehension practice. The Online Workbook provides instant feedback for students on hundreds of activities, as well as easy-to-use tools for teachers to monitor student progress.
NEW! Video Program	Videos for each unit offer compelling, thought-provoking content in a variety of real-life genres that reinforce and extend the language presented in the Student's Book. The photocopiable Video Activity Worksheets include comprehension and discussion activities, while the Video Notes include detailed teaching suggestions for both the worksheets and video projects.
NEW! Presentation Plus	Presentation Plus classroom presentation software makes it easy to plan and deliver more effective and engaging lessons and can be used on an interactive whiteboard, portable interactive software technology, or with a computer and projector. It is intended for classroom use and includes the complete Student's Book, Workbook, Video Activity Worksheets, Class Audio, and Video Program.
NEW! *Passages* Online Vocabulary Accelerator	The interactive Online Vocabulary Accelerator is a free self-study application that increases the speed and ease of acquiring *Passages* vocabulary through an innovative and dynamic environment. It includes the pronunciation, definition, and usage examples for every vocabulary item presented in each unit.
NEW! Online and Print Placement Test Programs	The Placement Test programs for *Passages* are available either in combination with *Interchange* or with *Four Corners* for the lower levels. The programs are available both in print and online, each including multiple versions of the test.

For a complete list of components, visit www.cambridge.org/passages3 or contact your local Cambridge University Press representative.

Student's Book overview

Passages Third Edition is a two-level course that helps high-intermediate and advanced students take their English to a whole new level.

Passages includes a range of activities that will:
- progressively **expand students' language abilities** in both formal and conversational contexts,
- **develop vocabulary** through collocations and word building exercises,
- **sharpen listening skills** through naturalistic recordings based on real-life interactions,
- **stimulate discussion** with thought-provoking topics and reading texts drawn from authentic sources,
- **build academic writing** ability.

The Student's Book is comprised of 12 units of instruction and practice, plus 4 communicative review units. A **Grammar Plus** section, conveniently located in the back of the book, includes more grammar explanations and practice, while a new **Vocabulary Plus** section provides additional controlled vocabulary activities. *Passages* also provides access to more interactive **vocabulary practice online**.

Each unit consists of two four-page lessons, each offering a variety of language-expanding activities. Below are representative sample pages from a typical unit.

4 SUPERSTITIONS AND BELIEFS
LESSON A ▶ Superstitions

1 STARTING POINT
The things people believe!

A Read the list of superstitions. Do you believe in any of them?

Beliefs Across Cultures

In Turkey, many people agree that when someone goes on a journey, you should pour water on the ground behind him or her to bring the person back safely.

In Brazil, people claim you should enter a place using your right foot to have good fortune.

In Russia, looking into a broken mirror will bring bad luck.

In Italy, many people believe that if visitors toss a coin into the Trevi Fountain in Rome, they will return to that city in the future.

In Japan, it is very bad luck to give a present that consists of four pieces.

In Venezuela, some people say that if someone passes a broom over your feet, you will never get married.

In Greece, you should place your shoes with the soles on the floor when you take them off because overturned shoes are considered unlucky.

B Pair work Which superstitions do some people in your culture believe?

2 VOCABULARY
Expressions with *luck*

A Match the statements with the replies containing *luck*.

1. "I've got to go. I have a big test tomorrow." ____
2. "I'm out of cash. Is there an ATM nearby?" ____
3. "He won the first game of chess he ever played!" ____
4. "He lost his job and house, and now he's sick." ____
5. "Are you going to Europe this summer?" ____
6. "How did you win those soccer tickets?" ____
7. "Thanks for the $20. Can I have $40 more?" ____

a. "That was beginner's luck."
b. "No such luck. I'm staying home."
c. "I'm afraid you're out of luck."
d. "Wow! He's got bad luck."
e. "Well, best of luck!"
f. "Don't push your luck."
g. "It was the luck of the draw."

B Pair work Use the expressions with *luck* to write short conversations. Act them out with your partner.

"I really want tickets to the Jay Z concert."
"I'm afraid you're out of luck. They sold out in 10 minutes!"

VOCABULARY PLUS see page 133

28 UNIT 4 Superstitions and beliefs

STARTING POINT
- Introduces the lesson's topic
- Presents new grammar in both formal and conversational contexts
- Gets students talking right away

VOCABULARY
- Presents vocabulary related to the lesson topic
- Emphasizes collocations, phrasal verbs, idioms, and prefixes and suffixes
- Helps students employ new vocabulary right away in meaningful spoken contexts
- More vocabulary practice provided in the new Vocabulary Plus section in the back of the book and in *Passages* Online Vocabulary Accelerator

GRAMMAR

- Presents the lesson's target grammar with clear examples and explanations
- Helps students notice examples of the target grammar in context and discuss reasons behind grammar rules
- Practices the grammar in communicative contexts
- More in-depth grammar work provided in the Grammar Plus section in the back of the book

SPEAKING

- Helps students use the target grammar and vocabulary in personalized tasks
- Expands students' talking time
- Teaches important discourse expressions such as disagreeing, showing empathy, and building consensus

LISTENING

- Provides pre-listening tasks, as well as opportunities for post-listening discussion
- Develops a variety of listening skills, such as listening for main ideas and details and inferring meaning from intonation
- Exposes students to realistic features of spoken English, such as verbal pauses

Introduction   xiii

6 WRITING
Persuasive writing

In persuasive writing, you take a position on an issue and try to convince the reader that your position is correct. To do so, you present both sides of the issue, providing arguments, reasons, and examples that support your point of view and show weaknesses of the opposing point of view.

A Read the article. What is the writer's position? What are the arguments for the opposing view? What arguments, reasons, and examples does the writer give to support his position and to show the weakness of the opposing viewpoint?

Every Student Should Be Required to Study a Foreign Language
by Leo Fernández

Recently, a student organization at our university proposed that we do away with our foreign language requirement, which mandates that all students complete two years of foreign language study. The main reason for this proposal seems to be to eliminate unnecessary courses; however, the proponents of this change are overlooking the great benefits foreign language study provides to students of any major.

Students who oppose the language requirement argue that university study should be more career focused. They feel that the language requirement steals time that could be spent on courses directly related to a student's major. This is a shortsighted position. Statistics suggest that candidates proficient in two languages have an increased chance of finding work. For example, . . .

Another point often made by the proponents of the change is that a large number of students who study a language for two years rarely use it again in their lives. While this may be true in some cases, study of a foreign language has been shown to further develop native language skills. In addition, the understanding of oneself and one's own culture is increased through contact with another language and its culture. Students who . . .

In conclusion, it is crucial that we keep the foreign language requirement. To eliminate it would be doing a great disservice to our university and its students. Foreign language learning benefits us in concrete and subtle ways as it broadens our minds and expands our opportunities.

B Pair work With a partner, take a position on one of these issues or use your own idea. Then brainstorm reasons supporting your position and weaknesses of the opposing view. Which reasons are the strongest?

- Schools should teach a second language starting in kindergarten.
- Every foreign language student should be required to study abroad.
- Institutions should be created to preserve dying languages.

C Write an article of at least four paragraphs supporting your position. Use the reasons you have brainstormed to support your position. Make sure to argue against the opposing view.

D Pair work Exchange articles. Discuss ways the writing could be made more persuasive and the arguments stronger.

WRITING

- Builds academic writing skills step-by-step, from writing a topic sentence to crafting an effective conclusion
- Gives students clear models for each writing task
- Reinforces process writing skills through writing tips, analysis of models, and peer-editing activities

---

6 READING
Technology and friendship

A Pair work Discuss these questions. Then read the article to compare your ideas with the author's.

1. What are some ways that interacting online might encourage people to connect in real life?
2. How could social media help shy students participate more in class?

HOW SOCIAL MEDIA "FRIENDS" TRANSLATE INTO REAL-LIFE FRIENDSHIPS

When social media first gained attention, I heard many people say online connections couldn't possibly be real friends. Some even feared people might trade face-to-face interaction for a virtual life online. But now the majority of the people I know consider at least some of their online friends to be like extended family. Which made me wonder – does social media actually encourage people to connect "in real life"?

One example of online life translating into real-life interaction happens on *Mashable*'s Social Media Day, when thousands of people attend in-person meet-ups to celebrate the power of online connections. Another example is location-based apps that help users connect face-to-face by allowing them to see who else has checked in at the same store, restaurant, or party – or even who is living in a city they plan to visit. They might then decide to seek each other out "in real life."

A Pew Internet and American Life Project report found that people using social networking sites have more close relationships and receive more support than others. They are also more likely to reconnect with old friends and use social networking to keep up with those they are already close to.

Other research shows that social media may also deepen what could otherwise be passing relationships. A study by Dr. Rey Junco found that college students who interacted with each other and their professors on Twitter were more likely to meet outside class to study. They also developed unexpected real-life connections and were also more likely to ask questions in class.

"What I find most fascinating is that I've consistently seen that students who start a course being more introverted and not speaking up during class discussions become more extroverted and participate more when encouraged to communicate through social media with their professors and their classmates," Junco said.

However, if social media does increase the likelihood of real-life interaction, it can also sometimes complicate it. When fans of social media meet face-to-face, their computers and mobile devices may actually make the meeting less productive. Instead of looking at each other, they may be glued to their screens!

Source: "How Social Media 'Friends' Translate Into Real-Life Friendships," by Terri Thornton, *Mediashift*

B Group work Discuss these questions. Then share your answers with the class.

1. In what ways are virtual friendships similar to and different from real-life friendships?
2. Would you be more or less willing to share ideas on social media than you would in class? Why?
3. What other issues and complications might come up when online friends meet face-to-face?

LESSON B Make new friends, but keep the old . . . 9

READING

- Presents a variety of text types drawn from authentic sources
- Includes pre-reading and post-reading tasks that develop skills such as skimming, scanning, and making inferences
- Promotes active discussion through personalization and critical thinking

xiv Introduction

GRAMMAR PLUS

- Explores each lesson's grammar concepts in greater depth
- Practices the grammar with controlled exercises
- Can be completed in class or assigned as homework

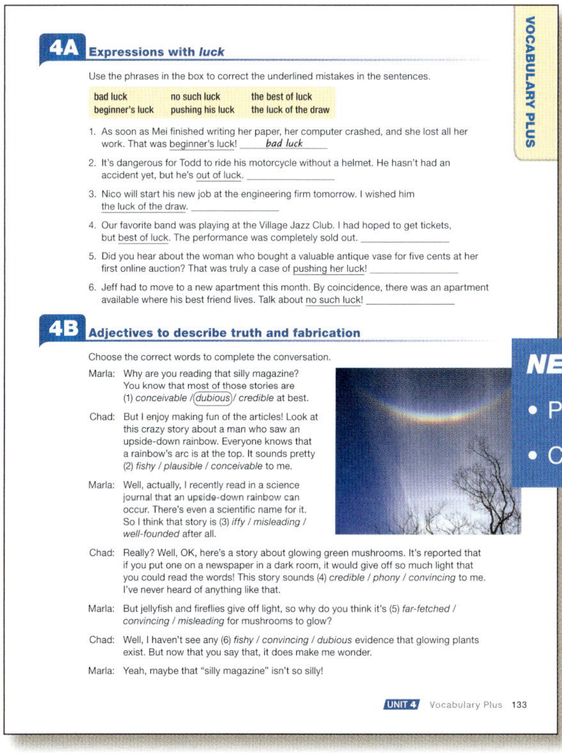

4A Reporting clauses

In reporting clauses, verbs such as *admit, agree, announce, comment, complain, confess, disclose, explain, inform,* and *reveal* are frequently followed by an indirect object. In this case, *that* should be retained for clarity.
Several people **agreed with me that** logic, not superstition, is the best way to make decisions.
Max **explained to the teacher that** a black cat never means bad luck in his country.

The following nouns are also often used in reporting clauses. Here, too, *that* is helpful in making the meaning clear and should be retained.

| accusation | assertion | comment | explanation | response |
| argument | claim | decision | remark | suggestion |

Bill made the **assertion that** he'd have no luck at all if it weren't for bad luck.
Liliana repeated her **argument that** only foolish people believe in magic.
The class rejected Niran's **suggestion that** we cancel class on Friday the 13th.

1 Using the words in parentheses, rewrite these sentences with reporting clauses in the simple past.

1. He had an irrational fear of spiders. (Luis / admit / his friend)
   Luis admitted to his friend that he had an irrational fear of spiders.
2. Some people really are luckier than others. (Min / agree / me)
3. There are too many pigeons in the park. (many people / complain / park staff)
4. He had spent his father's lucky dollar on candy. (Marco / confess / his mother)
5. It's bad luck to step on a crack in the sidewalk. (Marcie / explain / her little sister)
6. The day he met his wife was the luckiest day of his life. (Felix / announce / his wedding guests)

2 Combine the sentences using a reporting clause with one of the nouns from the grammar box.

1. Kim accused Anna of being a superstitious person. Anna didn't agree.
   Anna didn't agree with Kim's accusation that she was a superstitious person.
2. Gianna argues that everything happens for a reason. Many people disagree.
3. Leslie asserted that superstition is based in fear. Carlos didn't understand.
4. Jae-woo decided that a trip to Las Vegas was what he needed. We were surprised.
5. Ernesto commented that hard work is more important than luck. Lily repeated what he said.
6. Hiroshi claimed he had won the chess game thanks to beginner's luck. Sandra didn't believe him.
7. Patrick remarked that Tanya probably shouldn't push her luck. Tanya ignored what he said.
8. Mr. Wang responded that actions speak louder than words. I understood him.

4A Expressions with *luck*

Use the phrases in the box to correct the underlined mistakes in the sentences.

| bad luck | no such luck | the best of luck |
| beginner's luck | pushing his luck | the luck of the draw |

1. As soon as Mei finished writing her paper, her computer crashed, and she lost all her work. That was beginner's luck! **bad luck**
2. It's dangerous for Todd to ride his motorcycle without a helmet. He hasn't had an accident yet, but he's out of luck. _____
3. Nico will start his new job at the engineering firm tomorrow. I wished him the luck of the draw. _____
4. Our favorite band was playing at the Village Jazz Club. I had hoped to get tickets, but best of luck. The performance was completely sold out. _____
5. Did you hear about the woman who bought a valuable antique vase for five cents at her first online auction? That was truly a case of pushing her luck! _____
6. Jeff had to move to a new apartment this month. By coincidence, there was an apartment available where his best friend lives. Talk about no such luck! _____

4B Adjectives to describe truth and fabrication

Choose the correct words to complete the conversation.

Marla: Why are you reading that silly magazine? You know that most of those stories are (1) *conceivable /* **dubious** */ credible* at best.
Chad: But I enjoy making fun of the articles! Look at this crazy story about a man who saw an upside-down rainbow. Everyone knows that a rainbow's arc is at the top. It sounds pretty (2) *fishy / plausible / conceivable* to me.
Marla: Well, actually, I recently read in a science journal that an upside-down rainbow can occur. There's even a scientific name for it. So I think that story is (3) *iffy / misleading / well-founded* after all.
Chad: Really? Well, OK, here's a story about glowing green mushrooms. It's reported that if you put one on a newspaper in a dark room, it would give off so much light that you could read the words! This story sounds (4) *credible / phony / convincing* to me. I've never heard of anything like that.
Marla: But jellyfish and fireflies give off light, so why do you think it's (5) *far-fetched / convincing / misleading* for mushrooms to glow?
Chad: Well, I haven't see any (6) *fishy / convincing / dubious* evidence that glowing plants exist. But now that you say that, it does make me wonder.
Marla: Yeah, maybe that "silly magazine" isn't so silly!

NEW VOCABULARY PLUS

- Practices the vocabulary with controlled exercises
- Can be completed in class or assigned as homework

NEW ONLINE VOCABULARY ACCELERATOR

- Increases the speed and ease of acquiring new vocabulary
- Provides pronunciation, definitions, and examples of all the items presented in the Vocabulary sections of the Student's Book

Introduction xv

Workbook overview

The *Passages Third Edition* Workbook provides students with additional opportunities to practice the language taught in the Student's Book outside of the classroom. Each unit of the Workbook includes additional practice with grammar, vocabulary, writing, and reading.

GRAMMAR
Reinforces the unit grammar through both controlled and freer, personalized practice

VOCABULARY
Provides vocabulary practice based on the unit topic

WRITING
- Practices the writing skills presented in the Student's Book in step-by-step activities
- Includes model text for analysis and emulation
- Provides extra opportunity for freer, personalized practice

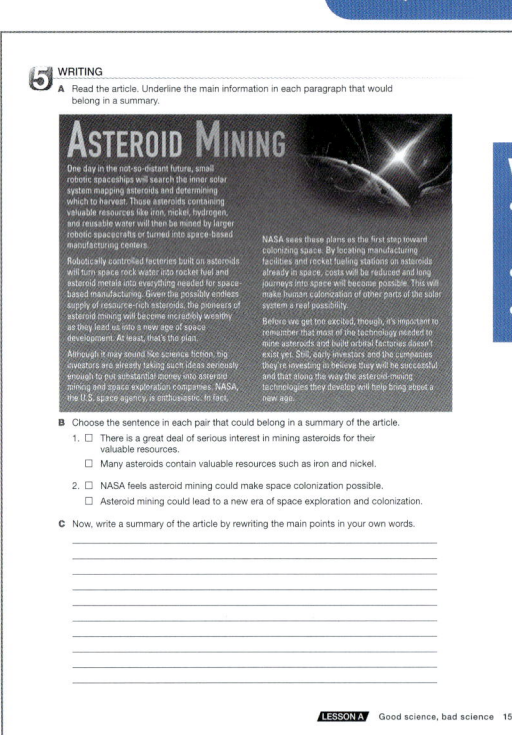

READING
- Gives additional reading practice based on the theme of the unit
- Introduces the text with a pre-reading task
- Reinforces reading skills used in the Student's Book

xvi   Introduction

Online Workbook overview

The *Passages Third Edition* Online Workbook provides additional activities to reinforce what is presented in the corresponding Student's Book. It provides all the familiarity of a traditional print workbook with the ease of online delivery. The Online Workbook includes:

- A variety of interactive activities, including video and listening comprehension, which correspond to each Student's Book lesson, allowing students to interact with workbook material in a fresh, lively way.

- Instant feedback for hundreds of activities, challenging students to focus on areas for improvement.

- Simple tools for teachers to monitor students' progress, such as scores and attendance, providing instant information, and saving valuable time for teachers.

- Intuitive navigation and clear, easy-to-follow instructions, fostering independent study practice.

The *Passages Third Edition* Online Workbooks can be purchased in a variety of ways. Please contact your local Cambridge University Press representative for more details.

Teacher's Edition overview

The Teacher's Edition provides complete support for teachers who are using *Passages Third Edition*. It includes every Student's Book page and comprehensive teaching notes for the units and review units.

It also contains answer keys for the Student's Book and Workbook, the Student's Book audio scripts, language summaries, photocopiable video activity worksheets, video teaching notes, and video scripts.

UNIT SUMMARY
Outlines the grammar and key topics and functions covered in the unit

TEACHING NOTES
- Include the learning aims for each exercise
- Provide step-by-step lesson plans
- Include answers and vocabulary definitions
- Indicate the Class Audio tracks and page numbers for the scripts

TEACHING NOTES
- Provide grammar notes and culture notes that give teachers more context for explanations

TEACHING NOTES
- Suggest optional activities for expansions and alternative presentations
- Indicate fresh ideas for alternative ways to present and review exercises and worksheets with fun games, extra readings, and projects
- Suggest materials students can use for further practice outside the classroom

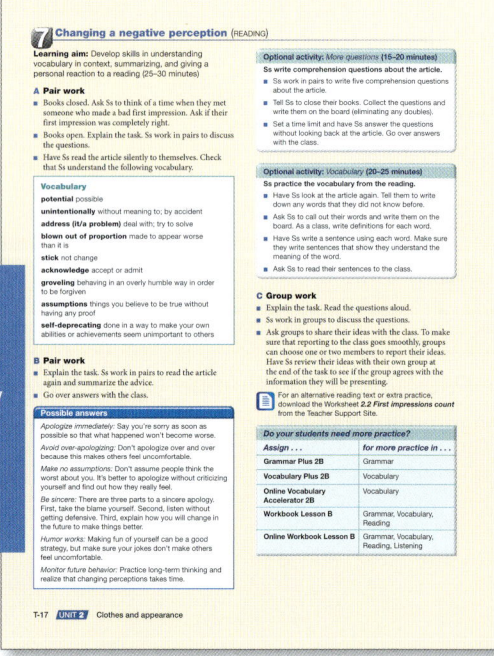

xviii   Introduction

The Assessment Audio CD/CD-ROM included in the Teacher's Edition contains oral quizzes, written quizzes, and progress tests, as well as the support audio, audio scripts, and answer keys. Administration guides and supporting materials are also included.

All the quizzes, tests, audio scripts, and answer keys are available both as ready-to-print PDFs and editable Microsoft Word files.

The audio is available both as MP3 files and as regular audio on the CD.

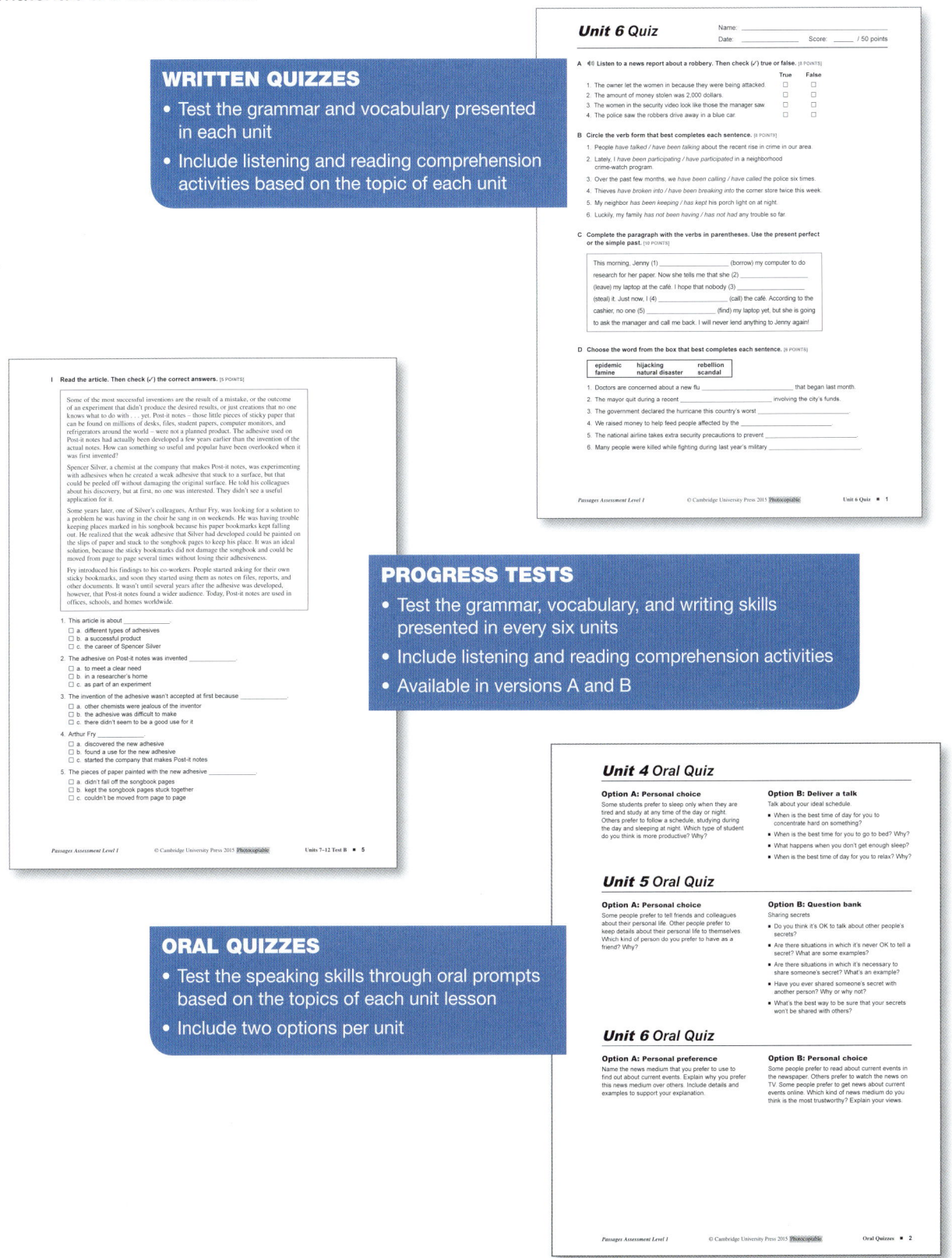

WRITTEN QUIZZES
- Test the grammar and vocabulary presented in each unit
- Include listening and reading comprehension activities based on the topic of each unit

PROGRESS TESTS
- Test the grammar, vocabulary, and writing skills presented in every six units
- Include listening and reading comprehension activities
- Available in versions A and B

ORAL QUIZZES
- Test the speaking skills through oral prompts based on the topics of each unit lesson
- Include two options per unit

Video Program overview

The **Passages Third Edition** Video Program complements each unit of the Student's Book, providing further practice with unit topics, grammar, and vocabulary in a relevant context.

The Video Program uses real-world genres, such as news reports, documentaries, video diaries, how-to clips, and interviews, as well as natural, real-life language. The videos model authentic spoken English, provide invaluable listening practice, create opportunities for discussion, and motivate students to make their own video projects.

Each video is supported by a video activity worksheet, video teaching notes, and the video script – all available in the Teacher's Edition.

VIDEO ACTIVITY WORKSHEETS

- Designed to facilitate effective use of the video in the classroom
- Include pre-viewing, viewing, and post-viewing activities that provide students with step-by-step support and guidance for understanding the events and language of the video segment:

  The *Before you watch* section activates previous knowledge and introduces the context and vocabulary necessary to understand and engage with the video.

  The *While you watch* section offers interesting activities to help students notice important facts, information, and events while watching the video.

  The *After you watch* section contains review and overall comprehension activities, as well as personalization activities that expand upon the content from the Student's Book and video.

- Available as photocopiables in the Teacher's Edition, as well as for classroom presentation in Presentation Plus

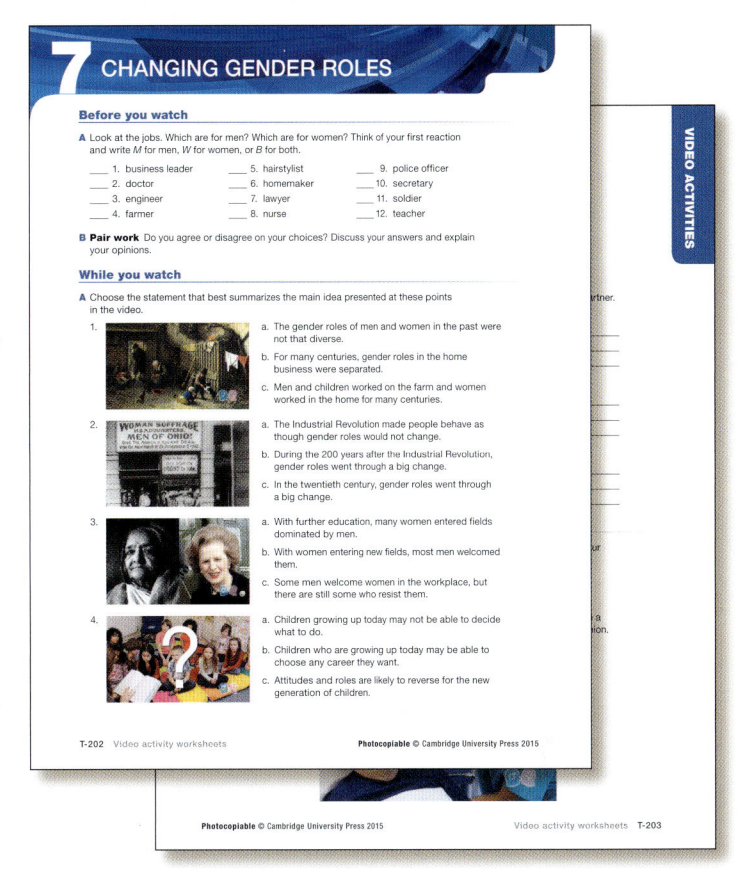

VIDEO NOTES

- Available in the Teacher's Edition
- Provide short summaries of the video and language points used
- Suggest step-by-step instructions and optional teaching ideas to work with the Video Activity Worksheets
- Include a Video Project assignment for each unit:

  The video project teaching notes provide step-by-step instructions and are structured into *Write the script* and *Make and share the video* sections to guide students as they create their own videos.

  They also include brainstorming tips, organizational ideas, and other suggestions for script writing and video making.

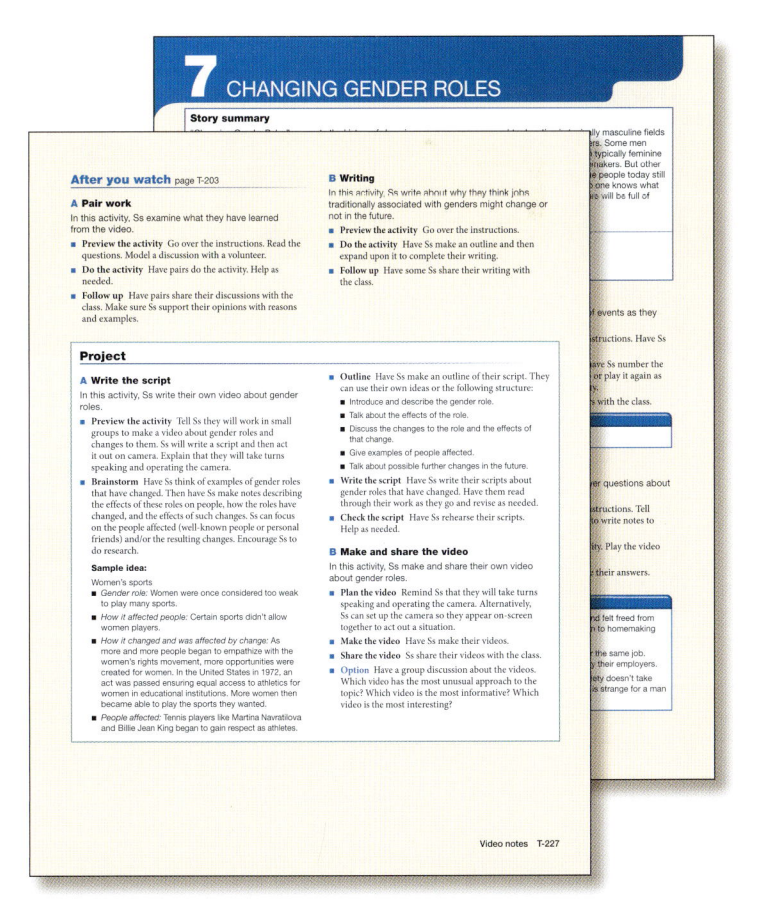

Introduction xxi

Presentation Plus overview

Passages Third Edition Presentation Plus combines the contents of the Student's Book, the Workbook, the Video Activity Worksheets, the Class Audio, and the Video Program into a convenient one-stop classroom presentation solution.

Plan, Save, and Go! Use this software to plan and create lively, engaging lessons ahead of time, which can be saved and uploaded later to any computer.

This software provides an effective medium to focus students' attention on the content being presented and practiced. It can also help promote their participation and interaction with the material in a more dynamic way.

This component simplifies several of the teaching tasks that take place in the classroom. You can use the software to play audio or video without having to use a separate CD or DVD player, reveal answers, zoom in on a page to more efficiently focus students' attention on an activity or image, annotate pages for future lessons, and even embed links to additional content.

xxii Introduction

Placement Test Program overview

The **Passages** Placement Test Program is available in combination with either the *Interchange* program or the *Four Corners* program. Each Placement Test Program is available both in print and online.

The print format provides three versions of an Objective Placement Test with Listening, three versions of a Placement Essay Test, and a Placement Speaking Assessment. An audio program, audio scripts, answer keys, and guidelines for administering the tests are included.

In the online version, all the questions have been optimized for Web delivery. The test also features a built-in reporting system to help you obtain students' placement test results immediately.

Please contact your local Cambridge University Press representative for more details.

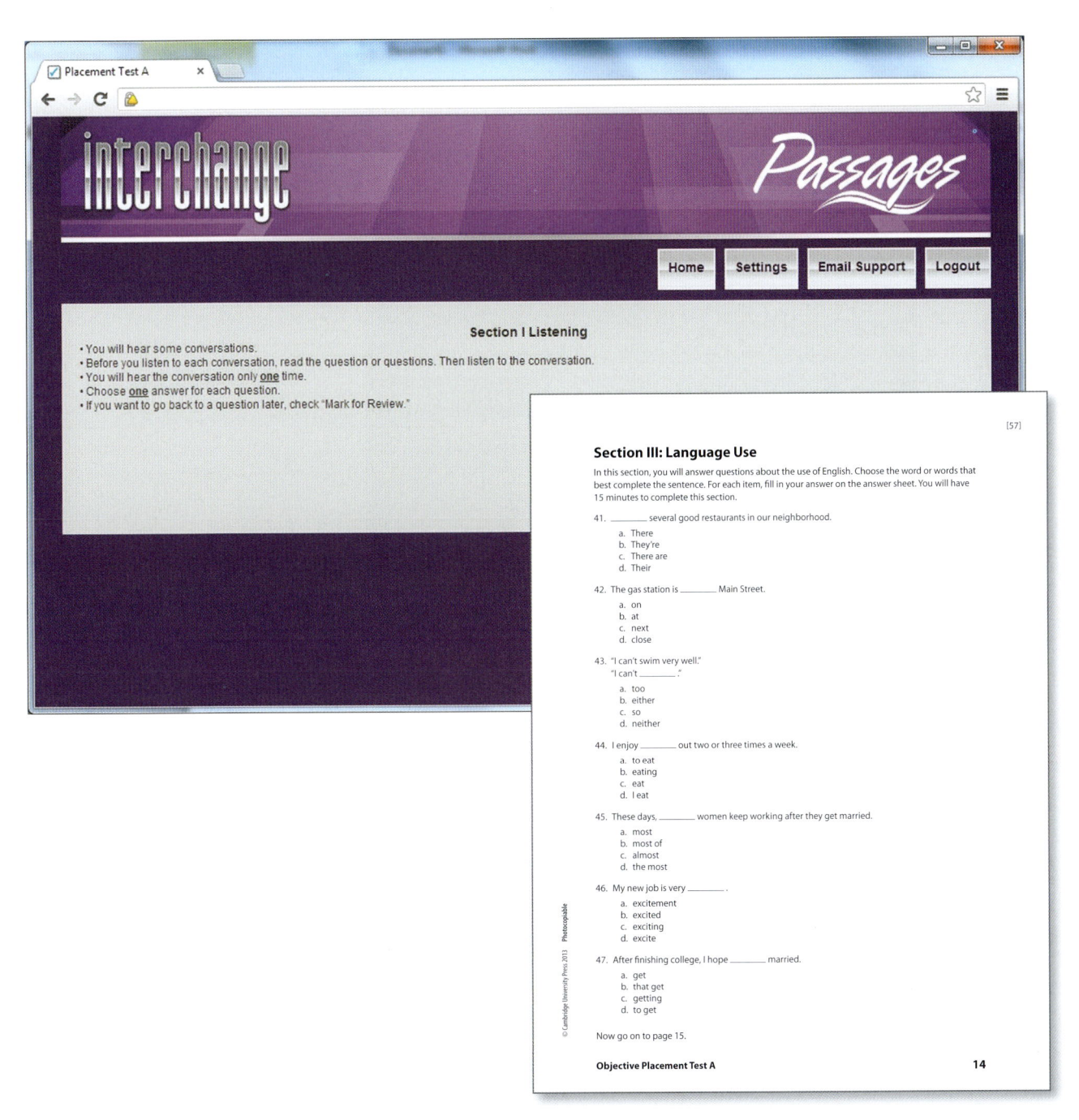

Introduction xxiii

Teacher Support Site overview

The **Passages** Teacher Support Site offers a variety of materials to assist the teachers using the series. It includes practical articles; author videocasts on methodology; correlations; language summaries; fresh ideas for optional alternative presentations and optional activities; and a number of downloadable worksheets with communicative games and activities, extra readings, and projects.

VIDEOCASTS
Provide useful information on methodology and practical tips

WORKSHEETS
- Game worksheets provide stimulating and fun ways to review or practice grammar, vocabulary, and speaking skills
- Project worksheets are engaging group research projects that offer collaborative and challenging task-based activities for students
- Reading worksheets give teachers an optional task for students to expand their reading skills
- All the downloadable worksheets are available both as ready-to-print PDFs and editable Microsoft Word files

FRESH IDEAS
Innovative ways to teach a variety of exercises in the Student's Book for more interactive and lively classes

Visit: www.cambridge.org/passages3

Introduction to the CEFR

Introduction to the Common European Framework of Reference (CEFR)

The overall aim of the Council of Europe's Common European Framework of Reference (CEFR) is to provide objective criteria for describing and assessing language proficiency in an internationally comparable manner. The Council of Europe's work on the definition of appropriate learning objectives for adult language learners dates back to the '70s. The influential Threshold series (J. A. van Ek and J. L. M. Trim, Cambridge University Press, 1991) provides a detailed description – in functional, notional, grammatical, and sociocultural terms – of what a language user needs to be able to do in order to communicate effectively in the sort of situations commonly encountered in everyday life.

Three levels of proficiency are identified: Waystage, Threshold, and Vantage (roughly corresponding to Elementary, Intermediate, and Upper Intermediate).

The Threshold series was followed in 2001 by the publication of the Common European Framework of Reference, which describes six levels of communicative ability in terms of competences or "can do" statements: A1 (Breakthrough), A2 (Waystage), B1 (Threshold), B2 (Vantage), C1 (Effective Operational Proficiency), and C2 (Mastery). Based on the CEFR descriptors, the Council of Europe also developed the European Language Portfolio, a document that enables learners to assess their language ability and to keep an internationally recognized record of their language learning experience.

Passages Third Edition and the Common European Framework of Reference

The table below shows how *Passages Third Edition* correlates with the Council of Europe's levels and with some major international examinations. A detailed correlation of *Passages* to the CEFR is available on the Teacher Support Site for download.

Interchange	Four Corners	CEFR	Council of Europe	Cambridge ESOL	IELTS	TOEFL iBT	TOEIC
Level Intro	Level 1	A1	Breakthrough				120+
Level 1	Level 1 / Level 2	A2	Waystage				225+
Level 2	Level 2						
Level 3	Level 3 / Level 4	B1	Threshold	KET (Key English Test)	4.0–5.0	57–86	550+
				PET (Preliminary English Test)			
Passages							
Level 1		B2	Vantage	FCE (First Certificate in English)	5.5–6.5	87–109	785+
Level 2		C1	Effective Operational Efficiency	CAE (Certificate in Advanced English)	7.0–8.0	110–120	490+ (Listening) 445+ (Reading)

Sources: http://www.cambridgeesol.org/about/standards/cefr.html
http://www.ets.org/Media/Research/pdf/CEFR_Mapping_Study_Interim_Report.pdf
http://www.sprachenmarkt.de/fileadmin/sprachenmarkt/ets_images/TOEIC_Can-do-table_CEFR_2008.pdf

1 RELATIONSHIPS
LESSON A ▶ The best of friends

1 STARTING POINT
The nature of friendship

A Read these statements about friendship. Can you explain what they mean? What other statements would you add to the list?

WHAT IS A Friend?

1. A friend is someone who brings out the best in you.
2. Good friends are always happy to help when you run into a problem.
3. A friend is someone who cheers you up when you're feeling bad.
4. True friends don't drift apart even after many years of separation.
5. A real friend will always stand up for you when others are putting you down.
6. Never be afraid to open up and ask a friend for advice. A true friend will never turn you down.
7. Make new friends, but hang on to the old ones.
8. Good friends are hard to come by, harder to leave, and impossible to do without.

"The first statement means a friend inspires you to show all your positive qualities."

B **Group work** Consider the statements in part A. What makes a good friend? Discuss with your group.

"In my opinion, a good friend is someone who makes you a better person. It's someone who brings out the best in you."

Useful expressions

Expressing opinions
In my opinion, . . .
I have to say that . . .
The way I see it, . . .
Personally, I (don't) think . . .

2 LISTENING & SPEAKING
Friendship among women and men

A Listen to a professor talk about author Deborah Tannen's ideas. In Tannen's opinion, what is the main difference between friendship among men and friendship among women?

B Listen again. According to Tannen, which of these things do male friends often do (*M*) and which do female friends often do (*F*)? Write the correct letter.

____ 1. are direct and to the point ____ 4. prefer to share factual information
____ 2. discuss daily life at length ____ 5. value activities over talk
____ 3. reveal private thoughts ____ 6. talk as a way to better understand their lives

C **Group work** Do you agree or disagree with Tannen's ideas about friendship? Why or why not?

"I have to say that I think some of her ideas seem to be accurate . . ."

1 RELATIONSHIPS
LESSON A ▶ The best of friends

> In this unit, Ss use phrasal verbs to describe and define friendships. They also practice gerund and infinitive constructions.

1 The nature of friendship (STARTING POINT)

Learning aim: Discuss the qualities of a good friendship and see phrasal verbs in context (10–15 minutes)

A
- Books closed. Introduce the topic by asking Ss to think of one of their good friends. Ask: *What positive qualities does he or she have?* Have Ss brainstorm and call out as many qualities as they can. Write them on the board.
- Books open. Explain the task. Read the statements and the example sentence aloud.
- Ss work in pairs or small groups to discuss the questions. Have Ss share their ideas and their own statements with the class.

B Group work
- Explain the task. Read the example opinion aloud.
- Point out the Useful Expressions box. Give an example of how to use each phrase.
- Ss work in groups to do the activity.
- Have groups share their opinions with the class.

> **Optional activity:** *Proverbs* (10–15 minutes)
>
> **Ss talk about friendship proverbs.**
> - Write the word *proverb* on the board. Explain that it is an old saying that usually gives advice for living our lives. Give a few examples of proverbs about friendship:
>   *A friend in need is a friend indeed.*
>   *Make new friends, but keep the old. One is silver, and the other is gold.*
> - Ss work in pairs or groups to think of other proverbs about friendship that they know.
> - Have groups share their proverbs with the class.

2 Friendship among women and men (LISTENING & SPEAKING)

Learning aim: Develop skills in listening for the main idea and details in a lecture (20–25 minutes)

A 🔊 [CD 1, Track 2]
- Explain the task. Read the question aloud.
- Tell Ss to listen for the answer to the question. Play the recording as Ss listen for the answer. Replay as many times as needed. Ss listen and check their answer.
- Go over the answer with the class.

> **Answer**
> According to Tannen, the main difference between friendship among men and friendship among women is that men and women communicate differently.

Audio script: See page T-164.

B 🔊 [CD 1, Track 3]
- Explain the task. Tell Ss to read the list of things male friends often do and female friends often do. Go over any unfamiliar vocabulary.
- Play the recording once as Ss listen. Play the recording again while Ss write the correct answers.
- Go over answers with the class.

> **Answers**
> 1. M   2. F   3. F   4. M   5. M   6. F

Audio script: See page T-164.

C Group work
- Explain the task. Read the example answer aloud.
- Ss work in groups to do the activity. Remind Ss to use the Useful Expressions from Exercise 1B.
- Have groups share their opinions with the class.

3 Phrasal verbs (GRAMMAR)

Learning aim: Practice using phrasal verbs to talk about friendship (20–25 minutes)

> **Grammar notes**
>
> Phrasal verbs are very common in English. The two-word verbs *show up* and *show off* illustrate how the meaning of a phrasal verb varies greatly depending on the particle.
> *I showed up late to my friend's party.*
> (Meaning: *I arrived late to my friend's party.*)
> *I was excited to show off my new ring.*
> (Meaning: *I was excited to attract attention to my new ring.*)
>
> Remind Ss that a transitive verb needs an object. An intransitive verb does not.
>
> Although intransitive verbs do not take an object, certain intransitive phrasal verbs followed by a preposition can take one. Compare:
> *When I look back, there are some great memories.*
> *When I look back on my childhood, there are some great memories.*

- Books closed. Write on the board:

  I showed up late to my friend's party.

  I was excited to show off my new ring.

- Have a S read the two sentences. Ask Ss to identify the particle in each phrasal verb. (Answers: *up* in *showed up*; *off* in *show off*)
- Books open. Discuss the information in the grammar box and read the example sentences.

A

- Have Ss look at the Starting Point on page 2 again. Explain the task and read the questions aloud. Go over answers with the class.

> **Answers**
>
> Separable:
> bring out, cheer up, put down, turn down
>
> Inseparable:
> run into, drift apart, stand up for, open up, hang on to, come by, do without
>
> Three-word verbs:
> stand up for, hang on to
>
> Intransitive:
> drift apart, open up

B

- Explain the task. Go over the example with the class. Ask Ss why both answers are possible. (Answer: because the phrasal verb *bring out* is separable)
- Ss work individually to complete the activity.
- Go over answers with the class.

> **Answers**
>
> 1. brought out the worst / brought the worst out
> 2. run into a friend
> 3. stand up for your friends
> 4. do without a cell phone
> 5. turn them down
> 6. hang on to your old friends
> 7. put down their friends / put their friends down

C Pair work

- Explain the task. Ss work in pairs. Have one pair read the example conversation to the class. Remind Ss to ask follow-up questions.
- Have pairs share their conversations with the class.

> **Optional activity:** *More phrasal verbs* (15–20 minutes)
>
> Ss practice more phrasal verbs.
>
> - Ss work in groups to brainstorm other phrasal verbs that they know. Write them on the board and go over the meaning of each one with the class.
> - Then have Ss return to their groups to write sentences for six or seven of the phrasal verbs on the board. Tell them to leave the phrasal verbs blank, in a similar way as the sentences in part B.
> - Have groups exchange papers. Give Ss a time limit to complete the sentences.
> - Have groups read their completed sentences aloud. Go over answers with the class.

To help Ss with the grammar in this exercise, download the Fresh Idea **Language hunters** from the Teacher Support Site.

T-3 UNIT 1 Relationships

3 GRAMMAR

Phrasal verbs

A phrasal verb is a verb plus a particle, such as *down*, *into*, *out*, or *up*.
The meaning of a phrasal verb is usually different from the meaning of its parts.

Separable phrasal verbs can take objects before or after the particle.
If the object is a pronoun, it always appears before the particle.
A friend is someone who **brings out** the best in you.
A friend is someone who **brings** the best **out** in you.
A friend is someone who **cheers** you **up** when you're feeling bad.

With inseparable phrasal verbs, the object cannot go between the verb and the particle.
Good friends are always happy to help when you **run into** a problem.

Three-word phrasal verbs have a particle and a preposition.
Make new friends, but **hang on to** the old ones.

Intransitive phrasal verbs don't take objects.
True friends don't **drift apart**.

GRAMMAR PLUS *see page 106*

A Look at the Starting Point on page 2 again. Can you find the phrasal verbs? Which are separable, inseparable, and/or three-word verbs? Which are also intransitive? Write them in the chart.

Separable	Inseparable	Three-word verbs	Intransitive

B Complete the questions with the phrasal verbs and objects in parentheses. Sometimes more than one answer is possible.

1. Have you ever had a friend who ___brought out the worst / brought the worst out___ (bring out / the worst) in you?

2. Have you ever _____ (run into / a friend) that you hadn't seen in a long time?

3. Do you usually _____ (stand up for / your friends) when other people criticize them?

4. Can you _____ (do without / a cell phone) and still keep in touch with friends?

5. When friends ask you for a favor, do you usually say yes, or do you _____ (turn down / them)?

6. Do you _____ (hang on to / your old friends) or do you drift apart as time goes by?

7. Some people like to _____ (put down / their friends) by insulting them. How would you feel if a friend did that to you?

C Pair work Discuss the questions in part B.

"Have you ever had a friend who brought out the worst in you?"
"Yeah, I once had a really messy roommate. She made me so angry."

LESSON A The best of friends 3

4 VOCABULARY
Describing friendship

A **Pair work** Complete the chart with the correct parts of speech.

	Verb	Adjective		Verb	Adjective
1.	admire		4.	empathize	
2.		beneficial	5.	endure	
3.	clash		6.		harmonious

B Choose the word from the chart in part A that best replaces the boldfaced words. Compare answers with a partner.

1. Ryan and Tina work to keep their friendship **free of conflict**. *(harmonious)*
2. Sometimes their opinions **are very different**, but they still get along.
3. They work to make their friendship **valuable and constructive**.
4. Having the same background helps them **understand and identify** with each other.
5. Ryan and Tina **think very highly of** each other's accomplishments.
6. Their friendship will certainly **last a long time**.

VOCABULARY PLUS see page 130

5 DISCUSSION
What should friends have in common?

A Look at the statements about friendship below. Do you agree with the statements? Add a statement of your own.

>> PEOPLE... Agree Disagree

1. who are close in age empathize with each other better.
2. with similar social backgrounds have more harmonious friendships.
3. who have similar values and beliefs have stronger connections.
4. with similar personalities have the most enduring friendships.
5. benefit from having friends with the same educational background.
6. should only mingle with friends who have the same interests.
7. from different cultures often clash with each other.
8. _____.

B **Group work** Share your opinions and explain your reasons.

"The way I see it, people who are close in age can empathize better with each other. They share many of the same experiences and understand each other."

"I see your point, but I don't think age is that important. If people like doing similar things, they can be good friends."

C **Group work** How many people agreed or disagreed with each statement? Report your findings to the class.

"Three of us agreed that friends who are close in age empathize with each other better..."

Useful expressions

Disagreeing politely
I see your point, but . . .
I see what you mean, but . . .
I'm not sure I agree.
Do you think so?

UNIT 1 Relationships

4 Describing friendship (VOCABULARY)

Learning aim: Learn and practice using verbs and adjectives to describe friendships (10–15 minutes)

A Pair work

- Explain the task. Read the words in the chart aloud. Ask Ss to suggest suffixes that indicate what part of speech a word is (e.g., *-ize* = verb; *-ous*, *-al*, *-able*, *-ic*, *-ing* = adjective).
- Ss work in pairs to complete the activity. Go over answers with the class.

Answers	
1. admire, admirable	4. empathize, empathetic
2. benefit, beneficial	5. endure, enduring
3. clash, clashing	6. harmonize, harmonious

B

- Explain the task. Read the sentences and example answer aloud. Answer any questions about vocabulary. Ss work individually to complete the activity.
- Ss work in pairs to compare answers. Go over answers with the class.

Answers	
1. harmonious	4. empathize
2. clash	5. admire
3. beneficial	6. endure

> **Optional activity:** *Best friends* **(10–15 minutes)**
>
> **Ss describe a relationship with a best friend.**
>
> - Tell Ss to think of one of their best friends, either from the present or past. Ask them to make a list of reasons why the friendship works (e.g., It's a harmonious relationship because we understand each other's moods and we have a lot in common.).
> - Ss work in groups to describe the friendship. Have Ss ask follow-up questions. Brainstorm follow-up questions as a class, if necessary.
> - Alternatively, have Ss think of two other people they know who are best friends and describe what they think makes the friendship so successful.

5 What should friends have in common? (DISCUSSION)

Learning aim: Talk about what friends should have in common and practice the lesson vocabulary (15–20 minutes)

A

- Books closed. Ask: *What does it take for two people to become good friends?* Have Ss call out their ideas. Write them on the board.
- Books open. Explain the task. Read the statements aloud. Make sure Ss understand the words *values* and *mingle*. Ask Ss to give a definition, an example, or a synonym for each.
- Ss work individually to complete the activity. Have a few Ss read the statement they added to the class.

B Group work

- Explain the task. Point out the Useful Expressions box. Give an example of how to use each phrase. Have one pair of Ss read the example conversation to the class.
- Ss work in groups to share their opinions and explain their reasons. Remind Ss to discuss the statement they added in part A and to ask follow-up questions.

C Group work

- Keep Ss in their groups. Explain the task. Read the example aloud.
- Ss work in groups to complete the activity. Have a S from each group report the group's findings to the class.

> **Optional activity:** *My friend and I* **(10–15 minutes)**
>
> **Ss talk about what they like to do with their best friend.**
>
> - Write on the board:
>
>   *Friends who play together stay together.*
>
>   Ask Ss to explain what the statement means.
> - Ss work in groups to talk about the kinds of activities they do with their best friends.
> - Have Ss report their answers to the class. Determine which three activities are the most popular with the class.

For more practice discussing this topic, download the Worksheet **1.1 Quotes about friendship** from the Teacher Support Site.

UNIT 1 Relationships T-4

6 Developing a thesis statement (WRITING)

Learning aim: Write a composition about a close friend and use a thesis statement (40–50 minutes)

A

- Tell Ss to read the information in the box at the top of the page. Ask: *What is a thesis statement?* (Answer: the sentence containing the main idea of the composition)
- Remind Ss that a thesis statement can be found at the beginning or at the end of the first paragraph and often includes a main idea or opinion that is further explained in the rest of the composition. Make sure Ss understand that each body paragraph of a composition should focus on only one aspect of the main idea. Each of those paragraphs has a topic sentence to present that aspect of the main idea.
- Explain the task. Ss work individually to read the composition and underline the thesis statement.
- Go over the answer with the class.

> **Answer**
>
> Our friendship shows that people who are very different can still have similar interests.

B

- Explain the task. Ss work individually to match the phrases with the correct paragraph.
- Go over answers with the class.

> **Answers**
>
> 4 why we have a close friendship
> 3 what we have in common
> 2 how we are different

> **Language note**
>
> Explain that the examples in the book show typical paragraph structure for a composition in English. Each paragraph has a topic sentence with the main idea, and the rest of the paragraph contains one or more examples to illustrate the main idea.

C

- Explain the writing task. Read the questions aloud. Remind Ss that after they finish their compositions, they should be able to answer those questions.
- Give Ss time to think of a thesis statement for their composition. Have several Ss tell the class their thesis statement. Have the rest of the class give any suggestions on how to improve each thesis statement.
- Ss work individually to write their paragraphs.
- Go around the class and help as needed.
- Ss work in pairs to exchange compositions and take turns answering the questions.
- Ss ask and answer follow-up questions and ask their partner about anything in the composition they don't understand.

> **Optional activity:** *Tell me more* (20 minutes)
>
> Ss write a paragraph about their partner's friend.
>
> - Keep Ss in pairs and have them take turns asking and answering questions about each other's friend. As a class, brainstorm questions to ask, if necessary.
> - Have Ss write a paragraph about their partner's friend based on the new information. Remind Ss to include a topic sentence.

Do your students need more practice?	
Assign . . .	for more practice in . . .
Grammar Plus 1A	Grammar
Vocabulary Plus 1A	Vocabulary
Online Vocabulary Accelerator 1A	Vocabulary
Workbook Lesson A	Grammar, Vocabulary, Writing
Online Workbook Lesson A	Grammar, Vocabulary, Writing

6 WRITING
Developing a thesis statement

> The first paragraph of a composition contains a thesis statement, which presents the main idea. The remaining paragraphs each have a single focus expressed in a topic sentence that develops the thesis statement.

A Read the composition. Underline the thesis statement in the first paragraph.

B Match each of the other paragraphs with the phrase below that best summarizes its focus.

___ why we have a close friendship   ___ what we have in common   ___ how we are different

1 My best friend, Eva, and I are different in many ways, but we have one important thing in common – we love to travel. Whenever I have the urge to explore a new place, I can always count on Eva to go with me. Our friendship shows that people who are very different can still have similar interests.

2 The differences between Eva and me are significant. Eva is an artist who loves to take photographs and draw pictures of the interesting things she sees. I am a marketing representative for a pharmaceutical company and spend a lot of my time estimating sales figures. Eva is a very impulsive person, and I'm very organized. She's very quiet, but I'm a very talkative person who enjoys telling stories.

3 Eva and I are both adventurous and love traveling. We discovered this shortly after we met several years ago. One day we were talking about vacations, and we found we had both visited many of the same places. We immediately made a plan to go to a nearby historical city the following weekend.

4 Although we are quite different in many ways, Eva and I have become close over the years, and we now have a very special and enduring friendship. Every time we get together, we always have so much to talk about and have the best time. One reason for this is that we share a love of travel and adventure. The other reason is that our differences complement each other, so we always get along well whenever we travel together.

C Write a composition about a close friend. Then exchange your composition with a partner, and answer these questions.

1. What is the thesis statement? Underline it.
2. Does each paragraph have a single focus? Write the focus for each in the margin of the text.
3. What else would you like to know about your partner's friend? Ask at least two questions.

LESSON A The best of friends 5

LESSON B ▶ Make new friends, but keep the old . . .

1 STARTING POINT
Meeting new people

A Read about how Yuan Lin, Brandon, and Jacob met new people. Which way of meeting people do you think is best?

Yuan Lin
"I decided to move to England last year. I felt really lonely at first. In fact, I regretted moving here. But I never gave up trying new things. Then, I saw an ad for a Chinese-English language exchange. It was a great way to meet cool people!"

Brandon
"I'd been planning to take a class, but was putting off enrolling. Well, last month I started taking a cooking class. I never expected to meet so many nice people! Some of us get together at each other's homes and practice what we learn. We've become really good friends!"

Jacob
"I didn't know many people at my new job, but I kept being invited by my co-workers to a lunchtime yoga class. I'm so glad I finally said yes! A couple of my colleagues play soccer, too, and they're considering starting a company team!"

"A language exchange is a great idea. You can meet people who are interested in languages and culture, so everyone already has something in common."

B Group work What other ways of meeting new people can you suggest to someone in these situations? Add another situation to the list.

Someone who . . .

- moved to a new neighborhood
- has little free time
- started a new job
- is very shy
- is over 65 years old
- _____

2 LISTENING
A chance meeting

A Pair work When was the last time you unexpectedly ran into someone you know? Tell your partner about your experience.

🔊 **B** Listen to Dena talk about how she met her friend Kate. Where were they when they first met? Where did they meet again?

🔊 **C** Listen again. Then answer the following questions.

1. Why were Dena and Kate going to Los Angeles?
2. What did Dena regret after she said good-bye to Kate?
3. How much time passed between their first and second meetings?
4. How did Samantha, the guest at the party, know Kate?

6   UNIT 1   Relationships

LESSON B ▶ Make new friends, but keep the old . . .

1 Meeting new people (STARTING POINT)

Learning aim: Discuss ways of meeting new people and see gerund and infinitive constructions in context (10–15 minutes)

A

- Books closed. Ask: *What are some good places to meet new friends?* Write Ss' ideas on the board.
- Books open. Have Ss look at the pictures. Ask them where they think each person met their friends.
- Read the texts aloud. Check that Ss understand the following vocabulary.

> **Vocabulary**
>
> **language exchange** the practice in which speakers of different languages meet to talk first in one language, then in the other
>
> **putting off** not doing (something) until a later time
>
> **enrolling** signing up for
>
> **yoga** physical and mental exercises; originated in India
>
> **colleagues** people who work together

- Have a S read the example answer aloud. Ss work individually to think of their answers to the question.
- Have Ss report their answers to the class.

> **Culture note**
>
> In the United States, it is common to make friends at work and in school. Other popular ways include joining book discussion clubs, playing sports, joining a gym, or doing volunteer work (e.g., working at an animal shelter, helping a local charity, or cleaning up local parks).

B Group work

- Explain the task. Read the situations aloud. Brainstorm another situation as a class, if necessary.
- Ss work in groups to add another situation to the list and suggest ways to meet people in each situation.
- Have groups report their suggestions to the class.

2 A chance meeting (LISTENING)

Learning aim: Develop skills in listening for gist and details (15–20 minutes)

A Pair work

- Ask Ss to define *chance meeting*. (Answer: meeting someone without first planning to do so) Ask Ss to give examples.
- Explain the task and read the question. Ss work in pairs to tell each other about their experiences.
- Have Ss share their partner's experience with the class.

B 🔊 [CD 1, Track 4]

- Explain the task. Read the questions aloud. Ask Ss to predict what kinds of things Dena will talk about. Check that Ss understand the following vocabulary.

> **Vocabulary**
>
> **a bunch** a group
>
> **to make a long story short** a common expression that means the whole story is longer and has more detail, but the speaker is only going to tell the end result

- Play the recording as Ss listen for the answers to the questions. Replay as many times as needed. Ss listen and check their answers.

- Go over answers with the class.

> **Answers**
>
> They first met on a plane.
> They met again at a party.

Audio script: See page T-164.

C 🔊 [CD 1, Track 5]

- Explain the task. Read the questions aloud.
- Play the recording as Ss listen for the answers to the questions. Replay as many times as needed. Ss listen and check their answers.
- Go over answers with the class.

> **Answers**
>
> 1. Dena was going to Los Angeles for work. Kate was going to Los Angeles to take a connecting flight to Monterey.
> 2. Dena regretted that she had forgotten to ask for Kate's email address or telephone number.
> 3. Three months.
> 4. They had been roommates in college.

Audio script: See page T-164.

3 Gerund and infinitive constructions (GRAMMAR)

Learning aim: Practice using gerund and infinitive constructions (20–25 minutes)

> **Grammar notes**
> In verb + verb complement constructions, the first verb can be followed by a gerund, an infinitive, or either one. This depends on what the first verb is.
>
> Some verbs (e.g., *love*, *hate*) can be followed by either a gerund or an infinitive with no difference in meaning.
>
> Some other verbs can be followed by either a gerund or an infinitive but have a difference in meaning. For example, when the verb *regret* is followed by the infinitive of verbs such as *say* or *announce*, it is a formal way of introducing bad news.
> *I regret to say she's not coming home.*
> (*I'm sorry to say she's not coming home.*)
> However, when *regret* is followed by a gerund, it means to be sorry for something that has been said or done.
> *I regret telling her that.*
> (*I'm sorry I told her that.*)
>
> In passive sentences, *being* or *to be* follows the first verb. The past participle of the second verb follows *being / to be*.

- Books closed. Write the terms *gerund* and *infinitive* on the board and review how to form them.
- Write these categories on the board:
  sports   hobbies   other activities
  Ss work in groups to think of as many verbs as they can for each category. Have a S from each group report the group's list to the class.
- Tell Ss to use the verbs they brainstormed to talk about activities they love, hate, or like. Explain that these verbs can be followed by a gerund or an infinitive. Give Ss a few examples: *I hate camping. I love to swim in the ocean.* Have groups make as many sentences as they can within a time limit.
- Books open. Discuss the information in the grammar box and read the example sentences.

A
- Have Ss look at the Starting Point on page 6 again. Explain the task and read the question aloud. Go over answers with the class.

> **Answers**
> regretted (followed by a gerund)
> planning (followed by an infinitive)

B
- Explain the task. Ss work individually to choose the correct form of each verb.
- Then Ss work in pairs to compare their answers. Go over answers with the class.

> **Answers**
> 1. to have
> 2. to make
> 3. changing
> 4. trying
> 5. to create
> 6. to wear / wearing
> 7. to change
> 8. leaving
> 9. to move
> 10. sharing
> 11. having

C Pair work
- Explain the task. Read the beginning of each sentence and have a S read the example sentence aloud. Tell Ss to use their own ideas to complete the sentences and add details.
- Ss work individually to complete the activity. Then Ss work in pairs to share their answers. Go over answers with the class.

> **Optional activity:** *Sentence correction* **(15 minutes)**
> Ss have additional practice with gerunds and infinitives.
> - Collect Ss' sentences from part C. Write several of the sentences on the board, but change some of them so that the gerund or infinitive is used incorrectly.
> - Set a time limit and have Ss work individually to decide which sentences are correct and to revise the incorrect ones.
> - Go over answers with the class and see which S has the most correct answers.

3 GRAMMAR

Gerund and infinitive constructions

These verbs are normally followed by a gerund: *appreciate, consider, enjoy, give up, keep, put off, suggest*.
They're **considering starting** a company team!

These verbs are normally followed by an infinitive: *ask, decide, expect, intend, need, refuse, seem, tend*.
I never **expected to meet** so many nice people!

These verbs are followed by either a gerund or an infinitive: *begin, bother, continue, hate, prefer, start*.
Last month I **started taking / to take** a cooking class.

Infinitives and gerunds can also occur in the passive voice. They follow the pattern subject + verb + *being / to be* + past participle.
I **kept being invited** by my co-workers to a lunchtime yoga class.
She **asked to be chosen** for the job.

GRAMMAR PLUS see page 107

A Look at the Starting Point on page 6 again. Can you find another verb followed by a gerund and another verb followed by an infinitive?

B Choose the correct form of the verbs. Sometimes both answers are possible.

Monday, March 18

I've never been a really popular guy. I'm the type of person who tends **1** *to have / having* one or two good friends rather than lots of acquaintances. Well, when I moved away from my hometown after getting a job in Denver, I really needed **2** *to make / making* some new friends. Because I'm shy, I considered **3** *to change / changing* my personality to become more outgoing. But that was very difficult for me. Just the same, I didn't give up **4** *to try / trying*. I decided **5** *to create / creating* a new image for myself. I bought myself some new shoes, new clothes, and I even got a new haircut and started **6** *to wear / wearing* contact lenses. However, it didn't seem **7** *to change / changing* anything. I was beginning to regret **8** *to leave / leaving* my hometown when, all of a sudden, I got a call from my old friend Jim. He was planning **9** *to move / moving* here pretty soon. He wanted some advice about finding an apartment in the city, and I suggested **10** *to share / sharing* an apartment with me. Well, he agreed! I really enjoy **11** *to have / having* someone to spend time with, and together we've made a lot of new friends.

Posted by DenverDan **2 COMMENTS**

C **Pair work** Complete these sentences with your own information, and add details. Then compare with a partner.

1. I don't like it when friends refuse . . .
   to do small favors for me, like lending me a book. It's so rude.
2. It can be annoying when friends expect . . .
3. I couldn't say no if a friend suggested . . .
4. When I'm with my good friends, I don't bother . . .

LESSON B Make new friends, but keep the old . . . 7

4 VOCABULARY
re- verbs

A Which word best completes these sentences? Write the correct letter.

a. rebuild   c. reconnect   e. rehash   g. replace
b. recall   d. redefine   f. rekindle   h. resurface

1. You can _f_ old friendships by sharing memories.
2. Don't ___ old arguments over and over.
3. People often ___ themselves, but they're essentially the same.
4. A close friend is impossible to ___.
5. Can you ___ the first time you met your best friend?
6. Friends you think are gone forever sometimes ___ unexpectedly.
7. Visit your hometown and ___ with your roots.
8. It takes time to ___ a damaged friendship.

B **Pair work** What other *re-* verbs do you know? How would you define them? Compare your list with a partner.

Recapture, reconsider, . . .

VOCABULARY PLUS see page 130

5 DISCUSSION
Friendship maintenance

A Look at these ideas for maintaining friendships. Choose three that you think are the most important.

Advice for Maintaining FRIENDSHIPS

▶ Praise your friends often and keep a positive, optimistic attitude when you're around them.
▶ Never betray a friend's trust – it can cause real resentment.
▶ Try to be completely honest with your friends at all times.
▶ Don't hold unkind words against a friend. Consider any problems he or she has that might be the cause of the hurtful words.
▶ Use social media to help you feel connected to friends but not to replace face time.
▶ Be a good listener and try to empathize with your friends.
▶ Respect your friends' point of view even when you disagree. Don't rehash old arguments.
▶ Watch out for "unhealthy" friendships. Sometimes it's better to end a friendship and move on with your life.

B **Group work** Tell your group which three pieces of advice you chose, and explain why. Then share any other ideas you have about maintaining friendships.

"Well, I think it's important to always be completely honest with your friends. If you aren't honest with your friends, they might not be honest with you."

Useful expressions

Agreeing on importance
Well, I think it's important . . .
Yeah, that's true, but even more important is . . .
And let's not forget . . .
You're right . . . is also quite important.

4 re- verbs (VOCABULARY)

Learning aim: Learn and practice using the prefix *re-*
(10–15 minutes)

A

- Books closed. Write on the board:

  paint, repaint   make, remake

  Explain that a prefix is added to the start of a root word to change the word's meaning. Give an example sentence for each *re-* word on the board. Ask: *What does the prefix* re- *mean in these examples?* (Answer: do again)

- Write on the board: *return.* Tell Ss that *re-* can also give the idea of *back*. Tell Ss that when they return to a place, they "turn back" to it.

- Books open. Explain the task. Read the verbs aloud and go over any unfamiliar vocabulary.

- Ss work individually to complete the activity. Go over answers with the class.

Answers			
1. f	3. d	5. b	7. c
2. e	4. g	6. h	8. a

B Pair work

- Explain the task. Provide definitions and/or example sentences for the example verbs, if necessary (e.g., *recapture* means take something into your possession again; *The police recaptured the criminal after he escaped.*).

- Ss work individually to make a list of *re-* verbs with their definitions or example sentences. Tell Ss that their example sentences should show that they understand the meaning of the word. Ss then work in pairs to compare their lists.

- Have Ss report their partner's list to the class. Write the words on the board.

> **Language note**
>
> Explain that *re-* is not always a prefix. Some English words simply start with the letters *re-* (e.g., *reality, regular, recent*, etc.).

> **Optional activity:** Re- *words* (10–15 minutes)
>
> Ss think of other words with the prefix *re-*.
>
> - Ask Ss to think of other *re-* words that are not verbs, such as nouns and adjectives (e.g., *replacement, recycled*, etc.). Brainstorm a list as a class and write them on the board, if necessary.
>
> - Set a time limit and have Ss write as many sentences as they can using the *re-* words. Explain that the sentences must show that they understand the meaning of the words. For example: The sentence *His recollection was not good* does not show an understanding of *recollection*, but the following sentences do: *His recollection of their childhood together was not good. She had to remind him of many things.*
>
> - Have Ss read their sentences to the class.

5 Friendship maintenance (DISCUSSION)

Learning aim: Talk about maintaining a friendship
(15–20 minutes)

A

- Books closed. Ask: *What does "maintain a friendship" mean?* Elicit answers. Ask: *How do you maintain your friendships?* Have Ss call out their ideas, and write them on the board.

- Books open. Explain the task. Read the advice aloud. Check that Ss understand the following vocabulary.

> **Vocabulary**
>
> **betray (a person's) trust** fail to help someone or keep someone's secrets when needed
>
> **face time** time spent with someone in person
>
> **unhealthy** not good for emotional or psychological well-being (in this context)

- Ss work individually to complete the activity.

B Group work

- Explain the task. Point out the Useful Expressions box. Give an example of how to use each phrase. Have a S read the example answer aloud.

- Ss work in groups to discuss their choices from part A.

- Have a S from each group report on the group's discussion to the class.

> For more practice discussing this topic, download the Worksheet **1.2 The meaning of friendship** from the Teacher Support Site.

UNIT 1 Relationships T-8

6 Technology and friendship (READING)

Learning aim: Develop skills in understanding vocabulary in context, making inferences, and giving a personal reaction to a reading (25–30 minutes)

A Pair work

- Books closed. Ask Ss what social media sites they use. Ask them what they use the sites for and how often they use them.
- Books open. Explain the task. Ss work in pairs to discuss the questions.
- Ask Ss to share their answers with the class.
- Have Ss read the article silently to themselves. Check that Ss understand the following vocabulary.

Vocabulary

virtual life doing everything online; interacting with others and doing everyday actions only through a computer, not face-to-face

extended family relatives

in-person meet-ups a meeting with people in real, face-to-face situations

passing temporary and superficial

introverted shy, quiet

extroverted outgoing

likelihood the chance that something will happen

be glued to be looking at something without paying attention to anything else

- Go over the answers with the class. Ask Ss if they were surprised by what they read.

Possible answers

1. On *Mashable*'s Social Media Day, there are in-person meet-ups. Location-based apps help users connect face-to-face when they see who else has checked in at the same location.
2. Shy students who get to know their professors and classmates better as they communicate more through social media become more extroverted and participate more in class.

B Group work

- Explain the task. Read the questions aloud.
- Ss work in groups to discuss the questions.
- Ask groups to share their ideas with the class. To make sure that reporting to the class goes smoothly, have groups choose one or two members to report their ideas. Ask Ss to review their ideas with the group at the end of the task to see if the group agrees with the information they will be presenting.

Possible answers

1. Both virtual and real-life friends can seem like extended family members. Virtual interactions can deepen real-life friendships that might have otherwise been short-term. People may connect with old friends online that they otherwise would not have. Virtual friends may never meet face-to-face. If they don't live close to one another, they'll rarely, if ever, hang out together or go to a celebration together.
2. *Answers will vary*.
3. People may not feel as connected once they actually meet face-to-face, and the situation could be awkward. Their mobile devices may make the meeting less productive, as the "friends" might not look at each other but be glued to their screens. People may assume things about others online, and others may not live up to their expectations when they meet in person.

Optional activity: Class debate (15–20 minutes)

Ss have a debate about how technology is changing friendships.

- Write on the board:

    Technology is hurting friendships by making them more superficial.

- Divide the class into two groups: A and B. Tell group A to think of as many reasons as they can in favor of the statement. Tell group B to think of as many reasons as they can against the statement.
- Give Ss time to think of reasons individually. Then Ss work in groups to discuss their reasons.
- Have each group take turns presenting their ideas to the class.

Do your students need more practice?

Assign . . .	for more practice in . . .
Grammar Plus 1B	Grammar
Vocabulary Plus 1B	Vocabulary
Online Vocabulary Accelerator 1B	Vocabulary
Workbook Lesson B	Grammar, Vocabulary, Reading
Online Workbook Lesson B	Grammar, Vocabulary, Reading, Listening

6 READING
Technology and friendship

A Pair work Discuss these questions. Then read the article to compare your ideas with the author's.

1. What are some ways that interacting online might encourage people to connect in real life?
2. How could social media help shy students participate more in class?

HOW SOCIAL MEDIA "FRIENDS" TRANSLATE INTO REAL-LIFE FRIENDSHIPS

When social media first gained attention, I heard many people say online connections couldn't possibly be real friends. Some even feared people might trade face-to-face interaction for a virtual life online. But now the majority of the people I know consider at least some of their online friends to be like extended family. Which made me wonder – does social media actually encourage people to connect "in real life"?

One example of online life translating into real-life interaction happens on *Mashable*'s Social Media Day, when thousands of people attend in-person meet-ups to celebrate the power of online connections. Another example is location-based apps that help users connect face-to-face by allowing them to see who else has checked in at the same store, restaurant, or party – or even who is living in a city they plan to visit. They might then decide to seek each other out "in real life."

A Pew Internet and American Life Project report found that people using social networking sites have more close relationships and receive more support than others. They are also more likely to reconnect with old friends and use social networking to keep up with those they are already close to.

Other research shows that social media may also deepen what could otherwise be passing relationships. A study by Dr. Rey Junco found that college students who interacted with each other and their professors on Twitter were more likely to meet outside class to study. They also developed unexpected real-life connections and were also more likely to ask questions in class.

"What I find most fascinating is that I've consistently seen that students who start a course being more introverted and not speaking up during class discussions become more extroverted and participate more when encouraged to communicate through social media with their professors and their classmates," Junco said.

However, if social media does increase the likelihood of real-life interaction, it can also sometimes complicate it. When fans of social media meet face-to-face, their computers and mobile devices may actually make the meeting less productive. Instead of looking at each other, they may be glued to their screens!

Source: "How Social Media 'Friends' Translate Into Real-Life Friendships," by Terri Thornton, *Mediashift*

B Group work Discuss these questions. Then share your answers with the class.

1. In what ways are virtual friendships similar to and different from real-life friendships?
2. Would you be more or less willing to share ideas on social media than you would in class? Why?
3. What other issues and complications might come up when online friends meet face-to-face?

LESSON B   Make new friends, but keep the old . . .

2 CLOTHES AND APPEARANCE
LESSON A ▶ *The way we dress*

1 STARTING POINT
Fashion sense

A What's your approach to fashion? Complete this survey.

Clothing Survey

		Agree	Disagree
1	When I choose clothes, I tend to think of comfort first and appearance second.	☐	☐
2	I hate choosing my outfits in the morning. I just put on anything I can find.	☐	☐
3	Celebrities sometimes inspire me to change the way I look.	☐	☐
4	Companies should discourage employees from wearing casual clothes to work.	☐	☐
5	I don't like to draw attention to myself, so I wear pretty conventional clothes.	☐	☐
6	I enjoy shopping for clothes. I don't mind spending hours in clothing stores.	☐	☐
7	High prices rarely prevent me from buying quality clothing.	☐	☐
8	Peer pressure sometimes compels me to wear brand-name clothing.	☐	☐

B **Group work** Discuss your answers to the survey.

"I tend to think of comfort first when I choose clothes. When I'm comfortable, I feel good, and that's more important to me than looking good."

2 DISCUSSION
Judging by appearances

A **Pair work** Read these famous quotations. In your own words, explain to a partner what they mean. Do you agree with the quotations?

> It's always the badly dressed people who are the most interesting.
> – Jean Paul Gaultier

> You're never fully dressed without a smile.
> – Martin Charnin

> Three-tenths of good looks are due to nature; seven-tenths to dress.
> – Chinese proverb

"I think the first one means interesting people focus on more meaningful things than clothes. I think it's often true. For example, scientists and inventors don't always dress very well."

B **Group work** Discuss these questions. Explain your answers.

1. Do you think it's fair for people to judge you by the way you dress?
2. If you had an unlimited clothing budget, would you change your style?
3. Would you change the way you dress to please someone else?

2 CLOTHES AND APPEARANCE

LESSON A ▶ The way we dress

> In this unit, Ss use different verb patterns to talk about clothing. They also practice cleft sentences with *what*.

1 Fashion sense (STARTING POINT)

Learning aim: Discuss fashion choices and shopping for clothes, and see verb patterns in context (10–15 minutes)

A

- Books closed. Introduce the topic by asking Ss what they like to wear when they go out with friends to different places. Ask them if they tend to choose clothing to look good or to feel comfortable.
- Books open. Explain the task. Read the survey aloud. Check that Ss understand the following vocabulary.

Vocabulary

outfits sets of clothes that are worn together

discourage try to persuade someone not to do something

draw attention to get people to notice

conventional usual, traditional, or accepted type

peer pressure the influence that other people of the same age or social group have on someone

compel force (a person to do something)

- Ss work individually to complete the survey.

B Group work

- Explain the task. Read the example answer aloud.
- Ss work in groups to discuss their answers to the survey.
- Have Ss share their group's discussion with the class.

2 Judging by appearances (DISCUSSION)

Learning aim: Talk about people's appearance and what it says about them (15–20 minutes)

A Pair work

- Books closed. Write this proverb on the board:

  You can't judge a book by its cover.

  Ask Ss what they think it means. (Answer: You can't judge a person or thing only by outward appearance.)
- Books open. Explain the task. Read the quotations aloud. Answer any questions about the vocabulary.

Culture note

Jean Paul Gaultier: famous French fashion designer

Martin Charnin: American lyricist. One of his most famous works is the Broadway musical *Annie*. The quotation comes from one of the songs in this musical.

- Ask a S to read the example answer aloud. Ss work in pairs to do the activity.
- Have Ss share their partner's answers with the class.

Possible answers

It's always the badly dressed . . . could mean that interesting people have more important things to think about than clothes. Or it could mean that people who don't follow the fashion trends and look different might be more interesting.

You're never fully dressed . . . means that your positive attitude is as important a part of your appearance as the clothes you wear.

Three-tenths of good looks are due . . . means that we are born with a certain amount of attractiveness, but through fashion and style, we can become more attractive.

B Group work

- Explain the task. Read the questions aloud.
- Ss work in groups to do the activity.
- Have groups share their answers with the class.

UNIT 2 Clothes and appearance T-10

3 Review of verb patterns (GRAMMAR)

Learning aim: Practice using different verb patterns (25–30 minutes)

> **Grammar notes**
> In pattern b (verb + object + infinitive), the object is a direct object, and it is the object of the main verb, not the infinitive. Direct objects of the infinitive normally follow the infinitive.
> *I want my sister to buy a new coat.*
>
> The infinitive can be followed by both a direct and an indirect object. The indirect object precedes the direct object if it is present without a preposition. The indirect object follows the direct object if the preposition is used.
> *I want to buy my sister a new coat.*
> *I want to buy a new coat for my sister.*

- Books closed. Write on the board:
  1. *I like to dress in bright colors.*
  2. *He wants her to buy a new shirt.*
  3. *They enjoy going to fashion shows.*
  4. *She told me about making her own clothes.*
- Have Ss come to the board and label the parts of each sentence (e.g., verb, infinitive, gerund, preposition, object).
- Books open. Discuss the information in the grammar box and read the example sentences.

A
- Have Ss look at the Starting Point on page 10 again. Explain the task and read the question aloud. Go over answers with the class.

> **Answers**
>
> Pattern a:
> 5. *I don't like to draw attention to myself, . . .*
>
> Pattern b:
> 8. *Peer pressure sometimes compels me to wear . . .*
>
> Pattern c:
> 6. *I enjoy shopping for clothes . . .*
>
> Pattern d:
> 4. *Companies should discourage employees from wearing . . .*

B Pair work
- Explain the task. Read the sentences aloud. Answer any questions about vocabulary.
- Ss work in pairs to complete the activity.
- Go over answers with the class.

> **Answers**
>
> | 1. c | 3. a | 5. b | 7. d |
> |------|------|------|------|
> | 2. a | 4. c | 6. d | 8. b |

C Pair work
- Explain the task. Ask Ss if sentence 1 is true for them. Ask them why or why not.
- Keep Ss in pairs to do the activity. Have a few Ss share their partner's answers with the class.

D Pair work
- Explain the task. Read the verbs aloud. Answer any questions about vocabulary.
- Go over the example with the class. Keep Ss in pairs to complete the activity. Go over answers with the class.

> **Possible answers**
>
> 1. Some schools <u>require</u> students to wear <u>school uniforms</u>. They think that students will spend more time studying and less time thinking about clothes.
> 2. Parents often <u>discourage</u> their children from <u>staying out late</u>. They don't want them to get into trouble.
> 3. Some restaurants don't <u>allow</u> customers to <u>dine barefoot</u>. They don't mind people wearing flip flops.
> 4. I <u>try</u> to wear clothes that <u>make me look thin</u>. It's easier than going on a diet.
> 5. Experts <u>advise</u> people against wearing <u>stripes and patterns together</u>. They are distracting to look at.
> 6. My clothes always <u>seem</u> to make me look <u>too young</u>. I'm going to change my style so I look my age.
> 7. I <u>don't mind</u> buying expensive <u>jewelry</u>. It helps me to feel special.
> 8. Young people <u>tend</u> to be concerned about <u>trends</u>. They don't mind following the crowd.

> **Optional activity:** *More practice* (10–15 minutes)
>
> Ss practice the verb patterns.
> - Ss work in groups to write eight sentences using the patterns reviewed in Exercise 3. Tell them to leave the gerund or infinitive blank but to include a word box with possible choices.
> - Have groups exchange papers. Give Ss a time limit to complete the sentences. Have Ss read their completed sentences aloud and go over answers with the class.

T-11 UNIT 2 Clothes and appearance

3 GRAMMAR

Review of verb patterns

Study the following common verb patterns.

a. verb + infinitive
When I choose clothes, I **tend to think** of comfort first and appearance second.

b. verb + object + infinitive
Celebrities sometimes **inspire me to change** the way I look.

c. verb + gerund
I **hate choosing** my outfits in the morning.

d. verb + object + preposition + gerund
High prices rarely **prevent me from buying** quality clothing.

GRAMMAR PLUS see page 108

A Look at the Starting Point on page 10 again. Can you find another example of each verb pattern above?

B Pair work Which verb patterns from the box do these sentences follow? Write *a*, *b*, *c*, or *d*.

____ 1. I enjoy making a statement with my clothes.
____ 2. I like to wear unusual color combinations.
____ 3. I refuse to shop with my friends.
____ 4. I can't help being critical of what others wear.
____ 5. Parents should allow their children to wear whatever they want.
____ 6. My friends usually advise me against spending too much on clothes.
____ 7. My parents have always discouraged me from wearing sloppy clothes.
____ 8. Advertising definitely convinces me to buy certain articles of clothing.

C Pair work Which statements above are true for you? Explain and give examples.

D Pair work Complete each sentence with a verb from the box and your own ideas. Then add a follow-up comment, and compare with a partner.

| advise | discourage | encourage | require | tend |
| allow | don't mind | permit | seem | try |

1. Some schools ____*require*____ students to wear ____*school uniforms*____.
   They think that students will spend more time studying and less time thinking about clothes.
2. Parents often _____ their children from _____.
3. Some restaurants don't _____ customers to _____.
4. I _____ to wear clothes that _____.
5. Experts _____ people against wearing _____.
6. My clothes always _____ to make me look _____.
7. I _____ buying expensive _____.
8. Young people _____ to be concerned about _____.

LESSON A The way we dress 11

4 VOCABULARY
Your taste in clothes

A Look at the words below. Do some have similar meanings? Which ones would you use to describe your own style?

| chic | conservative | fashionable | formal | functional | quirky | sloppy | stylish |
| classic | elegant | flashy | frumpy | funky | retro | stuffy | trendy |

B Pair work What do you think of these styles? Describe the people in the picture.

Holly   Hugo   Heather   Bruce   Ryan   Erica

"Erica's outfit is pretty functional. She's probably going to the gym."
"Yes, but I'd say it's fashionable, too. The colors and design are stylish, and it fits her well."

VOCABULARY PLUS see page 131

5 LISTENING
Fashion developments

A Pair work Was your style the same five years ago? In what ways has your style changed? In what ways has it remained the same?

B Listen to Mark, Shelby, and Carlos describe how their tastes in fashion have changed. What was their style, and what is their style now?

	Then	Now
1. Mark		
2. Shelby		
3. Carlos		

C Listen again. Write the items of clothing or accessories you hear for each of the looks below.

grunge _____   bohemian _____
urban _____   sporty _____
goth _____   preppy _____

12   UNIT 2   Clothes and appearance

4 Your taste in clothes (VOCABULARY)

Learning aim: Learn and practice using adjectives to talk about personal style in clothes (10–15 minutes)

A
- Explain the task. Read the words in the box aloud. To check understanding, have Ss name a celebrity whose style could be described by each of the words.
- Ss work individually to do the activity. Go over answers with the class.

Answers
Yes. The following have similar meanings:
chic, classic, elegant
fashionable, stylish, trendy
funky, quirky
conservative, stuffy

- Have a few Ss describe their own style.

B Pair work
- Explain the task. Have one pair of Ss read the example conversation to the class.
- Ss work in pairs to discuss the question and describe the people in the picture using the words from part A.
- Ask Ss to share their partner's answers with the class.

Possible answers
Holly: chic, elegant, formal
Hugo: classic, conservative, stuffy
Heather: trendy, fashionable, funky, quirky
Bruce: stylish, flashy, sloppy
Ryan: sloppy
Erica: functional, fashionable, trendy

5 Fashion developments (LISTENING)

Learning aim: Develop skills in listening for gist and details (15–20 minutes)

A Pair work
- Ask Ss what kinds of styles were popular five years ago. Have them give specific examples.
- Explain the task. Ss work in pairs to tell each other about the ways their style has changed and the ways it has remained the same.
- Have Ss share their partner's answers with the class.

B 🔊 [CD 1, Track 6]
- Explain the task. Tell Ss to look at the chart and determine the information they need to complete it. Then read the six words that describe looks in part C aloud.
- Tell Ss to listen for the answers to complete the chart. Play the recording as Ss listen for the answers. Replay as many times as needed. Ss listen and check their answers.
- Ss work in pairs to compare answers. Go over answers with the class.

Answers		
Mark:	Then: grunge	
	Now: urban, hip-hop	
Shelby:	Then: conservative, stuffy, boring, then goth	
	Now: bohemian	
Carlos:	Then: sporty	
	Now: preppy, classic	

Audio script: See page 164.

C 🔊 [CD 1, Track 7]
- Explain that Ss will listen again and write the items of clothing or accessories mentioned for each of the looks.
- Play the recording as many times as needed.
- Go over answers with the class. Go over any unfamiliar vocabulary. Use the illustrations in Exercise 4B to help, if necessary.

Answers
grunge: ripped jeans, checked flannel shirts, wool cap
urban: baggy jeans, oversized T-shirts, hooded sweatshirts, baseball cap
goth: long black dresses, heavy black boots, dark makeup
bohemian: long flowing floral skirts and dresses, long tunics
sporty: sweatpants, jogging suit, jerseys with numbers
preppy: light-colored slacks, polo shirt, sweater

Audio script: See page T-164.

6 Writing about personal beliefs (WRITING)

Learning aim: Write a composition about personal beliefs about fashion using a thesis statement and giving examples to support the thesis (40–50 minutes)

A

- Tell Ss to read the information in the box at the top of the page. Ask: *What is a thesis statement?* (Answer: the sentence containing the main idea of a composition)
- Remind Ss that a thesis statement can be found at the beginning or end of the first paragraph and often includes a main idea or opinion that is further explained in the rest of the composition. Also remind Ss that each body paragraph of a composition should focus on only one aspect of the main idea. Each of those paragraphs has a topic sentence to present that aspect of the main idea.
- Explain the task. Read the mottos aloud. Ask: *In the first motto, what does "make a statement" mean?* (Answer: choose clothes that will create a certain impression about your personality)
- Ss work individually to do the activity. Then Ss work in pairs to share their ideas.
- Have Ss share their partner's ideas with the class.

B

- Explain the task. Read the example thesis statement aloud. Ask Ss which motto from part A it matches. (Answer: *Don't just get dressed. Make a statement.*)
- Ss work individually to write their thesis statement. Then Ss work in pairs to compare their thesis statements and, if necessary, suggest ways each thesis statement could be improved.

C

- Explain the writing task. Ask Ss to read the example composition and identify the thesis statement. (Answer: *They [clothes] should make a statement about who you are.*)
- Ss work individually to write their compositions. Go around the class and help as needed.

D Pair work

- Explain the task. Read the questions aloud. Ss work in pairs to exchange compositions and take turns answering the questions.
- Go around the class and help as needed. Encourage Ss to ask and answer follow-up questions about the compositions and to ask about anything in the composition they don't understand.

Optional activity: *The contest* (20 minutes)

Ss vote on the best composition.

- Gather Ss' compositions and divide them according to the four different mottos used to write the thesis statements. Ss work in groups that correspond to their thesis statement.
- Tell Ss that they will pretend to be an editor of a magazine. The magazine is looking for stories about how people dress. Each group reads all the compositions with the same thesis statement and decides which one should be included in the magazine.
- Have a S from each group read the winning composition to the class.

Do your students need more practice?	
Assign . . .	for more practice in . . .
Grammar Plus 2A	Grammar
Vocabulary Plus 2A	Vocabulary
Online Vocabulary Accelerator 2A	Vocabulary
Workbook Lesson A	Grammar, Vocabulary, Writing
Online Workbook Lesson A	Grammar, Vocabulary, Writing

6 WRITING
Writing about personal beliefs

> In a composition about a personal belief, clearly state that belief in a thesis statement in the first paragraph. In the following paragraphs, give examples to support your thesis.

A Look at these fashion mottos. Which motto best reflects your opinion about fashion? Why? Share your ideas with a partner.

Don't just get dressed. Make a statement.

Why look like everyone else?

Feel comfortable. That's all that matters.

Don't live in the past. Wear today's styles!

B Use the motto you chose as the basis for a thesis statement about your personal belief about fashion. Compare your ideas with a partner.

> Your clothes should make a statement about who you are.

C Use your thesis statement to develop a composition of about 200 words in three paragraphs that describes your approach to clothes.

> I believe that clothes should be more than functional. They should make a statement about who you are. Before you get dressed or go shopping for clothing, it's important to think about what kind of message your clothes will send to others.
>
> I think of my clothes as a reflection of my personality. When people look at me and my clothes, they can get an idea of the kind of person I am. I'm interested in the arts, and I'm concerned about environmental issues. Therefore, I not only wear colorful clothes that are a bit unusual, but I also wear natural fabrics that are made locally. This is important to me.
>
> I don't follow trends because I don't like to look like everyone else. I'm unique, and I want my clothes to show it.

D Pair work Exchange compositions and answer these questions.

1. Does the thesis statement in the first paragraph clearly state the writer's point of view?
2. Do the examples given in the other paragraphs support the thesis statement and clarify the writer's point of view?
3. What else do you want to know about your partner's attitude toward clothes?

LESSON A The way we dress

LESSON B ▶ How we appear to others

1 STARTING POINT
Forming an impression

A Look at the statements about how people form a first impression of someone. Choose the statements that are true for you.

First Impressions
What People Notice First When They Meet Someone New

- ☐ What I notice is the other person's eyes.
- ☐ What's really important to me is a person's smile.
- ☐ What I always notice is a person's hands.
- ☐ I look at people's clothes first.
- ☐ What I notice is a person's figure (or physique).
- ☐ What strikes me first is the way people wear their hair.
- ☐ I always appreciate a nice pair of shoes.
- ☐ I have no idea what I notice first.

B **Group work** What other traits help you form an impression of a person? What are the three most important traits for the people in your group? Are they the same for men and women?

2 LISTENING
Important traits

A Listen to Gabriela, Joon, and Alice talk about what is important to them when forming an impression. Complete the chart.

	What is important
1. Gabriela	
2. Joon	
3. Alice	

B Listen again. Which speakers mention what is *not* very important to them? What do they mention? Complete the chart.

	What is not very important
1. Gabriela	
2. Joon	
3. Alice	

C **Pair work** Which speaker thinks the most like you? Share your reasons with a partner.

14 UNIT 2 Clothes and appearance

LESSON B ▶ How we appear to others

1 Forming an impression (STARTING POINT)

Learning aim: Discuss first impressions and see cleft sentences with *what* in context (10–15 minutes)

A

- Books closed. Write on the board:

  You never get a second chance to make a good first impression.

  Ask Ss what they think this saying means. Ask Ss if they think first impressions are important.

- Books open. Explain the task. Read the statements aloud and answer any questions about vocabulary. Ss work individually to complete the activity.

- Have a few Ss share their answers with the class.

> **Culture note**
>
> In the United States, first impressions are very important. When meeting someone for the first time, a warm smile and looking the other person in the eye are considered ways to make a good first impression. In a business setting, a firm handshake is also considered important.

B Group work

- Explain the task and read the questions aloud. Brainstorm other traits as a class, if necessary.
- Ss work in groups to do the activity.
- Have groups share their answers with the class.

2 Important traits (LISTENING)

Learning aim: Develop skills in listening for the general idea (15–20 minutes)

A 🔊 **[CD 1, Track 8]**

- Explain the task. Tell Ss to look at the chart and determine the information they need to complete it. Check that Ss understand the following vocabulary.

> **Vocabulary**
>
> **overall** general; whole, entire

- Tell Ss to listen for the things that are important to the speakers when forming an impression. Play the recording as Ss complete the chart. Replay as many times as needed. Ss listen and check their answers.
- Go over answers with the class.

> **Answers**
>
> 1. Gabriela: appearance, clothes
> 2. Joon: face (in a social setting); overall appearance, confidence (in a business setting)
> 3. Alice: eyes

Audio script: See page T-165.

B 🔊 **[CD 1, Track 9]**

- Explain the task. Read the questions aloud. Tell Ss to listen again to write what is *not* very important to the speakers when forming an impression.
- Play the recording. Ss listen for the answers and complete the chart. Replay as many times as needed.
- Ss work in pairs to compare answers. Go over answers with the class.

> **Answers**
>
> 1. Gabriela: personality
> 2. Joon: doesn't say
> 3. Alice: clothing, hair color

Audio script: See page T-165.

C Pair work

- Read the question aloud. Ss work in pairs to discuss the question.
- Have Ss share their partner's answer with the class.

UNIT 2 Clothes and appearance

3 Cleft sentences with *what* (GRAMMAR)

Learning aim: Practice using cleft sentences with *what* (20–25 minutes)

> **Grammar notes**
> Cleft sentences are used to focus attention on a particular piece of information. A speaker may use a cleft sentence to add emphasis.
> *He didn't buy a cheap car. What he bought was a Mercedes.*
>
> The noun clause starting with *what* is the subject of the sentence and takes a singular verb. In an informal style, a plural verb is possible if followed by a plural noun.

- Books closed. Write on the board:
  1. *Everyone always notices her smile.*
  2. *What everyone always notices is her smile.*

  Read the sentences aloud and ask Ss if the sentences mean the same thing. (Answer: yes) Ask how the sentences are different. (Answer: The second sentence puts more emphasis on *her smile*.)
- Books open. Discuss the information in the grammar box and read the example sentences.

A
- Have Ss look at the Starting Point on page 14 again. Explain the task and read the question aloud. Go over answers with the class.

> **Answers**
> *What I notice is the other person's eyes.*
> I notice the other person's eyes.
> *What I notice is a person's figure (or physique).*
> I notice a person's figure (or physique).
> *What strikes me first is the way people wear their hair.*
> The way people wear their hair strikes me first.

B
- Explain the task. Read the example answer aloud. Ss work individually to complete the activity.
- Ss work in pairs to compare their answers. Go over answers with the class.

> **Answers**
> 1. What I appreciate is a person with a good sense of humor.
> 2. What I always notice is the way people look at me.
> 3. What's important to me is a person's fashion sense.
> 4. What I pay attention to is / are people's manners.
> 5. What I really dislike is sarcasm.
> 6. What I'm interested in is / are the subjects people talk about.
> 7. What's appealing to me is a kind face.

4 Good first impressions (DISCUSSION)

Learning aim: Talk about making a good first impression and practice the lesson grammar (15–20 minutes)

A Pair work
- Books closed. Ask: *What can you do to make a good first impression?* Have Ss call out their ideas, and write them on the board.
- Books open. Explain the task. Read the tips aloud. Ss work individually to choose a tip. Then Ss work in pairs to explain their choice.

B Group work
- Explain the task. Have one pair of Ss read the example conversation to the class.
- Ss work in groups to discuss which tips from part A and which tips of their own are best for the situations.
- Have a S from each group report on the group's tips for the situations to the class.

> **Optional activity:** *Role play* (20–25 minutes)
> Ss role-play making a good first impression and a bad first impression.
> - Ss work in groups to role-play meeting a friend's parents for the first time. Have Ss work together to write two scenes: one where the person makes a good first impression and one where the person makes a bad first impression.
> - Have Ss perform their role plays for the class. Ask the class to take notes on what the person did right or wrong.
> - Discuss Ss' notes after each role play.

T-15 UNIT 2 Clothes and appearance

3 GRAMMAR

Cleft sentences with *what*

You can add *what* and a form of *be* to a sentence when you want to emphasize information. The resulting sentence is called a *cleft* sentence.

A person's smile **is really important to me**.   **What's really important to me is** a person's smile.

For sentences with verbs other than *be*, insert *what* at the beginning of the sentence and a form of *be* after the main verb.

I always notice a person's hands.   **What I always notice is** a person's hands.

GRAMMAR PLUS see page 109

A Look at the Starting Point on page 14 again. Can you find more cleft sentences? Try to change them into declarative sentences.

B Rewrite these sentences to add emphasis by beginning them with *what*. Which statements are true for you? Compare answers with a partner.

1. I appreciate a person with a good sense of humor.
   What I appreciate is a person with a good sense of humor.
2. I always notice the way people look at me.
3. A person's fashion sense is important to me.
4. I pay attention to people's manners.
5. I really dislike sarcasm.
6. I'm interested in the subjects people talk about.
7. A kind face is appealing to me.

4 DISCUSSION

Good first impressions

A Pair work Read these tips on making a good first impression. Choose the tip you think is the most useful. Then explain your choice to a partner.

QUICK TIPS for Making a Lasting Impression

1. Appearance matters. Dress a little nicer than you need to when meeting new people.

2. Occasionally, use the names of the people you are talking to, for example: *Amy, have you seen that movie yet?*

3. Break the silence with small talk about a topic that you think will interest others.

4. When it's in good taste, use humor. A joke can be a nice way to break the ice, but what you should avoid is sarcasm.

5. Everyone likes compliments, so give plenty of them. Just make sure you are sincere.

6. Be yourself, and be sure to smile. A friendly smile can make other people feel at ease.

B Group work What's the best way to make a good first impression in these situations? Discuss and add some tips of your own.

- a dinner party at a new friend's home
- an initial interview for a job you want
- the first day in a fitness class
- the first time you meet new neighbors

"At a dinner party with new friends, what's really important is good table manners."
"That's true. Also, what I always do is compliment my hosts on the food."

LESSON B How we appear to others

5 VOCABULARY
Adjectives to describe outward appearance

A Which adjectives seem to have a positive meaning, a negative meaning, or both? Write +, −, or +/−.

___ a. arrogant ___ d. innocent ___ g. sinister ___ i. sympathetic
___ b. dignified ___ e. intense ___ h. smug ___ j. trustworthy
___ c. eccentric ___ f. intellectual

B Now match the words with their definitions. Write the correct letter.

1. rational and studious ___
2. kind and understanding ___
3. worthy of respect or honor ___
4. reliable ___
5. forceful; with strong opinions ___
6. proud in an unpleasant way ___
7. self-satisfied; pleased with oneself ___
8. without blame; childlike and pure ___
9. strange or unusual in an amusing way ___
10. evil or ominous ___

C Pair work What famous people do you think the adjectives describe?

"To me, Johnny Depp looks intellectual."
"Oh, I don't know. He looks eccentric, in my opinion."

VOCABULARY PLUS see page 131

6 DISCUSSION
Faces matter

Psychologist Leslie Zebrowitz found that people are usually categorized by their faces. She gave résumés of equally qualified people to groups of business students, with photos attached. It was discovered that the students recommended baby-faced people for jobs that required more sympathetic and submissive people, while people with mature faces were seen as more dignified or intense and were recommended for high-powered jobs, like lawyers. "We found that the more baby-faced people had baby-faced jobs," Zebrowitz said. "People seemed to be chosen for jobs, or to select themselves into jobs, to match their appearance."

Source: "Judging Faces Comes Naturally," by Jules Crittenden, *Boston Herald*

Gisele Bündchen
Zooey Deschanel 
John Cho
Elijah Wood

Group work Answer these questions.

1. Which of the people above do you think have "baby faces"? What makes a baby face different from a mature face?
2. In what ways can having a baby face be useful? In what situations is it better to have a mature face?
3. In some countries, job applications sometimes require a recent photo of the candidate. Do you agree with this practice? Why or why not?

16 UNIT 2 Clothes and appearance

5 Adjectives to describe outward appearance (VOCABULARY)

Learning aim: Learn and practice using adjectives to describe someone's appearance (10–15 minutes)

A
- Books closed. Ask Ss to call out adjectives that can be used to describe people's appearance. Write them on the board. Then write on the board: *sensitive*. Ask Ss to give a definition. (Answer: easily affected by emotional situations) Ask Ss if they think this is a positive or a negative adjective and why. Discuss how some adjectives can be considered both positive and negative, depending on the person and the situation.
- Books open. Explain the task and read the list of adjectives aloud.
- Ss work individually to complete the activity. Go over answers with the class.

Answers			
a. –	d. +	g. –	i. +
b. +	e. +/–	h. –	j. +
c. +/–	f. +		

Optional activity: *Positive or negative?* **(10–15 minutes)**
Ss have additional practice with adjectives.
- Ss work in groups to discuss each of the adjectives from part A. Tell them to think of situations where each adjective could be positive or negative.
- Allow Ss time to think of other traits that could be positive or negative and give examples of each.
- Alternatively, do the activity as a class discussion.

B
- Explain the task. Ss work individually to complete the activity.
- Go over answers with the class.

Answers				
1. f	3. b	5. e	7. h	9. c
2. i	4. j	6. a	8. d	10. g

C Pair work
- Explain the task. Have one pair of Ss read the example conversation aloud. Ss work in pairs to discuss the question.
- Have Ss share their partner's answers with the class.

For more practice with vocabulary, download the Worksheet **2.1 Impressions** from the Teacher Support Site.

6 Faces matter (DISCUSSION)

Learning aim: Talk about how people perceive different kinds of faces and practice the lesson vocabulary (15–20 minutes)

Group work
- Books closed. Ask: *Which celebrity looks trustworthy? Which one looks too serious? Why?* Have Ss call out their ideas. Write Ss' answers on the board.
- Books open. Explain the task. Read the article aloud. Check that Ss understand the vocabulary on the right.
- Ss work in groups to discuss the questions.
- Have groups share their answers with the class.

Vocabulary

psychologist someone who studies the human mind and behavior

categorized put into a specific group based on certain qualities

qualified having the skills and/or experience to do a job well

baby-faced having a face that looks innocent and younger than the person's chronological age

submissive always doing what other people tell you to do

To help Ss with the discussion in this exercise, download the Fresh Idea **Catch!** from the Teacher Support Site.

UNIT 2 Clothes and appearance

7 Changing a negative perception (READING)

Learning aim: Develop skills in understanding vocabulary in context, summarizing, and giving a personal reaction to a reading (25–30 minutes)

A Pair work

- Books closed. Ask Ss to think of a time when they met someone who made a bad first impression. Ask if their first impression was completely right.
- Books open. Explain the task. Ss work in pairs to discuss the questions.
- Have Ss read the article silently to themselves. Check that Ss understand the following vocabulary.

> **Vocabulary**
>
> **potential** possible
>
> **unintentionally** without meaning to; by accident
>
> **address (it/a problem)** deal with; try to solve
>
> **blown out of proportion** made to appear worse than it is
>
> **stick** not change
>
> **acknowledge** accept or admit
>
> **groveling** behaving in an overly humble way in order to be forgiven
>
> **assumptions** things you believe to be true without having any proof
>
> **self-deprecating** done in a way to make your own abilities or achievements seem unimportant to others

B Pair work

- Explain the task. Ss work in pairs to read the article again and summarize the advice.
- Go over answers with the class.

> **Possible answers**
>
> *Apologize immediately:* Say you're sorry as soon as possible so that what happened won't become worse.
>
> *Avoid over-apologizing:* Don't apologize over and over because this makes others feel uncomfortable.
>
> *Make no assumptions:* Don't assume people think the worst about you. It's better to apologize without criticizing yourself and find out how they really feel.
>
> *Be sincere:* There are three parts to a sincere apology. First, take the blame yourself. Second, listen without getting defensive. Third, explain how you will change in the future to make things better.
>
> *Humor works:* Making fun of yourself can be a good strategy, but make sure your jokes don't make others feel uncomfortable.
>
> *Monitor future behavior:* Practice long-term thinking and realize that changing perceptions takes time.

> **Optional activity:** *More questions* (15–20 minutes)
>
> **Ss write comprehension questions about the article.**
>
> - Ss work in pairs to write five comprehension questions about the article.
> - Tell Ss to close their books. Collect the questions and write them on the board (eliminating any doubles).
> - Set a time limit and have Ss answer the questions without looking back at the article. Go over answers with the class.

> **Optional activity:** *Vocabulary* (20–25 minutes)
>
> **Ss practice the vocabulary from the reading.**
>
> - Have Ss look at the article again. Tell them to write down any words that they did not know before.
> - Ask Ss to call out their words and write them on the board. As a class, write definitions for each word.
> - Have Ss write a sentence using each word. Make sure they write sentences that show they understand the meaning of the word.
> - Ask Ss to read their sentences to the class.

C Group work

- Explain the task. Read the questions aloud.
- Ss work in groups to discuss the questions.
- Ask groups to share their ideas with the class. To make sure that reporting to the class goes smoothly, groups can choose one or two members to report their ideas. Have Ss review their ideas with their own group at the end of the task to see if the group agrees with the information they will be presenting.

For an alternative reading text or extra practice, download the Worksheet **2.2 First impressions count** from the Teacher Support Site.

Do your students need more practice?	
Assign . . .	for more practice in . . .
Grammar Plus 2B	Grammar
Vocabulary Plus 2B	Vocabulary
Online Vocabulary Accelerator 2B	Vocabulary
Workbook Lesson B	Grammar, Vocabulary, Reading
Online Workbook Lesson B	Grammar, Vocabulary, Reading, Listening

UNIT 2 Clothes and appearance

7 READING
Changing a negative perception

A Pair work In what ways could someone make a bad first impression? Once a bad impression is made, what can be done to change the negative perception? Discuss with a partner. Then read the article.

OVERCOMING A BAD FIRST IMPRESSION

Have any of these situations happened to you? Forgetting someone's name after you've just met, spilling coffee on your potential boss during an interview, or unintentionally insulting a co-worker on your first day? Ouch! You never have a second chance to make a first impression, so what happens when that first impression is a negative one? Here is how you can recover.

Apologize immediately. As soon as you realize that you may have offended someone, address it. The more time that passes, the more the story can become blown out of proportion. While first impressions stick, so do last impressions. Take control of the situation by making your last impression a positive one.

Avoid over-apologizing. Saying you're sorry is important, but overdoing it can create another uncomfortable situation. Your goal is to acknowledge your mistake and reposition yourself as being responsible and sensitive. If you repeatedly bring up the past, groveling and begging for forgiveness, you're defeating your purpose. It puts the other person in the uncomfortable position of having to constantly reassure you.

Make no assumptions. It's easy to assume that others think the worst of you, but usually what we imagine is far worse than reality. So, don't start out with, "You must think I'm a total idiot." Say something like, "I'm uncomfortable with how I behaved yesterday because I realized I might have offended you. Did you feel the same way?" The other person may think it was no big deal.

Be sincere. A sincere apology requires three steps. First, don't blame what happened on other people or circumstances. Second, acknowledge how your actions affected the other person – which means listening without defending yourself. Third, explain what you will do differently in the future to avoid making the same mistake. Such an apology might sound like, "I want to apologize for what I said yesterday. After speaking with you, I can hear how much my comments offended you and caused embarrassment. I want you to know that in the future I will be more sensitive."

Humor works. A little self-deprecating humor can save you, but make sure it is really only directed at yourself and does not increase anybody else's level of discomfort. Sometimes humor breaks the tension and provides an opening for you to recover.

Monitor future behavior. Communication has a cumulative effect. Every impression you make builds on the previous one. Overcoming a bad impression requires that all future behavior be consistent with how you want to be perceived. It will take time and trust to change perceptions, but it can be done!

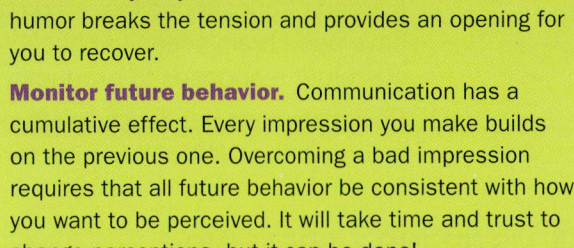

Source: "Overcoming a Bad First Impression," by Susan Fee, www.susanfee.com

B Pair work Read the article again. Then take turns summarizing the advice in your own words.

C Group work Discuss these questions. Then share your answers with the class.

1. How effective do you think the advice in the article would be in changing a bad first impression?
2. How could an incident get blown out of proportion if someone doesn't apologize right away?
3. Do you believe that time and trust can change a negative perception? Explain.

LESSON B How we appear to others 17

3 SCIENCE AND TECHNOLOGY

LESSON A ▶ Good science, bad science

1 STARTING POINT
What's new?

A Read about these advances in science. What are the possible benefits and dangers?

DNA for Information Storage
Incredibly, scientists can now synthesize DNA to hold digital information, such as a video or text. The information can later be read by machines called DNA sequencers. DNA offers the longest duration for digital storage, keeping data safe for tens of thousands of years.

Thought Identification
Technology can already identify thoughts from scans of activity patterns in the human brain. The first attempts identified simple thoughts, but researchers are finding ways to reveal more complex thoughts and intentions.

Animal Cloning
With just one cell from a live or dead animal, an exact copy of the animal can be created with a technique known as cloning. The technique has been used to clone various pets, and cloned horses can even take part in the Olympics now.

B Pair work Read more about the scientific advances in part A. Do you think each statement is a good idea (G) or a bad idea (B)? Discuss each statement with a partner.

____ 1. DNA storage could one day provide so much storage space that no data would ever need to be erased again.

____ 2. Instead of questionnaires, marketers have used brain scans to check customer responses to products.

____ 3. Scientists have successfully stored a song in the DNA of living bacteria.

____ 4. An application of thought-identification technology allows a person to type on a computer just by thinking.

____ 5. To avoid taking any more animals from the wild, some scientists hope to clone endangered animals for use in zoos.

____ 6. Scientists want to create a clone from the frozen remains of an extinct mammoth.

2 LISTENING & SPEAKING
The effects of technology

A Listen to a show about driverless car technology. Choose the areas in which the impact of the technology would be mostly positive according to the speakers.

☐ accidents   ☐ fuel consumption   ☐ car repair
☐ road construction ☐ parking   ☐ traffic

B Listen again and take notes about the impact of driverless car technology on the areas in part A. Then take turns describing the impact with a partner.

C Pair work Give an example of a new technology that has reshaped your daily life. What are the positive effects? What are the negative consequences?

18 UNIT 3 Science and technology

3 SCIENCE AND TECHNOLOGY

LESSON A ▶ Good science, bad science

> In this unit, Ss use indefinite and definite articles to talk about scientific advances. They also practice using -ing clauses.

1 What's new? (STARTING POINT)

Learning aim: Discuss advances in science and see indefinite and definite articles in context (10–15 minutes)

A
- Books closed. Ask Ss to define *scientific advances*. (Answer: a discovery or invention that significantly changes the way something is thought of or done) Ask Ss what they think are the most important scientific advances in the last 20 years. Write them on the board.
- Books open. Explain the task. Read the texts aloud. Check that Ss understand the vocabulary on the right.
- Give Ss time to think about their answer to the question. Then discuss the benefits and dangers of each advance with the class.

Vocabulary
storage a place where something is kept until needed
synthesize create a new substance through scientific manipulation
DNA sequencer machine that reads the sequence of bases that form the specific DNA

B Pair work
- Explain the task. Read the statements aloud.
- Ss work individually to write their answers. Then Ss work in pairs to discuss each statement.
- Have pairs share their discussion with the class.

2 The effects of technology (LISTENING & SPEAKING)

Learning aim: Develop skills in listening for main ideas and details and in note taking (20–25 minutes)

A 🔊 [CD 1, Track 10]
- Books closed. Ask Ss what they have heard about driverless cars.
- Books open. Explain the task. Read the areas aloud. Check that Ss understand the following vocabulary.

Vocabulary
laser scanners devices that tell the distance between the car and any object found nearby
navigation successful use of roads and highways
guardrails fence-like barriers along a road
mileage the number of miles per gallon of fuel
traffic congestion slow or blocked traffic due to too many cars on the road

- Tell Ss to listen for the answers. Play the recording as Ss choose the areas. Replay as many times as needed.
- Go over answers with the class.

Answers
accidents, road construction, fuel consumption, parking, traffic

Audio script: See page T-165.

B 🔊 [CD 1, Track 11]
- Explain the task. Play the recording again as Ss take notes about the positive and negative impacts of the new technology. Replay as many times as needed.
- Ss work in pairs to describe the impact of the technology. Go over answers with the class.

Answers
accidents: would decrease dramatically; businesses that profit from accidents would lose money
road construction: would be cheaper since lighting, guardrails, safety signs, etc. would be unnecessary
fuel consumption: efficient routes and better design would improve gas mileage; drop in sales for gas stations
parking: car sharing would mean fewer cars on the road and more parking spots
repair: the complex technology can't be repaired by the average mechanic at this point
traffic: fewer cars on the road due to car sharing would result in less traffic congestion

Audio script: See page T-165.

C Pair work
- Explain the task and read the questions aloud. Ss work in pairs to answer the questions.
- Have Ss share their partner's answers with the class.

UNIT 3 Science and technology T-18

3 Indefinite and definite articles (GRAMMAR)

Learning aim: Practice using indefinite and definite articles (20–25 minutes)

Grammar notes

Use the indefinite article *a* or *an* with generic nouns to make generalizations. A generic noun represents an entire class of things. It is not a specific thing; it is more like a symbol or a representative of a group of things.
A tree is an important part of the environment.

An indefinite article is not used if the generic noun is a plural countable noun or an uncountable noun.
Trees are an important part of the environment.
Clean water is an important part of the environment.

Use an indefinite article when talking about a thing that is not specifically identified. Use a definite article when talking about a specific thing.
I drive a car.
I drive the red car.

Use a definite article when you know that the speaker knows the noun you are talking about.
The car broke down today.

- Books closed. Write on the board:
  1. I'm riding in _____ car with no driver.
  2. I don't think they should clone _____ pets.
  3. _____ latest advance amazed _____ science world.
  4. In the future, there will be _____ robot that has emotions.

  Have Ss come to the board and write an indefinite, a definite, or no article in the blanks. (Answers: 1. *a*; 2. no article; 3. *The, the*; 4. *a*) Ask Ss to say what they remember about the rules for using definite and indefinite articles.

- Books open. Discuss the information in the grammar box and read the example sentences.

A

- Have Ss look at the Starting Point on page 18 again. Explain the task and read the question aloud.
- Go over answers with the class.

Answers

First rule:
. . . *to hold digital <u>information</u>, such as a video or text.*
<u>The information</u> can . . .

. . . can be created with <u>a technique</u> known as cloning.
<u>The technique</u> has been . . .

Second rule:
The information can later be read by <u>machines</u> . . .

Third rule:
. . . synthesize <u>DNA</u> to hold digital <u>information</u>, . . .
. . . keeping <u>data</u> safe . . .
<u>Technology</u> can already . . .

Fourth rule:
DNA offers <u>the longest duration</u> for . . .

B

- Explain the task. Read the sentences aloud. Answer any questions about vocabulary.
- Ss work individually to complete the activity.
- Go over answers with the class.

Answers

1. X, X	5. an, the
2. X	6. X
3. A, a	7. X
4. The, X	8. the, the / a

C Pair work

- Explain the task. Read the list of items aloud. Have one pair of Ss read the example conversation to the class. Brainstorm ideas for each item as a class, if necessary.
- Give Ss time to write statements individually about the items.
- Ss work in pairs to discuss their ideas.
- Have Ss share their partner's ideas with the class.

3 GRAMMAR

Indefinite and definite articles

Review these rules for the indefinite articles *a* and *an* and the definite article *the*.

Use an indefinite article (*a* or *an*) when you mention a singular countable noun for the first time, or no article for plural countable and uncountable nouns. When you refer to the same item again, use *the*.
With just one cell from **a** live or dead **animal**, an exact copy of **the animal** can be created.

If you use a plural noun to make a general statement, do not use an article. However, if you make the same statement using a singular noun, use *the* or *a / an*.
Technology can already identify thoughts from scans of activity patterns in **human brains**.
Technology can already identify thoughts from scans of activity patterns in **the / a human brain**.

When making a general statement, do not use an article with uncountable nouns (*technology, education, shopping, love*, etc.).
DNA offers the longest duration for digital **storage**.

Use *the* with superlatives and with sequence markers such as *first, last, next*, etc., but don't use *the* with time expressions such as *last night* or *next month*.
The first attempts identified simple thoughts.

GRAMMAR PLUS see page 110

A Look at the Starting Point on page 18 again. Can you find other examples of article usage for each rule in the grammar box?

B Complete these sentences with the correct article. Write *X* where none is needed.

1. Nowadays, _X_ tracking technologies enable ___ websites to trace what online shoppers buy.
2. In some countries, ___ brain-scan evidence has been used in court to help convict killers.
3. ___ robot at Stanford University has used tools to successfully assemble ___ bookcase.
4. ___ first microbes able to consume oil were created to help clean up ___ oil spills.
5. Cloning could bring ___ animal back from extinction provided that DNA of ___ animal is still available.
6. I'm sure that a new computer will be even less expensive ___ next year.
7. It's a fact that ___ wireless technology makes the Internet available on a much wider scale.
8. For me, ___ most interesting new transportation technology is ___ driverless car.

C Pair work Write statements about the items below. Then discuss your ideas with a partner.

1. the most interesting electronic device in stores
2. the most exciting app or software on the market
3. the greatest advance in medicine
4. the most amazing invention of the twentieth century

"For me, the most interesting electronic device is the personal 3-D viewer."
"Oh, yeah. I tried one in a store. It feels just like you're in a movie theater."

LESSON A Good science, bad science

4 VOCABULARY
A brave new world

A Match the words on the left with their definitions on the right.

1. audacious ____
2. confidential ____
3. frivolous ____
4. hazardous ____
5. problematic ____
6. prudent ____
7. unethical ____

a. silly and wasteful; carelessly self-indulgent
b. avoiding unnecessary risks
c. having a willingness to take risks
d. private or secret
e. against accepted beliefs about good behavior
f. dangerous
g. full of difficulties that are hard to solve

B Complete the sentences with the words in part A. Then compare your answers with a partner. Sometimes more than one answer is possible.

1. Sadly, much of our _____ personal information is now on the Internet.
2. While switching to driverless cars would have benefits, the possible disruption to the economy makes the switch _____.
3. Some _____ scientists think it would be wise to do more research before using genetically modified plants in food.
4. Some people feel that denying any patient access to medical technology due to cost is _____.
5. Due to its potential for serious accidents, many believe nuclear power is too _____ to use safely.
6. One bold and _____ dream of thought-identification researchers is to create a machine that can read all human thought.
7. With thousands of dogs and cats looking for homes, cloning additional ones for pets seems _____.

VOCABULARY PLUS see page 132

5 DISCUSSION
Pros and cons

Group work Look at these news headlines. Discuss the positive effects and negative consequences of the events in the headlines.

Cosmetic Surgery Better and Cheaper Than Ever
Many men and women today are considering

Use of Personal Data by Social Media Sites Raises Privacy Concerns
Concerns rise as more social media sites use

More Farmers Plant Genetically Engineered Crops to Save Money

Microchip Implant Allows Criminals to Be Followed 24 Hours a Day
There is a debate over whether or not microchip

"Too many people are having cosmetic surgery for frivolous reasons these days. They should think twice about all the potential risks."
"Well, I'm all for it as long as people are prudent."

Useful expressions

Expressing caution and confidence
I'm a bit leery of . . .
You should think twice about . . .
I'm all for . . .
I have every confidence that . . .

UNIT 3 Science and technology

4 A brave new world (VOCABULARY)

Learning aim: Learn and practice using adjectives to talk about technological advances (10–15 minutes)

A
- Explain the task and read the list of adjectives aloud. Ss work individually to complete the activity.
- Go over answers with the class.

Answers			
1. c	3. a	5. g	7. e
2. d	4. f	6. b	

B
- Explain the task. Ss work individually to complete the activity.
- Ss work in pairs to compare answers. Go over answers with the class.

Answers	
1. confidential	5. hazardous / problematic
2. problematic	6. audacious / problematic / unethical
3. prudent	7. frivolous / problematic / unethical
4. unethical	

Optional activity: *My opinion* **(20–25 minutes)**

Ss use the vocabulary to talk about their opinions.
- Have Ss write a general opinion about human cloning or another topic of their choosing. Then have Ss think of three or four ideas that support their opinion. Explain that they should use the words from part A in their sentences.
- Ss work in pairs to take turns presenting their opinion and supporting ideas to each other. Have Ss say if they agree or disagree with their partner's opinion.

For more practice with vocabulary, download the Worksheet *3.1 Inventions from 3010* from the Teacher Support Site.

5 Pros and cons (DISCUSSION)

Learning aim: Talk about the consequences of technological advances and practice the lesson vocabulary (15–20 minutes)

Group work
- Ask Ss what *pros and cons* means. (Answer: the advantages and disadvantages of something)
- Tell Ss they are going to evaluate the pros and cons of some technological advances. Read the headlines aloud. Make sure Ss understand the words *personal data, privacy, genetically engineered crops,* and *microchip.* Have them give definitions or examples of each word.
- Explain the task. Read the information in the Useful Expressions box aloud. Give an example of how to use each phrase. Then have one pair of Ss read the example conversation to the class.
- Ss work in groups to discuss the positive and negative consequences. Make sure that each S in the group has a chance to speak.
- Ask groups to share their ideas with the class.

Optional activity: *Class debate* **(15–20 minutes)**

Ss have a class debate.
- Write on the board:

  Teenagers should be able to have cosmetic surgery.

- Divide the class into two groups: A and B. Tell group A to think of as many reasons as they can in favor of the statement. Tell group B to think of as many reasons as they can against the statement.
- Give Ss time to think of reasons individually. Ss work in groups to discuss their answers.
- Have each group take turns presenting their ideas to the class.

UNIT 3 Science and technology T-20

6 Writing summaries (WRITING)

Learning aim: Write a summary reflecting the main points of the original text (40–50 minutes)

A

- Books closed. Ask Ss to think about instances in which summaries are useful (e.g., movie or book reviews or note taking).
- Books open. Tell Ss to read the information in the box at the top of the page. Ask: *What is a summary?* (Answer: a shorter version of a text which only includes its most important points)
- Remind Ss that when writing a summary, they should use their own words, not copy sentences exactly from the original text. Also, a summary should be shorter than the original text.
- Explain the task. Ss work individually to complete the task.
- Go over answers with the class.

Answers

Main points:
Animal cloning is the technique of creating an exact genetic copy of an animal from a single cell.

. . . the potential benefits of animal cloning are many.

Those who argue against cloning warn of its dangers.

B

- Explain the task. Read the summary aloud. Ss work individually to do the activity.
- Go over answers with the class.

Answers

From paragraph 2:
Cloning can produce animals that are unable to reproduce naturally.

From paragraph 3:
Cloning is too expensive.

C Pair work

- For Ss who don't have access to an article, bring in various articles about technology. Distribute them to pairs of Ss.
- Explain the task. Ss work individually to choose an important paragraph in the article and write the main idea. Go around the class and help as needed.
- Ss work in pairs to compare their paragraphs and main ideas. Have Ss take turns suggesting improvements to the main ideas.
- Alternatively, have both partners choose the same paragraph in an article. Ss work individually to write the main idea. Then they compare the main idea they wrote with their partner.

D

- Explain the writing task.
- Ss work individually to write their summary.
- Go around the class and help as needed.
- Go over the summaries with the class.

Optional activity: Story summaries (20 minutes)

Ss write summaries.

- Give Ss time to think individually of a story about something that happened to them or use their imaginations and make up a story. The story should not take more than a minute or two to tell.
- Ss work in groups. Have Ss take turns telling their stories to the group. The other Ss in the group listen carefully, take notes, and write a brief summary of the story.
- Have Ss compare their summaries.

Do your students need more practice?

Assign . . .	for more practice in . . .
Grammar Plus 3A	Grammar
Vocabulary Plus 3A	Vocabulary
Online Vocabulary Accelerator 3A	Vocabulary
Workbook Lesson A	Grammar, Vocabulary, Writing
Online Workbook Lesson A	Grammar, Vocabulary, Writing

6 WRITING
Writing summaries

> When you write a summary, state in your own words the main points of a text, leaving out most of the supporting details. The summary must accurately reflect the ideas of the original text.

A Read the article and underline the main points.

ANIMAL CLONING
BENEFITS AND CONCERNS

Animal cloning is the technique of creating an exact genetic copy of an animal from a single cell. It has previously been used to create copies of, for example, sheep, cows, and cats. While animal cloning is an amazing and powerful technology with possible benefits to science and humanity, many people are voicing concerns about the ethics and wisdom of this scientific innovation.

On the surface, animal cloning simply seems to be the "copying" of an animal, and it is difficult to see the benefits. However, the potential benefits of animal cloning are many. Cloned animals can be useful in the production of certain drugs to treat human illnesses. Through cloning, scientists can modify animal organs, such as heart valves, so that they can be safely transplanted into the human body. Cloning could also be very useful in saving endangered species. Two types of Asian cattle, the gaur and the banteng, have been helped in this way. Furthermore, cloning can be used to produce animals that are unable to reproduce naturally, such as mules.

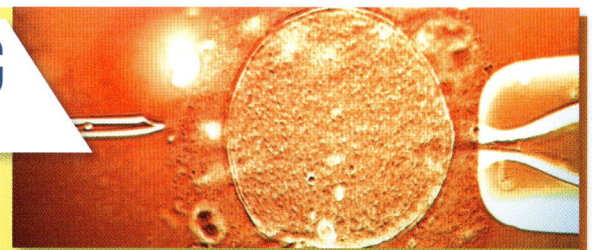

Those who argue against cloning warn of its dangers. Organs transplanted from animals to humans might not always be safe, and there is a risk of disease. Additionally, for every animal that is successfully cloned, there are frequently a number of others that are not healthy enough to live. Cloned animals can also be weaker than those born by normal reproduction. When it comes to saving endangered animals, critics argue that cloning is too expensive and takes the attention and resources away from the real problem – the destruction of animal habitat.

In conclusion, it is unlikely that people on the two sides of the animal cloning issue will arrive at an agreement any time soon. But, as scientific progress presents us with new technologies such as animal cloning, it is important to discuss their benefits and voice our concerns about their use.

B Read the summary. Some main points from the article are not included. What are they?

Summary

Animal cloning is a technique for creating a copy of an animal from a single cell. People who support animal cloning argue that it can be useful in the production of drugs and transplant organs for humans. They also point out its value in preserving endangered species. Those who are against animal cloning argue that its medical uses are actually unsafe, that it produces unhealthy animals, and that it distracts us from the real problems that endangered animals face.

C Pair work Find an article on technology or a related topic. Then choose an important paragraph, and write the main idea. Compare with your partner.

D Write a summary of all or part of the article in one or more paragraphs.

LESSON B ▶ Technology and you

1 STARTING POINT
Technology troubles

A Read about three people who had trouble with technology. How would you have felt in their situation? What would you have done?

Stan, 36

"Working from home one Friday, I opened my company network login page. Unfortunately, I'd forgotten the password my boss had given me, and he had taken the day off. Being too embarrassed to call him at home, I had to go to work after all to access the network."

Peter, 18

"I had dinner plans with my parents, but I was still out hiking when I was supposed to meet them at the restaurant. I kept trying to call them, but the calls were dropped before I could even say hello. Having gotten several calls from me, my parents became really worried. They were relieved when I finally got through an hour later."

Vera, 24

"I had a great presentation ready for the business class I'm taking. Being a perfectionist, I had prepared it in detail on my laptop. The next day in class, my laptop crashed opening the file. Trying to stay calm, I gave the presentation as best I could from memory."

B Pair work What technology gives you the most trouble? Tell your partner a story of a time you had trouble with technology.

"Sometimes my Wi-Fi stops working. It's really frustrating. I remember one day . . ."

2 LISTENING
The convenience of technology?

A Listen to a comedian talk about problems he had with technology. Write the types of technology and the problems he mentions in the chart.

	Technology	Problem	Example
1.			
2.			
3.			

B Listen again. What examples does he give of how the problems affected him? Complete the chart.

C Pair work Have you had similar problems with technology? How could the comedian have avoided them?

22 UNIT 3 Science and technology

LESSON B ▶ Technology and you

1 Technology troubles (STARTING POINT)

Learning aim: Discuss trouble with technology and see -ing clauses in context (10–15 minutes)

A

- Books closed. Ask Ss what technologies they use regularly (e.g., tablet, laptop, cell phone, etc.). Ask Ss if they ever have any problems with them.
- Books open. Explain the task. Read the texts aloud. Check that Ss understand the following vocabulary.

> **Vocabulary**
>
> **access** connect to
>
> **dropped (calls)** didn't connect; disconnected
>
> **perfectionist** someone who must do everything perfectly
>
> **crashed** stopped working completely

- Give Ss time to think about their answers to the questions.
- Ss work in pairs to discuss their answers. Alternatively, have a class discussion.

B Pair work

- Explain the task. Have a S read the example answer to the class.
- Ss work in pairs to do the activity.
- Have Ss share their partner's answers with the class.

2 The convenience of technology? (LISTENING)

Learning aim: Develop skills in listening for the main idea and details (15–20 minutes)

A 🔊 [CD 1, Track 12]

- Explain the task. Tell Ss to look at the chart and determine the information they need to complete it. Check that Ss understand the following vocabulary.

> **Vocabulary**
>
> **swipe** the act of moving your finger across the screen of a device or a card through a slot
>
> **not your everyday . . .** not common
>
> **rocketed** moved extremely quickly

- Tell Ss to listen for the types of technology and the problems the comedian mentions. Play the recording as Ss complete the first two columns of the chart. Replay as many times as needed. Ss listen and check their answers.
- Go over answers with the class.

> **Answers**
>
> 1. Autocorrect;
>   It doesn't always give the right words. / It overcorrects.
> 2. Voice recognition;
>   It doesn't recognize what he's saying.
> 3. Autofill;
>   It doesn't fill in the right information.

Audio script: See page T-166.

B 🔊 [CD 1, Track 13]

- Explain the task. Play the recording again. Ss complete the third column of the chart.
- Go over answers with the class.

> **Possible answers**
>
> 1. It typed "Mr. Coffee" instead of "Mr. Coffel."
> 2. It typed "I'd really like to go out for a romantic dinner with Sue" instead of "I'd really like to go out for a romantic dinner with you."
> 3. It filled in a group contact instead of just one friend and invited 20 people to dinner.

Audio script: See page T-166.

C Pair work

- Explain the task. Ss work in pairs to discuss the questions.
- Have pairs share their answers with the class.

3 -ing clauses (GRAMMAR)

Learning aim: Practice using -ing clauses
(20–25 minutes)

> **Grammar notes**
>
> Modifying phrases with -ing are reduced adverb clauses.
> *While I was walking down the street, I saw a car crash.*
> *While walking down the street, I saw a car crash.*
>
> An adverb clause can only be changed to a modifying phrase with -ing when the subject of the adverb clause and the subject of the main clause are the same.
>
> The adverb clause in the sentence below cannot be changed to a modifying phrase because the subject of the adverb clause is the word *I* and the subject of the main clause is *a car*.
> *While I was walking down the street, a car crashed into a pole.*

- Books closed. Write on the board:
    1. *She is on the computer downloading new software.*
    2. *Having finished my book, I returned it to the library.*
    3. *Listening to the story, I remembered my own experience.*
- Read the sentences aloud and ask Ss to identify the verbs in each clause. (Answers: 1. *is, downloading*; 2. *Having finished, returned*; 3. *Listening, remembered*) Ask if the actions are happening at the same time or if one is happening before the other. (Answers: 1. They happen at the same time.; 2. The action of finishing the book happens first.; 3. They happen at the same time.)
- Books open. Discuss the information in the grammar box and read the example sentences.

A

- Have Ss look at the Starting Point on page 22 again. Explain the task and read the question aloud. Have Ss complete the task individually.
- Go over answers with the class.

> **Answers**
>
> *Working from home one Friday,*
> *Being a perfectionist,*

B

- Explain the task. Read the example answer aloud. Ss work individually to combine the sentences using -ing clauses. Then Ss work in pairs to compare their answers.
- Go over answers with the class.

> **Answers**
>
> 1. Being unable to remember my password, I clicked the link to have it sent to my email.
> 2. My computer froze up streaming a movie I'd already paid for.
> 3. Being very clumsy, I tripped and broke my brand-new tablet.
> 4. Smiling from ear to ear, Zoe took a picture of herself to post on her website.
> 5. Harry invited some friends to join a club using a social networking site.
> 6. Having implanted the criminal with a microchip, the police easily tracked him to his hideout.
> 7. Wen learned a lot about cloud computing reading *TechToday* magazine.
> 8. Having just gotten her first smartphone, Mari now spends all of her extra money on apps.

C Pair work

- Explain the task. Read the beginning of each sentence and the example answer aloud. Ss work individually to complete the sentences with their own ideas.
- Ss work in pairs to compare their answers.
- Have Ss share their partner's answers with the class.

3 GRAMMAR

-ing clauses

To express two actions performed by the same person or thing in a single sentence, we can include an *-ing* clause. An *-ing* clause contains an *-ing* participle.

The two actions happen at the same time or one action happens during another action.
The next day in class, my laptop crashed **opening** the file.
(My laptop crashed while / when it was opening the file.)

Trying to stay calm, I gave the presentation as best I could from memory.
(I was trying to stay calm while I gave the presentation.)

She is at her desk **typing** a paper.
(She is at her desk, and she is typing a paper.)

When one action happens before another action, use *having* + past participle.
Having gotten several calls from me, my parents became really worried.
(My parents got several calls from me, and then they became really worried.)

Reasons and explanations for actions can also be expressed with *-ing* clauses.
Being too embarrassed to call him at home, I had to go to work after all to access the network.
(Because I was too embarrassed to call him at home, I had to go to work.)

GRAMMAR PLUS see page 111

A Look at the Starting Point on page 22 again. Can you find more examples of *-ing* clauses in the stories?

B Combine the sentences using an *-ing* clause. Then compare answers with a partner.

1. I was unable to remember my password. I clicked the link to have it sent to my email.
   Being unable to remember my password, I clicked the link to have it sent to my email.
2. My computer froze up. It was streaming a movie I'd already paid for.
3. I am very clumsy. I tripped and broke my brand-new tablet.
4. Zoe smiled from ear to ear. Zoe took a picture of herself to post on her website.
5. Harry invited some friends to join a club. Harry used a social networking site to do this.
6. The police implanted the criminal with a microchip. The police easily tracked him to his hideout.
7. Wen learned a lot about cloud computing. Wen was reading *TechToday* magazine.
8. Mari just got her first smartphone. Mari now spends all of her extra money on apps.

C Pair work Complete the sentences with your own ideas. Compare answers with a partner.

1. Having broken my . . .
   cell phone, I finally had a good reason to upgrade to a better one.
2. Being a creative person, . . .
3. Trying to keep up with new technologies, . . .
4. Having purchased a new . . .

LESSON B   Technology and you   23

4 VOCABULARY & SPEAKING
Different attitudes

A Look at these expressions. Which ones express a positive attitude, a negative attitude, or a neutral attitude? Write +, –, or ~.

____ 1. aware of
____ 2. curious about
____ 3. sick of
____ 4. fed up with
____ 5. familiar with
____ 6. suspicious of
____ 7. intimidated by
____ 8. knowledgeable about
____ 9. crazy about
____ 10. reliant on
____ 11. grateful for
____ 12. leery of

B **Group work** Look at the list of inventions and technologies. Can you think of more? What are your feelings about them? Discuss with your group.

1. spacecraft for private flights
2. touch-screen technology
3. speech-translation technology
4. video surveillance
5. wearable electronics
6. mobile apps
7. laser surgery
8. robots

"So, what do you think about spacecraft for private flights?"
"I'm a little intimidated by the idea of being in space. I'm curious about it, but I wouldn't try it."

VOCABULARY PLUS see page 132

5 DISCUSSION
Tech savvy?

A Are you a technophile or a technophobe? Complete the survey to find out.

TECHNOPHILE or TECHNOPHOBE?

	Agree (2 pts.)	Not Sure (1 pt.)	Disagree (0 pts.)
1. If technology permits it, I would favor the development of machines that surpass humans in intelligence.	☐	☐	☐
2. Governments need to generously fund research and development in technology.	☐	☐	☐
3. Everyone should try to stay informed about the latest innovations in technology.	☐	☐	☐
4. Genetic technologies should be used to gradually improve the human body over the course of generations.	☐	☐	☐
5. Science and technology will someday solve the world's problems of famine, war, disease, and overcrowding.	☐	☐	☐
6. It's important to acquire new technological devices shortly after they come out.	☐	☐	☐
7. Social media has a positive effect on people's social lives.	☐	☐	☐
8. Being connected to the Internet is a human right.	☐	☐	☐

SCORE

0–4 You are a technophobe, a person who has a strong mistrust of technology.

5–8 While not in love with technology, you see the need for it in our world.

9–12 You're a fan of technology and may be showing some signs of being a geek.

13–16 You're a technophile, a person who is crazy about technology.

B **Group work** Discuss your answers to the survey. Talk about the reasons for your choices and whether or not you agree with your score.

4 Different attitudes (VOCABULARY & SPEAKING)

Learning aim: Learn and practice using expressions to talk about different attitudes toward technology (15–20 minutes)

A

- Explain the task. Read the list of expressions aloud. Go over any unfamiliar vocabulary. Ss work individually to complete the activity.
- Ss work in pairs to compare answers. Go over answers with the class.

Answers					
1. ~	3. –	5. ~	7. –	9. +	11. +
2. +	4. –	6. –	8. +	10. ~	12. –

B Group work

- Explain the task. Read the list of inventions and technologies. Have one pair of Ss read the example conversation to the class. Check that Ss understand the following vocabulary.

Vocabulary

spacecraft for private flights aircraft that flies regular individuals (not astronauts) as passengers into space

speech-translation technology a device or system that instantly translates something spoken in one language into another language

wearable electronics electronic devices designed to be worn (as clothes, accessories, etc.)

- Ss work individually to add more items. Give Ss time to think about how they feel about each item.
- Ss work in groups to discuss their ideas. Tell Ss to use the new vocabulary from part A when possible.
- Have a S from each group share their group's discussion with the class.

> **Optional activity:** *I can't live without . . .* **(15 minutes)**
>
> Ss have additional practice talking about technology.
>
> - Ss work in groups to discuss which piece of technology is the one that people today can't live without. Tell Ss to use the list from part B or their own ideas.
> - Have a S from each group report the group's decision to the class.
> - If time allows, have a class discussion about which item is the most important. Have groups defend their answers.

💡 To help Ss with vocabulary in this exercise, download the Fresh Idea *Bleep! Bleep!* from the Teacher Support Site.

5 Tech savvy? (DISCUSSION)

Learning aim: Talk about opinions and attitudes toward technology and practice the lesson vocabulary (15–20 minutes)

A

- Books closed. Ask Ss what they think the suffixes -*phile* and -*phobe* mean. (Answer: -*phile* means likes or has a strong interest in; -*phobe* means dislikes or is afraid of) Ask Ss if they know any words with these suffixes. Have Ss call out their ideas. Write them on the board.
- Books open. Explain the task. Read the survey items aloud. Check that Ss understand the following vocabulary.

Vocabulary

surpass go beyond

innovations new ideas or methods

genetic having to do with DNA

overcrowding too many people in one place

mistrust not believing or having confidence in

- Ss work individually to complete the survey. Ss add up their points and read what their score means. Explain that in this context a *geek* is someone who is very interested in technology.

B Group work

- Explain the task. Ss work in groups to discuss their answers to the survey and their score.
- Have a S from each group report on the group's discussion to the class.

> **Optional activity:** *Class survey* **(10–15 minutes)**
>
> Ss write a new survey about technology.
>
> - Ss work in groups to make five new survey questions, similar to the ones in part A.
> - Write the questions on the board and have the class take the new survey.
> - Have Ss tell the class their scores to see who is the biggest technophobe and who is the biggest technophile.

UNIT 3 Science and technology

6 A holiday from technology (READING)

Learning aim: Develop skills in understanding vocabulary in context, reading for specific information, making inferences, and giving a personal reaction to a reading (25–30 minutes)

A Pair work

- Books closed. Ask Ss to think about how important technology is in their lives. Ask Ss which piece of technology they could give up.
- Books open. Explain the task. Have Ss scan the article and then work in pairs to discuss the questions.
- Have Ss read the article silently to themselves. Check that Ss understand the following vocabulary.

Vocabulary

ceased stopped

take action do something about a situation

initiated began

banned said something was forbidden

confronted faced a problem and tried to deal with it

transform change completely

deprivation not having something that is usually considered necessary

technologically literate able to understand and use technology

succumbed accepted a situation that one was initially opposed to

intermittent happening occasionally, but not at regular times

straightens your head out helps you think clearly

B Group work

- Explain the task. Read the questions aloud. Give Ss time to think about their answers individually. Then have Ss work in groups to discuss the questions.
- Have a S from each group report on the group's discussion to the class.

Possible answers

1. The family ate together more often, talked more, played games, and went on outings. Anni began studying in the university library. Bill started playing his saxophone again and became interested in reading novels. Yes, it was a success.
2. They all had to learn how to entertain themselves without the Internet. They read more, began studying in different ways, and rediscovered old hobbies. *Answers to the second question will vary.*
3. Answers will vary.

Optional activity: *Vocabulary* (15–20 minutes)

Ss practice the vocabulary from the reading.

- Have Ss look at the article again. Tell them to write down any words that they did not know before.
- Ask Ss to call out their words, and write them on the board. As a class, write definitions for each word.
- Have Ss write a sentence using each word. Make sure they write sentences that show they understand the meaning of the word.
- Ask Ss to read their sentences to the class.

Optional activity: *More questions* (15–20 minutes)

Ss write their own comprehension questions about the article.

- Ss work in pairs to write five comprehension questions about the article.
- Tell Ss to close their books. Collect the questions and write them on the board (eliminating any doubles).
- Set a time limit and have Ss answer the questions without looking back at the article. Go over answers with the class.

For an alternative reading text or extra practice, download the Worksheet **3.2 Living off-grid** from the Teacher Support Site.

Do your students need more practice?

Assign . . .	for more practice in . . .
Grammar Plus 3B	Grammar
Vocabulary Plus 3B	Vocabulary
Online Vocabulary Accelerator 3B	Vocabulary
Workbook Lesson B	Grammar, Vocabulary, Reading
Online Workbook Lesson B	Grammar, Vocabulary, Reading, Listening

6 READING
A holiday from technology

A **Pair work** Scan the article. Which of the technologies mentioned do you use? How would your life change if you stopped using them for six months? Discuss with a partner. Then read the article.

I Took My Kids Offline

Susan Maushart was fed up. All she usually saw of her 15-year-old son, Bill, was the back of his head as he played video games. Her elder daughter, Anni, 18, had become overly reliant on social networking sites, and 14-year-old Sussy seemed physically attached to her laptop, often staying logged on to the Internet through the night.

"My concern," she says, "was that we had ceased to function as a family. We were just a collection of individuals who were very connected outwards – to friends, business, school, and sources of entertainment and information. But we simply weren't connecting with one another in real space and time in any sort of authentic way."

Having decided to take action, Maushart came up with a plan. She initiated an "experiment in living" and banned all technology at home for six months. Her kids really didn't believe her at first, but once they realized their mother was serious, they adapted well to an offline world.

Anni, Bill, and Sussy confronted boredom – something that they were previously unfamiliar with because of their endless access to online entertainment. They found out that it made them resourceful. Indeed, their mother thinks boredom is fundamentally important in terms of creativity: "If nothing's wrong, you're never motivated to change, to move out of that comfort zone."

Maushart had high expectations for her experiment: "I hoped that it would transform our lives – that we would become a closer family, read more, sit around the table to eat and play more music . . . that we would feel closer to one another." To her delight, many of these expectations were met.

During their half-year of technological deprivation, the family did eat together more regularly. They talked more. They played board games. They went on outings to the cinema and restaurants. Anni started studying in the university library. Bill rediscovered his saxophone and got into reading novels. Sussy, as the youngest and most technologically literate, struggled more, but eventually succumbed.

The family hasn't remained app-free, but there have been permanent changes. Because they'd come to understand how it was interfering with their social life, her older two teenagers have both taken holidays from Facebook. Bill sold his game console to buy a new saxophone, and Anni still prefers to study in the library, in a social-networking-free zone.

Maushart's children have all expressed a willingness to go offline again. It is something she too would love to do. "I'd look forward to a technology vacation," she says, "just like I look forward to going on a yoga retreat. I see it as an intermittent thing that straightens your head out, not a way of life."

Source: "Family: I Unplugged My Kids," by Melissa McClements, *The Guardian*

B **Group work** Discuss these questions. Then share your answers with the class.

1. What effects did Maushart's experiment have on her family? Was it a success?
2. How did being bored increase Anni, Bill, and Sussy's resourcefulness? Would it increase yours?
3. Would taking a "holiday from technology" be beneficial to most people? Why or why not?

COMMUNICATION REVIEW
UNITS 1–3

SELF-ASSESSMENT

How well can you do these things? Choose the best answer.

I can . . .	Very well	OK	A little
▶ Understand a conversation about people's appearance and personality (Ex. 1)	☐	☐	☐
▶ Take part in a discussion about attitudes toward clothes and fashion (Ex. 2)	☐	☐	☐
▶ Take part in a discussion about the impact of technology on people's lives (Ex. 3)	☐	☐	☐
▶ Take part in a discussion about issues associated with technology (Ex. 4)	☐	☐	☐

Now do the corresponding exercises. Was your assessment correct?

1 LISTENING
Class reunion

A Listen to a conversation between two friends. What is Karla trying to do? Choose the correct answer.

☐ a. She's trying to set up her personal profile on a social networking site.
☐ b. She's using a website to organize a class reunion.
☐ c. She's replying to messages she got from ex-classmates.

B Listen again. Are these statements true or false? Choose the correct answer.

	True	False
1. Karla is intimidated by the website technology.	☐	☐
2. Lucy isn't sure that the reunion will be completely harmonious.	☐	☐
3. Neither woman liked Andrew very much.	☐	☐
4. Renée's fashion taste has changed since she was in high school.	☐	☐
5. Mike's style has changed since he was in high school.	☐	☐

2 SPEAKING
Fashion statements

A Which of these statements about clothing do you agree with most?

- What you wear is who you are.
- People often discriminate against others because of the way they dress.
- Buying new clothes all the time is unethical.
- Clothes are like art that you wear.
- People who are interested in fashion are shallow and superficial.

B Group work Compare and explain your answers to part A. Try to find two statements that you all agree with.

Units 1–3
COMMUNICATION REVIEW

> Ss assess how well they have learned the communication skills in Units 1–3.

✓ Self-assessment

Review aim: Ss assess how well they have learned the material in Units 1–3 (10–15 minutes)

- Books closed. List or elicit from Ss the language and topics covered in Units 1–3.
- Books open. Explain the task. Read the list of skills aloud.
- Ss work individually to do the assessment.
- Tell Ss they will review their assessment after doing the activities in this unit.

1 Class reunion (LISTENING)

Review aim: Develop skills in listening to gerund and infinitive constructions and to adjectives and phrasal verbs to describe people and styles (20–25 minutes)

A 🔊 [CD 1, Track 14]

> **Culture note**
> In the United States, school reunions are very popular for high school and college graduates. They are usually held every five or ten years after the year of graduation. High school reunions tend to be big parties for one evening. College reunions tend to be parties and/or events that take place over a whole weekend.

- Explain the task. Tell Ss to read the possible answers. Check that Ss understand the following vocabulary.

> **Vocabulary**
> **neat** clever
> **personality clashes** disagreements between people who have different personalities that aren't compatible
> **getting dressed up** putting on formal clothes

- Tell Ss to listen for the answer to the question. Play the recording as Ss choose the correct answer. Replay as many times as needed. Ss listen and check their answer.

- Go over the answer with the class.

> **Answer**
> b. She's using a website to organize a class reunion.

Audio script: See page T-166.

B 🔊 [CD 1, Track 15]

- Explain that Ss will listen again, decide if the statements are true or false, and then choose the correct answer. Read the statements aloud and answer any questions about vocabulary.
- Play the recording and have Ss complete the activity. Replay as many times as needed. Ss listen and check their answers.
- Ss work in pairs to compare answers. Go over answers with the class.

> **Answers**
> 1. False   3. True   5. True
> 2. True   4. False

Audio script: See page T-166.

- To review the grammar, make copies of the audio script and have Ss work in pairs to underline all the gerunds, infinitives, adjectives, and phrasal verbs they can find.

2 Fashion statements (SPEAKING)

Review aim: Talk about attitudes toward fashion and practice cleft sentences (20–25 minutes)

A
- Explain the task. Read the statements aloud.
- Have Ss think individually about their answers.

B Group work
- Explain the task. Ss work in groups to discuss their answers to part A.
- Have a S from each group report on the group's answers to the class.

UNITS 1–3 Communication review T-26

3 Technological advances (DISCUSSION)

Review aim: Discuss technological issues and practice using articles (20–25 minutes)

A
- Focus Ss' attention on the pictures. Ask Ss to explain what they see.
- Explain the task and read the question aloud. Give Ss time to think individually of their answers.

B Pair work
- Explain the task. Have one pair of Ss read the example conversation to the class. Point out the definite and indefinite articles, and also the nouns that have no article.
- Ss work in pairs to compare their answers. Ask a few pairs to report on their discussion to the class.

> **Optional activity:** *Class poll* (15–20 minutes)
> Ss vote for their favorite technological advance.
> - Write the technological advances from part A on the board in a column. Ask Ss to vote for their favorite and tally the votes on the board.
> - Have a class discussion about why Ss think the technological advance with the most points is so popular.

4 Is technology good or bad? (DISCUSSION)

Review aim: Identify the main issues and express opinions about the positive and negative effects of technology (20–25 minutes)

A
- Explain the task. Read the opinions aloud. Check that Ss understand the following vocabulary.

> **Vocabulary**
> **dispose of** get rid of something you no longer need or want
> **flawed** has problems
> **overeager** more enthusiastic than is good or necessary
> **compactness** being small and efficiently arranged
> **flashiness** being too big, bright, and/or expensive-looking

- Ss work individually to identify the main issues. Go over answers with the class.

> **Answers**
> The main issue in the first opinion is that technology should be an improvement on what it replaces.
>
> The main issue in the second opinion is that people are more concerned with what's new rather than with what's useful.

- Give Ss time to think individually about their own points of view on the issues.

B Group work
- Explain the task. Ss work in groups to discuss their points of view on the issues in part A.
- Have a S from each group report on the group's answers to the class and write them on the board.
- Determine which points of view are the most common and have a class discussion about these.

✓ Have Ss look at their answers to the self-assessment at the beginning of this review unit. As a class, discuss which skills were easy and which were more difficult and why.

3 DISCUSSION
Technological advances

A Which of these advances in technology has had the most positive or negative impact on our lives?

social media

internal combustion engine

genetically modified food

large-scale farming

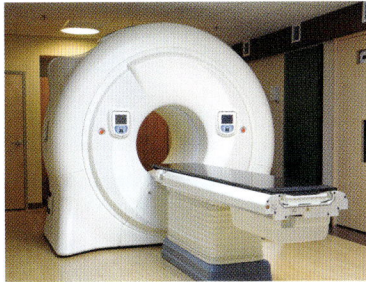

medical technology

renewable energy technology

B Pair work Compare your answers with a partner.

"I think social media has had the most positive impact on our lives. We are so much more connected than we were a few years ago."

"Well, that's true, but medical technology has had more of a positive influence on people around the world."

4 DISCUSSION
Is technology good or bad?

A Read these opinions about technology. What are the main issues they raise? What's your own point of view on these issues?

When you are ready to invest in a new technology, there are a few questions you should ask yourself. First, is the new item cheaper than what it replaces? Does it save space? Will it make your life easier? Is it energy efficient? Will you be able to recycle it or at least dispose of it properly? If not, don't buy it.

— Kwang-hyun Lee, Busan, Korea

How we think about technology is flawed. We are overeager to have the newest gadget. We are too impressed by speed, noise, compactness, and general flashiness. We need a more mature and cautious way of thinking about technology. New is not always better.

— Inés Candia, Asunción, Paraguay

B Group work Compare your ideas. Are your points of view similar? How?

UNITS 1–3   Communication review   27

4 SUPERSTITIONS AND BELIEFS
LESSON A ▶ Superstitions

1 STARTING POINT
The things people believe!

A Read the list of superstitions. Do you believe in any of them?

Beliefs Across Cultures

In Turkey, many people agree that when someone goes on a journey, you should pour water on the ground behind him or her to bring the person back safely.

In Brazil, people claim you should enter a place using your right foot to have good fortune.

In Russia, looking into a broken mirror will bring bad luck.

In Italy, many people believe that if visitors toss a coin into the Trevi Fountain in Rome, they will return to that city in the future.

In Japan, it is very bad luck to give a present that consists of four pieces.

In Venezuela, some people say that if someone passes a broom over your feet, you will never get married.

In Greece, you should place your shoes with the soles on the floor when you take them off because overturned shoes are considered unlucky.

B Pair work Which superstitions do some people in your culture believe?

2 VOCABULARY
Expressions with *luck*

A Match the statements with the replies containing *luck*.

1. "I've got to go. I have a big test tomorrow." ____
2. "I'm out of cash. Is there an ATM nearby?" ____
3. "He won the first game of chess he ever played!" ____
4. "He lost his job and house, and now he's sick." ____
5. "Are you going to Europe this summer?" ____
6. "How did you win those soccer tickets?" ____
7. "Thanks for the $20. Can I have $40 more?" ____

a. "That was beginner's luck."
b. "No such luck. I'm staying home."
c. "I'm afraid you're out of luck."
d. "Wow! He's got bad luck."
e. "Well, best of luck!"
f. "Don't push your luck."
g. "It was the luck of the draw."

B Pair work Use the expressions with *luck* to write short conversations. Act them out with your partner.

"I really want tickets to the Jay Z concert."
"I'm afraid you're out of luck. They sold out in 10 minutes!"

VOCABULARY PLUS see page 133

28 UNIT 4 Superstitions and beliefs

4 SUPERSTITIONS AND BELIEFS

LESSON A ▶ *Superstitions*

> In this unit, Ss use reporting clauses to talk about superstitions and beliefs. They also practice reporting clauses in the passive.

1 The things people believe! (STARTING POINT)

Learning aim: Discuss superstitions from different cultures and see reporting clauses in context (10–15 minutes)

A
- Books closed. Write a superstition that most Ss will know on the board. For example:

  Don't walk under a ladder.

  Ask Ss if they know what is supposed to happen if you walk under a ladder. (Answer: It will bring you bad luck.) Ask Ss if they think this kind of thing is true.
- Books open. Have Ss cover the superstitions below the pictures. Then ask Ss what each picture illustrates.
- Explain the task. Read the list of superstitions aloud. Go over any unfamiliar vocabulary.
- Give Ss time to think about their answer to the question.
- Have a class discussion about which superstitions Ss believe, if any.

B Pair work
- Explain the task. Read the question aloud.
- Ss work in pairs to answer the question. Make sure that Ss take turns asking and answering follow-up questions.
- Have pairs share their answers with the class.

2 Expressions with *luck* (VOCABULARY)

Learning aim: Learn and practice using expressions about luck (10–15 minutes)

A
- Explain the task. Read the statements and the replies aloud. Go over any unfamiliar vocabulary.
- Ss work individually to complete the activity.
- Go over answers with the class.

Answers
1. e	2. c	3. a	4. d	5. b	6. g	7. f

B Pair work
- Explain the task. Have one pair of Ss read the example conversation to the class.
- Ss work in pairs to write their conversations. Go around the class and help as needed.
- Have pairs act out their conversations for the class.

UNIT 4 Superstitions and beliefs   T-28

3 Reporting clauses (GRAMMAR)

Learning aim: Practice using reporting clauses (20–25 minutes)

> **Grammar notes**
> Reporting verbs introduce what someone says or thinks. The object of the reporting verb is a noun clause. The clause can be introduced by *that*. However, *that* is often omitted, especially when speaking.

- Books closed. Write on the board:
  1. *Dan: "If you walk under a ladder, it will bring you bad luck."*
  2. *Dan believes (that) if you walk under a ladder, it will bring you bad luck.*

  Ask: *What is different about the two examples?* (Answer: Number 1 is someone expressing his belief in direct speech; number 2 is reporting what the person believes in reported speech.) Tell Ss that number 2 has a reporting clause – *Dan believes (that) . . .* – to introduce the reported speech.
- Books open. Discuss the information in the grammar box and read the example sentences.

A

- Have Ss look at the Starting Point on page 28 again. Explain the task and read the question aloud. Go over answers with the class.

> **Answers**
> Sentences with a reporting clause:
> *In Brazil, people claim . . .*
> *In Italy, many people believe that . . .*
>
> Possible answers rewritten with reporting clauses:
> In Russia, <u>some people feel that</u> looking into a broken mirror will bring bad luck.
> In Japan, <u>most people agree that</u> it is very bad luck to give a present that consists of four pieces.
> In Greece, <u>people say that</u> you should place your shoes with the soles on the floor . . .

B

- Explain the task. Read the sentences and the example answer aloud. Answer any questions about vocabulary.
- Ss work individually to complete the activity.
- Go over answers with the class.

> **Possible answers**
> 1. Many people agree that almost everyone is superstitious about a few things.
> 2. Some people say that it's fine to follow superstitions for fun but not to really believe in them.
> 3. Our teacher explained that superstitions are an important part of our cultural heritage.
> 4. Many people assert that superstitions are dangerous because they prevent people from thinking scientifically.
> 5. Sociologists believe that many holiday rituals are based on ancient beliefs and superstitions.
> 6. Many people claim that superstitions sometimes contain truths handed down from the past.

C Pair work

- Explain the task. Have a S read the example statement to the class.
- Ss work in pairs to share their answers from part B and to discuss their opinions.
- Have Ss share their partner's opinions with the class.

4 Everyday superstitions (DISCUSSION)

Learning aim: Talk about superstitions and practice the lesson grammar (15–20 minutes)

A Pair work

- Explain the task. Read the categories aloud.
- Ss work in pairs to do the activity. Brainstorm superstitions for each category as a class, if necessary.

B Group work

- Explain the task. Have one pair of Ss read the example conversation to the class.
- Put pairs together and have them discuss their answers from part A. Remind Ss to ask follow-up questions.

3 GRAMMAR

Reporting clauses

To report what someone says, thinks, believes, etc., you can use a sentence that includes a reporting clause. The use of the word *that* is optional.

In Turkey, **many people agree (that)** when someone goes on a journey, you should pour water on the ground behind him or her to bring the person back safely.

In Venezuela, **some people say (that)** if someone passes a broom over your feet, you will never get married.

The following verbs are often used in reporting clauses.
More formal: argue   assert   claim   report
More conversational: admit   agree   assume   believe   doubt   explain   feel   say

GRAMMAR PLUS *see page 112*

A Look at the Starting Point on page 28 again. Can you find two other sentences that contain reporting clauses? For the sentences that don't, add a reporting clause and rewrite the sentence.

B Rewrite each sentence with a reporting clause. Use a different reporting verb to introduce each one.

1. Everyone is superstitious about a few things.
   Many people agree that almost everyone is superstitious about a few things.
2. It's fine to follow superstitions for fun, but not to really believe in them.
3. Superstitions are an important part of our cultural heritage.
4. Superstitions are dangerous because they prevent people from thinking scientifically.
5. Many holiday rituals are based on ancient beliefs and superstitions.
6. Superstitions sometimes contain truths handed down from the past.

C Pair work Share your answers with your partner. Then give your opinions about the statements.

"Many people agree that almost everyone is superstitious about a few things. It's true! When I spill some salt, I always throw a little over my left shoulder so I don't have bad luck."

4 DISCUSSION

Everyday superstitions

A Pair work Do you know any superstitions connected with these things? Describe them to your partner.

- animals and plants
- days, dates, or months
- household objects
- clothing
- food
- colors
- money
- numbers
- weddings

B Group work Join another pair and compare your answers. Ask follow-up questions.

"In parts of Great Britain, people who aren't feeling well sometimes stick coins into the trunk of a tree that has fallen down."
"Why is that?"
"Well, some people believe that if you put a coin in wood, it can make illnesses go away. They call these trees 'wishing trees.'"

LESSON A Superstitions

5 LISTENING
Common explanations

A Listen to people talk about superstitions. What superstitions are they talking about? How is each superstition explained?

B Listen again. Answer these questions.

1. How did the woman with allergies react to the man's explanation?
2. Why did the son feel it was necessary to say that he was only kidding?
3. Why does the man suggest not telling Mr. Wilson that being left-handed was once thought to be suspicious?

6 DISCUSSION
Are you superstitious?

A Pair work Take turns interviewing each other, and complete the questionnaire. Then calculate your scores.

Lucky or Unlucky?

	YES (1 pt.)	NO (0 pt.)
1. Is it unlucky not to say something like "Bless you!" when someone sneezes?	☐	☐
2. Are there any particular days that you consider unlucky?	☐	☐
3. Do you have any lucky numbers?	☐	☐
4. Do you think some colors bring good luck?	☐	☐
5. Do you avoid walking under a ladder because it might bring you bad luck?	☐	☐
6. Are there any animals you consider unlucky?	☐	☐
7. Do you believe that certain actions before a wedding bring good or bad luck?	☐	☐
8. Do you carry any good luck charms or have any in your house?	☐	☐
9. Do you have a piece of clothing that brings you good luck?	☐	☐
10. Do you avoid having specific items in your house because they might bring bad luck?	☐	☐

SCORE
- 0–1 Life is not a matter of luck to you!
- 2–4 You're not very superstitious, but . . .
- 5–7 You're fairly superstitious, aren't you?
- 8–10 Wow! You're really superstitious!

B Group work Compare your scores. Then explain some of the things you're superstitious about. Is there anything else that you think brings good or bad luck?

"Well, when I talk about something that's going well, I say 'knock on wood.'"
"Really? Why do you do that?"
"Well, they say that if you knock on something made of wood, your luck will continue."

5 Common explanations (LISTENING)

Learning aim: Develop skills in listening for the main ideas and details, and in paraphrasing (15–20 minutes)

A [CD 1, Track 16]

- Explain the task. Read the questions aloud. Check that Ss understand the following vocabulary.

> **Vocabulary**
>
> **automatically** without thinking
>
> **(you're) in for** (you are) going to experience something, usually unpleasant
>
> **suspicious** making you think that something is wrong or strange about someone or a situation

- Tell Ss to listen for the answers to the questions. Play the recording as Ss listen for the answers. Replay as many times as needed. Ss listen and check their answers.
- Go over answers with the class.

> **Possible answers**
>
> 1. Saying "Bless you" when someone sneezes:
>   People would bless a person who sneezed as a way to ensure the return of life or to encourage the person's heart to continue beating.
> 2. Breaking a mirror causing seven years of bad luck:
>   Once a mirror is broken, the person can't see himself or herself as a whole person in it, so people thought something really bad was going to happen to them for seven years, since this was the time they believed it would take for the body to become whole again.
> 3. Getting up on the wrong side of the bed:
>   Since most people are right-handed, people in the past thought being left-handed was suspicious.

Audio script: See page T-167.

B [CD 1, Track 17]

- Explain that Ss will listen again and answer the questions. Read the questions aloud.
- Tell Ss to listen for the answers to the questions. Play the recording as Ss listen for the answers. Replay as many times as needed. Ss listen and check their answers.
- Go over answers with the class.

> **Answers**
>
> 1. She seemed unconcerned by the explanation.
> 2. He joked that his mother was going to have seven years of bad luck, and his mother reacted with concern.
> 3. Mr. Wilson is left-handed, and since he is in a bad mood, he might not like being called suspicious.

Audio script: See page 167.

> **Optional activity:** *Scrambled* **(20 minutes)**
>
> **Ss practice understanding conversations.**
>
> - Write one of the conversations from the audio script on a separate piece of paper. Make enough copies for each pair of Ss. Cut the paper into strips so that each of the sentences is on a separate strip of paper.
> - Ss work in pairs. Give each pair the papers and have them unscramble the conversation.
> - Play the recording again for Ss to check their answers.

6 Are you superstitious? (DISCUSSION)

Learning aim: Talk about belief in superstitions (15–20 minutes)

A Pair work

- Explain the task. Read the questionnaire aloud. Make sure Ss understand *good luck charm*. Have them give a definition or examples.
- Ss work in pairs to do the activity.
- Have Ss share their partner's answers with the class.

B Group work

- Explain the task. Have one pair of Ss read the example conversation to the class.
- Ss work in groups to discuss their scores for the questionnaire and what else they think brings good luck or bad luck.
- Have a S from each group report on the group's discussion to the class.

> For more practice discussing this topic, download the Worksheet *4.1 Superstitions* from the Teacher Support Site.

UNIT 4 Superstitions and beliefs

7 Restating a thesis (WRITING)

Learning aim: Write a composition with a thesis statement and supporting examples, and restate the thesis in the last paragraph (40–50 minutes)

A

- Tell Ss to read the information in the box at the top of the page. Ask: *What is a thesis statement?* (Answer: the sentence containing the main idea of a composition) Ask: *What can you find in the first paragraph of a composition?* (Answer: the thesis statement and sometimes general supporting examples)
- Remind Ss that a thesis statement often includes a main idea or opinion that is further explained in the rest of the composition. If necessary, also remind Ss that each body paragraph of a composition should focus on only one aspect of the main idea. Each of those paragraphs has a topic sentence to present that aspect of the main idea.
- Explain the task. Have Ss read the composition silently to themselves. Check that Ss understand the following vocabulary.

Vocabulary

concerning about

fake not real

panics feels extremely upset and nervous to the point of losing self-control

level-headed having good judgment, able to be calm even in difficult situations

goes out of his way to makes a special effort to

- Ss work individually to complete the activity.
- Go over answers with the class.

Answers

Thesis statement:
Superstitions concerning both good and bad luck are part of everyone's life in the United States – even if you don't believe in them, they are difficult to ignore.

Supporting example:
Even people who claim not to believe in superstitions sometimes use phrases such as "knock on wood" when they speak.

Restatement of the thesis:
Superstitions are just a part of life, whether you believe them or not.

B

- Explain the writing task.
- Ss work individually to write their compositions. Remind Ss to make sure their first and last paragraphs follow the guidelines.
- Go around the class and help as needed.

C Pair work

- Ss work in pairs to exchange compositions and take turns answering the questions.
- Go around the class and help as needed. Encourage Ss to ask and answer follow-up questions about the compositions, and to ask about anything in the composition they don't understand.

> To help Ss with writing in this exercise, download the Fresh Idea *Collective texts* from the Teacher Support Site.

Do your students need more practice?	
Assign . . .	for more practice in . . .
Grammar Plus 4A	Grammar
Vocabulary Plus 4A	Vocabulary
Online Vocabulary Accelerator 4A	Vocabulary
Workbook Lesson A	Grammar, Vocabulary, Writing
Online Workbook Lesson A	Grammar, Vocabulary, Writing

7 WRITING
Restating a thesis

> The first paragraph of a composition provides the thesis statement and sometimes gives general examples. The last paragraph restates the thesis statement.

A Read this composition. Find the thesis statement and a supporting example in the first paragraph. Then look at the last paragraph. Which sentence restates the thesis statement?

SUPERSTITIONS: HARD TO IGNORE

Some people think that certain objects bring them good luck; others avoid certain things or situations that they believe might bring them bad luck. Even people who claim not to believe in superstitions sometimes use phrases such as "knock on wood" when they speak. Superstitions concerning both good and bad luck are part of everyone's life in the United States – even if you don't believe in them, they are difficult to ignore.

It's easy to find superstitions relating to good luck. For example, my friend Irene carries a fake rabbit's foot in her pocket to bring her good luck. Another friend, who plays baseball, panics whenever his mother washes his "lucky" baseball socks. My mother believes that nine is her lucky number, and even my level-headed father has hung a horseshoe over the entrance of our home to bring us good luck and good fortune.

Superstitions concerning bad luck are just as common. My mother believes that certain days are bad for events like marriages and ceremonies, while my uncle always says "knock on wood" and then looks for something made of wood to knock on with his hand. Then there's my friend who goes out of his way to avoid black cats. My sister never puts her bag on the floor because she thinks doing so will bring her bad luck.

Personally, I am not very superstitious. I don't have any lucky socks, and I don't have any lucky or unlucky numbers. Still, I find myself avoiding black cats, and I knock on wood every now and then. Superstitions are just a part of life, whether you believe them or not.

B Write a composition about superstitions and good and bad luck in your culture. Do your first and last paragraphs follow the guidelines stated in the box above?

C Pair work Exchange your composition with a partner, and answer these questions.

1. Does the first paragraph contain a thesis statement and give general examples?
2. How well do the examples in the middle paragraphs support the thesis? Are there enough examples?
3. Does the last paragraph restate the thesis?

LESSON B ▶ Believe it or not

1 STARTING POINT
Fact or fiction?

A Three of these news stories are true and one is false. Decide which one is false.

1 A company has produced a device designed to chase away loitering children and teenagers. It was explained that the device emits a sound that irritates young people.

2 It's been confirmed that if an egg is placed directly between two cell phones that are in "talk mode," the egg will be cooked in about an hour.

3 A candy company is selling lollipops with a variety of insects inside, including crickets, ants, and scorpions. It is claimed that the lollipops are actually quite tasty.

4 It was reported that a website broadcast live video of a wheel of cheddar cheese as it ripened. It is said that the video ran for over nine months.

B Pair work Tell your partner your choice and explain why you think it is false. (For the answer, see page 142.)

2 VOCABULARY & SPEAKING
That sounds fishy!

A Which of these words describe something likely to be true? Which describe something likely to be fabricated? Divide them into two groups. Then add two more items to each group.

| believable | convincing | dubious | fishy | misleading | plausible |
| conceivable | credible | far-fetched | iffy | phony | well-founded |

B Use the words in part A to write about each story in the Starting Point.

The article about the candy company sounds completely phony to me. It's just not a plausible story.

C Group work Take turns making statements, some true and some false, about yourself to your group. Respond using the words describing truth and fabrication.

"I have a very good singing voice, and I sing with a band on the weekend."
"Well, your speaking voice is very nice, so that seems pretty believable to me."

VOCABULARY PLUS see page 133

32 UNIT 4 Superstitions and beliefs

LESSON B ▶ Believe it or not

1 Fact or fiction? (STARTING POINT)

Learning aim: Discuss news stories and see reporting clauses in the passive in context (10–15 minutes)

A

- Books closed. Ask Ss where they usually get their news from (e.g., the Internet, TV, newspapers, radio, magazines, etc.). Ask them if they ever read tabloid news sites or newspapers – sites or newspapers that publish news stories that are usually false or sensational. Ask Ss how reliable they think various news sources are.
- Books open. Explain the task. Read the stories aloud. Check that Ss understand the vocabulary on the right.

> **Vocabulary**
>
> **loitering** remaining in one place and not doing anything
>
> **emits** sends out into the air
>
> **wheel of (cheddar) cheese** a large round piece of cheese; the form it comes in before it is cut and sold
>
> **ripen** to age so that the proper color, texture, and taste are achieved

- Give Ss time to think about their answer.

B Pair work

- Explain the task. Ss work in pairs to do the activity.
- Have Ss share their partner's answers with the class.
- Ask Ss to check the answer on page 142. (Answer: Story 2 is false.)

2 That sounds fishy! (VOCABULARY & SPEAKING)

Learning aim: Learn and practice using adjectives to discuss if something is true or false (15–20 minutes)

A

- Books closed. Ask Ss to guess the meaning of *That sounds fishy!* (Answer: That seems suspicious/untrue.) If necessary, give Ss a hint by asking them what bad fish smells like and what kind of feeling the smell evokes.
- Books open. Explain the task and read the list of adjectives aloud. Ss work individually to complete the activity.
- Have Ss compare answers with a partner. Go over answers with the class.

> **Answers**
>
> Likely to be true:
> believable, conceivable, convincing, credible, plausible, well-founded
> (Possible additions: persuasive, possible)
>
> Likely to be fabricated:
> dubious, far-fetched, fishy, iffy, misleading, phony
> (Possible additions: doubtful, unlikely)

B

- Explain the task. Have a S read the example sentence to the class.
- Ss work individually to complete the task. Have Ss read their sentences to the class.

C Group work

- Explain the task. Have one pair of Ss read the example conversation to the class. Then demonstrate the task by saying two true statements about yourself and one false one. Have Ss comment on each statement using words from the list in part A. Give Ss time to think about statements that they could make about themselves.
- Ss work in groups to do the activity.
- Have a S from each group share the most surprising true statement that they heard with the class.

> **Optional activity:** *Be a tabloid writer* (20 minutes)
>
> Ss write a story for a tabloid news site and present it to the class.
>
> - Have Ss look again at the four stories in Exercise 1A. Tell them that they are going to write a similar story for a tabloid news site. Encourage them to use their imaginations to write a completely unbelievable and funny story. Remind Ss that a news story usually answers the questions *who*, *what*, *when*, *where*, and sometimes *why*.
> - Ss work individually to write their stories.
> - Have Ss present their stories to the class. Have the class vote on the best one.

UNIT 4 Superstitions and beliefs   T-32

3 Reporting clauses in the passive (GRAMMAR)

Learning aim: Practice using reporting clauses in the passive (20–25 minutes)

> **Grammar notes**
>
> *It* + the passive form of a reporting verb (e.g., *argue, claim, assert, assume, believe, estimate, feel, report, say*) is often used to report a general claim or an opinion.
>
> The agent (*by* + noun) is often omitted in reporting clauses in the passive because it is understood to mean *some people* or *many people*.

- Books closed. Write on the board:
  1. *Gorillas can learn to use sign language.*
  2. *It is believed that gorillas can learn to use sign language.*

  Read the sentences aloud and ask Ss where they might see the second sentence. (Possible answers: in more formal or academic texts, or in a newspaper or magazine)

- Books open. Discuss the information in the grammar box and read the example sentences.

A

- Have Ss look at the Starting Point on page 32 again. Explain the task and read the question aloud. Go over answers with the class.

> **Answers**
>
> Story 2:
> *It's been confirmed that if an egg is placed . . .*
>
> Story 3:
> *It is claimed that the lollipops are . . .*
>
> Story 4:
> *It was reported that a website broadcast . . .*

B

- Explain the task. Read the example answer aloud.
- Ss work individually to rewrite the sentences using reporting clauses in the passive.
- Ss work in pairs to compare their answers. Go over answers with the class.

> **Possible answers**
>
> 1. It is estimated that 50 percent of the population believes in ghosts.
> 2. It is said that the idea of horseshoes being lucky dates back to the ancient Greeks.
> 3. It is claimed that some people can communicate with plants.
> 4. It was once thought (that) the sun moved around the earth.
> 5. It has been reported that practical jokes on April 1 are becoming less common.
> 6. It is argued that people create Internet hoaxes for a wide variety of reasons.
> 7. It is thought that people developed the first superstitions in an attempt to gain control over things they didn't understand.
> 8. It is too easily assumed that just because something is in print, it's true.

C Pair work

- Explain the task. Read the facts and example answer aloud. Go over any unfamiliar vocabulary.
- Read the information in the Useful Expressions box aloud. Give an example of how to use each phrase.
- Ss work in pairs to talk about the facts. Make sure they use reporting clauses in the passive and the expressions.
- Have Ss share some of their sentences with the class.

> **Possible answers**
>
> 1. Get this – it's been reported that a company makes a bicycle that seats seven people.
> 2. Believe it or not, it has been claimed that a 33-year-old man . . .
> 3. Did you hear what happened? It was admitted that a flight was denied permission to land . . .
> 4. Get this – it is believed that butterflies . . .
> 5. Believe it or not, it is claimed that you can send a coconut through the mail in the . . .
> 6. Did you hear what happened? It was reported that a crocodile measuring over six meters long was found . . .
> 7. Get this – it was reported that the world's first webcam was used to let staff . . .

D Pair work

- Explain the task. Give Ss time to complete the statements with their own information.
- Ss work in pairs to compare their statements.
- Have Ss share their partner's answers with the class.

3 GRAMMAR

Reporting clauses in the passive

To report a general claim or opinion, you can use a passive form of a reporting verb and *it*.
Notice that the agent is often omitted and understood to be "some people" or "many people."
It was explained (that) the device emits a sound that irritates young people.
It is said (that) the video ran for over nine months.

GRAMMAR PLUS see page 113

A Look at the Starting Point on page 32 again. Can you find other examples of reporting clauses in the passive?

B Rewrite these statements with a reporting clause in the passive with *it*.

1. People estimate that 50 percent of the population believes in ghosts.
   It is estimated that 50 percent of the population believes in ghosts.

2. Some sources say that the idea of horseshoes being lucky dates back to the ancient Greeks.

3. Many claim that some people can communicate with plants.

4. People once thought the sun moved around the earth.

5. Some sources have reported that practical jokes on April 1 are becoming less common.

6. Experts argue that people create Internet hoaxes for a wide variety of reasons.

7. Sociologists think that people developed the first superstitions in an attempt to gain control over things they didn't understand.

8. People too easily assume that just because something is in print, it's true.

C **Pair work** Use reporting clauses in the passive to talk about these interesting facts.

1. A company makes a bicycle that seats seven people.
2. A 33-year-old man married a 104-year-old woman.
3. On April 1, 2006, a flight was denied permission to land because the air traffic controller was on a tea break.
4. Butterflies can taste with their feet.
5. You can send a coconut through the mail in the United States without any wrapping.
6. A crocodile measuring over six meters long was found in the Philippines.
7. The world's first webcam was used to let staff in a university computer department see the office coffee pot.

"Get this – it's been reported that a company makes a bicycle that seats seven people."

Useful expressions

Reporting something surprising
Get this – . . .
Believe it or not, . . .
Did you hear what happened?

D **Pair work** Complete these statements about beliefs using your own information. Compare your statements with a partner.

1. People don't believe this anymore, but it used to be said that . . .
2. Recently, it has been reported in the news that . . .

LESSON B Believe it or not

4 LISTENING
Shocking news

A Look at the map of Belgium. What do you know about this country?

B Listen to a conversation about a journalistic hoax that affected many people in Belgium. What was the hoax?

C Listen again. Which events actually happened? Choose the correct answers.

☐ 1. The king and queen left the country.
☐ 2. People panicked.
☐ 3. A television station website crashed.
☐ 4. Foreign ambassadors called the Belgian authorities.

5 DISCUSSION
Internet hoaxes

A **Pair work** Have you ever read or heard about something on the Internet that was a hoax? Tell your partner about it.

B **Pair work** Read these claims found on the Internet. Choose the ones you think are hoaxes. Then discuss with a partner. (For the answers, see page 142.)

Website Claims

	HOAX?
1. A man offers $10,000 to anyone who can find him a wife.	☐
2. There is a group dedicated to preventing cruelty to insects throughout the world.	☐
3. Each year, the Internet must be shut down for 24 hours to allow authorities to clean it.	☐
4. There is a new chewing gum that you can recharge with flavor when the taste fades.	☐
5. An 85-year-old woman is training to climb Mount Everest with her little dog.	☐
6. An adventure company is now reserving seats for a trip to the center of the earth.	☐
7. A new technology allows you to get a suntan from your computer screen.	☐
8. A company can deliver tacos to homes using delivery robots.	☐

C **Group work** Discuss these questions with your group.

1. Which of the website claims seems the most plausible to you? Which seems the most iffy? Why?
2. Why do you think people create hoax websites and hoax emails?
3. Do you think people who create Internet hoaxes should be punished?

4 Shocking news (LISTENING)

Learning aim: Develop skills in listening for gist and details (15–20 minutes)

A
- Books closed. Ask Ss what a *hoax* is. (Answer: a trick to make people believe something that isn't true) Ask them if they know of any famous hoaxes.
- Books open. Have Ss look at the map. Have the class answer the question.

> **Possible answers**
> Belgium is in Europe, between France, the Netherlands, and Germany. Belgians speak French, Dutch (or Flemish), and/or German. Belgium is famous for chocolate, french fries, and waffles. The capital is Brussels. Belgium has a monarchy.

B [CD 1, Track 18]
- Explain the task. Read the question aloud. Check that Ss understand the following vocabulary.

> **Vocabulary**
> **April Fools'** April 1, traditionally a day when people play harmless tricks on one another. A person who believes the trick is known as an "April Fool."
> **pranks** tricks meant to be funny and not harm anyone
> **declared independence** separated from a central government and became an independent state
> **frantic** almost out of control because of extreme emotions such as worry or fear
> **cooked up** invented (a story)

- Tell Ss to listen for the answer to the question. Play the recording as Ss listen for the answer. Replay as many times as needed. Ss listen and check their answers.
- Go over the answer with the class.

> **Answer**
> A TV station reported that the northern/Dutch-speaking half of Belgium had declared independence.

Audio script: See page T-167.

C [CD 1, Track 19]
- Explain that Ss will listen again and choose the events that actually happened.
- Read the statements aloud and answer any questions about vocabulary.
- Play the recording and have Ss complete the activity.
- Ss work in pairs to compare answers. Go over answers with the class.

> **Answers**
> 2, 3, 4

Audio script: See page T-167.

5 Internet hoaxes (DISCUSSION)

Learning aim: Talk about Internet hoaxes and practice the lesson vocabulary (15–20 minutes)

A Pair work
- Explain the task. Ss work in pairs to discuss the question. Alternatively, if some Ss don't know of any Internet hoaxes, have a class discussion. Have Ss who know about Internet hoaxes tell the class about them.

B Pair work
- Explain the task. Read the website claims aloud. Check that Ss understand the following vocabulary.

> **Vocabulary**
> **dedicated to** giving a lot of time and energy to a cause
> **fades** loses strength

- Ss work individually to do the activity.
- Ss then work in pairs to discuss their answers.
- Have Ss share their partner's answers with the class.
- Tell Ss to check their answers on page 142. (Answer: All are hoaxes.)

C Group work
- Explain the task. Read the questions aloud.
- Ss work in groups to discuss the questions.
- Have a S from each group report on the group's discussion to the class.

For more practice with this topic, download the Worksheet *4.2 Origins of superstitions* from the Teacher Support Site.

UNIT 4 Superstitions and beliefs T-34

6 Athletes and their superstitions (READING)

Learning aim: Develop skills in understanding vocabulary in context, reading for specific information, making inferences, and giving a personal reaction to a reading (25–30 minutes)

A Pair work

- Books closed. Ask Ss if they believe in good luck charms. Then ask if they know what a *lucky ritual* is. (Answer: an action performed to bring good luck or success) Discuss whether Ss think they generally have good or bad luck.
- Books open. Explain the task. Ss work in pairs to discuss the question. Go over answers with the class.

Possible answer

Carrying a good luck charm might make a person feel secure or confident. Following a lucky ritual might be relaxing.

- Have Ss read the article silently to themselves. Check that Ss understand the following vocabulary.

Vocabulary

jinxing doing something to cause bad luck (to someone)

hurdler an athlete who jumps over a type of fence while running around a track

podium small raised platform

psycho (slang) very unusual behavior

prevalence frequency, commonness

foul shot free throw given to a basketball team because of something wrong the opposing team did

triggers causes to start

mindset way of thinking

B

- Explain the task. Read the statements aloud. Ss work individually to complete the activity.
- Go over answers with the class. Ask Ss to provide the extract from the article that supports the corrected false statements.

Answers

1. F; Angela Whyte considers her ritual of not carrying her podium clothes to the track rather irrational. (Paragraph 2: *It's a little psycho, but it worked!*)
2. F; Those with an avid interest in sports are likely to be influenced by superstitions. (Paragraph 3: *. . . the greater the interest in sports, the more superstitious a person is likely to be.*)
3. NG
4. T
5. T

Optional activity: Questions (20 minutes)

Ss write questions about the article.

- Ss work in pairs to write five questions about the article.
- Tell Ss to close their books. Collect the questions and write them on the board (eliminating any doubles).
- Set a time limit and have Ss answer the questions without looking back at the article. Go over answers with the class.

Optional activity: Vocabulary (15–20 minutes)

Ss practice the vocabulary from the reading.

- Have Ss look at the article again. Tell them to write down any words that they did not know before.
- Ask Ss to call out their words and write them on the board. As a class, write definitions for each word.
- Have Ss write a sentence using each word. Make sure they write sentences that show they understand the meaning of the word.
- Ask Ss to read their sentences to the class.

C Group work

- Explain the task. Read the questions aloud.
- Ss work in groups to discuss the questions.
- Ask groups to share their ideas with the class. To make sure that reporting to the class goes smoothly, groups can choose one or two members to report their ideas. Have Ss review their ideas with their own group at the end of the task to see if the group agrees with the information they will be presenting.

Do your students need more practice?	
Assign . . .	for more practice in . . .
Grammar Plus 4B	Grammar
Vocabulary Plus 4B	Vocabulary
Online Vocabulary Accelerator 4B	Vocabulary
Workbook Lesson B	Grammar, Vocabulary, Reading
Online Workbook Lesson B	Grammar, Vocabulary, Reading, Listening

T-35 UNIT 4 Superstitions and beliefs

6 READING
Athletes and their superstitions

A **Pair work** Research suggests that good luck charms and lucky rituals can actually have an effect on an athlete's performance. Why might this be so? Discuss with a partner. Then read the article.

DO GOOD LUCK CHARMS REALLY WORK IN COMPETITIONS?

To avoid jinxing herself, Canadian hurdler Angela Whyte never carries her podium clothes with her to the track at international competitions. But before the 100-meter hurdle final at the Commonwealth Games in New Delhi, Ms. Whyte faced a dilemma, because her roommate – whom she would usually ask to bring them – was gone for the day.

"I packed the podium clothes in a separate backpack, so they wouldn't touch the competition gear," she laughed, after winning a silver medal. "It's a little psycho, but it worked!"

Ms. Whyte isn't alone in her faith in the power of superstition. Numerous studies have examined the prevalence of "magical thinking" among athletes, finding that the greater the interest in sports, the more superstitious a person is likely to be.

Intrigued by stories about athletes such as Michael Jordan, who wore his old college shorts under his uniform throughout his professional career, Dr. Lysann Damisch led a study in which she found that following a lucky ritual enhances self-confidence. This leads one to set higher goals and be more persistent, ultimately achieving greater success.

Not all athletic rituals work this way, though. Dr. Damisch claims that routines such as bouncing a basketball exactly three times immediately before shooting a foul shot does more than simply boost confidence. This routine actually serves to focus attention and also triggers well-learned motor sequences. Other apparent superstitions may have more to do with creating a relaxed and positive mindset. Ms. Whyte, for example, always travels to competitions with a teddy bear named O.T. – but not because she believes O.T. brings her luck. "I've had him since I was two years old," she explains, "so he reminds me of my home and family when I'm traveling. He's my security blanket."

The effectiveness of superstitious rituals may explain why they have persisted across cultures and eras, Dr. Damisch points out. But there are limits to their power. Following such rituals "doesn't mean you win, because of course winning and losing is something else."

Source: "Do Good Luck Charms Really Work In Competitions?" by Alex Hutchinson, The Globe and Mail

B Read the article again. Are the statements true (*T*), false (*F*), or is the information not given (*NG*) in the article? Write the correct letters and correct the false statements.

____ 1. Angela Whyte considers her ritual of not carrying her podium clothes to the track completely rational.

____ 2. Those with an avid interest in sports are not likely to be influenced by superstitions.

____ 3. Dr. Damisch was fascinated by Michael Jordan's professional career.

____ 4. An increase in self-confidence can make people set and reach more challenging goals.

____ 5. Some lucky rituals actually help the brain and body prepare for performance.

C **Group work** Discuss these questions. Then share your answers with the class.

1. What other good luck charms and lucky rituals used in sports do you know about? How do they relate to the findings of the research mentioned in the text?
2. What things do you do to increase confidence and keep a positive mindset? Which is most effective?

5 MOVIES AND TELEVISION
LESSON A ▶ Movies

1 STARTING POINT
Movies today

A Read the statements about some movie trends. Which of these trends have you noticed?

Movie Trends

Unquestionably, studios are interested in producing a lot more movies about superheroes, because these are so popular with audiences! That's good news if you love superhero movies as much as I do! —**Maura B., Ireland**

For a long time, box office hits were predictably followed by sequels. But nowadays, the production of prequels has become a pretty exciting trend. —**Alejandro H., Mexico**

Box office profits will possibly continue to fall in the United States. Fortunately, for the movie studios, revenues continue to increase in several overseas markets. —**Naomi S., the United States**

Independent filmmakers often go into debt producing their movies, so many now turn to crowdsourcing websites for funding. Many fans like me make donations to film projects they support. —**Masako N., Japan**

Seemingly, there have been more women cast in leading roles in successful movies. Honestly, I hope that having more courageous heroines will be a trend that lasts and not just a passing fad. —**Leonard W., Canada**

Overall, the animated movies I take my children to see these days are visually spectacular and have sophisticated humor and storylines. Not surprisingly, the other adults I see at the theater also enjoy these movies as much as the kids do. —**Lucas M., Brazil**

B Pair work What other movie trends have you noticed? Discuss them with your partner.

"It seems to me that quite a few plays and musicals are being made into movies lately."

2 VOCABULARY
Reacting to movies

A Do these adjectives have a positive or a negative meaning? Mark them + or –.

____ a. clichéd   ____ d. inspiring   ____ g. predictable
____ b. engrossing   ____ e. mediocre   ____ h. riveting
____ c. formulaic   ____ f. moving   ____ i. touching

B Complete the sentences with the adjectives from part A. Sometimes more than one answer is possible.

1. _____ movies affect your emotions or bring tears to your eyes.
2. A/An _____ movie completely captures your attention.
3. A/An _____ movie isn't very good, and probably not worth watching.
4. A movie is _____ if its plot is obvious and you can guess the ending.

VOCABULARY PLUS see page 134

36 UNIT 5 Movies and television

5 MOVIES AND TELEVISION
LESSON A ▶ Movies

> In this unit, Ss use sentence adverbs to discuss movie trends. They also use *such . . . that* and *so . . . that* to make exclamatory statements about TV.

1 Movies today (STARTING POINT)

Learning aim: Discuss movie trends and see sentence adverbs in context (10–15 minutes)

A

- Books closed. Ask Ss how often they watch movies and where they normally watch them. Then ask: *Why do you watch movies?* (e.g., to escape, to relax, to laugh, etc.)
- Books open. Explain the task. Read the question and statements aloud. Check that Ss understand the vocabulary on the right.
- Give Ss time to think about which trends they have noticed. Then have a class discussion.

> **Vocabulary**
> **box office hits** movies that are successful at theaters
> **sequel** a movie that continues the story from an earlier one
> **prequel** a movie that shows the story preceding that of an earlier one
> **profits** money earned after paying expenses
> **revenues** amount of money earned by a company
> **crowdsourcing** requesting ideas, services, or funds from a large group of people, especially online
> **passing fad** something that is popular for a short time
> **storyline** what the movie is about; the plot

B Pair work

- Explain the task. Have a S read the example answer to the class.
- Ss work in pairs to do the activity.
- Have Ss share their partner's answers with the class.

2 Reacting to movies (VOCABULARY)

Learning aim: Learn and practice using adjectives to talk about movies (15–20 minutes)

A

- Explain the task. Read the adjectives aloud.
- Ss work individually to complete the activity.
- Go over answers with the class. Have Ss use each word in a sentence that shows they understand what the word means.

Answers

a. –	d. +	g. –
b. +	e. –	h. +
c. –	f. +	i. +

B

- Explain the task. Ss work individually to complete the sentences with adjectives from part A.
- Go over answers with the class.

> **Answers**
> 1. Moving / Touching
> 2. riveting / engrossing
> 3. mediocre / predictable
> 4. clichéd / formulaic / predictable

> **Optional activity:** *When I was young . . .* (15–20 minutes)
> Ss talk about movies they liked when they were young.
> - Ss work in pairs to talk about their favorite movie when they were young.
> - Have Ss summarize or explain their partner's movie to the class.

3 Sentence adverbs (GRAMMAR)

Learning aim: Practice using sentence adverbs (20–25 minutes)

> **Grammar notes**
>
> Sentence adverbs modify the whole sentence.
>
> They commonly occur in three positions: at the beginning of a sentence, before the auxiliary verb, or after the auxiliary verb.
>
> When a sentence adverb is located at the beginning of the sentence, it is set off by a comma.
> *Obviously, it's too late now.*
>
> In colloquial English, it is common for sentence adverbs to appear at the end of the sentence.
> *It's too late now, obviously.*

- Books closed. Write on the board:
  1. *He will definitely call me.*
  2. *He will supposedly call me.*
  3. *He will probably call me.*

  Read the sentences aloud and ask Ss to identify what is different in each sentence. (Answer: the adverb) Ask if the sentences mean the same thing. (Answer: No. The adverb changes the degree of certainty.)

- Books open. Discuss the information in the grammar box and read the example sentences.

A

- Have Ss look at the Starting Point on page 36 again. Explain the task and read the questions aloud. Go over answers with the class.

> **Answers**
>
> For a long time, box office hits were <u>predictably</u> followed by sequels.
>
> <u>Fortunately</u>, for the movie studios, revenues continue to increase in several overseas markets.
>
> Possible answers to the second question:
> *Predictably* expresses the attitude that sequels to box office hits were no surprise and had come to be expected.
>
> *Fortunately* expresses the attitude that it's a good thing for the movie studios that revenues continue to increase in several overseas markets.

B Pair work

- Explain the task. Read the example answer aloud.
- Ss work individually to rewrite the sentences using sentence adverbs.
- Ss work in pairs to compare their answers. Go over answers with the class.

> **Possible answers**
>
> 1. Not surprisingly, movie attendance is declining in the United States due to the many forms of home entertainment available.
> 2. Supposedly, men prefer action movies while women favor romantic ones.
> 3. More and more independent films will probably win awards in the future.
> 4. Honestly, many people enjoy engrossing movies full of action and special effects.
> 5. Clearly, in the future, nearly all movies will be shot and projected using digital technology instead of film.
> 6. Young filmmakers may potentially never use film.
> 7. Amazingly, studios routinely spend hundreds of millions of dollars to make a movie.
> 8. Possibly, watching violent movies can make some children more aggressive.

C Group work

- Explain the task. Read the list of areas aloud. Have one pair of Ss read the example conversation to the class. As a class, brainstorm what the trends are in each area, if necessary.
- Ss work in groups to discuss their attitudes about the trends. Make sure they use sentence adverbs.
- Have a S from each group report on the group's discussion to the class.

3 GRAMMAR

Sentence adverbs

Sentence adverbs modify a whole sentence, not just part of it. Many adverbs can be used in this way. Sentence adverbs express the speaker's attitude, opinion, or reason for speaking.

Certainty: *clearly, definitely, obviously, unquestionably*
Unquestionably, studios are interested in producing a lot more movies about superheroes.

Less certainty: *apparently, seemingly, supposedly*
Seemingly, there have been more women cast in leading roles in successful movies.

Possibility and probability: *possibly, potentially, probably*
Box office profits will **possibly** continue to fall in the United States.

Talking honestly and directly: *frankly, honestly, seriously*
Honestly, I hope that having more courageous heroines will be a trend that lasts and not just a passing fad.

Summarizing: *basically, essentially, fundamentally, mainly, overall*
Overall, the animated movies I take my children to see these days are visually spectacular.

Other attitudes: *amazingly, surprisingly, not surprisingly, predictably, fortunately, unfortunately*
Not surprisingly, the other adults I see at the theater also enjoy these movies as much as the kids do.

GRAMMAR PLUS *see page 114*

A Look at the Starting Point on page 36 again. Can you find other sentences with adverbs from the grammar box? What attitude or opinion do they convey?

B Pair work Rewrite each sentence using one of the adverbs from the grammar box. Compare with a partner.

1. No one is surprised that movie attendance is declining in the United States due to the many forms of home entertainment available.
   Not surprisingly, movie attendance is declining in the United States due to the many forms of home entertainment available.

2. It's been said that men prefer action movies while women favor romantic ones.

3. It's likely that more and more independent films will win awards in the future.

4. In truth, many people enjoy engrossing movies full of action and special effects.

5. It's clear that in the future nearly all movies will be shot and projected using digital technology instead of film.

6. A potential result is that young filmmakers may never use film.

7. It's amazing that studios routinely spend hundreds of millions of dollars to make a movie.

8. It's possible that watching violent movies can make some children more aggressive.

C Group work Use sentence adverbs to express your attitude about trends in the areas below, or use your own ideas. Listen to your classmates' reactions.

- shopping
- television
- music
- smartphones
- transportation
- computers
- magazines
- video games
- language learning

"You can supposedly get discounts from stores by indicating you like them on social media sites."

"Really? I'll have to give that a try. Frankly, I hate paying full price for anything."

4 LISTENING
Behind all good movies . . .

A **Pair work** Look at the movie genres. What elements do you consider essential for each genre? Discuss with a partner.

animated movies   musicals   romantic comedies   sci-fi movies

B Listen to four people talk about key elements of the movie genres in part A. Complete the chart with the genre each speaker is talking about.

	Movie genre	Key elements
1. Heather		
2. Josh		
3. Felipe		
4. Dana		

C Listen again. What three elements does each person consider essential for each movie genre? Complete the chart. Are their opinions similar to yours?

5 DISCUSSION
Movie genre preferences

A **Pair work** Discuss the results of this survey on movie genre preferences. Do you think the preferences are the same where you live?

Movie Genre Preferences of Men and Women

Men	Women
1. comedy	1. comedy
2. action/adventure	2. drama
3. suspense/thriller	3. romantic comedy
4. sci-fi	4. suspense/thriller
5. drama	5. romance

Source: "Opening Our Eyes," a study by Northern Alliance and Ipsos MediaCT for the British Film Institute

B **Group work** Discuss different aspects of each movie genre in the survey. What is it about them that men, women, or both might like?

"Thriller movies often have riveting action scenes. I think that's more of a guy thing."

"I don't agree. I think both genders enjoy thriller movies because of the element of surprise that many of them have."

C **Group work** Name actors and actresses who have starred in the various movie genres. Discuss their performances and whether the genre suits them.

"I think Will Smith is perfect in sci-fi movies. He can be serious and funny, which makes the movies riveting and entertaining."

"That's true. But I think he's better suited for comedies – when he's not serious at all!"

4 Behind all good movies . . . (LISTENING)

Learning aim: Develop skills in listening for main ideas and details, and in making inferences (15–20 minutes)

A Pair work

- Explain the task. Ss work in pairs to discuss the elements they consider essential for each genre.
- Have each pair share their discussion with the class.

B 🔊 [CD 2, Track 2]

- Explain the task. Tell Ss they will not hear the name of the genre but infer it from what the people say. Check that Ss understand the following vocabulary.

> **Vocabulary**
>
> **reflect** give a correct picture
>
> **appeal** attract interest
>
> **engaging** interesting in a way that holds your attention
>
> **dynamic** continuously moving forward
>
> **setting** when and where the story takes place
>
> **one-dimensional (character)** too simple and uninteresting, showing only one aspect of (the person's personality)
>
> **drive** keep (something) moving
>
> **conflict** disagreement between people

- Tell Ss to listen for the answers. Play the recording as Ss write the genres in the first column of the chart. Replay as many times as needed. Ss listen and check their answers.
- Go over answers with the class.

Answers	
1. romantic comedy	3. sci-fi movie
2. animated movie	4. musical

Audio script: See page T-168.

C 🔊 [CD 2, Track 3]

- Explain that Ss will listen again and write the key elements in the chart.
- Tell Ss to listen for the answers. Play the recording as Ss complete the chart. Replay as many times as needed. Ss listen and check their answers.
- Ss work in pairs to discuss their answers. Go over answers with the class.

> **Answers**
>
> 1. good storyline, combination of humor and realism, appeals to both men and women
>
> 2. appeals to all ages (with sophisticated humor and well-thought-out stories), makes people forget they're not watching real people or objects (through quality computer graphics, dynamic plot, attractive setting, interesting characters), talented people for the characters' voices (so that they are credible)
>
> 3. outstanding special effects, realness of the characters, talented director
>
> 4. talented actors (good singing, dancing, and acting) pleasurable and memorable soundtrack, some sort of conflict

Audio script: See page T-168.

5 Movie genre preferences (DISCUSSION)

Learning aim: Talk about movie preferences and practice the lesson vocabulary (15–20 minutes)

A Pair work

- Books closed. Ask Ss what kinds of movies they tend to watch. Then ask Ss what attracts them to those kinds of movies.
- Books open. Explain the task. Read the movie genres aloud. Check that Ss understand all the genres listed.
- Ss work in pairs to discuss the question.
- Have Ss share their partner's answers with the class.

B Group work

- Explain the task and read the question. Have one pair of Ss read the example discussion to the class.
- Ss work in groups to discuss the question. Go around the class and help as needed.
- Have a S from each group share their group's opinions with the class.

C Group work

- Explain the task. Have one pair of Ss read the example discussion to the class. Give Ss time to think of their answer.
- Ss work in groups for the discussion.
- Have a S from each group report the group's discussion to the class.

> For more practice with discussion, download the Worksheet *5.1 Must-see movie* from the Teacher Support Site.

6 Writing a movie review (WRITING)

Learning aim: Write an effective movie review
(40–50 minutes)

A

- Books closed. Ask Ss if they ever read movie reviews before selecting a movie to watch. Ask what kind of information they would expect to find in a review.
- Books open. Tell Ss to read the information in the box at the top of the page. Ask: *What is included in a movie review?* (Answer: information about the movie, a summary of the plot, a recommendation)
- Explain the task. Read the questions aloud. Ss work individually to complete the activity. Check that Ss understand the following vocabulary.

Vocabulary

indie film movie made by an independent filmmaker, not associated with a large studio; movie in the style of such films

offbeat unusual and unexpected in an interesting way

long to want very much to do something

classified ad advertisement in a newspaper or online used to find, buy, or sell something

would-be wanting or trying to be something

- Go over answers with the class.

Answers

1. Safety Not Guaranteed *is an offbeat romantic comedy* . . .

2. *I'm a huge fan of both indie films and movies about time travel, so choosing to watch* Safety Not Guaranteed *was an easy decision to make and a very good one.*

3. *It's about time travel, but it's also about why people long to revisit the past and about why some people are willing to believe in the impossible.*

4. . . . *Kenneth (played by Mark Duplass), the would-be time-traveler,* . . .
   . . . *Darius (Aubrey Plaza), one of the reporters,* . . .
   . . . *Jeff (Jake Johnson), another one of the reporters,* . . .
   . . . *Arnou (Karan Soni), the third reporter,* . . .
   Directed by Colin Trevorrow . . .

5. . . . *the movie is charming, likable, and funny. Every line of its clever script either makes you laugh or moves the story in a new direction. Best of all, it's a movie so magical that it might make you want to believe in time travel yourself. Highly recommended.*

B

- Explain the task. Tell Ss that a review is similar to other types of composition – each body paragraph should be about only one main idea. One body paragraph could be about the actors; another could be about the plot. Tell Ss they could organize each body paragraph using the questions in part A.
- Ss work individually to make notes to answer the questions in part A. Then Ss use their notes to write their reviews.
- Go around the class and help as needed.

C Pair work

- Explain the task. Read the information in the Useful Expressions box aloud. Give an example of how to use each phrase.
- Ss work in pairs to exchange reviews and take turns answering the questions.
- Go around the class and help as needed. Encourage Ss to ask and answer follow-up questions about the review and to ask about anything in the review they don't understand.

Do your students need more practice?	
Assign . . .	for more practice in . . .
Grammar Plus 5A	Grammar
Vocabulary Plus 5A	Vocabulary
Online Vocabulary Accelerator 5A	Vocabulary
Workbook Lesson A	Grammar, Vocabulary, Writing
Online Workbook Lesson A	Grammar, Vocabulary, Writing

6 WRITING
Writing a movie review

> An effective movie review generally provides information about the movie, summarizes the plot, and offers a recommendation based on the writer's opinion.

A Read the questions and the movie review. Underline the answers to the questions in the review and write the number of the question.

1. What is the title of the movie, and what genre is it?
2. What made you decide to watch the movie? What is your general impression?
3. What is the movie about?
4. Who are the main characters and actors? Who is the director?
5. Would you recommend this movie to others? Why or why not?

MOVIE REVIEW: Safety Not Guaranteed

1 — I'm a huge fan of both indie films and movies about time travel, so choosing to watch *Safety Not Guaranteed* was an easy decision to make and a very good one. *Safety Not Guaranteed* is an offbeat romantic comedy with an original storyline, an excellent cast, and an unexpected ending. It's about time travel, but it's also about why people long to revisit the past and about why some people are willing to believe in the impossible.

Three magazine reporters from Seattle head out on an assignment to interview a guy who placed a classified ad looking for a partner to travel back in time with him. They think it's a joke, but as the movie progresses, they gradually discover that Kenneth (played by Mark Duplass), the would-be time-traveler, actually believes he's built a working time machine. Along the way, Darius (Aubrey Plaza), one of the reporters, falls in love with Kenneth. Meanwhile, Jeff (Jake Johnson), another one of the reporters, does some time-traveling of his own as he takes time off to look up an old girlfriend and teach Arnou (Karan Soni), the third reporter, a little bit about love. In the end, it all comes together in a marvelous way.

Directed by Colin Trevorrow, the movie is charming, likable, and funny. Every line of its clever script either makes you laugh or moves the story in a new direction. Best of all, it's a movie so magical that it might make you want to believe in time travel yourself. Highly recommended.

B Think of a movie you've seen recently, and make notes to answer the questions in part A. Then use your notes to write a movie review.

C Pair work Exchange your movie review with a partner, and answer these questions.

1. Does your partner's review answer all of the questions in part A? Find the answers.
2. Is the information in the review organized effectively? How could it be improved?
3. What else would you like to know about the movie reviewed? Ask at least two questions.
4. Would you follow the recommendation in your partner's review after reading it? Why or why not?

> **Useful expressions**
>
> **Suggesting improvements**
> It might be better if you . . .
> I think what it needs is . . .
> You might want to . . .
> It'd be even better if . . .

LESSON A Movies 39

LESSON B ▶ Television

1 STARTING POINT
TV time

A Read these posts about TV programs. Which program would you most like to watch? Which one would least interest you? Why?

What's On? A Blog for TV Lovers

Today's Question: What TV shows could you watch over and over again?

Posted at 9:24 by Donna
House is such a riveting show that I could watch it again and again. Frankly, Dr. Gregory House (played by Hugh Laurie) is so foul-tempered that I hated him when I first started watching the show. But the amazing plots combining medical mysteries and detective work really drew me in. It's such a great show that I bought all eight seasons and have watched many episodes more than once.

Posted at 9:03 by Justin
I could watch many sitcoms forever, but my busy schedule leaves me so little TV time that I don't want to waste it watching mediocre sitcoms. So, I watch only the best ones, like *The Big Bang Theory*. It centers on the hilarious lives of four geeky scientists. The show's intelligent, witty dialogue is packed with so many great jokes that it's nonstop laughs from beginning to end.

Posted at 8:46 by Franco
I never get tired of watching *CSI*. The unique murder investigations are always thrilling! They include so many scientific details that I always learn something. Plus, I love the humor, and the chemistry between the characters is great! Some of my favorite actors are on *CSI New York*, so those are the episodes I stream the most.

B Pair work What are your favorite TV shows of all time? Why do you like them?

"One of my favorite shows is Law and Order, a crime drama series. The plots are always engrossing with lots of surprising twists."

2 VOCABULARY
Types of TV programs

A Pair work Look at the different types of TV programs. Select the ones that you know. Then ask a partner about the ones you don't know.

- ☐ 1. game show
- ☐ 2. soap opera
- ☐ 3. sitcom
- ☐ 4. cartoon
- ☐ 5. documentary
- ☐ 6. drama series
- ☐ 7. sports program
- ☐ 8. talk show
- ☐ 9. sketch comedy show
- ☐ 10. cooking show
- ☐ 11. reality TV show
- ☐ 12. news program

B Group work Which types of TV shows do you watch? Give an example of each.

VOCABULARY PLUS see page 134

LESSON B ▶ Television

1 TV time (STARTING POINT)

Learning aim: Discuss TV shows and preferences and see *such . . . that* and *so . . . that* in context (10–15 minutes)

A
- Books closed. Ask Ss if they watched TV last night and, if they did, what they watched.
- Books open. Explain the task and read the questions aloud. Check that Ss understand the following vocabulary.

> **Vocabulary**
>
> **foul-tempered** easily annoyed, usually in a bad mood
>
> **drew me in** attracted me to
>
> **hilarious** very funny
>
> **witty** clever and funny
>
> **packed with** full of
>
> **unique** very unusual in some way
>
> **chemistry** relationship between people
>
> **stream** get continuous sound and moving images sent from the Internet to a computer or mobile device

- Have Ss read the text silently to themselves.
- Give Ss time to think about their answers to the questions. Then have a class discussion about the questions.

B Pair work
- Explain the task. Read the questions and example answer aloud.
- Ss work in pairs to do the activity.
- Have Ss share their partner's answers with the class.

2 Types of TV programs (VOCABULARY)

Learning aim: Learn and practice vocabulary for different types of TV programs (10–15 minutes)

A Pair work
- Explain the task. Read the types of TV programs aloud.
- Ss work individually to select the types of programs they know. Then Ss work in pairs to talk about the program types they don't know.

B Group work
- Explain the task.
- Ss work in groups to discuss the types of shows they watch from part A and to give an example of each type of program.
- Have a S from each group tell the class the group's answers.

> **Optional activity:** *TV programs* (10–15 minutes)
>
> **Ss choose their ideal TV programming.**
>
> - Ss work in pairs. Tell them that all the TV companies have decided to let viewers stream eight programs for free for one day only.
> - Have each pair decide on eight programs that they would stream. Tell Ss they should choose at least six different types of shows and that both Ss in each pair should either like the TV shows or at least be interested in watching them for the first time.
> - Have each pair present and explain their choices to the class.

3 Such . . . that and so . . . that (GRAMMAR)

Learning aim: Practice using *such . . . that* and *so . . . that* (20–25 minutes)

Grammar notes

Such is followed by a noun, which is usually modified by an adjective.
That sitcom was such an exciting show (that) I recommended it to everyone I know.

So is followed by an adjective or adverb.
That sitcom was so exciting (that) I recommended it to everyone I know.

So few and *so many* are followed by countable nouns.
So much and *so little* are followed by uncountable nouns.
We downloaded so many shows (that) it took us weeks to watch them all.
We were having so much fun (that) we forgot to eat.

When *such* is followed by a singular countable noun, the noun is preceded by the indefinite article.
It was such an interesting movie (that) I watched it three times.

When *such* is followed by a plural countable noun or an uncountable noun, no article is used.
That TV show got such good ratings (that) it won an award.
The athlete showed such joy (that) the crowd suddenly cheered.

In colloquial English, *that* is often omitted.

- Books closed. Write on the board:
  1. *The show was so funny that I laughed nonstop.*
  2. *It was such a funny show that I laughed nonstop.*
- Ask: *Do the sentences mean the same thing?* (Answer: yes) *What is different about the two sentences?* (Answer: In sentence 1, *so* is used before an adjective. In sentence 2, *such* is used before an adjective + noun.)
- Review countable and uncountable nouns. Write on the board:
  There is so little choice on cable TV that I prefer to watch my shows online.
  There are so few good shows on cable TV that I prefer to watch my shows online.
  Ask Ss why the first sentence uses *little* and the other uses *few*. (Answer: The word *little* precedes the uncountable noun *choice*. The word *few* precedes the countable noun *shows*.) If necessary, give Ss a hint by asking what kind of noun follows *little* and *few* in the sentences.
- Books open. Discuss the information in the grammar box and read the example sentences.

A

- Have Ss look at the Starting Point on page 40 again. Explain the task and read the questions aloud.
- Go over answers with the class.

Answers

Pattern a:
House is such a riveting show that I could watch it again and again.

Pattern c:
They include so many scientific details that I always learn something.

B

- Explain the task. Read the example aloud and answer any questions about vocabulary.
- Ss work individually to complete the activity.
- Go over answers with the class.

Answers

| 1. so much | 3. so little | 5. so much |
| 2. so many | 4. so many | 6. so few |

C

- Explain the task. Read the sentences and the example aloud. Answer any questions about vocabulary.
- Ss work individually to complete the activity. Then Ss work in pairs to compare answers.
- Go over answers with the class.

Answers

1. The referee did such a terrible job during the soccer game that my father was yelling at the TV set.
2. There are so many TV programs available on the Internet that I'm using my TV set less and less.
3. That new sitcom was so well reviewed that I wouldn't be surprised if it won an award.
4. Certain singers attract such huge audiences that they charge ridiculously high prices for concert tickets.
5. Some documentaries today deal with such critical social issues that they can have a political effect.

To help Ss with grammar in this exercise, download the Fresh Idea **1, 2, or 3?** from the Teacher Support Site.

T-41   UNIT 5   Movies and television

3 GRAMMAR

Such . . . that and so . . . that

So and *such*, *such . . . that*, *so . . . that*, *so much / little . . . that*, and *so many / few . . . that* are commonly used to express extremes in exclamatory sentences.

a. *Such* is followed by a noun (usually modified by an adjective).

   It's **such** a great show **that** I bought all eight seasons.

b. *So* is followed by an adjective or adverb.

   Dr. House is **so** foul-tempered **that** I hated him when I first started watching the show.

c. *So many* and *so few* are followed by countable nouns.

   The dialogue is packed with **so many** jokes **that** it's nonstop laughs from beginning to end.

d. *So much* and *so little* are followed by uncountable nouns.

   My busy schedule leaves me **so little** TV time **that** I don't want to waste it watching mediocre sitcoms.

GRAMMAR PLUS see page 115

A Look at the Starting Point on page 40 again. Can you find more sentences with *so* and *such*? Which patterns do the sentences follow?

B Complete these sentences with *so many*, *so few*, *so much*, or *so little*.

1. My brother watches _____**so much**_____ reality TV that he hardly does anything else.
2. There are _____ fans of that drama series that it's consistently the highest rated show on TV.
3. There was _____ interest in the cartoon that the network canceled it.
4. Bob knows _____ useless facts that he should go on a trivia game show.
5. Ads for that new talk show generated _____ hype that most viewers were disappointed once it came out.
6. There are _____ trustworthy news programs that I've started going to reliable websites instead.

C Rewrite these sentences using *such . . . that* or *so . . . that*. Then compare with a partner.

1. The referee did a terrible job during the soccer game. My father was yelling at the TV set.
   The referee did such a terrible job during the soccer game that my father was yelling at the TV set.
2. There are many TV programs available on the Internet. I'm using my TV set less and less.
3. That new sitcom was well reviewed. I wouldn't be surprised if it won an award.
4. Certain singers attract huge audiences. They charge ridiculously high prices for concert tickets.
5. Some documentaries today deal with critical social issues. They can have a political effect.

LESSON B Television

4 LISTENING
New TV shows

A Listen to some TV network employees discuss ideas for new shows with their boss, Rick. Write the type and the basic idea of each show in the chart.

	Café People	*Serve Yourself!*	*New Borders*
Type of show			
Basic idea			
Accepted?			
Reasons			

B Listen again. Were the show ideas accepted? Write *Yes* or *No* and Rick's reasons for the decisions in the chart.

C Pair work Make a list of three TV shows that are popular in your community. Then discuss the reasons why these programs are so popular.

"Modern Family is a really popular comedy show. I think that's because it lets people laugh at problems all families have, and it's presented in an interesting fake documentary style."

5 DISCUSSION
Your own TV show

A Pair work Work with your partner to develop a new TV show. Choose one of the genres in the form below or add one. Brainstorm ideas for the show. Then complete the form with your best ideas.

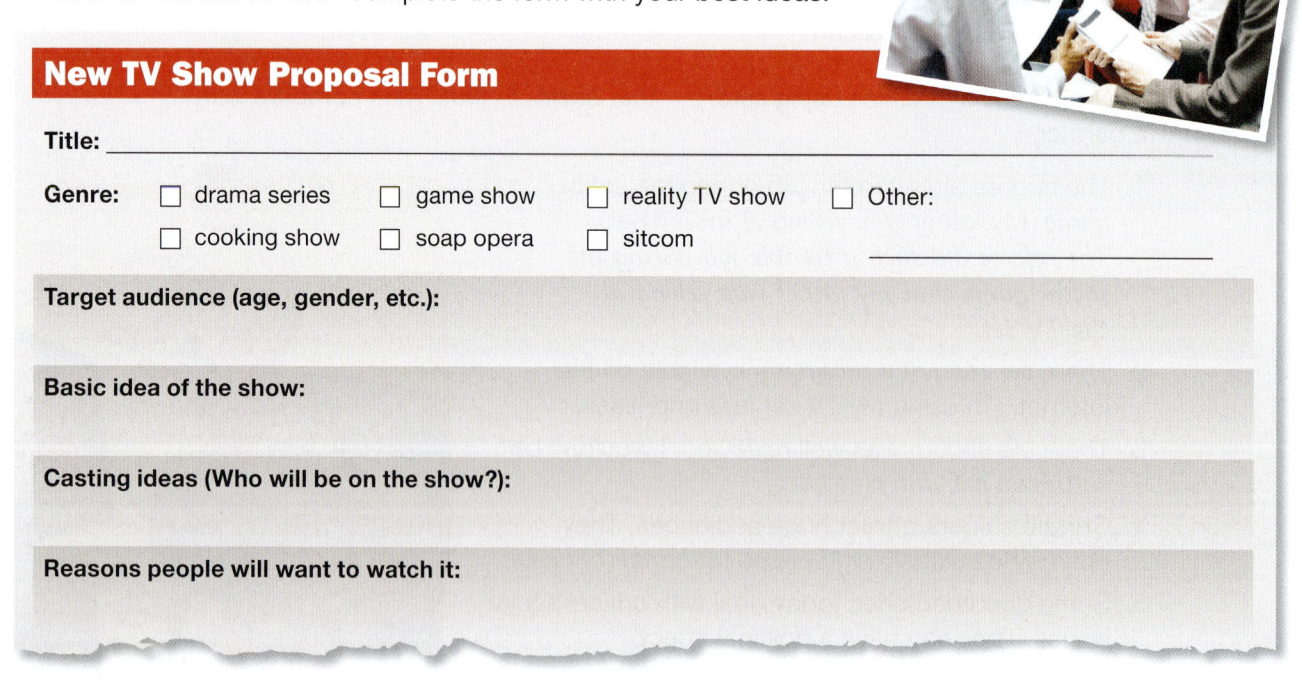

New TV Show Proposal Form

Title: _____

Genre: ☐ drama series   ☐ game show   ☐ reality TV show   ☐ Other: _____
        ☐ cooking show   ☐ soap opera   ☐ sitcom

Target audience (age, gender, etc.):

Basic idea of the show:

Casting ideas (Who will be on the show?):

Reasons people will want to watch it:

B Group work Role-play a meeting at a TV network. Present your show idea to the group and try to convince them to produce it. Then decide whose idea was the best.

4 New TV shows (LISTENING)

Learning aim: Develop skills in listening for gist and details (20–25 minutes)

A [CD 2, Track 4]

- Explain the task. Tell Ss to look at the chart and determine the information they need to complete it. Check that Ss understand the following vocabulary.

> **Vocabulary**
>
> **network** a large TV or radio broadcasting company
> **aspirations** things you hope to achieve
> **in the meantime** meanwhile
> **stuck working** unable to move out of a job
> **kitchenette** small kitchen
> **academic** related to education
> **capture** record something (on video)
> **exotic** unusual, interesting, and often foreign
> **accomplish** succeed at reaching a goal
> **a win** a success

- Tell Ss to listen for the type and basic idea of each show. Play the recording once as Ss listen. Play the recording again while Ss write their answers. Replay as many times as needed. Ss listen and check their answers.
- Go over answers with the class.

> **Answers**
>
> *Café People:* sitcom; A group meets at a café to discuss their job aspirations and experiences.
> *Serve Yourself!:* (reality) cooking show; Young people make simple, inexpensive recipes in a college dorm kitchen.
> *New Borders:* reality TV show; People learn languages and then live in foreign countries as part of a competition.

Audio script: See page T-168.

B [CD 2, Track 5]

- Explain that Ss will listen again and write *Yes* or *No* and the reasons for the decisions.
- Tell Ss to listen for the answers. Play the recording as Ss complete the rest of the chart. Replay as many times as needed. Ss listen and check their answers.
- Ss work in pairs to compare answers. Go over answers with the class.

> **Answers**
>
> *Café People:* No; Viewers are interested in something less predictable and formulaic.
> *Serve Yourself!:* Yes; The online aspect is what viewers want, and the how-to approach should be a big hit.
> *New Borders:* Yes; It's what the network is looking for, and most of their viewers are interested in traveling and learning about other cultures.

Audio script: See page T-168.

C Pair work

- Explain the task. Read the example answer aloud.
- Ss work in pairs to think of three popular TV shows and talk about the reasons for their popularity.
- Have Ss share their answers with the class. Write the most common answers on the board and have the class vote for the best and worst shows.

5 Your own TV show (DISCUSSION)

Learning aim: Talk about and develop ideas for a TV show (20–25 minutes)

A Pair work

- Explain the task. Read the information in the proposal form aloud. Answer any questions about vocabulary.
- Have pairs decide on a genre and complete the form with their best ideas.

B Group work

- Explain the task.
- Ss work in groups to role-play a meeting with a TV network. Each pair presents their idea for a show from part A. Make sure they try to convince the group.
- Have a S from each group report the winning TV show proposal to the class.

> For more practice discussing this topic, download the Worksheet **5.2 TV mania** from the Teacher Support Site.

6 A movie starring everyone (READING)

Learning aim: Develop skills in understanding vocabulary in context, making inferences, and giving a personal reaction to a reading (25–30 minutes)

A Pair work

- Explain the task. Ask: *What is a time capsule?* (Answer: a container filled with objects that are considered to be typical of the present time) Explain that time capsules are usually buried in order to be opened at a later date so that the contents can be studied.
- Have Ss discuss the questions in pairs. Then have the pairs share their ideas with the class.
- Have Ss read the article silently to themselves. Check that Ss understand the following vocabulary.

Vocabulary

footage a piece of video (showing an event)
broadcast (project) intended for TV or radio
feature-length (movie that is) 90 or more minutes long
awkward difficult
fusion combination
editorial process the process of preparing the final movie (in this context)
organically naturally
underscore emphasize the importance of something
grounded gave a firm base to
wide-ranging including a large number of subjects
grassroots from ordinary people
painstakingly carefully, with great attention to detail
tap into make sense of (something, such as beliefs or attitudes)
derives from develops from
indulge allow to have something enjoyable

B Group work

- Explain the task. Read the questions aloud. Ss work in groups to discuss the questions.
- Ask groups to share their ideas with the class. To make sure that reporting to the class goes smoothly, groups can choose one or two members to report their ideas. Have Ss review their ideas with their own group at the end of the task to see if the group agrees with the information they will be presenting.

Possible answers

1. Someone in each country had to organize volunteers. Volunteers then had to find and film people in their countries. Ruddick and Litman had to go through thousands of hours of footage to create the film.
2. Answers will vary.
3. Answers will vary.

Optional activity: *Your movie* (20 minutes)

Ss plan their own footage for the *One Day on Earth* project.

- Ss work in pairs and imagine they have been asked to film something for the *One Day on Earth* project. Ss decide what to film about their lives and/or their community. Tell Ss they should provide reasons for their decisions.
- Have each pair present their plan to the class. Make sure each pair gives reasons for their decisions.

Optional activity: *Vocabulary* (15–20 minutes)

Ss practice the vocabulary from the reading.

- Have Ss look at the article again. Tell them to write down any words that they did not know before.
- Ask Ss to call out their words, and write them on the board. As a class, write definitions for each word.
- Have Ss write a sentence using each word. Make sure Ss write sentences that show they understand the meaning of the word.
- Ask Ss to read their sentences to the class.

Do your students need more practice?

Assign . . .	for more practice in . . .
Grammar Plus 5B	Grammar
Vocabulary Plus 5B	Vocabulary
Online Vocabulary Accelerator 5B	Vocabulary
Workbook Lesson B	Grammar, Vocabulary, Reading
Online Workbook Lesson B	Grammar, Vocabulary, Reading, Listening

6 READING
A movie starring everyone

A **Pair work** How could someone make a movie showing what life is like on a single day in every country on earth? What would a project like that involve? Discuss with a partner. Then read the article.

One Day on Earth:
A Time Capsule of Our Lives

It is considered one of the most audacious documentary film projects ever made: a film shot in every country of the world on the same day, involving 3,000 hours of footage in 70 languages from 19,000 volunteer filmmakers around the world. The 104-minute film, *One Day on Earth*, is a visual poem starring everyone on the planet. It's about you and me, the times we live in, and our place in the puzzle of humanity.

Director Kyle Ruddick and executive producer Brandon Litman are the two young forces behind *One Day on Earth*. They met at the University of Southern California, where Ruddick studied film and Litman majored in business. Although both had worked on short-length commercial and broadcast projects, they had never attempted anything like *One Day on Earth* – their first feature-length film – and neither had anyone else.

Ruddick and Litman came up with the idea for the film in 2008 at a world music festival, where they heard musicians who had never met before play together for the first time. After a few awkward attempts, the musicians soon discovered a way to create a beautiful fusion of music. In a similar way, "the editorial process was a process of discovery," said Ruddick. "You couldn't make this sort of film without being completely open to what you receive."

Common themes arose organically, and the filmmakers structured the documentary around film clips that underscore larger global issues. A sense of communal experience further grounded the wide-ranging film as the grassroots filmmakers worked to painstakingly capture the beauty and tragedy of the human experience.

In one of the more touching moments of *One Day on Earth*, a man looks into the camera and says, "I want to thank you for recording this story of my life and replaying it for others." He says he hopes the viewer may find a lesson in it. His words tap into greater truths about this time-capsule art – about how the drive to understand others often derives from a more personal need to understand ourselves.

The film is also about a need to reaffirm just how alike we are despite our outward differences. "The world is a vast spectacle that we indulge and love and also struggle through," said Ruddick. "We're born, we're young, we dance, we sing, and despite all of that, we have incredible challenges." Yet, "cinema is this universal language that anyone can understand and relate to," Ruddick said. "It goes beyond borders."

Source: "'One Day on Earth' Debuts Worldwide, Offers Time Capsule of Our Lives," by Mark Johanson, *International Business Times*

B **Group work** Discuss these questions. Then share your answers with the class.

1. What factors do you think had to come together to make *One Day on Earth* possible?
2. Do you agree with Ruddick that film is a universally understood language? Why or why not?
3. In your opinion, is it true that people all over the world are alike despite our outward differences? Explain.

6 MUSICIANS AND MUSIC
LESSON A ▶ *A world of music*

1 STARTING POINT
Taste in music

A Read the statements expressing different views on music. Which ones do you agree with?

Overheard on the Streets

1. "I think the more you like to dance, the more you appreciate music with a Latin beat."

2. "At first, I didn't like rap music. But the more I listened to the lyrics, the more I understood its powerful social message."

3. "Some of the greatest music is in movie soundtracks. The more exciting the soundtrack, the better the movie seems."

4. "Radio stations kill music sales by overplaying songs. The more I hear a pop song on the radio, the less I feel like buying it."

5. "I'm interested in how a band plays, not how it looks. The more a band focuses on its appearance, the less interesting the music is."

6. "Classical music has many layers of complexity. The more knowledgeable you are about it, the more you'll be able to enjoy it."

7. "TV commercials often feature a catchy tune – and the catchier the tune, the more likely you are to remember the name of the product."

8. "A lot of my friends like to go to clubs with really loud music, but not me. The louder the music gets, the sooner I feel like leaving."

B Pair work What kinds of things do you look for in new songs or artists? What makes certain songs more successful than others?

"I love sampling. You know, when artists mix older songs with new music and lyrics."

"Me, too. I like recognizable tunes, but with a new twist."

> **Useful expressions**
>
> **Asking about opinions**
> What do you think of/about . . . ?
> How do you feel about . . . ?
> Are you into . . . ?

2 LISTENING
Awesome tunes

🔊 **A** Listen to Adam and Lisa talk about music. What are they doing?

🔊 **B** Listen again. What are the three types of music Adam and Lisa listen to? What do they think about the types of music they hear? Complete the chart.

	Type of music	Lisa's opinion	Adam's opinion
1.			
2.			
3.			

44 UNIT 6 Musicians and music

6 MUSICIANS AND MUSIC
LESSON A ▶ *A world of music*

> In this unit, Ss use double comparatives to talk about music and *will* and *would* to talk about habits and general truths.

1 Taste in music (STARTING POINT)

Learning aim: Discuss different tastes in music and see double comparatives in context (10–15 minutes)

A
- Books closed. Ask Ss to call out different music genres. Write them on the board.
- Have Ss call out the names of several musicians or music groups. Write them on the board under the correct genre. Try to include names for all the genres listed.
- Books open. Explain the task. Read the question and statements aloud. Check that Ss understand the following vocabulary.

> **Vocabulary**
>
> **social message** an opinion about social issues expressed through art
>
> **overplaying** playing too often
>
> **catchy** pleasing and easy to remember

- Give Ss time to think about their answer to the question. Then have a class discussion.

B Pair work
- Explain the task. Have one pair of Ss read the example conversation to the class. Go over the information in the Useful Expressions box. Give an example of how to use each question.
- Ss work in pairs to do the activity. Remind Ss to use the expressions in their conversations.
- Have Ss share their partner's answers with the class.

2 Awesome tunes (LISTENING)

Learning aim: Develop skills in listening for gist and details (15–20 minutes)

A 🔊 [CD 2, Track 6]
- Explain the task. Read the question aloud. Check that Ss understand the following vocabulary.

> **Vocabulary**
>
> **weird** strange

- Tell Ss to listen for the answer to the question. Play the recording as Ss listen for the answer. Replay as many times as needed. Ss listen and check their answer.
- Go over the answer with the class.

> **Answer**
>
> They are listening to music on a website.

Audio script: See page T-169.

B 🔊 [CD 2, Track 7]
- Explain the task. Tell Ss to look at the chart and determine the information they need to complete it.
- Tell Ss to listen for the answers. Play the recording as Ss complete the chart. Replay as many times as needed. Ss listen and check their answers.
- Ss work in pairs to compare answers. Go over answers with the class.

> **Answers**
>
> 1. Type of music: reggae
>   Lisa's opinion: She's not crazy about it.
>   Adam's opinion: He's not crazy about it.
>
> 2. Type of music: bluegrass
>   Lisa's opinion: It's sort of cool. She kind of likes it.
>   Adam's opinion: He thinks it's kind of interesting but a little weird.
>
> 3. Type of music: hip-hop
>   Lisa's opinion: She thinks it's amazing.
>   Adam's opinion: He loves it.

Audio script: See page T-169.

UNIT 6 Musicians and music   T-44

3 Double comparatives (GRAMMAR)

Learning aim: Practice using double comparatives
(20–25 minutes)

> **Grammar notes**
> In double comparatives, a conditional relationship is expressed. This condition is always expressed in the first clause. Compare the different meanings of these two sentences:
> *The more I paint, the more confidence I gain.*
> (If I paint more, I gain more confidence.)
> *The more confidence I gain, the more I paint.*
> (If I gain more confidence, I paint more.)
>
> The verb *be* can be omitted if it is the main verb in the first clause.
> *The more experienced the musicians (are), the more confidence they have.*

- Books closed. Write on the board:

  the more I practice guitar

  the better I become

  Ask Ss which clause is a condition for the other, and have Ss say the full sentence. (Answer: The first clause is the condition for the other. *The more I practice guitar, the better I become.*)

- Books open. Discuss the information in the grammar box and read the example sentences.

A

- Have Ss look at the Starting Point on page 44 again. Explain the task and read the question aloud.
- Go over the answers with the class, having Ss identify and call out each of the eight double comparatives.

> **Answers**
>
> Eight double comparatives:
> 1. *I think the more you like to dance, the more you appreciate music with a Latin beat.*
> 2. *But the more I listened to the lyrics, the more I understood its powerful social message.*
> 3. *The more exciting the soundtrack, the better the movie seems.*
> 4. *The more I hear a pop song on the radio, the less I feel like buying it.*
> 5. *The more a band focuses on its appearance, the less interesting the music is.*
> 6. *The more knowledgeable you are about it, the more you'll be able to enjoy it.*
> 7. *. . . and the catchier the tune, the more likely you are to remember the name of the product.*
> 8. *The louder the music gets, the sooner I feel like leaving.*

B Pair work

- Explain the task. Read the clauses aloud. Answer any questions about vocabulary.
- Go over the example answer as a class. Ss work individually to complete the activity.
- Ss work in pairs to compare and discuss answers.
- Go over answers with the class.

> **Answers**
>
> 1. c   2. d   3. e   4. b   5. a

- Have pairs discuss the statements they agree with and explain why.
- Have a few pairs share their answers with the class.

C

- Explain the task. Read the beginning of each sentence aloud and answer any questions about vocabulary.
- Ss work individually to complete the sentences and add further information to clarify or support the statements.

D Pair work

- Explain the task. Have one pair of Ss read the example conversation to the class.
- Ss work in pairs to discuss their answers.
- Have a few Ss share their opinions with the class.

> **Optional activity:** *Double comparatives* **(20 minutes)**
>
> **Ss practice writing sentences with double comparatives.**
>
> - Ss work individually to write three first clauses with comparatives using part B as a guide.
> - Ss work in pairs to exchange papers and complete each sentence with a second comparative clause.

T-45   UNIT 6   Musicians and music

3 GRAMMAR

Double comparatives

You can use two comparatives, each preceded by *the*, in order to show how one quality or amount is linked to another. The first comparative expresses a condition for the second comparative.
The more you like to dance, **the more** you appreciate music with a Latin beat.
The more I hear a pop song on the radio, **the less** I feel like buying it.
The more exciting the soundtrack, **the better** the movie seems.
The louder the music gets, **the sooner** I feel like leaving.
The less 80s pop music I hear, **the better**.

GRAMMAR PLUS see page 116

A Look at the Starting Point on page 44 again. How many double comparatives can you find?

B Pair work Match the clauses to make logical statements. Then compare answers with a partner. Which statements do you agree with?

1. The more types of music you try to listen to, _c_
2. The more often you go to dance clubs, ___
3. The more companies a new artist sends a demo recording to, ___
4. The more you study the history of American popular music, ___
5. The less emphasis schools place on music, ___

a. the fewer new musicians will be developed.
b. the more you realize how much influence African music has had on it.
c. the more likely you are to enjoy a wide variety of genres.
d. the greater your chance of suffering some hearing loss.
e. the better his or her chances are of getting a recording contract.

"I agree with the first statement. Listening to lots of different genres naturally leads you to appreciate more of them."

C Complete these sentences with your own ideas. Can you add further information to clarify or support the statements you wrote?

1. The earlier children start playing music, . . .
2. The more famous a recording artist becomes, . . .
3. The catchier the melody of a pop song, . . .
4. The more expensive a musical performance is, . . .
5. The more thoughtful the song's lyrics are, . . .
6. The older I get and the more I listen to music, . . .

D Pair work Compare and discuss the sentences you wrote above. Share your opinions with the class.

"The earlier children start playing music, the better. Research suggests that music improves memory and increases attention."

"I agree. I think that sometimes we just think of math or language classes as being beneficial, but in fact, . . ."

LESSON A A world of music

4 VOCABULARY
Describing music

A Look at the collocations below. Match the adjectives used to describe music with their definitions.

1. a **soothing** rhythm _e_
2. a **monotonous** beat ___
3. an **exhilarating** tempo ___
4. **evocative** music ___
5. a **frenetic** pace ___
6. a **haunting** melody ___
7. **mellow** sounds ___
8. a **catchy** tune ___

a. fast and energetic, and rather uncontrolled
b. sadly beautiful and difficult to forget
c. bringing to mind a strong emotion or image
d. pleasing and easy to remember
e. relaxing, calming, and comforting
f. cool, laid-back, and smooth
g. following the same pattern; unchanging
h. making you feel very excited and happy

B **Pair work** Which of the adjectives from part A could you use to describe these types of sounds, music, and performances?

- a live performance by a punk rock band
- the sound of rain and howling wind
- the soundtrack to an action movie
- the sound of ocean waves
- fast-paced techno music
- classical music played by an orchestra
- soft jazz with a slow beat
- a children's nursery rhyme

VOCABULARY PLUS see page 135

5 DISCUSSION
Music everywhere

A **Pair work** What kind of music would you expect to hear in these places or at these events? What purpose does music serve in each situation?

- the street
- a wedding
- a clothing store
- a café
- a supermarket
- a gym
- a sports event
- a birthday party

"On the street, I would expect to hear musicians playing catchy or evocative tunes in order to convince passersby to donate some money."

B **Group work** What are some of the ways that music is or could be used in these fields? Discuss the benefits and drawbacks.

- education
- health care
- advertising
- entertainment

"I think music, especially if it's mellow, can be used in the classroom to focus students' attention."
"Yes, but I think people are different, and some require silence to concentrate."

4 Describing music (VOCABULARY)

Learning aim: Learn and practice collocations for talking about music (10–15 minutes)

A

- Books closed. Ask Ss if they know what a *collocation* is. (Answer: two or more words that are often used together)
- Books open. Explain the task. Read the collocations and the definitions aloud.
- Ss work individually to complete the activity. Go over answers with the class.

Answers			
1. e	3. h	5. a	7. f
2. g	4. c	6. b	8. d

Optional activity: *My life's soundtrack* (15 minutes)

Ss describe music that is important to them.

- Ask Ss to think of songs that remind them of important time periods or specific events in their life. Have Ss make a list of the songs and write reasons why these are important to them.
- Ss work in pairs to take turns telling each other about their lists and describing the songs. Make sure Ss use the collocations from part A to describe the songs. As a class, brainstorm other words to describe songs, if necessary.

B Pair work

- Explain the task. Read the types of sounds, music, and performances aloud. Go over any unfamiliar vocabulary with the class.
- Ss work in pairs to complete the activity. Go over answers with the class.

Possible answers

performance by a punk rock band: exhilarating, frenetic

rain and howling wind: haunting, exhilarating, frenetic

soundtrack to an action movie: exhilarating, frenetic

ocean waves: soothing, mellow, haunting, monotonous

techno music: catchy, monotonous, exhilarating, frenetic

classical music played by an orchestra: soothing, mellow, evocative

soft jazz with a slow beat: mellow, soothing

children's nursery rhyme: evocative, soothing, catchy

For more practice with vocabulary, download the Worksheet **6.1 What music is best?** from the Teacher Support Site.

5 Music everywhere (DISCUSSION)

Learning aim: Talk about the use of music and practice the lesson vocabulary (15–20 minutes)

A Pair work

- Explain the task. Have one S read the list of places and events and another the example opinion to the class.
- Ss work in pairs to do the activity. Remind Ss to include the purpose the music serves in each situation.
- Have Ss share their partner's answers with the class.

B Group work

- Explain the task. Read the four fields aloud. Have one pair of Ss read the example conversation to the class.
- Ss work in groups to discuss different ways music is or could be used in each field and the benefits and drawbacks. Remind Ss to give reasons for their answers.
- Have a S from each group report the group's discussion to the class.

6 Compare-and-contrast essays (WRITING)

Learning aim: Write a compare-and-contrast essay (40–50 minutes)

A

- Books closed. Ask Ss what they know about the Beatles and the Rolling Stones. Ask them what they think the similarities and the differences are between the groups.
- Books open. Tell Ss to read the information in the box at the top of the page. Ask: *What information does a compare-and-contrast essay present?* (Answer: similarities and differences of two or more things)
- Explain that in a compare-and-contrast essay, as with other compositions, each body paragraph should only have one main idea. So one paragraph could be about similarities and another about differences. Alternatively, the body paragraphs could also be organized so that the similarities and differences of *one* aspect are discussed in each paragraph.
- Have Ss read the essay silently to themselves. Check that Ss understand the following vocabulary.

Vocabulary
cutting-edge the very newest (style, idea, technology, etc.)
debut first public appearance
clean-cut clean and neat, usually conservative looking
rocks is extremely good

- Have Ss circle the thesis statement and match the paragraphs with the headings. Remind Ss to also underline the words showing comparison or contrast.
- Go over answers with the class.

Answers
Thesis:
Although the Beatles and the Rolling Stones have both been called the "greatest rock 'n' roll band of all time," the prize should go to the Rolling Stones.

1 introduction 4 conclusion
3 differences 2 similarities

Words that show comparison or contrast:
<u>Although</u> the Beatles and the Roling Stones have <u>both</u> . . .
<u>While both</u> bands have had . . .
<u>Both</u> the Beatles and the Rolling Stones began . . .
<u>The two</u> bands released . . .
. . . and <u>both</u> featured . . .
<u>Like</u> the Rolling Stones, . . .
. . . and <u>both</u> bands were known . . .
<u>In contrast</u>, the Rolling Stones had . . .
. . . <u>but</u> the Stones' first big hit was . . .
<u>While</u> the Beatles were . . .
<u>However</u>, the Rolling Stones were . . .

B

- Explain the task. As a class, brainstorm types of things to compare and contrast in an essay about two bands, singers, or musical styles.
- Ss work individually to do the activity.
- Go around the class and help as needed.

C

- Explain the writing task.
- Using their thesis statement and list from part B, Ss work individually to write their essays.
- Go around the class and help as needed.

D Pair work

- Ss work in pairs and take turns reading their own essays aloud and guessing their partner's point of view. Remind Ss not to read their thesis statement.
- Go around the class and help as needed. Encourage Ss to ask and answer follow-up questions about the essay and to ask about anything in the essay they don't understand.

Do your students need more practice?	
Assign . . .	**for more practice in . . .**
Grammar Plus 6A	Grammar
Vocabulary Plus 6A	Vocabulary
Online Vocabulary Accelerator 6A	Vocabulary
Workbook Lesson A	Grammar, Vocabulary, Writing
Online Workbook Lesson A	Grammar, Vocabulary, Writing

T-47 UNIT 6 Musicians and music

6 WRITING
Compare-and-contrast essays

> A compare-and-contrast essay presents the similarities and differences of two or more things. The thesis statement expresses your position on the subject, and it is followed by supporting paragraphs that discuss similarities and differences.

A Read the essay and circle the thesis statement. Then match each paragraph to the headings below. Underline the words that show comparison or contrast.

___ introduction   ___ differences   ___ conclusion   ___ similarities

THE BEATLES vs. THE ROLLING STONES

1 Although the Beatles and the Rolling Stones have both been called the "greatest rock 'n' roll band of all time," the prize should go to the Rolling Stones. While both bands have had a huge influence on popular music, the Beatles broke up in 1970, and the Rolling Stones went on recording and performing for over 50 years.

2 Both the Beatles and the Rolling Stones began as four-member British bands that first became popular in the 1960s. The two bands released their first records within a year of each other, and both featured a pair of talented songwriters: Paul McCartney and John Lennon for the Beatles, and Mick Jagger and Keith Richards for the Rolling Stones. Like the Rolling Stones, the Beatles were famous for their cutting-edge style at the time of their debut, and both bands were known for their energetic stage performances.

3 In the beginning, the Beatles were clean-cut boys with short hair who wore suits. In contrast, the Rolling Stones had a "bad boy" image – they dressed in funky clothes and acted like rebels. One of the Beatles' first major hits was the catchy love song "I Want to Hold Your Hand," but the Stones' first big hit was a rock song called "Satisfaction." While the Beatles were pop stars, the Rolling Stones were rockers.

4 It's true that the Beatles did amazing things during the short time they were together, and their innovations are still apparent in today's music. However, the Rolling Stones were the first band to offer the world "real" rock music, and even after all these years, their music still rocks. That says it all.

B Choose two bands, singers, or musical styles to compare and contrast, and make a list of similarities and differences. Then compose a thesis statement that expresses your view.

C Write a four-paragraph essay. Make sure it has an introduction with a clear thesis statement, two paragraphs describing similarities and differences, and an effective conclusion.

D **Pair work** Take turns reading your essays. Do not read your thesis statement. Can your partner guess your point of view?

LESSON A A world of music 47

LESSON B ▶ Getting your big break

1 STARTING POINT
Music success stories

A Read about these three music success stories. Do you know these singers? Do you know how any other famous singers began their music careers?

Bruno Mars

Bruno Mars, born Peter Gene Bayot Hernández Jr., grew up in a very musical family in Hawaii. At age four, he would play with his family's band five days a week. When he was only 17, he moved to L.A. to write and produce music. At concerts, you'll see this multi-talented musician sing and play the piano or the guitar with ease.

Adele

From a very young age, Adele would perform for her mother, impersonating her favorite singers. She went to a performing arts academy in her teens, and, while there, a friend posted some of her songs online. Two years later, recording companies started noticing her. Despite her fame, Adele will still sometimes suffer from stage fright before a performance.

Rihanna

As a girl in Barbados, Robyn Rihanna Fenty would sell clothes at a street stall. She loved to sing with neighbors and friends. True talent will always be noticed. In 2003, a visiting music producer discovered her. Today, superstar Rihanna will often reinvent her look with startling new hairstyles and clothes.

B Pair work What qualities and opportunities does a person need to have in order to be a success in the popular music industry? Share your ideas with a partner.

"I think it's important to have an established person in the business take an interest in your talent and help you get your start."

2 VOCABULARY
Breaking into the business

A Look at these expressions related to show business and fame. Write them in the chart below. Compare with a partner.

be a big hit	make it big	get your big break	break into the business
be a has-been	be washed up	make a comeback	make a name for yourself
be discovered	pay your dues	be a one-hit wonder	get your foot in the door

Just starting out	Currently successful	No longer successful
	be a big hit	

B Pair work Talk about famous people you know. How did they start out? Which ones are still successful? Which ones are has-beens?

"Mark Wahlberg has really made a name for himself. He went from singer to model to Oscar-nominated actor."

VOCABULARY PLUS see page 135

48   UNIT 6   Musicians and music

LESSON B ▶ Getting your big break

1 Music success stories (STARTING POINT)

Learning aim: Discuss music success stories and see *will* and *would* for habits and general truths in context (10–15 minutes)

A

- Books closed. Ask Ss what someone needs to do in order to become a famous pop singer or musician (e.g., take music lessons; have positive influences when they are children; have a mentor; win a talent show such as *American Idol, X-Factor,* etc.).

- Books open. Explain the task. Have Ss read the stories silently to themselves. Check that Ss understand the following vocabulary.

> **Vocabulary**
>
> **impersonating** intentionally copying someone else's voice, behavior, or appearance
>
> **stage fright** nervousness before or during a performance in front of an audience
>
> **reinvent** change something in order to appear different
>
> **startling** very surprising

- Read the questions aloud. Ss work in pairs to discuss the questions. Alternatively, have a class discussion.

B Pair work

- Explain the task and read the question aloud. Have a S read the example answer to the class.
- Ss work in pairs to do the activity.
- Have Ss share their partner's answers with the class.

2 Breaking into the business (VOCABULARY)

Learning aim: Learn and practice vocabulary to talk about show business and fame (10–15 minutes)

A

- Explain the task. Read the expressions aloud.
- Ss work individually to complete the activity.
- Go over answers with the class. To check understanding, have Ss use each expression in a sentence that shows they understand what it means.

> **Answers**
>
> Just starting out:
> be discovered, get your big break, break into the business, make a name for yourself, get your foot in the door, pay your dues
>
> Currently successful:
> be a big hit, make it big, make a comeback, pay your dues
>
> No longer successful:
> be a has-been, be washed up, be a one-hit wonder

B Pair work

- Explain the task. Read the questions and example aloud. Ss work in pairs to do the activity.
- Have Ss share their answers with the class. Write the names of the famous people on the board.
- Have a class discussion. Ask Ss if they agree or disagree with the answers.

UNIT 6 Musicians and music

3 Will and would for habits and general truths (GRAMMAR)

Learning aim: Practice using *will* and *would* for habits and general truths (20–25 minutes)

> **Grammar notes**
> *Would* is used to express a habitual action that is in the past. It has the same meaning as *used to*.
>
> When *used to* expresses a situation that existed in the past, *would* cannot be substituted. *Would* is only for habitual actions in the past and cannot be used with stative verbs.
> Correct: *When I was young, I used to be very shy.*
> Incorrect: *When I was young, I ~~would~~ be very shy.*

- Books closed. Write on the board:
  1. *He will sing in the choir tomorrow.*
  2. *Practicing the songs every day will always make a choir sound better.*
  3. *He would sing in the choir every Sunday.*
  4. *Would you sing with us?*
- Ask Ss to identify how *will* and *would* are used in each sentence. (Answer: In sentence 1, *will* is used to show a future action. In sentence 2, *will* is used to express a general truth. In sentence 3, *would* is used to express a habitual action in the past. In sentence 4, *would* is used to make a polite request.)
- Books open. Discuss the information in the grammar box and read the example sentences.

A
- Have Ss look at the Starting Point on page 48 again. Explain the task and read the question aloud. Go over answers with the class.

> **Answers**
> . . . he would play with his family's band five days a week.
>
> At concerts, you'll see this multi-talented musician sing and play the piano or the guitar with ease.
>
> . . . Adele will still sometimes suffer from stage fright before a performance.
>
> As a girl in Barbados, Robyn Rihanna Fenty would sell clothes at a street stall.

B
- Explain the task. Read the example answer aloud. Ss work individually to complete the sentences.
- Ss work in pairs to compare their answers. Go over answers with the class.

> **Answers**
> 1. would play
> 2. will practice
> 3. would compose
> 4. will plug
> 5. would perform
> 6. would gain

C
- Explain the task. Read the descriptions and example answer aloud.
- Ss work individually to complete the activity.
- Go over answers with the class.

> **Possible answers**
> 1. He would take it with him wherever he went.
> 2. He will spend a whole day researching them online.
> 3. We would sing songs and play games.
> 4. She would listen mainly to disco.
> 5. She will teach in the morning and perform in the evening.

D Pair work
- Explain the task. Have a S read the example sentence to the class. Ss work individually to complete the sentences with true information, and then write follow-up sentences with *would* or *will*.
- Ss share their answers with a partner.
- Have Ss share their partner's answers with the class.

3 GRAMMAR

Will and *would* for habits and general truths

You can use *would* to express habitual actions in the past. *Would* is more formal than *used to* and is frequently used in past narratives. *Would* needs to be clearly associated with a time in the past.
From a very young age, Adele **would** perform for her mother.

You can use *will* to express personal habits or characteristic behavior in the present.
Today, superstar Rihanna **will** often reinvent her look with startling new hairstyles and clothes.

Will is also used to express facts that are generally true.
True talent **will** always be noticed.

GRAMMAR PLUS see page 117

A Look at the Starting Point on page 48 again. Which other habitual actions are expressed using *would* and *will*?

B Complete these sentences using the verb in parentheses and *would* or *will*.

1. In my younger days, I ____would play____ (play) in a band at local clubs.
2. I love playing the piano. I _____ (practice) every chance I get.
3. After he went deaf, Beethoven _____ (compose) music in his head.
4. My son loves to play his electric guitar. Whenever he can, he _____ (plug) it in and play a few songs.
5. When she was only 11 years old, Japanese violinist Midori Goto _____ (perform) in front of large audiences with confidence.
6. As a young man in Britain, singer-songwriter James Morrison _____ (gain) valuable experience by performing for people on the street.

C Read these descriptions of people. Then use your own ideas to write sentences describing their habitual actions with *would* or *will*.

1. When Ricky was a little boy, he was crazy about his violin.
   He would take it with him wherever he went.
2. Evan is really interested in learning all he can about today's top musicians.
3. Our teacher used to have lots of good ideas to pass the time on monotonous school bus trips.
4. The music Helen listened to as a teen was very different from what's popular these days.
5. The key to Jennifer's successful music career is that she teaches and performs.

D Pair work Complete these statements with true information. Then write a follow-up sentence using *would* or *will*. Share your answers with a partner.

1. I really enjoy listening to . . .
2. When I was young, I loved . . .
3. It's true that musicians today . . .

"I really enjoy listening to techno music. I'll listen to it when I'm feeling tired or sad, and it will always make me feel better."

LESSON B Getting your big break 49

4 LISTENING
Guitar blues

A Pair work You are going to listen to Paul, a young musician, talk to Theresa about his career. What do you think some of his concerns might be? Tell your partner.

🔊 **B** Now listen to the conversation between Paul and Theresa. What's Paul's biggest problem?

🔊 **C** Listen again. What advice does Theresa give Paul regarding each of these four areas? Complete the chart.

	Theresa's advice
1. His parents	
2. His opinion of himself	
3. His appearance	
4. The possibility of failure	

5 DISCUSSION
The secrets of success

A Group work Discuss the following questions with your group.

1. What are some of the ways that some actors and singers have made it big?
2. What are some of the things that successful people have in common?
3. What is your definition of *success*?

B Read the advice for success below. Choose the three pieces of advice that you think are most useful.

Advice *for* Success

1. **Don't be afraid to dream.** You don't need to accept limitations others put on you.
2. **Don't talk about your plans too much.** Spend that energy making things happen.
3. **Take yourself seriously.** Pursue your dreams with conviction.
4. **Don't try to do it all alone.** Seek out the people and resources you need.
5. **Always appear confident** – even if you don't always feel that way inside.
6. **Think positively.** Don't let yourself have negative thoughts for very long.
7. **Don't be afraid to fail.** All successful people will fail – and learn a lot from it.
8. **Dress for success.** Figure out how you need to look to get what you want.

C Group work Tell your group which three pieces of advice you chose. Explain why you think they are useful.

4 Guitar blues (LISTENING)

Learning aim: Develop skills in listening for gist and details (15–20 minutes)

A Pair work

- Explain the task. Ss work in pairs to discuss their answer to the question.
- Have pairs share their answers with the class.

B [CD 2, Track 8]

- Explain the task. Read the question aloud. Check that Ss understand the following vocabulary.

> **Vocabulary**
>
> **frustrated** annoyed because things aren't going the way you want
>
> **creating buzz** causing positive reactions and excitement
>
> **bug** annoy, pester
>
> **gigs** paid musical performances

- Tell Ss to listen for the answer to the question. Play the recording as Ss listen for the answer. Replay as many times as needed. Ss listen and check their answer.
- Go over the answer with the class.

> **Possible answer**
>
> He's been unable to break into the music business, and he seems to be losing his parents' support and his confidence.

Audio script: See page T-169.

C [CD 2, Track 9]

- Read the question aloud. Explain that Ss will listen again and write the advice given for each area in the chart.
- Tell Ss to listen for the answers. Play the recording as Ss complete the chart. Replay as many times as needed. Ss listen and check their answers.
- Ss work in pairs to compare answers. Go over answers with the class.

> **Answers**
>
> 1. Tell them you need a little more time.
> 2. Don't doubt yourself. You have to take yourself seriously.
> 3. Look confident.
> 4. Even if you fail sometimes, you've got to keep going and not give up.

Audio script: See page T-169.

💡 To help Ss with listening in this exercise, download the Fresh Idea *What's next?* from the Teacher Support Site.

5 The secrets of success (DISCUSSION)

Learning aim: Talk about the secrets of success and practice the lesson vocabulary (15–20 minutes)

A Group work

- Books closed. Ask Ss how long they think it takes to make a name for oneself. Ask if they think there are many famous people who were overnight sensations.
- Books open. Explain the task. Read the questions aloud.
- Ss work in groups to discuss the questions.
- Have a S from each group report the group's answers to the class.

B

- Explain the task. Have a few Ss read the pieces of advice aloud. Answer any questions about vocabulary.
- Ss work individually to complete the activity.

C Group work

- Explain the task. Ss work in groups to discuss their choices from part B.
- Have a S from each group report the group's most common choices and reasons to the class.

> **Optional activity:** *The best advice* (15–20 minutes)
>
> **Ss talk about good advice they have received.**
>
> - Ss work in groups to take turns telling each other the best advice they ever received about how to be successful in life. Make sure Ss ask follow-up questions (e.g., *Who gave you the advice? How has the advice helped you?*).
> - Have a S from each group share the best advice with the class.

UNIT 6 Musicians and music T-50

6 Famous without knowing it (READING)

Learning aim: Develop skills in understanding vocabulary in context, reading for specific details, and giving a personal reaction to a reading (25–30 minutes)

A Pair work

- Books closed. Ask: *Before the Internet was available, how do you think people used to share or hear about music for the first time?* (Possible answers: on the radio, on TV, in music magazines, from friends)
- Books open. Explain the task. Ss work in pairs to discuss the question.
- Have Ss read the article silently to themselves. Check that Ss understand the following vocabulary.

> **Vocabulary**
>
> **without a trace** completely
> **bootleg** made or sold illegally
> **wound up** ended up
> **reputation** people's opinion of someone
> **stumbled on** discovered by chance
> **astonishing** very surprising
> **went wild** got very excited about something
> **went platinum** sold thousands of copies and received the music industry platinum certification award
> **frenzy** almost out-of-control excitement

B

- Explain the task. Read the statements aloud.
- Ss work individually to complete the activity.
- Go over answers with the class.

> **Answers**
>
> 1. T
> 2. NG
> 3. T
> 4. F; Bendjelloul heard about Rodriguez while in Cape Town, South Africa.
> 5. F; Rodriguez was astonished about how he was greeted in Cape Town.
> 6. NG

> **Optional activity:** *Questions* (15 minutes)
>
> Ss write comprehension questions about the article.
>
> - Ss work in pairs to write five comprehension questions about the article.
> - Collect the questions and write them on the board (eliminating any doubles).
> - Set a time limit and have Ss answer the questions without looking back at the article. Go over answers with the class.

> **Optional activity:** *Vocabulary* (15–20 minutes)
>
> Ss practice the vocabulary from the reading.
>
> - Have Ss look at the article again. Tell them to write down any words that they did not know before.
> - Ask Ss to call out their words and write them on the board. As a class, write definitions for each word.
> - Have Ss write a sentence using each word. Make sure Ss' sentences show they understand the meaning of the word.
> - Ask Ss to read their sentences to the class.

C Group work

- Explain the task. Read the questions aloud.
- Ss work in groups to discuss the questions.
- Ask groups to share their ideas with the class. To make sure that reporting to the class goes smoothly, groups can choose one or two members to report their ideas. Have Ss review their ideas with their own group at the end of the task to see if the group agrees with the information they will be presenting.

For an alternative reading text or extra practice, download the Worksheet **6.2 A song stuck in the head** from the Teacher Support Site.

Do your students need more practice?	
Assign . . .	for more practice in . . .
Grammar Plus 6B	Grammar
Vocabulary Plus 6B	Vocabulary
Online Vocabulary Accelerator 6B	Vocabulary
Workbook Lesson B	Grammar, Vocabulary, Reading
Online Workbook Lesson B	Grammar, Vocabulary, Reading, Listening

6 READING
Famous without knowing it

A **Pair work** How could a musician possibly become famous without knowing it? Discuss with a partner. Then read the article.

ON THE TRAIL OF SIXTO RODRIGUEZ

Sixto Rodriguez, a Mexican-American construction worker from Detroit, used to perform his songs in the city's small clubs in the late sixties. Known simply as Rodriguez, he would perform with his back to the audience. "There was something mysterious about him," says one local who saw him back then.

During that period, Rodriguez recorded and released two albums – *Cold Fact* and *Coming From Reality*. Sales, though, were small, and the albums disappeared without a trace. Since he'd never had a big hit, no one in the United States thought much more about Rodriguez after that.

But in South Africa, a bootleg copy of *Cold Fact* wound up being distributed on a small South African record label and some songs got played on the radio. Those songs became incredibly popular, and Rodriguez's reputation spread – along with the myths about him.

In those pre-Internet days, there was no information from the United States about this long-forgotten artist. Most people thought he had died, and the mystery surrounding Rodriguez just increased his incredible popularity in South Africa.

Documentary filmmaker Malik Bendjelloul stumbled on the Rodriguez story in 2006 while in Cape Town, where "every other person knew and loved Rodriguez," he recalls. "He was huge there – bigger than the Rolling Stones."

However, a decade earlier, two of his biggest South African fans, Cape Town record store owner Steve Segerman and music journalist Craig Bartholomew, had already set out to find out what had happened to Rodriguez.

The two men studied every Rodriguez lyric to establish where he might have lived and then found the producer of Rodriguez's album *Cold Fact*. Finally, the truth was revealed: Rodriguez was alive, had three adult daughters, and was still living in the same house in Detroit and doing construction work. Rodriguez knew nothing of his astonishing popularity in South Africa.

Segerman finally spoke with Rodriguez from Cape Town. The next step was for Rodriguez to perform there. He flew from the States with his daughters and was astonished to find a limousine waiting for him. On that first tour, Rodriguez played six sold-out concerts in a 5,000-seat hall. Crowds went wild, and *Cold Fact* went platinum, selling half a million copies in South Africa.

Footage of those first concerts, and the fan frenzy they inspired, can be seen in *Searching for Sugar Man*, Bendjelloul's documentary that tells the story of Rodriguez. Finally, his work will be heard widely.

Source: "Sixto Rodriguez: On the Trail of the Dylan of Detroit," by David Gritten, *The Telegraph*

B Read the article again. Are these statements true (*T*), false (*F*), or is the information not given (*NG*)? Correct the false statements to make them true.

____ 1. In the United States, Rodriguez's recordings were not commercially successful in the 1960s.

____ 2. *Cold Fact* sold more copies in the United States than *Coming From Reality* did.

____ 3. Rodriguez's songs helped Segerman and Bartholomew find the musician.

____ 4. Bendjelloul had heard about Rodriguez before he went to South Africa.

____ 5. Rodriguez was not really surprised about how he was greeted in Cape Town.

____ 6. Tickets for the first Rodriguez tour of South Africa were incredibly expensive.

C **Group work** How do you think instant fame affects people? Does age matter? How do you think Rodriguez's life changed after his trip to South Africa? Discuss your answers.

LESSON B Getting your big break

COMMUNICATION REVIEW
UNITS 4–6

✓ SELF-ASSESSMENT

How well can you do these things? Choose the best answer.

I can . . .	Very well	OK	A little
▶ Describe and evaluate television shows (Ex. 1)	☐	☐	☐
▶ Take part in a discussion about movies and movie-related topics (Ex. 2)	☐	☐	☐
▶ Understand a radio program about superstitions (Ex. 3)	☐	☐	☐
▶ Describe and evaluate music and songs (Ex. 4)	☐	☐	☐
▶ Take part in a decision-making discussion about music and songs (Ex. 4)	☐	☐	☐

Now do the corresponding exercises. Was your assessment correct?

1 DISCUSSION
My kind of show

A Think of an example of each type of television show. For each show, write at least one good point about it and one change that would improve it.

Type of show	Example	Good points	Changes you'd make
game show			
reality TV show			
soap opera			
talk show			
drama series			

B Pair work Compare your ideas with a partner. Use sentence adverbs.

"For me, CSI is unquestionably the best TV show ever."

"I like it, too. Apparently, some of the episodes are based on real crimes. But one thing I'd change is . . ."

2 DISCUSSION
You have to see this!

A Think about your movie-viewing habits. Give an example for each of these topics.

1. a movie you would recommend
2. the most interesting character you've ever come across in a movie
3. a book you would like to see made, or that has already been made, into a movie
4. a movie that you would rather see in a theater than at home

B Pair work Discuss your ideas with a partner.

"I recommend Life of Pi. It's so moving that it actually made me cry."

Units 4–6
COMMUNICATION REVIEW

> Ss assess how well they have learned the communication skills in Units 4–6.

✓ Self-assessment

Review aim: Ss assess how well they have learned the material in Units 4–6 (10–15 minutes)

- Books closed. List or elicit from Ss the language and topics covered in Units 4–6.

- Books open. Explain the task. Read the list of skills aloud.
- Ss work individually to do the assessment.
- Tell Ss they will review their assessment after doing the activities in this unit.

1 My kind of show (DISCUSSION)

Review aim: Describe and evaluate TV shows and practice sentence adverbs (15–20 minutes)

A
- Read the types of television shows aloud. Ask Ss to give a definition for each one.
- Explain the task. Ss work individually to complete the chart. Fill in the chart for one type of television show as a class, if necessary.

B Pair work
- Explain the task. Have one pair of Ss read the example conversation to the class. Point out that the example conversation includes sentence adverbs.
- Ss work in pairs to compare their ideas using sentence adverbs.
- Ask a few pairs to report their ideas to the class.

> **Optional activity:** *Class poll* (15–20 minutes)
>
> Ss vote for their favorite TV shows.
>
> - Write the types of shows from part A on the board in a column. Ask Ss to share their favorite TV shows for each type listed on the board. Tally the results and write the most popular answer for each type of show on the board.
> - Have a class discussion on the good points for each show and what changes should be made.
> - Have Ss vote for their favorite TV show.

2 You have to see this! (DISCUSSION)

Review aim: Discuss movie viewing and practice using *so . . . that* and *such . . . that* (20–25 minutes)

A
- Explain the task. Read the topics aloud.
- Ss work individually to think about their movie-viewing habits and give examples for each topic.

B Pair work
- Explain the task. Read the example answer aloud. Ss work in pairs to discuss their ideas. Remind Ss to use *so . . . that* and *such . . . that* in their discussions.
- Have Ss share their partner's ideas with the class. Write them on the board.
- Have the class discuss the ideas on the board. Ask Ss which movies, characters, and books are familiar to them and which are unfamiliar. Have Ss ask questions about the ones they don't know about and tell the class about the ones they are familiar with.

3 Superstitious actors (LISTENING)

Review aim: Develop skills in listening for the main idea and details, and for sentence adverbs and examples of *will* for habits (20–25 minutes)

A

- Explain the task. Read the question aloud.
- Discuss the question as a class. Write some of the Ss' answers on the board.

B 🔊 [CD 2, Track 10]

- Explain the task. Tell Ss to read the answer choices. Check that Ss understand the following vocabulary.

> **Vocabulary**
>
> **looked down on** thought of as bad or inferior in some way
>
> **felt cut off from** felt separated from or not welcomed in a particular part of society
>
> **nibbling** taking small bites out of something

- Tell Ss to listen for the answer to the question. Play the recording once as Ss listen. Play the recording again while Ss choose the correct answer. Replay as many times as needed. Ss listen and check their answer.
- Go over the answer with the class.

> **Answer**
>
> a. They used to feel isolated from the rest of society.

Audio script: See page T-170.

C 🔊 [CD 2, Track 11]

- Explain the task. Read the statements aloud.
- Play the recording again while Ss choose the theater superstitions they hear. Replay as many times as needed. Ss listen and check their answers.
- Ss work in pairs to compare answers. Go over answers with the class.

> **Answers**
>
> 1. a   2. b   3. a   4. b

Audio script: See page T-170.

- To review the grammar, make copies of the audio script and have Ss work in pairs to underline all the sentence adverbs and the examples of *will* and *would* for habits they can find.

4 Hit songs (SPEAKING)

Review aim: Give opinions about music (20–25 minutes)

A Pair work

- Explain the task. Ss work in pairs to complete the activity. Brainstorm songs from the last three years as a class, if necessary.
- Go around the class and help as necessary. Remind Ss to support their choices with reasons. Make sure all pairs have a list of five songs they both agree on.

B Group work

- Explain the task. Have one pair of Ss read the example conversation to the class.
- Put pairs together to share their lists and agree on which three songs are the very best.
- Have a S from each group report on the group's list to the class. Ask Ss if there is one song that appears on every group's list.

> ✓ Have Ss look at their answers to the self-assessment at the beginning of this review unit. As a class, discuss which skills were easy and which were more difficult and why.

3 LISTENING
Superstitious actors

A You are going to listen to a show about superstitions in the acting profession. Why do you think actors might be more superstitious than non-actors?

B Now listen to the program. What is the main reason Jeffrey gives for superstition among actors? Choose the correct answer.

- ☐ a. They used to feel isolated from the rest of society.
- ☐ b. They are insecure.
- ☐ c. They travel a lot.

C Listen again. Choose the theater superstition you hear in each pair.

1. ☐ a. Black cats are considered lucky.
   ☐ b. Black cats are considered unlucky.

2. ☐ a. A costume is unlucky if a cat has slept on it.
   ☐ b. A costume is unlucky unless a cat has slept on it.

3. ☐ a. The number 13 is believed to be lucky.
   ☐ b. The number 13 is believed to be unlucky.

4. ☐ a. It is unlucky to act in the play *Macbeth*.
   ☐ b. It is unlucky to say the name of the play *Macbeth*.

4 SPEAKING
Hit songs

A **Pair work** What are the five best songs from the last three years? Support your choices with reasons. Make a list of five songs you both agree on.

B **Group work** Join another pair and share your lists. Then discuss which three songs are the very best. Create a new list you all agree on and share it with the rest of the class. Is there one song that appears on all the lists?

"How do you feel about . . . ?"

"Well, the more I hear it, the more I like it. It's pretty evocative. But I'm also into music with a mellow and soothing sound. What do you think about . . . ?"

7 CHANGING TIMES
LESSON A ▶ Lifestyles in transition

1 STARTING POINT
How we are changing

A People's lifestyles are changing more quickly than ever before. Have you noticed any of these trends in your community?

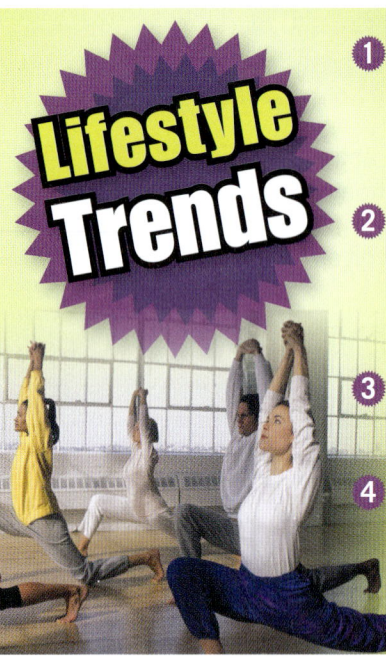

Lifestyle Trends

1. Social exercise programs that offer fun group workouts are on the rise. Enrollment in cycling, strength-training, dance, and yoga classes has never been higher.
2. Hybrid cars, powered by both gas and electricity, are an option that more people are choosing in order to save money and reduce pollution.
3. More professionals whose managers allow it are opting to telecommute, or work from home.
4. More and more shoppers are looking for recyclable products that companies can manufacture sustainably.
5. Children are learning foreign languages at earlier ages than ever before. Some elementary schools now offer classes for children whom they once considered too young.
6. A growing number of people who are concerned with the effects of pesticides on the environment are buying organic produce.
7. These days, people who are not happy with their bodies are more likely to resort to cosmetic surgery.
8. Tourists whose destinations are foreign countries are taking more trips, traveling greater distances, and spending more money.

B Pair work Discuss the good points and bad points of each trend. Which trends do you think are the most beneficial?

"Social exercise programs are great because they encourage more people to get fit."
"I think many people get a better workout by themselves. They exercise more and socialize less!"

2 DISCUSSION
Current trends

A Pair work Think of a current trend in your country, community, or among people you know for as many of these areas as you can.

- education / schools
- shopping / stores
- health / fitness
- science / technology
- nature / environment
- food / restaurants
- travel / tourism
- appearance / fashion

B Group work Join another pair. Share your ideas and choose the three most significant trends. Then prepare a short presentation for the class explaining the trends and why you think they are the most important.

"One trend we discussed is that a lot of people are into ecotourism lately. This is certainly an important and beneficial trend because . . ."

7 CHANGING TIMES
LESSON A ▶ Lifestyles in transition

> In this unit, Ss practice using optional and required relative pronouns to talk about lifestyle changes and using *as if*, *as though*, *as*, *the way*, and *like* to talk about personal changes.

1 How we are changing (STARTING POINT)

Learning aim: Discuss changing lifestyles and see relative pronouns in context (10–15 minutes)

A
- Books closed. Ask: *If people who lived 100 years ago could see your lifestyle today, would they be surprised? What changes would they notice?* Elicit ideas and write Ss' responses on the board.
- Books open. Focus Ss' attention on the picture. Ask Ss which trend they think is illustrated in the picture. (Answer: social exercise programs)
- Explain the task and read the text aloud. Check that Ss understand the vocabulary on the right.
- Give Ss time to think about their answer to the question. Then have a class discussion about the question. Ask: *Why are these changes occurring?*

Vocabulary
workouts series of physical exercises

strength-training exercises, such as weight lifting, that focus on making muscles stronger

sustainably with little or no damage to the environment

pesticides chemicals used to kill unwanted insects

organic produce fruits and vegetables grown without the use of harmful chemicals

resort to choose a way of doing something when other ways have not worked

B Pair work
- Explain the task and read the question aloud. Have a pair of Ss read the example conversation to the class.
- Ss work in pairs to do the activity.
- Have Ss share their partner's answers with the class.

2 Current trends (DISCUSSION)

Learning aim: Talk about current trends (15–20 minutes)

A Pair work
- Explain the task. Read the areas aloud. Ss work in pairs to do the activity. Brainstorm trends as a class, if necessary.
- Focus Ss' attention on the lifestyle changes listed on the board from Exercise 1A. Ask Ss which area each trend belongs to.

B Group work
- Explain the task. Make sure Ss understand that *significant* means important. Read the example aloud.
- Put pairs together and have them do the activity.
- Have groups share their presentations with the class.
- For more practice discussing this topic, download the Worksheet **7.1 Future trends** from the Teacher Support Site.

Possible answers
education / schools: Mobile devices are being used more frequently for educational purposes.

nature / environment: More people are using alternative energy sources, like wind and solar energy.

shopping / stores: "Brick and mortar" stores are having trouble competing with online shopping.

food / restaurants: People are buying more locally grown produce.

health / fitness: More people are becoming aware of the importance of daily exercise.

travel / tourism: Many people are vacationing locally.

science / technology: Internet connections are getting faster.

appearance / fashion: New technologies are playing a more important role in the development of fabrics for clothes.

3 Optional and required relative pronouns (GRAMMAR)

Learning aim: Practice using optional and required relative pronouns (20–25 minutes)

Grammar notes

Relative pronouns (e.g., *who*, *that*, *which*) introduce relative clauses. Relative clauses modify the nouns that precede them. The information in a defining relative clause further defines or gives essential information about the noun it is modifying. Defining relative clauses are not set off by commas.

Who, *that*, and *which* can act as subjects or objects of verbs in relative clauses. *Whom* can act as the object but not the subject. In informal English, *who* is often used instead of *whom*.

- Books closed. Write on the board:
  1. Many students who have finished high school are choosing to take a year off before college.
  2. A personal trainer is a professional whom people hire to help them get in shape.

  Underline the relative pronoun in both sentences and ask Ss what each refers to. (Answers: In sentence 1, *who* refers to *students*. In sentence 2, *whom* refers to *professional*.) Ask: *Is the relative pronoun needed in both sentences?* (Answer: It is needed in the first sentence, but not in the second sentence.)

- Books open. Discuss the information in the grammar box and read the example sentences.

A

- Have Ss look at the Starting Point on page 54 again. Explain the task and read the question aloud. Go over the answer with the class.

Answer

The relative pronoun is required in 1, 3, 6, 7, and 8.

1. Social exercise programs *that* offer fun group workouts . . .
3. More professionals *whose* managers allow it . . .
6. A growing number of people *who* are concerned with the effects of pesticides on the environment . . .
7. These days, people *who* are not happy with their bodies . . .
8. Tourists *whose* destinations are foreign countries . . .

B

- Explain the task. Read the sentences aloud. Answer any questions about vocabulary.
- Ss work individually to complete the activity.
- Go over answers with the class. Have Ss say which sentences are true for their community.

Answer

The relative pronoun is optional in 2, 6, and 8.

C

- Explain the task. Read the sentences aloud and answer any questions about vocabulary.
- Ss work individually to complete the activity.
- Go over answers with the class.

Answers

1. S   2. P   3. O   4. S   5. O   6. S

D Pair work

- Explain the task. Ss work in pairs to interview each other using the questions in part C.
- Have Ss share their partner's answers with the class.

3 GRAMMAR

Optional and required relative pronouns

In defining relative clauses, when the relative pronoun is the subject of the clause or it shows possession, the relative pronoun is required. When it is the object, it is usually optional.

Subject of clause (relative pronouns *that*, *which*, or *who* required)
People **who** / **that** are concerned with the effects of pesticides on the environment are buying organic produce.
Social exercise programs **that** / **which** offer fun group workouts are on the rise.

Showing possession (relative pronoun *whose* required)
More professionals **whose** managers allow it are opting to telecommute, or work from home.

Object of clause (relative pronouns *that*, *which*, *who*, or *whom* optional)
Hybrid cars are an option (**that** / **which**) more people are choosing.
Some elementary schools now offer classes for children (**who** / **whom** / **that**) they once considered too young.

GRAMMAR PLUS *see page 118*

A Look at the Starting Point on page 54 again. In which sentences is the relative pronoun required?

B Choose the sentences in which the relative pronoun is optional. Which sentences are true for your community?

☐ 1. Young families who dream of owning a house are finding they can't afford one.
☐ 2. The pressure that students feel to succeed in school is increasing.
☐ 3. People who used to go to theaters to watch movies now watch them at home.
☐ 4. People want exercise programs that are designed for their specific age group.
☐ 5. People are devoting more time to others who are less fortunate.
☐ 6. People are recycling many things which they would have thrown away in the past.
☐ 7. A lot of people who have grown tired of city life are moving to the country.
☐ 8. More college students are choosing majors that they think will lead to high-paying jobs.

C Is the relative pronoun in these sentences the subject of the clause (*S*), the object of the clause (*O*), or does it show possession (*P*)? Write the correct letter.

____ 1. Is the number of young people **who** opt for cosmetic surgery growing or shrinking?
____ 2. Who are some celebrities **whose** style has affected fashion or other trends?
____ 3. How have the foods **that** fast-food restaurants offer changed in recent years?
____ 4. What brand names **that** once were very popular are no longer as relevant?
____ 5. Are there any alternative therapies **that** you think are ineffective or even dangerous?
____ 6. Is it becoming more difficult for people **who** don't speak a foreign language fluently to get a job?

D Pair work Interview each other using the questions in part C.

LESSON A Lifestyles in transition 55

4 VOCABULARY & SPEAKING
Antonyms with prefixes

A The antonyms of these adjectives can be formed by adding the prefix *il-*, *im-*, *in-*, or *ir-*. Write the correct prefix in front of each adjective.

a. ___considerate c. ___decisive e. ___mature g. ___responsible
b. ___consistent d. ___logical f. ___proper h. ___tolerant

B Complete each opinion with one of the antonyms in part A. Write the correct letter.

1. "You can be 40 and still be ___ if you refuse to grow up and have the expected behavior for a person your age."
2. "People today just don't care about following correct rules or manners. They have such ___ behavior."
3. "Today's politicians are so ___. They just change their opinions and statements from one day to the next."
4. "Selfish people are often ___ of others and don't care about their feelings."
5. "___ people refuse to accept ideas and behavior different from their own."
6. "Many accidents happen when people are ___ and don't give careful thought to the results of their actions."
7. "Because young people lack wisdom and reason, they often make ___ decisions."
8. "Many young people are ___ about their future and unable to choose a course of action."

C Pair work Do you agree with the opinions? Discuss with a partner.

VOCABULARY PLUS see page 136

5 LISTENING
Generation Y

A Listen to a presentation by a corporate executive about two generations of employees. What audience is the presentation addressed to? What is the purpose?

B Listen again. Write the attitudes Generation Y has regarding each area in the chart. Then write what the company is planning to do to address each attitude.

	Generation Y's attitude	Plan
1. work and free time		
2. relationship to boss		
3. community involvement		

4 Antonyms with prefixes (VOCABULARY & SPEAKING)

Learning aim: Learn how to make antonyms with prefixes and practice using them to talk about trends (15–20 minutes)

A

- Explain the task. Read the adjectives aloud. To check understanding, have several Ss use each word in a sentence that shows that they understand its meaning.
- Ss work individually to complete the task. Go over answers with the class.

Answers			
a. in	c. in	e. im	g. ir
b. in	d. il	f. im	h. in

B

- Explain the task. Ss work individually to complete the activity.
- Ss work in pairs to compare answers. Go over answers with the class.

Answers			
1. e	3. b	5. h	7. d
2. f	4. a	6. g	8. c

C Pair work

- Explain the task. Give Ss time to think about whether or not they agree with each opinion and why.
- Ss work in pairs to discuss the opinions.
- Have Ss share their partner's answers with the class.

5 Generation Y (LISTENING)

Learning aim: Develop skills in listening for gist and details (20–25 minutes)

A 🔊 [CD 2, Track 12]

- Explain the task. Read the questions aloud. Check that Ss understand the following vocabulary.

Vocabulary

accommodating helping people by providing something they need

fall in (that category) belong to; are part of

transitioning changing from one style to another

hands-off not interfering; allowing others to work independently

(community) outreach program an organization or group that helps people with social, medical, or educational problems

instituting introducing, starting up (a new plan or system)

- Tell Ss to listen for the answers to the questions. Play the recording as Ss listen for the answers. Replay as many times as needed. Ss listen and check their answers.
- Ss work in pairs to compare answers. Go over answers with the class.

Answers

The presentation is addressed to managers in a company. Most of them are Generation X-ers.

The purpose is to discuss how the company is planning to focus on the needs of their Generation Y employees.

Audio script: See page T-170.

B 🔊 [CD 2, Track 13]

- Explain the task. Tell Ss to look at the chart and determine the information they need to complete it.
- Tell Ss to listen for the answers. Play the recording as Ss complete the chart. Replay as many times as needed. Ss listen and check their answers.
- Ss work in pairs to discuss their answers. Go over answers with the class.

Answers

1. work and free time:
   Generation Y's attitude: They are more flexible and tolerant when balancing work and private life.
   Plan: Create a corporate social networking website.

2. relationship to boss:
   Generation Y's attitude: They want to share opinions and ideas with their managers and want work-related comments and advice from them.
   Plan: Managers will make themselves available one hour a week to speak with staff informally.

3. community involvement:
   Generation Y's attitude: They are volunteer-minded and want to help others.
   Plan: Employees will be given up to 14 hours a year of paid time off to volunteer in the community.

Audio script: See page T-170.

6 Writing about a personal experience (WRITING)

Learning aim: Write a composition about a personal experience using background information and details (40–50 minutes)

A

- Books closed. Ask Ss if they ever write about their personal experiences. If so, ask where they do it. (Possible answers: on a social networking site, in a journal, etc.) Then ask Ss if they have ever written a composition about a personal experience. Ask Ss to tell the class what kind of information they included in their composition.

- Books open. Tell Ss to read the information in the box at the top of the page. Ask: *How does a composition about a personal experience usually begin?* (Answer: with a thesis statement and some observations or comments) *What is in the body of the composition?* (Answer: background information and details)

- Explain to Ss that in a composition about a personal experience, at least one body paragraph should be about the experience itself, and the other paragraphs should be about the background information and how the author feels about the experience.

- Explain the task. Tell Ss that the ellipses at the end of the three body paragraphs indicate that the paragraphs continue and words have been intentionally left out. Have Ss read the composition silently to themselves. Check that Ss understand the following vocabulary.

Vocabulary

giant step an action that causes a large amount of personal progress

assuming taking on

making up my mind deciding

- Ss work individually to underline the thesis statement and answer the questions.
- Ss work in pairs to compare answers.
- Go over answers with the class. Have some Ss share their answers to the third question with the class.

Answers

Thesis statement:
Last month I took a giant step and finally moved to a new apartment.

1. *In the beginning, I was a little scared . . . ; I was also a little concerned about feeling lonely, but I knew it was important to have the experience of being totally on my own.*

2. talking things over with the roommate before making a decision; looking at many apartments before making a decision; finding an affordable one-bedroom; decorating the apartment

3. *Answers will vary.*

B

- Explain the writing task.
- Ss work individually to write their compositions. Remind Ss to include an introductory paragraph, three detailed body paragraphs, and a conclusion.
- Go around the class and help as needed.

C Pair work

- Ss work in pairs to exchange paragraphs and take turns answering the questions.
- Go around the class and help as needed. Encourage Ss to ask and answer follow-up questions about the personal experience and about anything they don't understand.

Do your students need more practice?

Assign . . .	for more practice in . . .
Grammar Plus 7A	Grammar
Vocabulary Plus 7A	Vocabulary
Online Vocabulary Accelerator 7A	Vocabulary
Workbook Lesson A	Grammar, Vocabulary, Writing
Online Workbook Lesson A	Grammar, Vocabulary, Writing

6 WRITING
Writing about a personal experience

> A personal-experience composition usually begins with an introductory paragraph containing a thesis statement and some observations or comments. The body of the composition provides background information and gives details about what happened. The conclusion usually restates the thesis and presents the writer's feelings.

A Underline the thesis statement. Then read the composition and answer the questions below. Compare answers with a partner.

> Last month I took a giant step and finally moved to a new apartment. I had been sharing a two-bedroom apartment for two years with a friend who I'd known since childhood, and I decided that it was time to have my own place. In the beginning, I was a little scared because I would be assuming a great deal of financial responsibility. I was also a little concerned about feeling lonely, but I knew it was important to have the experience of being totally on my own.
>
> The first thing I wanted to do before making a final decision was to talk things over with my roommate. We had first moved in together because neither of us could afford . . .
>
> I looked at many apartments before making up my mind. I finally found one that I liked – an affordable one-bedroom in very good shape, with a lot of light. The apartment is . . .
>
> My new apartment is beginning to look like a home now. I've been looking at a lot of interior design websites, and I've managed to decorate my apartment. . . .
>
> Looking back, I definitely think that I made the right decision. I feel really good about having a place I can call my own. I feel more independent and responsible. Sometimes I feel a little lonely, but for the most part, I enjoy the privacy.

1. What observations or personal comments does the writer make in the first paragraph?
2. What details and background information does the body of the composition provide?
3. What additional information do you think the writer gives to complete the body paragraphs?

B Write a composition about something that has happened to you recently. Make sure to include an introductory paragraph, three body paragraphs with details, and a conclusion.

C **Pair work** Exchange papers and answer these questions.

1. Does your partner's introductory paragraph have a thesis statement?
2. Do all the details in the body of the composition support the thesis statement?
3. What other points or examples could be added?

LESSON A Lifestyles in transition

LESSON B ▶ A change for the better

1 STARTING POINT
Contemplating a change

A Pair work Read about the changes these people are thinking about. Do you think they'd be happy if they made the changes? Why or why not?

My public-relations job is secure and high paying. Still, I feel as though something is missing. My real passion is skiing, and today I saw an ad for a PR consultant at a ski resort. It seems like the job was made for me! I'd have to take a big pay cut, but it might be worth it.

My parents expect me to go to a four-year college the way they did. I'm not really sure that's for me. I mean, why go away for an education when there are so many online courses? It's as if my computer is a university! For some jobs I'm interested in, I only need a professional certificate, which I could earn online in less than a year.

I'm making ends meet thanks to my part-time jobs, but I guess I'm looking for more meaning in my life. I'm thinking of joining a volunteer program to help build houses for the needy as a few of my friends have. I'd get to travel, meet new people, and do something for others.

B Group work Tell your group about a change you are thinking of making. Respond to each other's ideas with advice about the changes and other suggestions.

"I'm thinking about changing careers and getting into fashion design."
"That's cool! Maybe taking online courses in fashion would be a good place to start."

2 LISTENING
Volunteering for a change

A You are going to listen to Jody speak to Mr. Turner about volunteering in a program called Houses for All. What kind of program do you think it is?

B Now listen to the conversation. Which of these things is Jody concerned about? Choose the correct answers.

☐ airfare   ☐ food   ☐ making friends
☐ culture shock ☐ job skills   ☐ visiting home

C Listen again. Write the three ways that Jody is hoping to benefit from the program.

1. _____
2. _____
3. _____

58 UNIT 7 Changing times

LESSON B ▶ A change for the better

1 Contemplating a change (STARTING POINT)

Learning aim: Discuss making lifestyle changes and see the lesson grammar in context (10–15 minutes)

A Pair work

- Books closed. Ask Ss if they know anyone who has made a change in their life recently. Ask Ss if they would or wouldn't make the same change and why.
- Books open. Explain the task. Read the questions aloud. Have a few Ss read the texts to the class. Check that Ss understand the following vocabulary.

> **Vocabulary**
>
> **public-relations (PR) job** working to get people to have a good opinion of a company or organization
>
> **making ends meet** having enough money to live on
>
> **the needy** the very poor

- Ss work in pairs to discuss their answers. Alternatively, have a class discussion.

> **Culture note**
>
> Four-year colleges have admission requirements. Successful completion of a set number of academic courses (credits) results in a bachelor's degree.
>
> A professional certificate is earned by passing an exam set up by an organization that sets the standards for a particular industry. The courses preparing for these exams usually have no admission requirements.

B Group work

- Explain the task. Ask one pair of Ss to read the example conversation to the class. Then tell Ss about a change you might make in your life and ask them for advice and suggestions.
- Ss work in groups to share their ideas and take turns responding, giving advice, and making suggestions.
- Have a S from each group report on the group's discussion to the class.

2 Volunteering for a change (LISTENING)

Learning aim: Develop skills in listening for the main idea and details (15–20 minutes)

A

- Explain the task and read the question aloud. Have several Ss share their answers with the class.

B 🔊 [CD 2, Track 14]

- Explain the task. Read the question and the topics aloud. Check that Ss understand the following vocabulary.

> **Vocabulary**
>
> **nonprofit** not established to make a profit; a charity organization in this context
>
> **cover their own airfare** pay for their own plane ticket
>
> **assigned** sent to a particular place for work
>
> **stand in my way** be an obstacle or a reason not to do something
>
> **sets them apart** shows that they are different
>
> **commitment** a promise to give time and energy to something
>
> **culture shock** a feeling of confusion or anxiety when in a new and different place, such as a foreign country

- Tell Ss to listen for the answers to the question. Play the recording as Ss choose the answers. Replay as many times as needed. Ss listen and check their answers.
- Go over answers with the class.

> **Answers**
>
> airfare, food, job skills

Audio script: See page T-171.

C 🔊 [CD 2, Track 15]

- Explain that Ss will listen again and write the three ways Jody is hoping to benefit from the program.
- Tell Ss to listen for the answers. Play the recording as Ss write their answers. Replay as many times as needed. Ss listen and check their answers.
- Go over answers with the class.

> **Answers**
>
> 1. help her get a good job in the future
> 2. gain confidence in herself
> 3. get a broader and more global world view

Audio script: See page T-171.

3 As if, as though, as, the way, and like (GRAMMAR)

Learning aim: Practice using *as if*, *as though*, *as*, *the way*, and *like* (25–30 minutes)

> **Grammar notes**
>
> In these clauses of manner, *as if* and *as though* are interchangeable.
>
> *Like* is often used in informal spoken American English, but in more formal situations (spoken and written), *as if*, *as though*, *as*, and *the way* are used more often.
>
> The past form of the verb is used after *as if* and *as though* when the clause is describing an unreal or hypothetical situation.
> *Andy talks about traveling as though he had the money to do it.*
> *My grandfather runs marathons as if he were 18 years old.*

- Books closed. Write on the board:
  1. Sometimes it looks as though I'll never reach my goal.
  2. Sometimes it looks like I'll never reach my goal.

  Read the sentences aloud and ask Ss which sentence is more formal. (Answer: the first one) Ask them to explain why. (Answer: *Like* has the same meaning as *as if* or *as though*, but it is more commonly used in informal spoken English.)

- Books open. Discuss the information in the grammar box and read the example sentences.

A

- Have Ss look at the Starting Point on page 58 again. Explain the task and read the question aloud. Go over the answer with the class.

> **Answer**
>
> It's <u>as if</u> my computer is a university!
> Rewritten with *like*:
> It's <u>like</u> my computer is a university!

B

- Explain the task. Read the sentences and the example aloud. Ss work individually to complete the activity.
- Ss work in pairs to compare their answers. Go over answers with the class.

> **Answers**
>
> 1. Lately, I'm trying to think more positively, <u>the way / as</u> I did when I was younger.
> 2. My father is trying to exercise more <u>the way / as</u> his doctor advised.
> 3. Sometimes I feel <u>as if / as though</u> the world is changing too fast.
> 4. To become a better listener, listen to people <u>as if / as though</u> everything they say is important.
> 5. My uncle needs to stop dressing <u>as if / as though</u> time has stood still for 20 years.
> 6. A friend of mine is teaching me to bake bread <u>the way / as</u> they do in France.

C Pair work

- Explain the task. Read the sentences and the example answer aloud.
- Ss work individually to complete the sentences and add a sentence with their own information.
- Ss work in pairs to compare their answers.

> **Possible answers**
>
> 1. I feel as though I don't have enough time to cook healthy food.
> 2. I don't feel the need to be online constantly as so many people do these days.
> 3. Young people today feel as though it's very difficult to succeed.
> 4. I wish I could still play sports the way I used to when I was younger.
> 5. People today would find it difficult to use horses for transportation as was necessary long ago.
> 6. *Answers will vary.*

D Group work

- Explain the task. Read the information in the Useful Expressions box aloud. Give an example of when to use each question. Have one pair of Ss read the example conversation to the class.
- Put pairs together and have them discuss their answers to part C.
- Have a S from each group report on the group's discussion to the class.

3 GRAMMAR

As if, as though, as, the way, and like

As if and *as though* often introduce clauses that describe impressions about feelings or behavior after verbs such as *act*, *behave*, *feel*, *look*, *seem*, and *talk*.
Still, I feel **as if / as though** something is missing.

As and *the way* introduce clauses that express a comparison.
I'm thinking of joining a volunteer program to help build houses for the needy **as / the way** a few of my friends have.

In informal English, the word *like* can be used instead of *as if / as though* and *as / the way*.
It seems **as though** the job was made for me!
It seems **like** the job was made for me!

GRAMMAR PLUS see page 119

A Look at the Starting Point on page 58 again. Can you find another expression you can rewrite with *like*?

B Rewrite these sentences to make them more formal using *as if*, *as though*, *as*, or *the way*. Compare your answers with a partner. More than one answer is possible.

1. Lately, I'm trying to think more positively, like I did when I was younger.
   Lately, I'm trying to think more positively, the way I did when I was younger.
2. My father is trying to exercise more like his doctor advised.
3. Sometimes I feel like the world is changing too fast.
4. To become a better listener, listen to people like everything they say is important.
5. My uncle needs to stop dressing like time has stood still for 20 years.
6. A friend of mine is teaching me to bake bread like they do in France.

C Pair work Complete these sentences so that they are true for you. Add another sentence with your own information, and compare with a partner.

1. I feel as though I don't have enough time to . . .
   cook healthy food.
2. I don't feel the need to . . . as so many people do these days.
3. Young people today feel as though . . .
4. I wish I could still . . . the way I used to when I was younger.
5. People today would find it difficult to . . . as was necessary long ago.
6. _____

D Group work Join another pair and share your answers. Ask for more specific information, and give your opinions.

"I really feel as if I don't have enough time to cook healthy food."
"What makes you say that?"
"Well, I'm so busy that there's too little time to go food shopping and make proper meals. It's easier just to grab fast food."

Useful expressions

Asking for more specific information
What makes you say that?
Why do you think that?
In what way(s)?

LESSON **B** A change for the better

4 VOCABULARY & SPEAKING
Collocations with *change*

A Look at the expressions with *change*. Match each expression with its definition.

1. anticipate ____		a. experience a change
2. avoid ____		b. expect a change
3. bring about ____		c. successfully deal with a change
4. cope with ____	(a) change	d. fight against a change
5. go through ____		e. escape or stay away from a change
6. resist ____		f. cause a change
7. welcome ____		g. invite and be happy about a change

B Pair work Use the expressions to discuss with your partner changes you would (not) . . .

1. avoid.   2. be able to cope with.   3. resist.   4. welcome.   5. bring about if you could.

"I'd try to avoid changes to my current lifestyle. I'm really happy with my life right now."
"That's good to hear. But would you also avoid changes that could make your life even better?"

VOCABULARY PLUS see page 136

5 DISCUSSION
How do you cope?

A Complete the survey. How true is each statement for you? Choose a number from 1 to 5. Then discuss the survey with a partner.

DO YOU RESIST OR WELCOME CHANGE?	Not true at all				Very true
1. I set realistic goals for myself and take steps to achieve them.	1	2	3	4	5
2. I am a curious person and enjoy new experiences.	1	2	3	4	5
3. I live in the present, appreciate the past, and focus on the future.	1	2	3	4	5
4. I listen to others and seek understanding.	1	2	3	4	5
5. When solving a problem, I seek advice and support from friends and family I trust.	1	2	3	4	5
6. I am highly flexible and easygoing.	1	2	3	4	5
7. I am creative and brainstorm solutions to challenges.	1	2	3	4	5
8. I stand up for myself and say "no" when I need to.	1	2	3	4	5
9. When I fail at something, I see it as a learning experience.	1	2	3	4	5
10. I try to find humor in all situations.	1	2	3	4	5

SCORE

10–20 You tend to avoid change. You need to learn to welcome change in your life.

21–30 You often resist change. Friends and family can help you cope with it.

31–40 You respond to change well. However, there is always room for improvement.

41–50 You are exceptionally adaptable. You bring about positive changes in your life.

B Pair work Think of a big change in your life. Tell your partner about your feelings and reactions at the time and how your life today is different because of it.

"Getting my driver's license was a welcome change. I felt independent and was thrilled to finally be able to go where I wanted when I wanted. . . ."

4 Collocations with *change* (VOCABULARY & SPEAKING)

Learning aim: Learn and practice using collocations with *change* (15–20 minutes)

A
- Ask Ss if they remember what a *collocation* is. (Answer: two or more words that often are used together) Ask Ss to give examples of collocations and write them on the board.
- Explain the task. Read the expressions and definitions aloud. Ss work individually to complete the activity.
- Go over answers with the class.

Answers
1. b   2. e   3. f   4. c   5. a   6. d   7. g

- Ask Ss if they can think of any other collocations with *change*. Allow them to use dictionaries or other resources. Write the collocations on the board and have Ss use them in a sentence. (Possible answers: *advocate, block, facilitate, initiate*)

B Pair work
- Explain the task. Have one pair of Ss read the example conversation to the class.
- Ss work in pairs to discuss changes.
- Have Ss share their partner's answers with the class.

Possible answers
1. I'd try to avoid changes to my current lifestyle.
2. I wouldn't be able to cope with a change to my neighborhood.
3. I'd resist changes to the volunteer program where I work.
4. I wouldn't welcome any changes to my job description. I like my job just as it is!
5. I'd bring about a change in driving laws if I could. The laws are too strict now.

To help Ss with vocabulary in this exercise, download the Fresh Idea *That reminds me of . . .* from the Teacher Support Site.

5 How do you cope? (DISCUSSION)

Learning aim: Discuss dealing with change and practice using collocations with *change* (20 minutes)

A
- Explain the task. Read the survey aloud.
- Ss work individually to complete the survey and then calculate their score.
- Ss work in pairs to discuss the survey and their results.
- Have Ss share their partner's results with the class.

B Pair work
- Explain the task. Have a S read the example to the class.
- Ss work in pairs to discuss a big change in their life. Brainstorm examples of big life changes as a class, if necessary.
- Have Ss share their partner's answers with the class.

Optional activity: *The biggest change* (20 minutes)
Ss talk about the biggest life change.
- Ss work in groups to discuss what they think are the top three most important life changes a person can experience. Tell them to write at least two reasons for each choice.
- Have each group tell the class about the changes they listed and their reasons. Write each group's ideas on the board.
- Have a class discussion about the most important life change. Have each group defend their ideas until the class can agree on the most important change a person can have.

6 Return to simplicity (READING)

Learning aim: Develop skills in understanding vocabulary in context, reading for specific information, making inferences, and giving a personal reaction to a reading (25–30 minutes)

A Pair work

- Books closed. Write on the board:

    rat race

    Ask Ss what the phrase means. (Answer: a way of life that is competitive, rushed, and stressful, usually in a city) Ask Ss if they think they are in the rat race or if they lead a simple life.

- Books open. Explain the task. Ss work in pairs to discuss the question.

- Have Ss read the article silently to themselves. Check that Ss understand the following vocabulary.

> **Vocabulary**
>
> **precious** extremely valuable
>
> **paralegal** a person who works in a lawyer's office and assists with researching cases
>
> **trial lawyer** a lawyer who defends or prosecutes clients in a courtroom
>
> **bed and breakfast** a small inn with a few bedrooms, typically a person's home, where guests can sleep and have breakfast
>
> **dishing out** serving (food)
>
> **mesa** a high, flat piece of land
>
> **phenomenon** something that is noticed because it is unusual or new
>
> **widespread** very common throughout a large area
>
> **frazzled** exhausting and stressful
>
> **gone way down** decreased a lot
>
> **potluck dinner** a dinner where each guest brings part of the meal
>
> **advocating** expressing support for
>
> **consumption patterns** the regular ways in which people buy and use resources
>
> **deprivation** the state of not having enough

B

- Ask Ss to define *summary*. (Answer: a short version of an article that gives only the main points) Explain the task.
- Ss work individually to complete the activity.
- Go over answers with the class.

> **Answers**
>
> 1. more precious   5. magazine
> 2. bed and breakfast   6. buy
> 3. cutting down on   7. money
> 4. her kids

> **Optional activity:** *Vocabulary* (15–20 minutes)
>
> Ss practice the vocabulary from the reading.
>
> - Have Ss look at the article again. Tell them to write down any words that they did not know before.
> - Ask Ss to call out their words and write them on the board. As a class, write definitions for each word.
> - Have Ss write a sentence using each word. Make sure they write sentences that show they understand the meaning of the word.
> - Ask Ss to read their sentences to the class.

C Group work

- Explain the task. Read the questions aloud.
- Ss work in groups to discuss the questions.
- Ask groups to share their ideas with the class. To make sure that reporting to the class goes smoothly, groups can choose one or two members to report their ideas. Have Ss review their ideas with their own group at the end of the task to see if the group agrees with the information they will be presenting.

For an alternative reading text or extra practice, download the Worksheet **7.2 Bright ideas** from the Teacher Support Site.

Do your students need more practice?	
Assign . . .	for more practice in . . .
Grammar Plus 7B	Grammar
Vocabulary Plus 7B	Vocabulary
Online Vocabulary Accelerator 7B	Vocabulary
Workbook Lesson B	Grammar, Vocabulary, Reading
Online Workbook Lesson B	Grammar, Vocabulary, Reading, Listening

6 READING
Return to simplicity

A **Pair work** Would you reduce your income by half in exchange for more free time and less stress? Discuss with a partner. Then read the article.

LEAVING THE Rat Race FOR THE Simple Life

Time is more precious than money for an increasing number of people who are choosing to live more with less – and welcoming the change.

Kay and Charles Giddens, a paralegal and a trial lawyer, respectively, sold their home to start a bed and breakfast. Four years later, the couple was dishing out banana pancake breakfasts, cleaning toilets, and serving homemade chocolate chip cookies to guests in a bed and breakfast surrounded by trees on a mesa known for colorful sunsets.

"Do I miss the freeways? Do I miss the traffic? Do I miss the stress? No," said Ms. Giddens. "This is a phenomenon that's fairly widespread. A lot of people are re-evaluating their lives and figuring out what they want to do."

Simple living ranges from cutting down on weeknight activities to sharing housing, living closer to work and commuting less, avoiding shopping malls, borrowing books from the library instead of buying them, and taking a cut in pay to work at a more pleasurable job.

Vicki Robin, a writer, tells us how she copes with the changes in her budget, now far less than she used to make.

"You become conscious about where your money is going and how valuable it is," Ms. Robin says. "You tend not to use things up. You cook at home rather than eat out. Your life is less frazzled, and you discover your expenses have gone way down."

Janet Luhrs, a lawyer, quit her practice after giving birth and leaving her daughter with a nanny for two weeks. "It was not the way I wanted to raise my kids," she says. "Simplicity is not just about saving money, it's about me sitting down every night with my kids to a candlelit dinner with classical music."

Mrs. Luhrs started editing a magazine called *Simple Living* and publishing tips on how to buy recycled furniture and shoes, organize potluck dinners instead of fancy receptions, and advocating changes in consumption patterns.

"It's not about poverty or deprivation," Mrs. Luhrs explains. "It's about conscious living and creating the life you want. The less stuff you buy, the less money goes out the door, and the less money you have to earn."

Source: "Living the Simple Life – and Loving It," by Julia Duin, *The Washington Times*

B Complete the summary of the article. Fill in each blank with words or phrases from the article.

Many people have come to think that time is (1) _____ than money. The Giddenses gave up their law careers to run a (2) _____, and they are happy they did. Others have chosen to simplify their lives by (3) _____ their activities and expenses. Janet Luhrs quit her job as a lawyer to spend more time with (4) _____. She started editing a (5) _____ called *Simple Living*. She understands that the less stuff you (6) _____, the less (7) _____ you need to earn.

C **Group work** Discuss these questions. Then share your answers with the class.

1. Do you think the people in the article have improved their lives? Why?
2. What changes would you make to live more simply? How would these changes simplify your life?

LESSON B A change for the better 61

8 CONSUMER CULTURE
LESSON A ▶ What's new on the market?

1 STARTING POINT
Smart shoppers

A Pair work Read about these four ways to find bargains. Which ones have you or your partner tried?

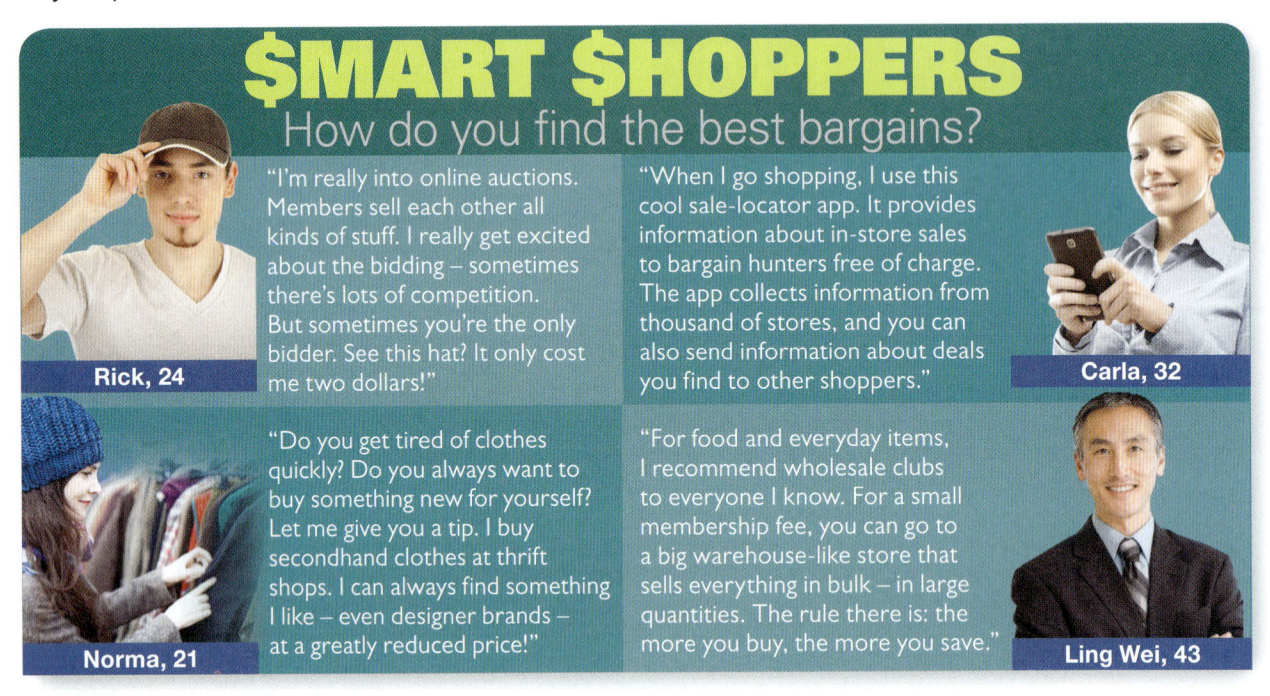

$MART $HOPPERS
How do you find the best bargains?

Rick, 24: "I'm really into online auctions. Members sell each other all kinds of stuff. I really get excited about the bidding – sometimes there's lots of competition. But sometimes you're the only bidder. See this hat? It only cost me two dollars!"

Carla, 32: "When I go shopping, I use this cool sale-locator app. It provides information about in-store sales to bargain hunters free of charge. The app collects information from thousand of stores, and you can also send information about deals you find to other shoppers."

Norma, 21: "Do you get tired of clothes quickly? Do you always want to buy something new for yourself? Let me give you a tip. I buy secondhand clothes at thrift shops. I can always find something I like – even designer brands – at a greatly reduced price!"

Ling Wei, 43: "For food and everyday items, I recommend wholesale clubs to everyone I know. For a small membership fee, you can go to a big warehouse-like store that sells everything in bulk – in large quantities. The rule there is: the more you buy, the more you save."

B Pair work What other ways do you find bargains? Can you remember an item you bought at a reduced price?

"There are some great discount websites that sell electronics, and you can find some awesome bargains. I got a great camera for half price from one of those sites."

2 LISTENING
Shopping preferences

A Listen to Ben and Anna talk about shopping online and in stores. Choose their preference and write three positive aspects they mention about it.

	Ben	Anna
Shopping preference	☐ online ☐ in stores	☐ online ☐ in stores
Positive aspects		
Negative aspects		

B Listen again. Write two negative aspects they mention in the chart.

C Pair work Do you prefer shopping online or in stores? Explain your preference.

8 CONSUMER CULTURE
LESSON A ▶ *What's new on the market?*

> In this unit, Ss practice placement of direct and indirect objects and use verbs in the subjunctive to talk about shopping and product marketing.

1 Smart shoppers (STARTING POINT)

Learning aim: Discuss finding bargains and see direct and indirect objects in context (10–15 minutes)

A Pair work
- Explain the task. Read the texts aloud. Check that Ss understand the following vocabulary.

Vocabulary
bidding offering to pay a particular price for an item, usually in competition with other people

thrift shop a store that sells used items for low prices

warehouse a very large building used to keep items before they go to the store and are sold to customers

- Give Ss time to think about their answer to the question. Then Ss work in pairs to discuss their answers.
- Have Ss share their partner's answers with the class.

B Pair work
- Explain the task. Read the example answer aloud.
- Ss work in pairs to do the activity.
- Have Ss share their partner's answers with the class.

2 Shopping preferences (LISTENING)

Learning aim: Develop skills in listening for gist and details (15–20 minutes)

A 🔊 **[CD 2, Track 16]**
- Explain the task. Check that Ss understand the following vocabulary.

Vocabulary
retailer company that sells items to the public in stores or online

sold out no longer available

shipping sending an item to a customer

drawback a problem or disadvantage

- Play the recording once as Ss listen. Play the recording again while Ss choose the preferences and write the positive aspects. Replay as many times as needed. Ss listen and check their answers.
- Go over answers with the class.

Answers
Ben: Shopping preference: online
Positive aspects: things are never sold out; there is a very wide selection; he gets a good price (because he can compare prices easily)

Anna: Shopping preference: in stores
Positive aspects: she can try on clothes; the personal touch of sales staff; a shopping trip is usually social

Audio script: See page T-171.

B 🔊 **[CD 2, Track 17]**
- Explain that Ss will listen again and write two negative aspects of Ben's and Anna's preferences in the chart.
- Tell Ss to listen for the answers. Play the recording as Ss complete the chart. Replay as many times as needed. Ss listen and check their answers.
- Ss work in pairs to compare their answers. Go over answers with the class.

Answers
Ben:
Negative aspects: shipping can be expensive; he has to wait for delivery, which can be unpredictable

Anna:
Negative aspects: stores get crowded during sales; when a store doesn't have what she needs, she has to go somewhere else

Audio script: See page T-171.

C Pair work
- Explain the task. Read the question aloud. Ss work in pairs to answer the question and explain their preference.
- Have Ss share their partner's answers with the class.

UNIT 8 Consumer culture T-62

3 Placement of direct and indirect objects (GRAMMAR)

Learning aim: Practice placement of direct and indirect objects (25–30 minutes)

> **Grammar notes**
>
> The position of an indirect object in a sentence depends on whether it is introduced by a preposition.
>
> If the indirect object is introduced by *to* and the direct object is a simple noun phrase, the indirect object follows the direct object:
>
>   D.O.   I.O.
> The teacher gave some difficult homework to his students.
>
> If the indirect object is not introduced by a preposition, it precedes the direct object.
>
>   I.O.   D.O.
> The teacher gave his students some difficult homework.

- Books closed. Write on the board:
  1. *The store offers sales to customers every Monday.*
  2. *The store offers customers sales every Monday.*

  Ask Ss to identify the direct and indirect object in each sentence. (Answers: direct object: *sales*; indirect object: *customers*) Ask them what is different between the two sentences. (Answer: the preposition *to* and the order of the objects) Then ask Ss if the sentences mean the same thing. (Answer: yes)

- Books open. Discuss the information in the grammar box and read the example sentences aloud.

A

- Have Ss look at the Starting Point on page 62 again. Explain the task and read the question aloud. Go over answers with the class.

> **Answers**
>
> Pattern A:
> *Do you always want to buy something new for yourself?*
> *. . . I recommend wholesale clubs to everyone I know.*
>
> Pattern B:
> *Members sell each other all kinds of stuff.*
> *Let me give you a tip.*

B

- Explain the task. Read the sentences and the example answer aloud. Answer any questions about vocabulary.
- Ss work individually to complete the activity.
- Go over answers with the class.

> **Answers**
>
> 1. Many companies use cartoon characters to sell products to children / children products.
> 2. If I'm not satisfied with a product, I never hesitate to return it to the store.
> 3. The Internet has made shopping much easier, but delivery costs people more money.
> 4. At restaurants, my wife thinks I ask the waiter too many questions.
> 5. At discount stores, when they lower prices, they always announce it to the shoppers.
> 6. When I told the baker the bread smelled good, he gave me a free sample / a free sample to me.
> 7. In most malls, there is a directory that shows the locations of all the stores to the shoppers / the shoppers the locations of all the stores.
> 8. Good salespeople convincingly explain the benefits of a product to their customers.

C Pair work

- Explain the task. Have one pair of Ss read the example conversation to the class.
- Ss work in pairs to do the activity. Remind Ss to ask follow-up questions.
- Have Ss tell the class about their conversation.

T-63 UNIT 8 Consumer culture

3 GRAMMAR

Placement of direct and indirect objects

For most verbs in English, including *get*, *give*, *lend*, *offer*, *sell*, *send*, *show*, *teach*, and *tell*, direct and indirect objects follow these patterns:

Pattern A
direct object + *to* / *for* + indirect object
You can send **information to other shoppers**.
You can send **information to them**.
You can send **it to other shoppers**.
You can send **it to them**.

Pattern B
indirect object + direct object
You can send **other shoppers information**.
You can send **them information**.

With verbs such as *announce*, *describe*, *explain*, *mention*, *provide*, *recommend*, *return*, and *say*, the indirect object cannot precede the direct object. Sentences follow Pattern A above.
It provides **information** about in-store sales **to bargain hunters** free of charge.
It provides **it to them** free of charge.

With verbs such as *allow*, *ask*, *cause*, and *cost*, the indirect object precedes the direct object and takes no preposition. Sentences follow Pattern B above.
It only cost **Rick two dollars**!
It only cost **him two dollars**!

GRAMMAR PLUS see page 120

A Look at the Starting Point on page 62 again. Find more sentences containing both a direct and an indirect object. Which pattern do they follow?

B Complete these sentences using the words in parentheses. Whenever possible, write the sentence in two different ways.

1. Many companies use cartoon characters to sell . . . (products / children)
   products to children. / children products.

2. If I'm not satisfied with a product, I never hesitate to return . . . (it / the store)

3. The Internet has made shopping much easier, but delivery costs . . . (more money / people)

4. At restaurants, my wife thinks I ask . . . (too many questions / the waiter)

5. At discount stores, when they lower prices, they always announce . . . (it / the shoppers)

6. When I told the baker the bread smelled good, he gave . . . (a free sample / me)

7. In most malls, there is a directory that shows . . . (the locations of all the stores / the shoppers)

8. Good salespeople convincingly explain . . . (the benefits of a product / their customers)

C **Pair work** Use the verbs below to talk about things you've bought recently. Ask follow-up questions.

| ask | describe | give | return |
| cost | explain | recommend | tell |

"A friend recommended a new discount store to me, and I finally went there last weekend."
"What kinds of things do they sell?"
"Mainly high-tech electronics and stuff like that."
"Did you buy anything?"
"Yeah. I bought a toy robot for my nephew."

LESSON A What's new on the market? 63

4 VOCABULARY & SPEAKING
Shopping experiences

A Pair work Match each expression with its meaning. Then compare with a partner.

1. go over your credit limit _g_
2. be a bargain hunter ___
3. be a compulsive shopper ___
4. have buyer's remorse ___
5. make an impulse buy ___
6. bid on an item ___
7. go on a shopping spree ___
8. go window-shopping ___

a. have regrets after making an unwise purchase
b. be unable to control your need to buy things
c. buy something suddenly without having planned to
d. spend lots of money shopping for pleasure
e. look at goods in stores without buying any
f. be a person who looks for low-priced products
g. charge more to your credit card than the allowed amount
h. offer money to buy an item at an auction

B Group work Which of these experiences related to shopping have you had? Share your experiences with the group. Use the expressions in part A where appropriate.

- You made an impulse buy.
- You resisted buying something you wanted.
- You bought something and later wished you hadn't.

"I'm usually a bargain hunter, but this outfit looked so good on the store mannequin that I just had to buy it."

VOCABULARY PLUS see page 137

5 DISCUSSION
Are you a compulsive shopper?

A Pair work Which statements are true for you? Choose *yes* or *no* for each statement. Then discuss your answers with a partner.

What Are Your SHOPPING HABITS?

	Yes	No
1. I can never go shopping without making an impulse buy.	○	○
2. I often buy things that I end up never wearing or using.	○	○
3. At home, I frequently feel tempted to go online and buy something.	○	○
4. When I visit a new city, I spend most of my free time shopping.	○	○
5. I always have buyer's remorse after going on a shopping spree.	○	○
6. I have gone over my credit limit at least once.	○	○
7. As soon as new fashions appear in the stores, I have to buy them.	○	○
8. After buying things, I sometimes lie to relatives and friends about the price.	○	○
9. I sometimes go shopping to forget my troubles.	○	○

B Group work Discuss these questions. Then share your ideas with the class.

1. What are some other characteristics of a compulsive shopper?
2. What other problems do compulsive shoppers face?
3. What would you do to help a compulsive shopper?

4 Shopping experiences (VOCABULARY & SPEAKING)

Learning aim: Learn and practice vocabulary for talking about shopping (15–20 minutes)

A Pair work

- Explain the task. Read the expressions and their meanings aloud.
- Ss work individually to do the matching activity.
- Ss work in pairs to compare answers. Go over answers with the class.

Answers			
1. g	3. b	5. c	7. d
2. f	4. a	6. h	8. e

B Group work

- Explain the task. Read the shopping experiences and example answer aloud.
- Ss work in groups to discuss the question.
- Have a S from each group tell the class about an amusing or unusual experience that the group talked about.

> **Optional activity:** *Make sentences* **(15–20 minutes)**
>
> Ss make sentences using vocabulary for talking about shopping.
>
> - Ss work in pairs to write sentences using each of the expressions in part A. Tell Ss to leave the expressions blank.
> - Have pairs exchange sentences with another pair and fill in the blanks with the correct expression.
> - Put the two pairs together to go over their answers.

5 Are you a compulsive shopper? (DISCUSSION)

Learning aim: Talk about shopping habits and practice the lesson vocabulary (15–20 minutes)

A Pair work

- Explain the task. Read the statements aloud.
- Ss work individually to complete the survey.
- Ss work in pairs to discuss their answers.
- Have Ss share their partner's answers with the class.

B Group work

- Explain the task. Read the questions aloud. Check that Ss understand that a compulsive shopper would probably have chosen "yes" to almost all the statements in the survey in part A.
- Ss work in groups to discuss the questions. Make sure Ss give reasons for their answers.
- Have a S from each group report on the group's discussion to the class.

> **Possible answers**
>
> 1. They don't look at prices and won't think about having a budget. They usually go shopping when bored or upset.
> 2. They may have problems with their relationships because they can't always be honest with family and friends about what they have bought. They are often in debt. It's a continuous problem and not something they just do around holiday times.
> 3. Help them get involved in a hobby.

For more practice discussing this topic, download the Worksheet *8.1 Shopaholics* from the Teacher Support Site.

6 Supporting an opinion (WRITING)

Learning aim: Write a composition to support an opinion (40–50 minutes)

A

- Books closed. Have a brief class discussion about credit cards. Ask Ss if they think credit cards are a good or bad thing and why.
- Books open. Tell Ss to read the information in the box at the top of the page. Ask: *When should you first present your opinion?* (Answer: in the thesis statement) *What is in the body of the composition?* (Answer: supporting examples and details)
- Explain to Ss that in a composition that supports an opinion, the first paragraph should state the opinion, and the body paragraphs should be about each of the supporting details.
- Explain the task. Read the questions aloud. Have Ss read the composition silently to themselves. Check that Ss understand the following vocabulary.

> **Vocabulary**
> **credit** amount of money someone is allowed to spend and pay back later
> **income** money that is earned from working or investments
> **run up debts** increase the amount of money you owe
> **go bankrupt** officially declare that you do not have any more money and that any money owed to credit card companies, stores, or banks cannot be paid back
> **accumulate** collect something gradually
> **absolute (credit limit)** very definite total (credit limit)

- Ss work individually to answer the questions.
- Ss work in pairs to compare answers. Go over answers with the class.

> **Answers**
> 1. There should be a limit to the total amount of credit people can have.
> 2. It is easy for people to be given credit they can't afford. They can get into debt. High debt leads to bankruptcy. It causes problems for the people they owe money to, as well.

B

- Explain the task. Ss work individually to complete one of the opinions and write their thesis statements. Brainstorm ideas for completing each opinion as a class, if necessary.
- Go around the class and help as needed.

C

- Explain the writing task. Have Ss make a list of details and examples supporting their thesis statements.
- Ss work individually to write their compositions. Remind Ss to include an introductory paragraph with their opinion, followed by at least one paragraph with supporting details and examples.
- Go around the class and help as needed.

D Pair work

- Ss work in pairs to exchange compositions and take turns answering the question.
- Go around the class and help as needed. Encourage Ss to ask and answer follow-up questions about anything they don't understand.

Do your students need more practice?	
Assign . . .	for more practice in . . .
Grammar Plus 8A	Grammar
Vocabulary Plus 8A	Vocabulary
Online Vocabulary Accelerator 8A	Vocabulary
Workbook Lesson A	Grammar, Vocabulary, Writing
Online Workbook Lesson A	Grammar, Vocabulary, Writing

6 WRITING
Supporting an opinion

When writing a composition that supports an opinion, first present the opinion in the thesis statement. Then support it in subsequent paragraphs with examples and details.

A Read the composition and discuss your answers to the questions.

1. What is the writer's opinion?
2. What are the reasons given to support the opinion?

   Having almost unlimited credit is certainly one of the many advantages of using credit cards. However, this benefit can easily turn into a major problem. With unlimited credit, people spend too much money. I think there should be a limit to the total amount of credit people can have. This way, the total amount of credit on all of their credit cards together could never go over a certain percentage of their income.
   Many compulsive shoppers run up such high debts that they go bankrupt, creating problems for their families as well as for the people to whom they owe money. Currently, it is easy for people to accumulate many credit cards. Although the credit cards have limits, the number of credit cards is not limited. People with 10 credit cards, each with a $5,000 limit, have $50,000 of credit, even though they might not be able to pay all of their bills. Such a situation can quickly lead to bankruptcy.
   People need to be given an absolute credit limit. If people were not permitted to go over this limit, they would have to be more responsible with their money and evaluate which purchases were most important to them. I think that the actual limit on credit card spending should be based on income so that credit would be based on the ability to pay.

B Complete one of these opinions on shopping or use one of your own. Then present your opinion in a thesis statement.

1. No one under 18 should be allowed to . . .
2. People with a lot of debt should . . .
3. Stores should never give cash refunds for . . .
4. Customers who break an item in a store should . . .
5. Shoplifters should do community service by . . .

C Make a list of details or examples to support your thesis statement. Then write a composition with an introductory paragraph containing your opinion, and at least one paragraph with supporting examples or details.

D Pair work Take turns reading each other's compositions. Can you think of additional examples or details your partner could use to be more persuasive?

LESSON A   What's new on the market?

LESSON B ▶ Consumer awareness

1 STARTING POINT
Print advertisements

A Pair work Look at the three advertisements. Which kind do you think is the most effective? Where else do you see advertisements?

magazine ads   *company logos*   *billboards*

B Pair work Read these opinions about advertisements. Do you agree with them? What do you think makes a good advertisement?

- "I think consumers need to insist that advertisements be truthful in every respect."
- "It seems to me that a good ad is a memorable ad – one that sticks in your head."
- "I believe it is essential that an ad be clever and witty in order to be effective."
- "Some ads seem to demand that the customer buy the product. I don't like a 'hard-sell' approach."
- "I think it's crucial that an ad clearly communicate the benefits of the product it is selling."

2 LISTENING
Radio ads

A Pair work What types of products or services are typically advertised on the radio? Do you think radio is an effective advertising medium?

B Listen to three radio advertisements. What products are they for? Write the name and type of each product in the chart in part C.

C Listen again. What benefits of the products are highlighted in the ads? Complete the chart.

	Name of product	Type of product	Benefit(s)
1.			
2.			
3.			

66   **UNIT 8**   Consumer culture

LESSON B ▶ Consumer awareness

1 Print advertisements (STARTING POINT)

Learning aim: Discuss advertisements and see subjunctive verbs in context (10–15 minutes)

A Pair work

- Books closed. Ask Ss to say how they feel about advertising in general. Do they think ads are fun, or are they annoying? Are there any ads that Ss like right now?
- Books open. Explain the task. Have Ss look at the types of ads and say which one they think is the most effective. Read the questions aloud.
- Ss work in pairs to do the activity.

B Pair work

- Explain the task. Read the questions and opinions aloud. Check that Ss understand the following vocabulary.

> **Vocabulary**
> **in every respect** in every way
> **witty** funny in an intelligent way
> **hard-sell** direct and aggressive selling
> **crucial** extremely important

- Ss work in pairs to discuss the opinions.
- Have Ss share their partner's answers with the class.

2 Radio ads (LISTENING)

Learning aim: Develop skills in listening for the main idea and details (15–20 minutes)

A Pair work

- Books closed. Ask Ss if they or someone they know listen to the radio and what kinds of radio programs they usually listen to. Ask them how they think advertising on the radio needs to be different from other kinds of advertising (e.g., print, Internet, and TV).
- Books open. Explain the task. Read the questions aloud. Ss work in pairs to discuss the questions.
- Have Ss share their partner's answers with the class.

B 🔊 [CD 2, Track 18]

- Explain the task. Read the question aloud. Ask Ss to predict what information they will hear in the advertisements. Check that Ss understand the following vocabulary.

> **Vocabulary**
> **appetite** the desire to eat
> **upgrade** change to an improved/newer version of technology

- Tell Ss to listen for the answers to the question. Play the recording as Ss write the name and type of each product in the chart in part C. Replay as many times as needed. Ss listen and check their answers.
- Ss work in pairs to compare answers. Go over answers with the class.

> **Answers**
> 1. Name of product: Healthy Go
>   Type of product: energy drink
> 2. Name of product: Meow Chow
>   Type of product: cat food
> 3. Name of product: Budget Talk
>   Type of product: a smartphone and service plan

Audio script: See page T-172.

C 🔊 [CD 2, Track 19]

- Read the question aloud. Explain that Ss will listen again for the benefits of each product.
- Tell Ss to listen for the answers. Play the recording as Ss write the benefits in the chart. Replay as many times as needed. Ss listen and check their answers.
- Ss work in pairs to discuss their answers. Go over answers with the class.

> **Answers**
> Benefits:
> 1. It has a lot of vitamins and minerals. It gives you energy.
> 2. It's organic with pure, high-quality ingredients and nothing artificial added.
> 3. The connection is fast and reliable. You get a free smartphone.

Audio script: See page T-172.

UNIT 8 Consumer culture

3 Verbs in the subjunctive (GRAMMAR)

Learning aim: Practice using verbs in the subjunctive (20–25 minutes)

> **Grammar notes**
> The subjunctive is used in a noun clause that follows certain verbs and expressions that stress the importance of something (e.g., *demand, recommend, suggest, it's crucial, it's imperative*).
> *Consumer groups demand that children's advertising follow certain rules.*
> *It is imperative that ads be honest.*
>
> The subjunctive uses the base form of the verb. In a negative sentence, *not* precedes the base form of the verb.
> *The parents insisted (that) the children not watch television at all.*
>
> The passive form of the subjunctive is formed with *be* + past participle.
> *The company demanded the commercial be pulled from television after the public outcry.*

- Books closed. Write on the board:

  It is important that an ad make a product seem useful.

  Read the sentence aloud and ask Ss to identify the verbs. Ask a S to underline the noun clause. (Answer: that an ad make a product seem useful) Ask: *What's unusual about* make *in this sentence?* (Answer: It is in its base form.) Explain to Ss that *make* is in the subjunctive.

- Books open. Discuss the information in the grammar box and read the example sentences.

A

- Have Ss look at the Starting Point on page 66 again. Explain the task and read the question aloud. Go over the answer with the class.

> **Answer**
> It seems to me that a good ad is a memorable ad – one that sticks in your head.

B

- Explain the task. Read the sentences and example answer aloud. Ss work individually to complete the activity.
- Ss work in pairs to compare their answers. Go over answers with the class.

> **Answers**
> 1. I suggest that companies advertise more to increase sales.
> 2. It is important that advertising agencies use humor in their ads.
> 3. I demand that cities tear down billboards that obstruct city views.
> 4. It is essential that the government regulate ads on the Internet.
> 5. I recommend that viewers skip the ads that precede online video clips.
> 6. It is crucial that the advertising of harmful products stop.
> 7. I propose that false advertising be treated as a serious crime.
> 8. It is vital that public television remain commercial free.

C Group work

- Explain the task. Read the problems aloud. Answer any questions about vocabulary. Read the information in the Useful Expressions box.
- Ss work in groups to take turns asking for and giving advice. Remind Ss to use the verbs and expressions in their discussions.
- Have a S from each group report on the group's discussion to the class.

> **Possible answers**
> 1. It is essential that you not believe everything you see in ads. They always make the product look better than the real thing.
> 2. I recommend you speak with someone in the store about the promotion before you buy anything.
> 3. I suggest you contact your email provider.

3 GRAMMAR

Verbs in the subjunctive

Certain expressions and verbs such as *demand*, *insist*, *propose*, *recommend*, *request*, and *suggest* are followed by the subjunctive. The subjunctive uses the base form of the verb. It is generally used in formal language to express a wish or necessity.

I think consumers need to insist (that) **advertisements be** truthful in every respect.
Some ads seem to demand (that) **the customer buy** the product.

These expressions are frequently followed by the subjunctive:

it is crucial	it is imperative	it is important
it is essential	it is vital	it is critical

I believe it is essential that **an ad be** clever and witty in order to be effective.

GRAMMAR PLUS see page 121

A Look at the Starting Point on page 66 again. Which opinion does not use the subjunctive?

B Use verbs followed by the subjunctive instead of *should* or *must* to rewrite these sentences without changing the meaning.

1. Companies should advertise more to increase sales. (I / suggest)
   I suggest that companies advertise more to increase sales.
2. Advertising agencies should use humor in their ads. (It is important)
3. Cities should tear down billboards that obstruct city views. (I / demand)
4. The government must regulate ads on the Internet. (It is essential)
5. Viewers should skip the ads that precede online video clips. (I / recommend)
6. The advertising of harmful products must stop. (It is crucial)
7. False advertising should be treated as a serious crime. (I / propose)
8. Public television should remain commercial free. (It is vital)

C Group work Use the verbs and expressions in the box below to give these people advice on their problems. Do you ever have similar problems? Ask your group for advice.

insist	it is crucial	it is essential
propose	recommend	suggest

Useful expressions

Asking for advice
What do you think I should do?
What would you do if you were me?
What would you do if you were in my position?

1 "The fast food in commercials and posters always looks great. It looks so good I can't resist buying some, but what they actually give me looks pretty bad and really unappetizing."

2 "I saw a clothing store with a big 'Going Out of Business' sign in the window last year, so I went in and bought a lot of clothes. Now, it's a year later, and the sign is still there."

3 "Several friends told me they have received spam emails from me offering to sell them diet pills. The thing is, I didn't send the emails. Someone must have hacked my email account!"

LESSON B Consumer awareness

4 VOCABULARY
Marketing strategies

A Look at the list of marketing strategies. Write the correct letter to complete the sentences below.

a. a free sample
b. coupon codes
c. product placement
d. comparative marketing
e. search-engine marketing
f. a celebrity endorsement
g. a loyalty program
h. word-of-mouth marketing

1. ___ gets attention for products when they are shown in movies or on TV shows.
2. ___ links the name and image of a famous person to a product.
3. ___ lets people try a product they weren't planning on buying.
4. ___ promotes a product or service related to your search on the results page.
5. ___ rewards customers for repeatedly purchasing products from one retailer.
6. ___ occurs when satisfied customers tell others about their positive experience.
7. ___ can be obtained at many websites and entitle customers to discounts.
8. ___ points out the superiority of a product over its competitors.

B Pair work With your partner, brainstorm an example from real life for as many of the marketing strategies as you can. How effective do you think they were?

VOCABULARY PLUS see page 137

5 DISCUSSION
The ethics of undercover marketing

A Pair work Look at the expressions in Exercise 4. Which of them describe undercover marketing strategies, in which people are not aware that they are being marketed to? Discuss your answers with your partner.

B Group work Read about undercover marketing. Then discuss the questions below with your group.

Undercover marketers (also called "stealth marketers") try to find ways to introduce products to people without actually letting them know that they are being marketed to. Here are three actual techniques that have been used for undercover marketing.

The product is a video gaming glove that allows gamers to control games with small finger movements. Unknown actors go into coffee shops and enthusiastically use the glove. This attracts interested people. The actor lets them try it out, never saying who he is.	A top cell phone company sent 60 actors to 10 cities with its latest model. The actors pretended to be tourists and asked people to take their picture with the phone. In this way, they put the new phone in people's hands and let them interact with it.	To attract attention and appear well established, a young firm had fake newspapers printed that had full back-page ads for the company. They then paid people to ride the subways in a major city, pretending to read the newspapers while holding up the ads for all to see.

1. Which of these three marketing techniques seems the most unethical to you? Why?
2. Do you think undercover marketing should be controlled by the government? Why or why not?

4 Marketing strategies (VOCABULARY)

Learning aim: Learn and practice expressions for talking about marketing strategies (15–20 minutes)

A

- Books closed. Ask Ss to say anything they know about marketing. Ask them how certain products, such as cars, candy, and household cleaners, are usually marketed.
- Books open. Explain the task. Read the list and sentences aloud.
- Ss work individually to complete the activity. Go over answers with the class.

Answers			
1. c	3. a	5. g	7. b
2. f	4. e	6. h	8. d

B Pair work

- Explain the task. Read the question aloud.
- Ss work in pairs to brainstorm examples for each strategy from part A and discuss the question. Brainstorm some examples as a class, if necessary.
- Have each pair share their examples and discussion with the class.

5 The ethics of undercover marketing (DISCUSSION)

Learning aim: Talk about the ethics of undercover marketing and practice the lesson vocabulary (15–20 minutes)

A Pair work

- Ask Ss to give a definition for *undercover*. (Answer: acting or done in secret) Explain the task. Ss work in pairs to discuss the question.
- Have Ss tell the class about their discussion. Go over answers with the class.

Answers

product placement, search-engine marketing, a loyalty program

B Group work

- Explain the task. Ss read the text about undercover marketing silently to themselves. Answer any questions about vocabulary.
- Ss work in groups to discuss the questions.
- Have Ss tell the class about their discussion.

Optional activity: *Undercover marketing* **(20 minutes)**

Ss think of ways to market a product.

- As a class, brainstorm different kinds of products. Write them on the board.
- Ss work in groups to think of an undercover marketing plan for one of the products, similar to the examples from part B.
- Have each group present their product and marketing plan to the class.

For more practice discussing this topic, download the Worksheet **8.2 Ad campaign** from the Teacher Support Site.

UNIT 8 Consumer culture T-68

6 Stealth advertising (READING)

Learning aim: Develop skills in understanding vocabulary in context, making inferences, and giving a personal reaction to a reading (25–30 minutes)

A Pair work

- Explain the task. Ss work in pairs to discuss the questions.
- Have Ss read the article silently to themselves. Check that Ss understand the following vocabulary.

> **Vocabulary**
>
> **crept** moved slowly
>
> **affluent** wealthy, rich
>
> **silhouetted** seen as a dark shape against a light or light surface
>
> **spontaneous** occurring in a natural way without any planning
>
> **fixtures** things such as sinks, bathtubs, and ceiling lights, which are fixed or attached to a building
>
> **clandestine** planned or done in secret
>
> **lurking** concealed or hidden with a purpose that may be considered threatening
>
> **went viral** became popular and spread very quickly

B Pair work

- Explain the task. Read the meanings aloud.
- Ss work in pairs to do the activity.
- Go over answers with the class.

> **Answers**
>
> 1. covert
> 2. amplified
> 3. tucked away
> 4. peddle
> 5. hyperconnected
> 6. pervasive

> **Optional activity:** *Fill in the blanks* (15 minutes)
>
> Ss write a cloze exercise.
>
> - Ss work in pairs to write three or four sentences about the article, leaving a word or two blank.
>   Example: *Some people object to _____ forms of marketing since they prefer an honest approach.*
> - Make sure Ss understand that they shouldn't copy sentences directly from the article; they should write about the article in their own words.
> - Tell Ss to close their books. Have pairs exchange sentences and fill in the blanks. Then have the pairs check each other's answers.

C Group work

- Explain the task. Read the questions aloud.
- Ss work in groups to discuss the questions.
- Ask groups to share their ideas with the class. To make sure that reporting to the class goes smoothly, groups can choose one or two members to report their ideas. Have Ss review their ideas with their own group at the end of the task to make sure the group agrees with the information they will be presenting.

To help Ss develop reading accuracy in this exercise, download the Fresh Idea *That's my point!* from the Teacher Support Site.

Do your students need more practice?	
Assign . . .	for more practice in . . .
Grammar Plus 8B	Grammar
Vocabulary Plus 8B	Vocabulary
Online Vocabulary Accelerator 8B	Vocabulary
Workbook Lesson B	Grammar, Vocabulary, Reading
Online Workbook Lesson B	Grammar, Vocabulary, Reading, Listening

UNIT 8 Consumer culture

6 READING
Stealth advertising

A Pair work What influences you most to try a new brand or product? How likely are you to use the same brands and products your friends use? Discuss with a partner. Then read the article.

Word-of-Mouth MARKETING

It was close to midnight as one truck after another crept down a quiet street in Laguna Beach, one of the most beautiful, affluent, and expensive communities in Southern California. Considering the time of night, it was unusual to see vehicles on the road. Yet several trucks stood silhouetted in the driveway and along the front curb as workers silently unloaded camera equipment and cardboard boxes, and then carried them inside the Morgenson family home.

What took place over the next eight weeks was inspired by a Hollywood movie called *The Joneses* about a family of stealth marketers who move into an upper-middle-class neighborhood to **peddle** their wares to unsuspecting neighbors. The idea was both simple and ambitious: to test the power of word-of-mouth marketing. By filming a "real" family in spontaneous, unscripted situations, my team and I would document how the Morgensons' circle of friends responded to specific brands and products the Morgensons brought into their lives. Would they want all the things that family has? Would this influence be so powerful as to make them actually go out and buy those things?

With the help of 35 video cameras and 25 microphones **tucked away** inside the furniture and fixtures, the clandestine operation revealed something shocking. The most powerful hidden persuader of all isn't in your TV or on the shelves of your supermarket or even lurking in your smartphones. It's a far more **pervasive** influence that's around you virtually every waking moment: your very own friends and neighbors. There's nothing quite so persuasive as observing someone we respect or admire using a brand or product.

Our analysis also found that the brands the Morgensons advocated went viral faster. Roughly one third of the Morgensons' friends began promoting these same brands to *their* friends and acquaintances. We also found that the brands their peers were most likely to buy at the Morgensons' subtle suggestion were the bigger and better-known ones. This confirmed my theory that conventional marketing and the more **covert** variety work well together. The most persuasive advertising strategies become that much more so when **amplified** by word-of-mouth advertising.

Whenever I meet with company executives, I remind them that the people who hold the *real* marketing power are **hyperconnected**, mouse-clicking consumers and their wide circles of virtual and real-life friends and acquaintances. In other words, the people who hold the real power are *us*.

Source: "Word-of-Mouth Marketing: We All Want to Keep Up with the Joneses," by Martin Lindstrom

B Pair work Write the expressions and words in boldface from the article next to their meanings.

1. undercover _____
2. strengthened _____
3. hidden _____
4. sell _____
5. always online _____
6. widespread and invasive _____

C Group work Discuss these questions. Then share your answers with the class.

1. In your opinion, what were the most interesting findings of the experiment described in the article?
2. Do you agree that there's nothing quite as persuasive as seeing people we admire and respect using a brand or product? Why or why not?
3. How ethical do you think covert word-of-mouth marketing is? Does the experiment described in the article present any dilemmas or limitations? Explain.

9 NATURE

LESSON A ▶ Animals in our lives

1 STARTING POINT
Amazing animals

A Read about these three famous animals. Have you heard of any of them before? Which do you think is the most impressive?

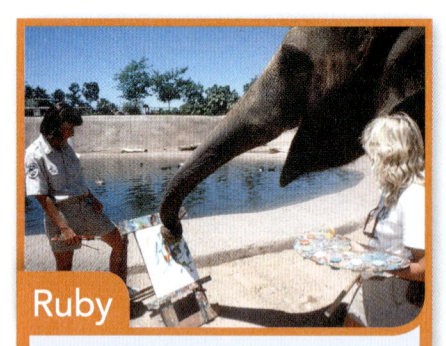

Ruby

Ruby was one of many elephants that learned to paint at the Phoenix Zoo. Wherever there are elephants painting, people are fascinated. Ruby was even more intriguing because she chose her own colors when she painted. Her works raised about $500,000 for the zoo.

Bart the Bear

Bart the Bear was a nine-foot Alaskan Kodiak bear. When he was a cub, he was raised by humans and trained to act in films. Whenever actors worked with him, they were always impressed. He worked with stars such as Brad Pitt and Steven Seagal.

Alex

Alex's name is usually mentioned whenever experts talk about language use by animals. It is claimed that this African grey parrot could categorize about 150 words, count numbers, and distinguish colors and shapes. He showed some of his skills on several nature shows on TV.

B Pair work Discuss these questions and share your ideas with the class.

1. Do you think animals should be trained for entertainment? Is it ethical?
2. What other interesting talents or skills do animals have?

"I think it's OK to train animals as performers, provided they don't suffer in any way when trained."

2 LISTENING
Helping hands

🔊 **A** Listen to these news reports on animals that help people. What kinds of people does each animal help?

🔊 **B** Listen again. How does each animal help the people? Write *M* for monkey, *D* for dog, or *NG* for information not given.

____ 1. fetching objects
____ 2. picking things up off the floor
____ 3. helping them to cross streets
____ 4. taking them places
____ 5. doing tricks to make them laugh
____ 6. sparking memories of pets
____ 7. giving them something to take care of
____ 8. scratching an itchy nose
____ 9. giving them something to look forward to

70   UNIT 9   Nature

9 NATURE
LESSON A ▶ Animals in our lives

> In this unit, Ss use *whenever* and *wherever* contrasted with *when* and *where* and noun clauses with *whoever* and *whatever* to talk about animals and about keeping in touch with nature.

1 Amazing animals (STARTING POINT)

Learning aim: Discuss famous animals and see *whenever* and *wherever* in context (10–15 minutes)

A
- Books closed. Ask Ss which wild animals they find the most interesting. Have Ss tell the class why the animals interest them.
- Books open. Explain the task. Read the questions and the descriptions aloud. Check that Ss understand the following vocabulary.

> **Vocabulary**
> **cub** a baby bear

- Give Ss time to think about their answers to the questions. Then Ss work in pairs to discuss their answers.

B Pair work
- Explain the task. Read the questions and the example answer aloud.
- Ss work in pairs to do the activity.
- Have Ss share their partner's answers with the class.

2 Helping hands (LISTENING)

Learning aim: Develop skills in listening for gist and details (15–20 minutes)

A 🔊 **[CD 3, Track 2]**
- Explain the task. Read the question aloud. Ask Ss to predict what kinds of information will be in the reports. Check that Ss understand the following vocabulary.

> **Vocabulary**
> **fetching** going to get and returning with something
> **foster families** families that care for an animal or a child for a limited period of time
> **nursing home** a place where elderly people who cannot care for themselves anymore can live and receive personal care
> **residents** people who live in a particular place
> **disposition** a person's or animal's usual way of feeling or behaving
> **spark** to inspire or cause
> **fond memories** happy memories

- Tell Ss to listen for the answer to the question. Play the recording as Ss listen for the answer. Replay as many times as needed. Ss listen and check their answers.
- Ss work in pairs to compare answers. Go over answers with the class.

> **Answers**
> 1. Monkeys help people who can't use their arms and legs (quadriplegics).
> 2. Dogs help elderly people in nursing homes.

Audio script: See page T-172.

B 🔊 **[CD 3, Track 3]**
- Explain that Ss will listen again and write the correct letters next to each task. Read the list of items aloud.
- Play the recording once as Ss listen. Play the recording again while Ss write the correct answers.
- Go over answers with the class.

> **Answers**
> 1. M   3. NG   5. NG   7. NG   9. D
> 2. M   4. NG   6. D   8. M

Audio script: See page T-172.

💡 To help Ss with listening in this exercise, download the Fresh Idea **Hands up!** from the Teacher Support Site.

UNIT 9 Nature T-70

3 Whenever and wherever contrasted with when and where (GRAMMAR)

Learning aim: Practice using *whenever* and *wherever* contrasted with *when* and *where* (20–25 minutes)

> **Grammar notes**
>
> *Whenever* and *wherever* are used when a sentence does not refer to a specific time or place.
>
> Sometimes *when* and *where* are interchangeable with *whenever* and *wherever*. However, *whenever* and *wherever* are used to convey *at any time* or *at any place*, and *when* and *where* should be used to convey a more specific time and place.
>
> If the adverbial clause with *whenever, wherever, when,* or *where* begins the sentence, a comma is required before the independent clause. No comma is necessary if the independent clause begins the sentence.
>
> *Whenever I go to the zoo, I take my camera.*
> *I take my camera whenever I go to the zoo.*
>
> *Wherever she goes, she takes her dog.*
> *She takes her dog wherever she goes.*

- Books closed. Write on the board:

    1. *Guide dogs can go wherever their owner goes.*
    2. *Dogs can't normally go where food is served in this hotel.*

    Ask: *Which sentence is talking about a specific place, and which sentence is talking about any place?* (Answer: Sentence 1 is about any place, and sentence 2 is about a specific place.) Underline the conjunctions *where* and *wherever*.

- Write on the board:

    3. *When I saw the gorillas yesterday, they looked unhappy.*
    4. *Whenever I go to the zoo, I always visit the gorillas.*

    Ask: *Which sentence is talking about a specific time, and which sentence is talking about any time?* (Answer: Sentence 3 is about a specific time, and sentence 4 is about any time.) Underline the conjunctions *when* and *whenever*.

- Discuss the information in the grammar box and read the example sentences.

A

- Have Ss look at the Starting Point on page 70 again. Explain the task and read the question aloud.
- Go over answers with the class.

> **Answers**
>
> *Wherever* (Where) *there are elephants painting, people are fascinated.*
>
> *Ruby was even more intriguing because she chose her own colors when* (whenever) *she painted.*
>
> *Whenever* (When) *actors worked with him, they were always impressed.*
>
> *Alex's name is usually mentioned whenever* (when) *experts talk about language use by animals.*

B

- Explain the task. Ss work individually to complete the activity.
- Go over answers with the class.

> **Answers**
>
> 1. when   3. Whenever   5. Where
> 2. wherever   4. Whenever   6. Whenever

C

- Explain the task. Read the clauses and the example answer aloud. Answer any questions about vocabulary.
- Ss work individually to complete the activity.
- Go over answers with the class.

> **Answers**
>
> 1. c We were very startled last night <u>when</u> a bat flew into the window.
> 2. f Parrots become very sad <u>when / whenever</u> they are separated from their owners.
> 3. d The sheep population grows quickly <u>where / wherever</u> there is plenty of grass to eat.
> 4. a A guide dog always stops <u>when / whenever</u> the traffic light is red.
> 5. b Police officers ride horses <u>where / wherever</u> cars can't conveniently go.
> 6. e Our helper monkey wakes us up <u>when</u> the sun comes up in the morning.

3 GRAMMAR

Whenever and *wherever* contrasted with *when* and *where*

Whenever and *wherever* mean "at any time" and "in any place." They are used to introduce adverbial clauses. Notice their position in the sentences.

Whenever experts talk about language use by animals, Alex's name is usually mentioned.
Alex's name is usually mentioned **whenever experts talk about language use by animals**.
Wherever there are elephants painting, people are fascinated.
People are fascinated **wherever there are elephants painting**.

When and *where* can replace *whenever* and *wherever* when they have the sense of "at any time" or "in any place."
Whenever / When actors worked with Bart the Bear, they were always impressed.
Wherever / Where there are elephants painting, people are fascinated.

Whenever and *wherever* cannot be used if the sentence refers to a specific time or location. In these cases, *when* and *where* are used.
Whenever actors worked with him, they were always impressed. *(any time)*
When Brad Pitt worked with Bart in *Legends of the Fall*, he was very impressed. *(specific time)*
Wherever there are elephants painting, people are fascinated. *(any place)*
There were a lot of people **where** the elephants were painting today. *(specific place)*

GRAMMAR PLUS see page 122

A Look at the Starting Point on page 70 again. In which sentences can *whenever* and *wherever* be used interchangeably with *when* and *where*?

B Complete the sentences with *whenever* or *wherever*. If the time or place is specific, use *when* or *where*.

1. Large animals, like tigers and bears, need to be trained _____ they are still very young.
2. Though large, trained elephants are obedient. They will usually go _____ they are led.
3. _____ someone has an unusual pet, serious problems can arise.
4. _____ you see a cat flatten its ears, you should assume it's upset.
5. _____ my sister and her family live now, tenants aren't allowed to have pets.
6. _____ a messenger pigeon is taken somewhere and released, it almost always find its way home.

C Match the clauses on the left with clauses on the right. Make logical sentences using *when*, *whenever*, *where*, or *wherever*.

1. We were very startled last night __c__
2. Parrots become very sad ____
3. The sheep population grows quickly ____
4. A guide dog always stops ____
5. Police officers ride horses ____
6. Our helper monkey wakes us up ____

a. the traffic light is red.
b. cars can't conveniently go.
c. a bat flew into the window.
d. there is plenty of grass to eat.
e. the sun comes up in the morning.
f. they are separated from their owners.

We were very startled last night when a bat flew into the window.

LESSON A Animals in our lives 71

4 VOCABULARY
Physical features of animals

A Pair work Look at this list of animal features. Which type(s) of animal do they belong to? Write them in the correct column(s) in the chart.

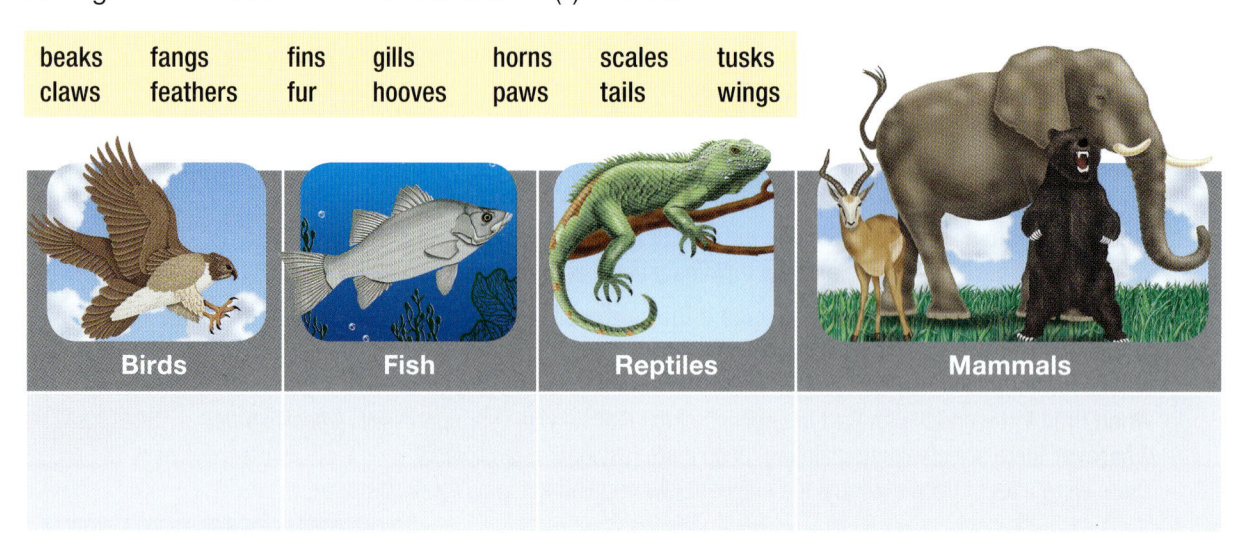

| beaks | fangs | fins | gills | horns | scales | tusks |
| claws | feathers | fur | hooves | paws | tails | wings |

Birds	Fish	Reptiles	Mammals

B Pair work Which animal features in part A do people make use of? Which animals do they come from, and what are the uses?

"Feathers are used in various ways. For example, many pillows are stuffed with duck or goose feathers."

VOCABULARY PLUS see page 138

5 DISCUSSION
Is it right to do that?

A Look at these ways humans use animals. How acceptable do you think they are? Add one idea of your own, and complete the chart.

ANIMAL ETHICS	I'm against it.	It depends.	I'm OK with it.
1. using ivory from elephant tusks in jewelry	☐	☐	☐
2. using rhinoceros horns for medicines	☐	☐	☐
3. using animals for medical research	☐	☐	☐
4. wearing animal fur and leather	☐	☐	☐
5. serving wild animal meat in restaurants	☐	☐	☐
6. using animals to test cosmetics	☐	☐	☐
7. training animals to perform in circuses	☐	☐	☐
8. _____	☐	☐	☐

B Group work Share your answers with the group, and explain your reasons. Who in your group seems to be the most "animal-friendly"?

"For me, using ivory from elephant tusks in jewelry depends on whether or not the ivory was taken from elephants that were killed illegally."

4 Physical features of animals (VOCABULARY)

Learning aim: Learn and practice using words for physical features of animals (15–20 minutes)

A Pair work

- Explain the task. Read the words aloud. Ask Ss for the singular of *hooves*. (Answer: hoof) Point out that some words can go in more than one column.
- Ss work in pairs to complete the chart.
- Go over answers with the class, asking Ss to point to the features shown in the pictures.

Answers
Birds: beaks, claws, feathers, tails, wings
Fish: fins, gills, scales, tails
Reptiles: beaks, claws, fangs, scales, tails
Mammals: claws, fangs, fur, hooves, horns, paws, tails, tusks

B Pair work

- Explain the task. Read the example answer aloud.
- Ss work in pairs to do the activity.
- Have Ss share their answers with the class.

Possible answers
Claws: jewelry, art
Feathers: pillows, fashion accessories (e.g., hats, jewelry)
Fins: food
Fur: clothing, fashion accessories
Hooves: hair products
Horns: traditional medicines
Paws: traditional medicines
Tusks: art, jewelry, buttons

Optional activity: *Guess the animal* (15 minutes)
Ss describe an animal, and other Ss guess which one it is.
■ Ss work in groups to make a list of five or six animals and write notes describing them.
■ Have groups take turns describing an animal while the other groups guess which one it is. Let the guessing groups use dictionaries, if necessary.

5 Is it right to do that? (DISCUSSION)

Learning aim: Talk about how humans use animals and practice the lesson vocabulary (15–20 minutes)

A

- Ask Ss to define *ethics*. (Answer: ideas and beliefs about what is morally right and wrong behavior)
- Explain the task. Read the survey aloud.
- Ss work individually to complete the survey and write one more idea. Brainstorm ideas as a class, if necessary.

B Group work

- Explain the task. Ss work in groups to discuss their answers to the survey in part A. Make sure they give reasons for their answers.
- Have a S from each group report on the group's discussion to the class.

Optional activity: *Class debate* (15–20 minutes)
Ss have a class debate.
■ Write on the board:
The world would be better if everyone were a vegetarian.
■ Divide the class into two groups: A and B. Tell group A to think of as many reasons as they can in favor of the statement. Tell group B to think of as many reasons as they can against the statement.
■ Give Ss time to think of reasons individually. Then have them discuss their reasons within their group.
■ Have each group take turns presenting their ideas to the class.

For more practice discussing this topic, download the Worksheet **8.1 Pet match** from the Teacher Support Site.

6 Classification essay (WRITING)

Learning aim: Write a classification essay using different categories (40–50 minutes)

A

- Tell Ss to read the information in the box at the top of the page. Ask: *What is a classification essay?* (Answer: an essay that organizes information into categories) *What is in the conclusion?* (Answer: an additional perspective on the overall topic)
- Explain to Ss that in a classification essay, the first paragraph introduces the overall topic and an overview of the categories included. Each body paragraph then provides details about only one category.
- Explain the task. Read the questions aloud. Have Ss read the essay silently to themselves. Check that Ss understand the following vocabulary.

> **Vocabulary**
>
> **companionship** the pleasant feeling you have when you spend time with someone/something
>
> **with special needs** with physical or mental disabilities and, therefore, needing help to do regular everyday tasks
>
> **devote** commit
>
> **visually impaired** having very poor sight due to a disability
>
> **harness** a piece of leather or other material that goes around an animal's body so the animal can be controlled by the owner
>
> **source** a thing that causes / emits something
>
> **mixed breeds** born of two or more different kinds of (dogs)
>
> **confined** forced to stay in something

- Ss work individually to answer the questions.
- Ss work in pairs to compare their answers.
- Go over answers with the class.

> **Answers**
>
> assistance dogs
>
> guide dogs, hearing dogs, and service dogs

B

- Explain the task. Ss work individually to choose a topic and classify it into three categories. Alternatively, have Ss brainstorm ideas in pairs before deciding on a topic.
- Go around the class and help as needed.

C

- Explain the writing task.
- Ss work individually to write their essay. Remind Ss to begin with an introduction; include three or more body paragraphs, each about a different category; and end with a conclusion.
- Go around the class and help as needed.

D Pair work

- Ss work in pairs to exchange essays and take turns answering the questions.
- Go around the class and help as needed. Encourage Ss to ask and answer follow-up questions about the essay and ask about anything they don't understand.

Do your students need more practice?	
Assign . . .	for more practice in . . .
Grammar Plus 9A	Grammar
Vocabulary Plus 9A	Vocabulary
Online Vocabulary Accelerator 9A	Vocabulary
Workbook Lesson A	Grammar, Vocabulary, Writing
Online Workbook Lesson A	Grammar, Vocabulary, Writing

6 WRITING
Classification essay

> A classification essay organizes information into categories. The first paragraph introduces the overall topic of the essay, includes a thesis statement, and gives an overview of the categories the writer will focus on. Each subsequent paragraph provides detailed information about one of the categories. A conclusion gives an additional perspective on the overall topic.

A Read this classification essay. What special kind of dog is the main topic of the essay? What three categories of this type of dog does the writer provide more information about?

Although most dogs offer their owners little more than companionship, assistance dogs are specially trained to assist people with disabilities or special needs. These dogs devote themselves to helping their owners live more independent lives. There are several types of assistance dogs, but the most common are guide dogs, hearing dogs, and service dogs.

Guide dogs help blind or visually impaired people get around their homes and communities. Most guide dogs are large breeds like Labrador retrievers and German shepherds, which wear a harness with a U-shaped handle to allow the dog and its human partner to communicate. The owner gives directional commands, and the dog's role is to ensure the human's safety, even if it means disobeying an unsafe command.

Hearing dogs alert a person who is deaf or hearing-impaired to sounds like doorbells, a baby's cries, and smoke alarms. They're trained to make physical contact and lead their owner to the source of the sound. Hearing dogs may be any size or breed, but they tend to be small to medium-sized mixed breeds because they are rescued from shelters. Hearing dogs can all be identified by their orange collar and vest.

Service dogs usually assist people who are confined to a wheelchair. The dogs are trained to pick up dropped objects, open and close doors, help in getting a person into or out of a wheelchair, and find help when needed. Because many of these tasks require strength, most service dogs are large breeds such as golden or Labrador retrievers. These dogs usually wear a backpack, harness, or vest.

Guide dogs, hearing dogs, and service dogs have one thing in common, however. Before being matched with a human partner, each type of assistance dog undergoes a one- to two-year training program. Once the dog and owner are matched, they begin to form a bond of trust with each other and often become an inseparable team.

B Choose one of these topics or one of your own. Brainstorm ways to classify your topic into at least three categories, and make a list of ideas for each.

- types of cats
- types of pets
- types of pet owners
- people who work with animals

C Write a classification essay that includes an introduction, three or more paragraphs – each one about a different category – and a conclusion.

D Pair work Read your partner's essay. Is the thesis statement clear? Are the categories distinct? Is each category described adequately? What other information would you want to have included?

LESSON A Animals in our lives

LESSON B ▶ In touch with nature

1 STARTING POINT
Careers in nature

A Read the job postings on this website. Do you know anyone who has one of these jobs? What else do you know about the jobs?

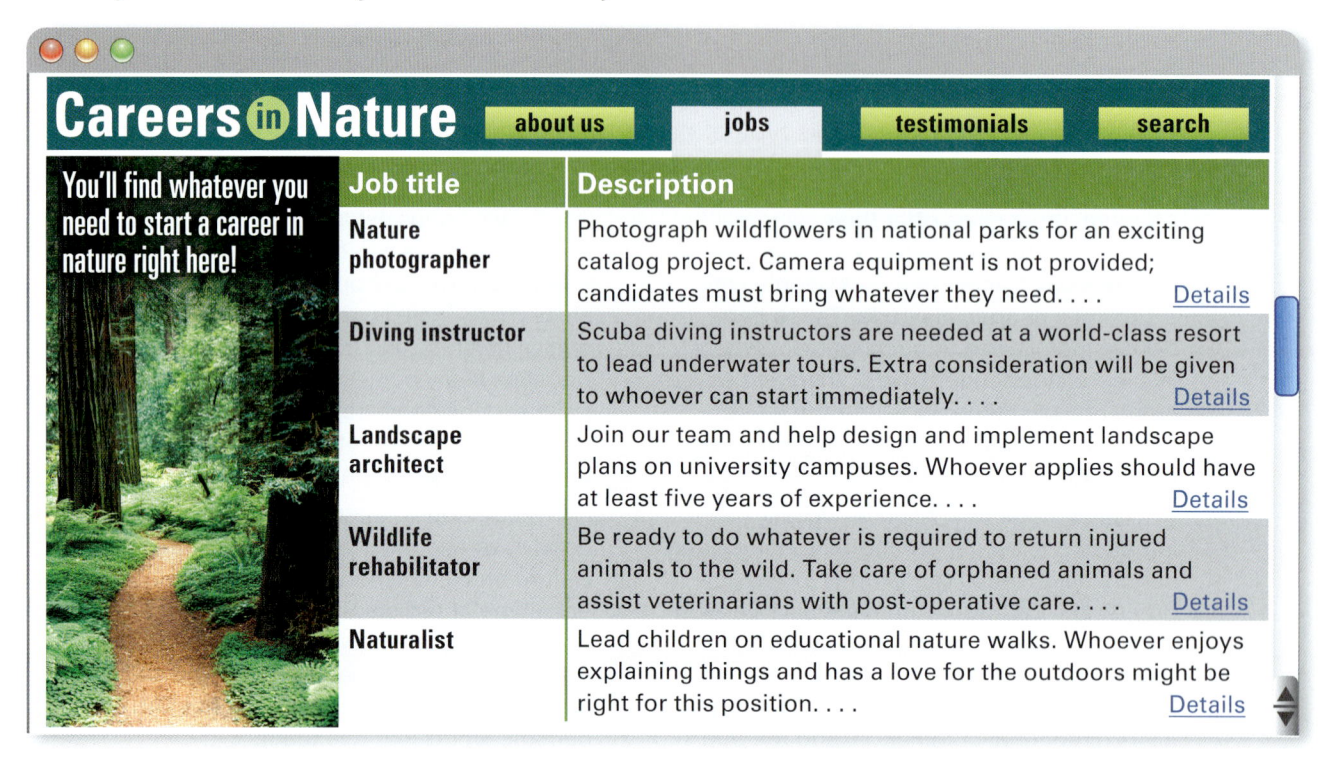

Careers in Nature — about us | jobs | testimonials | search

You'll find whatever you need to start a career in nature right here!

Job title	Description	
Nature photographer	Photograph wildflowers in national parks for an exciting catalog project. Camera equipment is not provided; candidates must bring whatever they need. . . .	Details
Diving instructor	Scuba diving instructors are needed at a world-class resort to lead underwater tours. Extra consideration will be given to whoever can start immediately. . . .	Details
Landscape architect	Join our team and help design and implement landscape plans on university campuses. Whoever applies should have at least five years of experience. . . .	Details
Wildlife rehabilitator	Be ready to do whatever is required to return injured animals to the wild. Take care of orphaned animals and assist veterinarians with post-operative care. . . .	Details
Naturalist	Lead children on educational nature walks. Whoever enjoys explaining things and has a love for the outdoors might be right for this position. . . .	Details

B Pair work Choose one of the jobs on the website or another nature-related job you might be interested in trying. Tell your partner what interests you about it.

2 LISTENING
An eco-resort

A Listen to a conversation with the manager of an eco-resort. Who is the manager speaking with? Choose the correct answer.

☐ a guest   ☐ a job applicant   ☐ a journalist   ☐ a nature guide

B Listen again. What is special about these features of the eco-resort? Complete the chart.

Eco-resort feature	Reasons it is special
1. Resort design	
2. Nature guides	
3. Spa	
4. Zip lines	

C Pair work If you were designing an eco-resort, which of the features in part B would you include in your resort? Why? What other features would you include?

74　UNIT 9　Nature

LESSON B ▶ In touch with nature

1 Careers in nature (STARTING POINT)

Learning aim: Discuss nature-related jobs and see noun clauses with *whoever* and *whatever* in context (10–15 minutes)

A
- Ask Ss if they know of any nature-related jobs and have them describe each one. Write Ss' ideas on the board.
- Explain the task. Read the questions and job postings aloud. Check that Ss understand the following vocabulary.

> **Vocabulary**
> **landscape architect** designer for gardens and parks
> **implement** make a plan start to happen
> **post-operative** immediately after surgery
> **naturalist** person who studies plants and animals

- Ss work in pairs to discuss their answers.

B Pair work
- Explain the task. Brainstorm other nature-related jobs as a class, if necessary. Add them to the list on the board.
- Ss work in pairs to do the activity.
- Have Ss share their partner's answers with the class.

> **Optional activity:** *The worst jobs* (10–15 minutes)
> Ss talk about nature-related jobs they would never want to have.
> - Ss work in groups to discuss nature-related jobs they would never want to have. Make sure Ss give reasons for each answer.
> - Have one S from each group share the group's answers with the class.
> - Have the class vote to see which job is the least popular.

2 An eco-resort (LISTENING)

Learning aim: Develop skills in listening for gist and details, and in making inferences (15–20 minutes)

A 🔊 [CD 3, Track 4]
- Ask: *What is an eco-resort?* (Answer: a vacation destination that emphasizes ecological responsibility through facilities that have little impact on the environment)
- Explain the task. Read the question and the choices aloud. Check that Ss understand the following vocabulary.

> **Vocabulary**
> **barriers** structures that keep someone or something from entering an area
> **in harmony** in peace together
> **orientation program** information and preparation for an activity, a job, or a situation
> **fumes** unpleasant and often dangerous gas or smoke
> **zoom** travel very fast
> **bird's eye view** a view from a very high place

- Play the recording as Ss listen for the answer. Replay as many times as needed. Ss listen and check their answer.

> **Answer**
> a journalist

Audio script: See page T-173.

B 🔊 [CD 3, Track 5]
- Explain that Ss will listen again for the reasons why each eco-resort feature is special.
- Tell Ss to listen for the reasons. Play the recording as Ss complete the chart. Replay as many times as needed. Ss listen and check their answers.

> **Possible answers**
> Resort design: It rises into the rain forest canopy. It was designed to make guests feel as if they are part of nature. It has no fences or barriers to keep animals out.
>
> Nature guides: They have lived and worked in the rain forest most of their lives. They educate the guests about living with the animals.
>
> Spa: It is world-class. It offers massage treatments using skin products made with local plants from the rain forest.
>
> Zip lines: They are eco-friendly. They don't disturb any wildlife, damage trees, use electricity, or emit fumes.

Audio script: See page T-173.

C Pair work
- Explain the task. Read the questions aloud.
- Ss work in pairs to do the activity.
- Have Ss share their partner's answers with the class.

3 Noun clauses with *whoever* and *whatever* (GRAMMAR)

Learning aim: Practice using noun clauses with *whoever* and *whatever* (20–25 minutes)

Grammar notes

Whoever refers to people. *Whatever* refers to things. *Whichever* (see Grammar Plus) refers to people or things.

Whoever and *whatever* function as pronouns.
Whoever crosses the line first wins the race.
I'll do whatever is necessary.

Whatever can also function as a determiner.
I like to eat whatever ice cream I can find in the freezer.

When *whoever* and *whatever* are used as the subject of a clause, they are considered third person singular, so the verbs that follow are in the third person singular.

- Books closed. Write on the board:
  1. <u>Anything</u> humans can do to protect the environment is worth considering.
  2. <u>The person who</u> designed this park is a great landscape architect.

  Have Ss rewrite the sentences by replacing the underlined words with *whoever* or *whatever*. (Answers: 1. <u>Whatever</u> humans can do to protect the environment is worth considering. 2. <u>Whoever</u> designed this park is a great landscape architect.) Then ask Ss to explain their answers. (Answers: Sentence 1 refers to a thing. Sentence 2 refers to a person.)

- Discuss the information in the grammar box and read the example sentences.

A

- Have Ss look at the Starting Point on page 74 again. Explain the task and read the questions aloud.
- Go over answers with the class.

Answers

Subject:

. . . *whoever* can start immediately.

Whoever applies should have at least five years of experience.

. . . *whatever* is required to return injured animals to the wild.

Whoever enjoys explaining things . . .

Object:

. . . *whatever* you need to start a career in nature right here!

. . . *whatever* they need.

B

- Explain the task. Ss work individually to complete the sentences.
- Ss work in pairs to compare their answers. Go over answers with the class.

Answers

1. whoever	5. Whoever
2. whoever	6. whatever
3. whatever	7. whatever
4. whatever	8. whoever

C Group work

- Explain the task. Read the beginning of each statement and example answer aloud. Answer any questions about vocabulary.
- Ss work individually to complete the statements.
- Ss work in groups to discuss their ideas.
- Have a S from each group report on the group's discussion to the class.

Possible answers

1. Whoever has a strong desire to help animals should consider volunteering some of their time at a wildlife center.
2. Whatever humans really need is provided by nature. For example, people can get water from ponds, lakes, streams, and rivers.
3. Hiking is a great pastime for whoever likes to exercise and be outdoors.
4. It's a bad idea to feed a pet whatever it wants. Instead, you should feed it healthy pet food.
5. Whoever is planning an excursion in nature should look into eco-tourism possibilities online.

3 GRAMMAR

Noun clauses with *whoever* and *whatever*

Whoever and *whatever* can begin noun clauses and function as either the subject or object of the clause.

Whoever = the person who / anyone who / everyone who
Whoever applies should have at least five years of experience.
Extra consideration will be given to **whoever** can start immediately.

Whatever = anything that / everything that
Be ready to do **whatever** is required to return injured animals to the wild.
You'll find **whatever** you need to start a career in nature right here!

GRAMMAR PLUS see page 123

A Look at the Starting Point on page 74 again. In which sentences are *whoever* or *whatever* used as the subject of a clause? In which are they the object of a clause?

B Complete the sentences with *whoever* or *whatever*. Then compare your answers with a partner.

1. Here's a warning to _____ is thinking about becoming a beekeeper: You *will* be stung!

2. The birds on that island are curious about people and approach _____ they see coming.

3. Nature photographers take pictures of landscapes and _____ they see in the wild.

4. It's a forest ranger's duty to immediately report _____ looks like smoke or fire.

5. _____ took this photo of Mount Everest is a talented nature photographer.

6. I'm sure a relaxing trip to the mountains will take your mind off _____ is bothering you.

7. Visitors must follow the rules and are not allowed to do _____ they want in nature reserves.

8. Wildflowers are protected by law in many places; _____ picks them is subject to a fine.

C **Group work** Complete the statements with your own ideas. Compare and discuss your ideas with your group.

1. Whoever has a strong desire to help animals . . .
   should consider volunteering some of their time at a wildlife center.
2. Whatever humans really need is provided by nature. For example, people can get . . .
3. Hiking is a great pastime for whoever . . .
4. It's a bad idea to feed a pet whatever it wants. Instead, . . .
5. Whoever is planning an excursion in nature . . .

LESSON B In touch with nature

4 VOCABULARY
Nature-related idioms

A Match the idioms in boldface with their meanings.

1. Her ideas are **a breath of fresh air** among so many outdated ones. _e_
2. Our contribution to the wildlife fund was just **a drop in the ocean**, but even small donations help. ___
3. His report on the wildfire is **as clear as mud**. I can't understand it. ___
4. This project is **a walk in the park**. The other one was so complex. ___
5. These are just initial ideas for the campaign. Nothing is **set in stone**. ___
6. This is just **the tip of the iceberg**. Things are much worse than that. ___
7. My son is **under the weather** today, so he can't go on the field trip. ___
8. The plans are still **up in the air**. Nothing has been decided yet. ___

a. easy
b. confusing; unclear
c. unchangeable
d. not feeling well
e. new, different, exciting
f. less/fewer than needed
g. undecided; uncertain
h. a small perceptible part of a much bigger problem

B Pair work Use the idioms to talk to your partner about nature-related issues.

"The new plan of turning that run-down area of the city into a park is a breath of fresh air. The previous plans were not very interesting."

VOCABULARY PLUS see page 138

5 DISCUSSION
The importance of nature

A How in touch with nature are you? Complete the survey to find out.

Are You in Touch with Nature?

	Agree	⟷	Disagree
1. Human beings are a part of nature, and therefore must interact frequently with nature to be healthy.	2	1	0
2. It's important to work or study in a space with indoor plants and large windows that let in sunlight.	2	1	0
3. Everyone needs at least one hobby, such as horseback riding or gardening, to keep in touch with nature.	2	1	0
4. When it comes to clothing and body care, it's best to wear natural fibers and use natural soaps and shampoos.	2	1	0
5. When I'm under the weather, I prefer to use all-natural treatments instead of synthetic drugs.	2	1	0
6. I would have been happier living in harmony with nature in a time before industry and technology.	2	1	0
7. Given a choice, I'd buy free-range poultry and meat products. I'd also buy wild fish instead of farmed varieties.	2	1	0
8. I recycle everything I can. Although my efforts might be just a drop in the ocean, I think I'm helping to preserve our natural resources.	2	1	0

SCORE
0–4 Like much of modern society, you may be out of touch with the natural world.
5–8 While nature isn't a priority for you, you do appreciate it when you experience it.
9–12 You see nature as an important part of your life and necessary for your well-being.
13–16 You're a nature lover who needs to be in constant contact with the natural world.

B Group work Discuss your answers to the survey. Talk about the reasons for your choices and whether or not you agree with your score.

4 Nature-related idioms (VOCABULARY)

Learning aim: Learn and practice using nature-related idioms (10–15 minutes)

A

- Books closed. Ask: *What's an idiom?* (Answer: an expression or group of words whose meaning is different from the meanings of the individual words)
- Write on the board:

  He can't see the forest for the trees.

  Ask what the idiom means. (Answer: He can't see the whole situation – the forest – clearly because he's thinking too much about the smaller details – the trees.)
- Books open. Explain the task. Read the sentences and the meanings of the idioms aloud.
- Ss work individually to complete the activity. Go over answers with the class.

Answers			
1. e	3. b	5. c	7. d
2. f	4. a	6. h	8. g

- Ask Ss which words helped them match the idioms to their meanings. (Possible answers: "Fresh air" is new air; "a drop" is a very small amount of water; "an ocean" is a very large amount of water; "mud" is not clear; "a walk" is usually a relaxing activity, and it's usually easy to walk in a "park"; something "set in stone" cannot be erased or changed; "an iceberg" is huge and mostly hidden under the water, so we can only see the "tip" – or a small part of it; something "up in the air" is not settled anywhere.)

B Pair work

- Explain the task. Read the example sentences aloud.
- Ss work in pairs to do the activity.
- Have Ss share their partner's ideas with the class.

> **Optional activity:** *Idioms quiz* **(15–20 minutes)**
> **Ss write a quiz with the new idioms.**
> - Ss work in groups to write one sentence with each idiom from part A. Tell them to leave the idiom blank in the sentence and list three possible answers under each sentence.
> - Go around the class and help as needed.
> - Have the groups exchange quizzes and do the activity.
> - Then have the groups check each other's answers.

5 The importance of nature (DISCUSSION)

Learning aim: Talk about people's relations with nature (15–20 minutes)

A

- Explain the task. Read the survey aloud. Check that Ss understand the following vocabulary.

> **Vocabulary**
>
> **natural fibers** fabrics made from natural materials, such as cotton or wool
>
> **free-range poultry** birds such as chickens and turkeys that have lived in the open, not in cages
>
> **farmed (fish)** fish raised in enclosed areas, not freely in the wild
>
> **natural resources** materials found in or on the earth, such as water, oil, minerals, and coal
>
> **priority** very important and needing to be dealt with before other things
>
> **well-being** state of being healthy, happy, and comfortable

- Ss work individually to do the activity and calculate their score.

B Group work

- Explain the task.
- Ss work in groups to discuss their answers to the survey, the reasons for their choices, and their scores.
- Have Ss share their group's discussion with the class.

6 Urban park rangers (READING)

Learning aim: Develop skills in understanding vocabulary in context, reading for specific information, making inferences, and giving a personal reaction to a reading (25–30 minutes)

A Pair work

- Ask Ss to look at the picture. Ask what they know about park rangers.
- Explain the task. Read the question aloud. Ss work in pairs to discuss the question.
- Have Ss read the article silently to themselves. Check that Ss understand the following vocabulary.

> **Vocabulary**
>
> **infiltrate** move slowly and secretly into a place without anyone noticing
>
> **distinguished marking** noticeable physical characteristic
>
> **corps** group of people who do the same job or activity
>
> **nightstick** a short stick that is carried as a weapon, usually by police officers
>
> **summonses** official orders to go to court
>
> **vexed** annoyed or worried
>
> **stunned** unable to move or focus
>
> **not so much** they don't or can't do something

> **Culture note**
>
> Smokey Bear, a brown bear that wears a park ranger hat, was created in 1944 as an advertising mascot. His mission is to educate the public about the dangers of forest fires and the care that should be taken to prevent them.

B Pair work

- Explain the task. Tell Ss that the words they are looking for do not appear in boldface in the text. Remind Ss to use the context to help them find the answers.
- Ss work in pairs to do the activity. Go over answers with the class.

> **Answers**
>
> 1. amiable
> 2. therapeutic
> 3. field
> 4. unnerved
> 5. yield
> 6. dumped

C Group work

- Explain the task. Read the questions aloud.
- Ss work in groups to discuss the questions.
- Have Ss report on their group's discussion to the class.

> **Possible answers**
>
> 1. They give nature walks, history talks, and children's craft classes. They answer people's questions about plants and animals. They explain to people how to interact with nature.
> 2. They are concerned about and don't understand normal animal behavior. For example, they mistakenly think that pigeons sunning themselves have broken wings, they worry about hawks hunting smaller birds, and they think ducks will drown.
>   *Answers to the second question will vary.*
> 3. Answers will vary.

> **Optional activity:** *Vocabulary* (15–20 minutes)
>
> Ss practice the vocabulary from the reading.
>
> - Have Ss look at the article again. Tell them to write down any words that they did not know before.
> - Ask Ss to call out their words, and write them on the board. As a class, write definitions for each word.
> - Have Ss write a sentence using each word. Make sure they write sentences that show they understand the meaning of the word.
> - Ask Ss to read their sentences to the class.

For an alternative reading text or extra practice, download the Worksheet **9.2 Dirt** from the Teacher Support Site.

Do your students need more practice?	
Assign . . .	for more practice in . . .
Grammar Plus 9B	Grammar
Vocabulary Plus 9B	Vocabulary
Online Vocabulary Accelerator 9B	Vocabulary
Workbook Lesson B	Grammar, Vocabulary, Reading
Online Workbook Lesson B	Grammar, Vocabulary, Reading, Listening

6 READING
Urban park rangers

A Pair work What are some of the daily tasks a park ranger might have to do in a city park? Discuss with a partner. Then read the article.

A SUMMER JOB that's a walk in the park

Every summer, curious creatures infiltrate New York City's biggest parks. They number in the dozens, walk on their hind legs, are khaki in color, and exceedingly amiable by nature. Their most distinguished markings are their wide-brimmed Smokey Bear hats.

They are Urban Park Ranger fellows, possessors of what may be the best, if not the most unusual, summer jobs in New York. "It's pretty laid back – kind of therapeutic," said Mohammed Alomeri, 22, who is from Midwood, Brooklyn, and works as a summer ranger at Fort Greene Park. "Every day, literally, is a walk in the park."

The summer fellows supplement the corps of year-round Urban Park Rangers – who also wear the Smokey Bear hats, but also carry nightsticks and can issue summonses – during the parks' busiest season. ...

Daily tasks can include, but are not limited to, giving nature walks, history talks, and children's craft classes; guiding people who have gotten lost; asking people to leash their dogs; getting outdoor chefs to move their barbecue grills away from trees; talking about why feeding chicken nuggets to birds is unhealthy; explaining that, yes, they are rangers, just like the ones in national parks; and posing for tourists' cameras. ...

Rangers field hundreds of calls from park visitors who are concerned about the behavior of wildlife, often when the animals in question are behaving naturally. They get reports from people who are unnerved by the sight of raccoons, or who mistakenly assume that pigeons sunning themselves have broken wings, or who grow vexed whenever an animal wanders onto a jogging path. The sight of hawks hunting smaller birds will invariably yield dozens of concerned calls.

"They call and say, 'You gotta get in there and get that pigeon out,'" said Richard Simon, who is citywide ranger captain and oversees the fellowship program. "That's when we explain, 'This is the food chain.'" ...

The rangers also get reports about animals that truly are hurt or in the wrong place. They are handed injured baby birds, alerted to exotic animals that have been dumped by their owners, or led to stunned squirrels that have fallen from trees. "They fall out of trees all the time," said Kathy Vasquez, a full-time, year-round ranger. "They usually land on their feet, but sometimes not so much." ...

The summer rangers program ends on Saturday, which means a return to a life indoors for most of the five dozen fellows. Mr. Alomeri, however, plans to apply for a position as a full-time ranger. He has only one semester left at Brooklyn College, where he is studying physics, and wants to put off graduate school. He has fallen in love with being a ranger, and delights at the way he can now identify trees and birds. ...

Source: "A Summer Job That Promises Nature Walks for Pay," by Cara Buckley, *The New York Times* (The ellipses indicate passages omitted from the original article.)

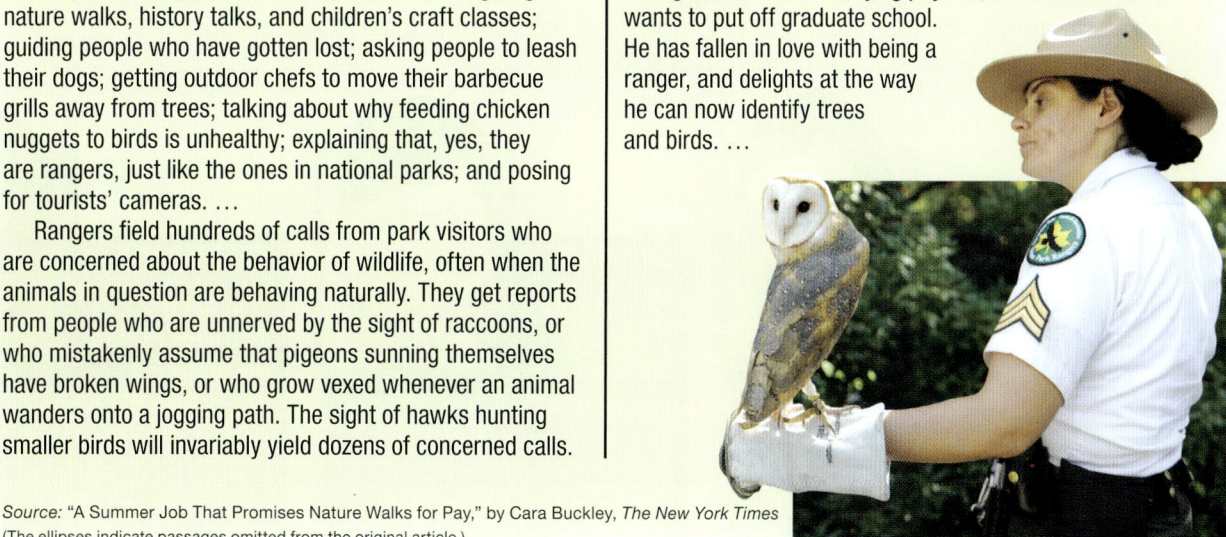

B Pair work Find the words in the article that match the meanings below.

1. friendly (paragraph 1) _____
2. healing (paragraph 2) _____
3. respond to (paragraph 5) _____
4. agitated (paragraph 5) _____
5. lead to (paragraph 5) _____
6. abandoned (paragraph 7) _____

C Group work Discuss these questions. Then share your answers with the class.

1. How do the Urban Park Ranger fellows help park visitors connect with nature?
2. What evidence from the article might lead you to assume that many park visitors are not familiar with nature? Is the same true about city dwellers where you're from? Explain.
3. Do you agree that being an Urban Park Ranger fellow would be laid back and therapeutic? Why?

COMMUNICATION REVIEW

UNITS 7–9

✓ SELF-ASSESSMENT

How well can you do these things? Choose the best answer.

I can . . .	Very well	OK	A little
▶ Take part in a discussion about recent trends and life choices (Ex. 1)	☐	☐	☐
▶ Take part in a decision-making discussion about marketing a new product or service (Ex. 2)	☐	☐	☐
▶ Give a persuasive presentation about a new product or service (Ex. 2)	☐	☐	☐
▶ Take part in a discussion about animals as pets (Ex. 3)	☐	☐	☐
▶ Understand an interview about animal caretaking (Ex. 4)	☐	☐	☐

Now do the corresponding exercises. Was your assessment correct?

1 DISCUSSION
Trends and attitudes

A Pair work Read what these people have to say about some trends. Who do you agree with the most, and who do you agree with the least? Discuss your ideas with a partner, and give reasons for them.

CARLOS
"I think it's great that so many companies allow employees to telecommute. It's illogical, even irresponsible, for companies to require employees who don't live nearby to come in to work every day."

HUI LIN
"Something that worries me is the way people risk their health by experimenting with alternative medicines and therapies that haven't been properly tested. No one really knows how safe they are."

STEPHANIE
"I'm hoping attitudes toward consumption – like constantly buying new clothes – are changing. Celebrities like actors, musicians, and athletes, whom young people look up to, need to set the right example and help bring about change."

"I disagree with Hui Lin. I don't think alternative medicines are dangerous. Many of them are traditional medicines that have been used for years. However, I agree with . . ."

B Group work Discuss how you feel about these life choices. Then share your answers with the class.

- adult children returning home to live with their parents
- people choosing to get married at a later age
- people socializing more online than they do in person
- senior citizens going back to school to earn degrees
- people choosing to spend more of their free time doing volunteer work

Units 7–9
COMMUNICATION REVIEW

> Ss assess how well they have learned the communication skills in Units 7–9.

✓ Self-assessment

Review aim: Ss assess how well they have learned the material in Units 7–9 (10–15 minutes)

- Books closed. List or elicit from Ss the language and topics covered in Units 7–9.

- Books open. Explain the task. Read the list of skills aloud.
- Ss work individually to do the assessment.
- Tell Ss they will review their assessment after doing the activities in this unit.

1 Trends and attitudes (DISCUSSION)

Review aim: Discuss trends using relative pronouns and adjectives (20–25 minutes)

A Pair work
- Explain the task. Read the question and the texts aloud. Check that Ss understand the following vocabulary.

> **Vocabulary**
> **alternative medicines** medicines not normally used by mainstream doctors but which may also be effective
> **therapies** treatments that are supposed to cure illness or medical problems
> **consumption** the amount of goods and/or services used

- Read the example answer aloud.
- Give Ss time to think individually of their answers.
- Ss work in pairs to discuss their answers. Make sure they give reasons for their answers.
- Have Ss share their partner's answers with the class.

B Group work
- Read the life choices aloud. Check that Ss understand the following vocabulary.

> **Vocabulary**
> **senior citizens** generally people age 65 and older

- Ss work in groups to discuss how they feel about the life choices.
- Have a S from each group share the group's answers with the class.

2 New products and marketing plans (DISCUSSION)

Review aim: Discuss ways of marketing new products using the subjunctive (20–25 minutes)

A Group work
- Explain the task. Have three Ss read the example conversation to the class. Brainstorm new products or services as a class, if necessary.
- Ss work in groups to do the activity.

B Class activity
- Explain the task. Have groups present their product or service and their marketing plans to the class.
- Have the class vote on the group with the best ideas.

3 Suitable pets? (SPEAKING)

Review aim: Give opinions about different wild animals as pets (10–15 minutes)

A
- Explain the task. Read the questions and captions aloud. Give Ss time to think of their answers to the questions.

B Pair work
- Explain the task. Read the example answer aloud.
- Ss work in pairs to discuss their answers to the questions in part A and explain their reasons.
- Have Ss share their partner's answers with the class.

4 Bird talk (LISTENING)

Review aim: Develop skills in listening for the main ideas and details (20–25 minutes)

A 🔊 [CD 3, Track 6]
- Explain the task. Read the requirements aloud. Check that Ss understand the following vocabulary.

> **Vocabulary**
>
> **reputable** well respected and highly thought of
>
> **captivity** the state of being in a cage or zoo, not in the wild
>
> **asthma** a medical problem that causes difficulty in breathing
>
> **groom** clean or neaten
>
> **affectionate** openly friendly (in words and actions)
>
> **vital** extremely important
>
> **stimulation** something that causes interest or excitement
>
> **supervised** watched over

- Play the recording while Ss choose the correct answers. Replay as many times as needed.
- Ss work in pairs to compare answers. Go over answers with the class.

Answers
a, c, d

Audio script: See page T-173.

B 🔊 [CD 3, Track 7]
- Explain that Ss will listen again, decide if the statements are true or false, and then choose the correct answer.
- Read the statements aloud and answer any questions about vocabulary.
- Play the recording and have Ss complete the activity.
- Ss work in pairs to compare answers. Go over answers with the class.

Answers		
1. True	3. True	5. True
2. False	4. True	6. False

Audio script: See page T-173.

✓ Have Ss look at their answers to the self-assessment at the beginning of this review unit. As a class, discuss which skills were easy and which were more difficult and why.

2 DISCUSSION
New products and marketing plans

A Group work Think of a new product or service you think would be successful. What is it? Who is it for? How does it work? What's the best way to advertise and promote it?

"Well, I'm thinking about a concierge service for people who are new in town. The concierge could provide the same services as a concierge in a hotel."
"I suggest we offer information and advice to help them cope with all the changes."
"Good idea. I recommend we advertise on the town's website. . . ."

B Class activity Present your product or service and marketing plans to the class. Which group has the best ideas?

3 SPEAKING
Suitable pets?

A Would you consider having any of these animals as pets? Why or why not?

tropical fish   boa constrictor   chimpanzee

B Pair work Compare your ideas with a partner. Explain your reasons.

"I really love tropical fish. Whenever I get the chance, I go snorkeling. I wouldn't have them as pets, though. I would rather see them in the ocean than in an aquarium."

4 LISTENING
Bird talk

A Listen to an interview with a parrot expert. She mentions three things that are important for a person to have before getting an African grey parrot. Choose the three basic requirements she mentions.

☐ a. time ☐ c. space ☐ e. children
☐ b. videos ☐ d. interest in parrots ☐ f. other birds

B Listen again. Are these statements true or false? Choose the correct answer.

	True	False
1. It is illegal to import wild African grey parrots.	☐	☐
2. Parrots cause asthma.	☐	☐
3. Parrots are intelligent and unpredictable.	☐	☐
4. Parrots need some time outside of their cage each day.	☐	☐
5. Research has been done on African grey parrots talking.	☐	☐
6. Parrots can eat all fruits and vegetables.	☐	☐

UNITS 7–9 Communication review

10 LANGUAGE
LESSON A ▶ Communication skills

1 STARTING POINT
Effective communicators

A Read about these effective communicators. What else do you know about them?

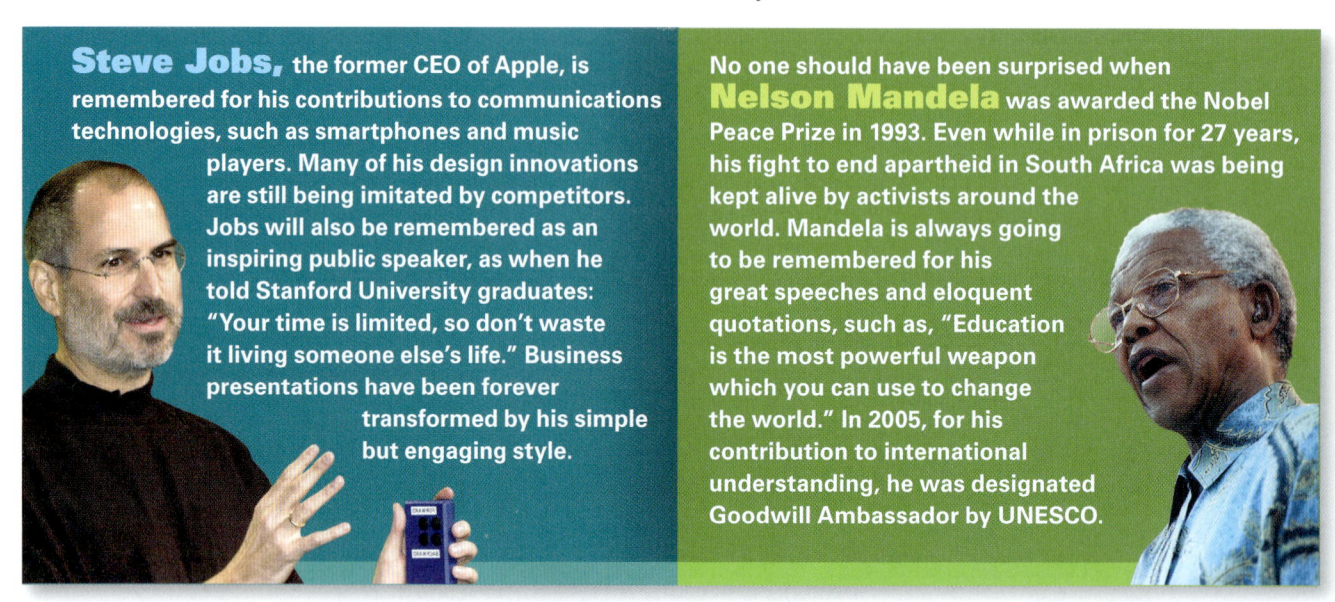

Steve Jobs, the former CEO of Apple, is remembered for his contributions to communications technologies, such as smartphones and music players. Many of his design innovations are still being imitated by competitors. Jobs will also be remembered as an inspiring public speaker, as when he told Stanford University graduates: "Your time is limited, so don't waste it living someone else's life." Business presentations have been forever transformed by his simple but engaging style.

No one should have been surprised when **Nelson Mandela** was awarded the Nobel Peace Prize in 1993. Even while in prison for 27 years, his fight to end apartheid in South Africa was being kept alive by activists around the world. Mandela is always going to be remembered for his great speeches and eloquent quotations, such as, "Education is the most powerful weapon which you can use to change the world." In 2005, for his contribution to international understanding, he was designated Goodwill Ambassador by UNESCO.

B Pair work Who are some effective communicators you know? What qualities make them effective?

2 DISCUSSION
Fear of public speaking

A Studies have shown that public speaking is many people's biggest fear. Do you share this fear? Complete the survey. Add a statement of your own.

Are you AFRAID to talk?

	Always true	Sometimes true	Never true
1 I can't sleep the night before a presentation.	☐	☐	☐
2 I rarely participate in discussions at work or in class.	☐	☐	☐
3 I avoid situations in which I might have to give an impromptu speech.	☐	☐	☐
4 When talking to others, I find it hard to look people in the eye.	☐	☐	☐
5 I can speak only from a prepared speech.	☐	☐	☐
6 I am intimidated by job interviews.	☐	☐	☐
7 I'd rather go to the dentist, pay taxes, or clean closets than give a presentation.	☐	☐	☐
8 _____	☐	☐	☐

Source: Schaum's Quick Guide to Great Presentation Skills

B Pair work Compare and explain your answers using examples from your life whenever possible. What do you have in common? How are you different?

10 LANGUAGE
LESSON A ▶ Communication skills

> In this unit, Ss use verbs in the passive and practice subject-verb agreement with quantifiers to talk about language and communication.

1 Effective communicators (STARTING POINT)

Learning aim: Discuss effective communicators and see passives in context (10–15 minutes)

A
- Books closed. Ask Ss to define *effective communicator*. Ask them whether or not they think they are effective communicators and why.
- Books open. Explain the task. Read the descriptions aloud. Check that Ss understand the following vocabulary.

> **Vocabulary**
>
> **CEO** chief executive officer; the highest position in a company
>
> **apartheid** official government policy that discriminated against nonwhite people in South Africa
>
> **activists** people who take one side of a political or social issue and work to make changes
>
> **eloquent** giving a clear and strong message fluently and expressively
>
> **designated** appointed or chosen for the purpose

- Give Ss time to think about their answer to the question. Then have Ss work in pairs to discuss their answers.
- Have Ss tell the class anything else they know about Steve Jobs or Nelson Mandela.

> **Culture note**
>
> **Steve Jobs** was born in San Francisco, California, in 1955. He co-founded Apple with Steve Wozniak in 1976. During the period Jobs was involved with Apple, the company developed groundbreaking and highly popular electronic products known for their elegant, simple, and user-friendly design. In 1986, Jobs bought the company that would become Pixar, a studio known for its innovative animated movies using high-end computer graphics.
>
> **Nelson Mandela** was born in 1918. He was an anti-apartheid activist and was sentenced to life imprisonment for sabotage. He spent 27 years in jail and became a symbol of the struggle against discrimination. He was released in 1990 and helped make South Africa into a multiracial democracy. He was president of South Africa from 1994 to 1999.

B Pair work
- Explain the task. Read the questions aloud. Ss work in pairs to do the activity.
- Have Ss share their partner's answers with the class.

2 Fear of public speaking (DISCUSSION)

Learning aim: Talk about speaking in public (15–20 minutes)

A
- Books closed. Ask Ss if they have ever had to speak or perform in public. Have them describe the circumstances and say whether or not they were nervous. Have Ss name different occupations where speaking in public is an important skill. (Possible answers: a lawyer, a teacher, a TV reporter)
- Books open. Explain the task. Read the survey aloud. Answer any questions about vocabulary.
- Ss work individually to do the activity and add a statement of their own. Brainstorm additional fears with the class, if necessary.

B Pair work
- Explain the task. Ss work in pairs to discuss what they have in common and how they are different.
- Have Ss share their partner's answers with the class.
- For further discussion, put pairs together to make a list of practical suggestions for overcoming the fear of public speaking.
- Have a S from each group read their list to the class. Ask other Ss if they have ever used any of the advice before.

> For more practice discussing this topic, download the Worksheet *10.1 Language survey* from the Teacher Support Site.

3 Overview of passives (GRAMMAR)

Learning aim: Practice using passives (20–25 minutes)

Grammar notes

In spoken English, many conversations involve the speaker as the "doer" of the action, so the actions are usually expressed using the active voice. For this reason, the passive voice is used less frequently than the active voice in spoken English.

The passive is generally used when the "doer" of the action (or the agent) is unknown, unimportant, or obvious from the context.

When the agent is relevant or important to the meaning of the sentence, it should be included after the preposition *by*.

The passive can be used with all verb forms, tenses, and modals, although it is rarely used with some forms, such as the present perfect continuous.

- Books closed. Write on the board:
   1. *My sister spilled the milk.*
   2. *The milk was spilled by my sister.*

   Ask Ss if the sentences mean the same thing. (Answer: yes) Ask what the differences are between the two sentences. (Answer: Sentence 1 is active; the subject is *My sister*. Sentence 2 is passive; the subject is *The milk*.) Tell Ss that in sentence 1, the speaker wants to emphasize that it was his or her sister who spilled something. In sentence 2, the speaker wants to emphasize that the spilled substance was the milk.
- Books open. Discuss the information in the grammar box and read the example sentences.

A

- Have Ss look at the Starting Point on page 80 again. Explain the task and read the questions aloud.
- Go over answers with the class.

Answers

. . . he was designated Goodwill Ambassador by UNESCO.

simple past

B

- Explain the task. Read the sentences and the example answer aloud. Answer any questions about vocabulary.
- Ss work individually to complete the activity.
- Go over answers with the class.

Answers

1. The way the world communicates has been changed by the Internet.
2. Presentations should be delivered confidently and cheerfully.
3. The students should have been told to speak louder during their speeches.
4. Married couples are being advised by counselors to communicate more openly.
5. Long ago, smoke signals were used to send simple messages in China.
6. After the ceremony, the scholarship recipients are being announced by the president.
7. The president's speech is going to be translated into 35 languages.
8. An announcement was being made by the principal when the microphone went dead.

C

- Explain the task. Read the beginning of each sentence and the example answer aloud. Brainstorm additional sentences in the passive with the class, if necessary.
- Ss work individually to complete the activity.
- Ss work in pairs to compare answers. Go over answers with the class. Have Ss share the sentence they added.

Possible answers

1. I've been told by many people that my English sounds quite formal.
2. My classmates and I are encouraged to speak by our teacher.
3. I hope that someday I will be complimented on how fluent my English is.
4. Students should be forced to take a foreign language.
5. Languages should be taught by someone who has a passion for language learning.
6. I've been advised to study Latin by my professor.
7. Not long ago, I was told that I have a very good French accent.
8. *Answers will vary.*

3 GRAMMAR

Overview of passives

Passive sentences focus on the receiver of the action by making it the subject of the sentence. The agent that performs the action can be omitted or follow *by* after the verb.

Passive = subject + form of *be* + past participle (+ *by* + agent)

Simple present: Steve Jobs **is remembered** for his contributions to communications technologies.
Present continuous: Many of his design innovations **are** still **being imitated** (by competitors).
Present perfect: Business presentations **have been** forever **transformed** by his simple but engaging style.
Simple past: Nelson Mandela **was awarded** the Nobel Peace Prize in 1993.
Past continuous: Mandela's fight **was being kept** alive (by activists) around the world.
Future with *going to*: Mandela **is** always **going to be remembered** for his great speeches.
Modals: Jobs **will** also **be remembered** as an inspiring public speaker.
Past modals: No one **should have been surprised**.

GRAMMAR PLUS *see page 124*

A Look at the Starting Point on page 80 again. Can you find another example of the passive? What verb form is it in?

B Change these active sentences to the passive. Keep or omit the agent as appropriate.

1. The Internet has changed the way the world communicates.
   The way the world communicates has been changed by the Internet.
2. People should deliver presentations confidently and cheerfully.
3. Someone should have told the students to speak louder during their speeches.
4. Counselors are advising married couples to communicate more openly.
5. Long ago, people used smoke signals to send simple messages in China.
6. After the ceremony, the president is announcing the scholarship recipients.
7. Translators are going to translate the president's speech into 35 languages.
8. The principal was making an announcement when the microphone went dead.

C Complete these sentences with information about language that is true for you. Then add another sentence of your own using a passive verb form.

1. I've been told by many people that . . .
   my English sounds quite formal.
2. My classmates and I are encouraged to . . .
3. I hope that someday I will be complimented on . . .
4. Students should / shouldn't be forced to . . .
5. Languages should be taught . . .
6. I've been advised . . .
7. Not long ago, I was told that . . .
8. _____

LESSON A Communication skills

4 VOCABULARY
Discourse markers

A Discourse markers are expressions that make communication flow more smoothly. Match each expression below with a function it serves. Sometimes more than one answer is possible.

a. to open a presentation c. to add information e. to introduce contrasts
b. to sequence information d. to introduce similarities f. to close a presentation

___ 1. in conclusion   ___ 5. nevertheless   ___ 9. likewise
___ 2. next   ___ 6. in addition   ___ 10. yet
___ 3. similarly   ___ 7. to sum up   ___ 11. first / second / third
___ 4. to begin   ___ 8. first of all   ___ 12. furthermore

B Pair work Complete each sentence with an expression from part A. Sometimes more than one answer is possible.

(1) _____, let me thank everyone for your interest and attention as I speak on the topic of petroleum dependency – our dependency on oil for our energy needs.

There are important reasons why we should be concerned about our dependency on petroleum. (2) _____, petroleum-based fuels contribute to both air pollution and global warming, two very serious problems today. (3) _____, there is a limited supply of oil in the world; therefore, we must reduce fuel consumption and be prepared to replace petroleum with other sources of energy.

There are many ways in which to do this on a large scale. First, we must produce fuel-efficient cars; (4) _____, we must encourage the use of public transportation. Finally, tax breaks could be offered to businesses that conserve fuel. (5) _____, homeowners could also be offered tax incentives for fuel conservation. It's true that cutting down on consumption is beneficial to the environment; (6) _____, we should keep in mind that cutting down too quickly could have a negative effect on the economy.

(7) _____, this problem has no simple answers, but if the government, corporations, and private citizens all work together, I feel we can solve the problem.

VOCABULARY PLUS see page 139

5 LISTENING
Getting your message across

🔊 **A** Listen to advice about speaking in public. Choose the items the speaker mentions.

	Advice		Advice
☐ the audience		☐ posture	
☐ the outline		☐ eye contact	
☐ pronunciation		☐ voice	
☐ practicing		☐ questions	
☐ humor		☐ speed	

🔊 **B** Listen again. Complete the chart with the advice you hear.

82 UNIT 10 Language

4 Discourse markers (VOCABULARY)

Learning aim: Learn and practice using discourse markers (10–15 minutes)

A
- Explain that *discourse* means communication in speech or writing.
- Explain the task. Read the expressions and the functions aloud.
- Ss work individually to do the activity.
- Go over answers with the class.

Answers
1. f	3. d	5. e	7. f	9. d	11. b
2. b	4. a, b	6. c	8. a, b	10. e	12. c

B Pair work
- Explain the task. Read the text aloud. Answer any questions about vocabulary.
- Ss work in pairs to complete the activity.
- Go over answers with the class.

Answers
1. First of all / To begin
2. First / First of all
3. Second / Next / Furthermore / In addition
4. second / next / furthermore / in addition
5. Similarly / Likewise
6. nevertheless / yet
7. In conclusion / To sum up

5 Getting your message across (LISTENING)

Learning aim: Develop skills in listening for main ideas and details (15–20 minutes)

A [CD 3, Track 8]
- Explain the task. Ask Ss to predict what kinds of advice they will hear.
- Focus Ss' attention on the chart. Read the items aloud. Explain that Ss should only choose the items they hear in the recording and not fill in any advice yet. Check that Ss understand the following vocabulary.

Vocabulary
go smoothly occur/happen without any problems

tedious extremely boring

one-on-one two people talking directly to each other, not in a group

- Play the recording. Ss choose the items the speaker mentions. Replay as many times as needed.
- Ss work in pairs to compare answers. Go over answers with the class.

Answers
the audience, the outline, practicing, humor, posture, eye contact, voice, questions

Audio script: See page T-174.

B [CD 3, Track 9]
- Explain that Ss will listen again and fill in the two columns with the advice the speaker gives.
- Play the recording as Ss complete the chart. Replay as many times as needed. Ss listen and check their answers.
- Ss work in pairs to compare answers. Go over answers with the class.

Answers
the audience: The presentation is for the audience. Keep in mind what they want to hear.

the outline: Include ideas for your introduction, main point, and conclusion. Keep it clear and simple.

practicing: Practice in front of a mirror, with a friend, or record the presentation and listen to it. Practice makes you more confident.

humor: Start with a joke or funny story. It puts the audience at ease.

posture: Try to look relaxed and natural.

eye contact: Move your eyes slowly around the room, from person to person.

voice: Your voice should sound friendly, natural, and expressive.

questions: Always welcome questions from the audience. Speak one-on-one to people who have many questions.

Audio script: See page T-174.

6 Persuasive writing (WRITING)

Learning aim: Write a persuasive essay by taking a position, looking at two sides of the argument, and using reasons and examples (40–50 minutes)

A

- Books closed. Have a brief class discussion about foreign languages. Ask Ss what other language they would like to learn and why. Ask them if they think learning a foreign language is important and why.
- Books open. Tell Ss to read the information in the box at the top of the page. Ask: *What does* persuasive *mean?* (Answer: convincing; making others agree with your opinion) *What should you provide in a persuasive essay?* (Answer: examples and reasons that support your opinion, the opposing view, and your argument against it)
- Explain to Ss that in the example essay, the first paragraph states the writer's opinion. Each of the next two body paragraphs contains an argument for the opposing view and the writer's counterargument. The final paragraph contains the writer's conclusion. Alternatively, in this kind of essay, the body paragraphs following the introduction can be about each of the supporting details, and one paragraph should include the opposite view and why the writer disagrees with it.
- Explain the task and read the questions aloud. Have Ss read the essay silently to themselves. Check that Ss understand the following vocabulary.

Vocabulary

proposed put forward (a plan, an offer, an idea, etc.)

do away with get rid of something

mandates makes something required/compulsory

proponents people who support and argue for an idea, cause, or plan

shortsighted unable to see how a situation will be in the future

proficient very good at

disservice something harmful or unhelpful

- Ss work individually to answer the questions.
- Ss work in pairs to compare their answers.
- Go over answers with the class.

Answers

Writer's position:
The writer believes that the university should keep the foreign language requirement.

Arguments for the opposing view:
It's more important for students to spend their time on courses that are focused on their careers than on a foreign language. Some people may study a language and never have to use it in later life.

Reasons and examples to support the writer's position:
People who speak two languages have an increased chance of getting a job. Study of a foreign language increases proficiency in native language skills and the understanding of one's own culture.

B Pair work

- Explain the task. Read the positions aloud.
- Ss work in pairs to do the activity. Brainstorm other positions as a class, if necessary.
- Go around the class and help as needed.

C

- Explain the writing task.
- Ss work individually to write their articles.
- Go around the class and help as needed.

D Pair work

- Ss work in pairs to exchange articles and take turns suggesting improvements.
- Go around the class and help as needed. Encourage Ss to ask and answer follow-up questions about the position taken in the article and about anything they don't understand.

Do your students need more practice?

Assign . . .	for more practice in . . .
Grammar Plus 10A	Grammar
Vocabulary Plus 10A	Vocabulary
Online Vocabulary Accelerator 10A	Vocabulary
Workbook Lesson A	Grammar, Vocabulary, Writing
Online Workbook Lesson A	Grammar, Vocabulary, Writing

6 WRITING
Persuasive writing

> In persuasive writing, you take a position on an issue and try to convince the reader that your position is correct. To do so, you present both sides of the issue, providing arguments, reasons, and examples that support your point of view and show weaknesses of the opposing point of view.

A Read the article. What is the writer's position? What are the arguments for the opposing view? What arguments, reasons, and examples does the writer give to support his position and to show the weakness of the opposing viewpoint?

Every Student Should Be Required to Study a Foreign Language
by Leo Fernández

Recently, a student organization at our university proposed that we do away with our foreign language requirement, which mandates that all students complete two years of foreign language study. The main reason for this proposal seems to be to eliminate unnecessary courses; however, the proponents of this change are overlooking the great benefits foreign language study provides to students of any major.

Students who oppose the language requirement argue that university study should be more career focused. They feel that the language requirement steals time that could be spent on courses directly related to a student's major. This is a shortsighted position. Statistics suggest that candidates proficient in two languages have an increased chance of finding work. For example, . . .

Another point often made by the proponents of the change is that a large number of students who study a language for two years rarely use it again in their lives. While this may be true in some cases, study of a foreign language has been shown to further develop native language skills. In addition, the understanding of oneself and one's own culture is increased through contact with another language and its culture. Students who . . .

In conclusion, it is crucial that we keep the foreign language requirement. To eliminate it would be doing a great disservice to our university and its students. Foreign language learning benefits us in concrete and subtle ways as it broadens our minds and expands our opportunities.

B Pair work With a partner, take a position on one of these issues related to language, or use your own idea. Then brainstorm reasons supporting your position and weaknesses of the opposing view. Which reasons are the strongest?

- Schools should teach a second language starting in kindergarten.
- Every foreign language student should be required to study abroad.
- Institutions should be created to preserve dying languages.

C Write an article of at least four paragraphs supporting your position. Use the best reasons you have brainstormed to support your position. Make sure you argue against the opposing view.

D Pair work Exchange articles. Discuss ways the writing could be made more persuasive and the arguments stronger.

LESSON A Communication skills

LESSON B ▸ Natural language

1 STARTING POINT
What's correct language?

A Read these statements about language. Choose the statements you agree with.

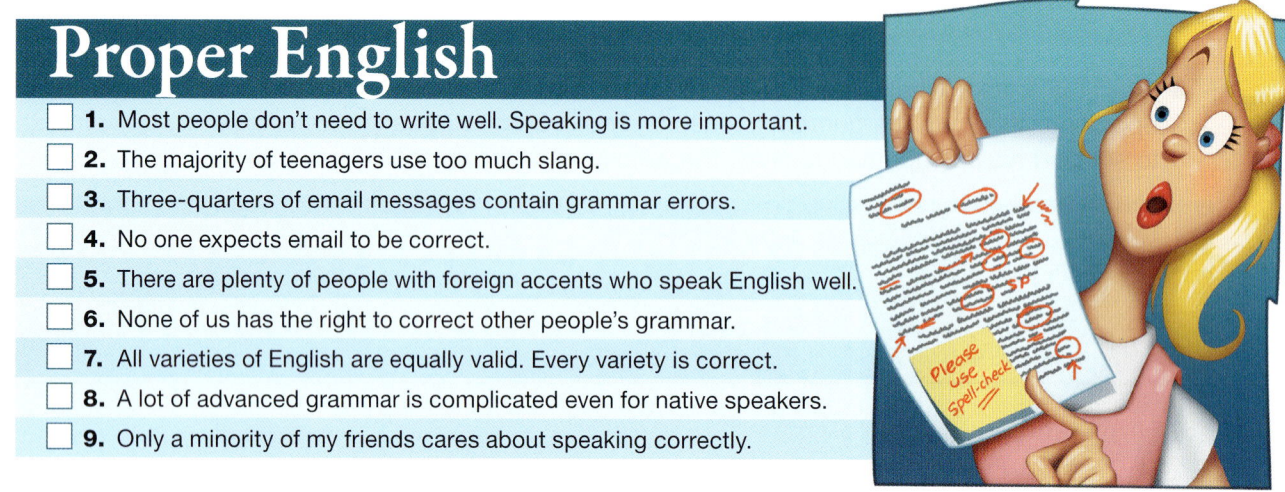

Proper English

☐ 1. Most people don't need to write well. Speaking is more important.
☐ 2. The majority of teenagers use too much slang.
☐ 3. Three-quarters of email messages contain grammar errors.
☐ 4. No one expects email to be correct.
☐ 5. There are plenty of people with foreign accents who speak English well.
☐ 6. None of us has the right to correct other people's grammar.
☐ 7. All varieties of English are equally valid. Every variety is correct.
☐ 8. A lot of advanced grammar is complicated even for native speakers.
☐ 9. Only a minority of my friends cares about speaking correctly.

B Pair work Discuss your opinions with a partner.

"I disagree with the first sentence. A lot of people need to write well for their jobs."

2 DISCUSSION
Text speak

A Pair work Read about "text speak." Then try to figure out what the six examples of text speak mean, and write the meanings. (For the answers, see page 142.)

"Text speak" refers to shortened forms of words commonly used in text messaging. When texting began, telephone companies would charge by the word, so fewer words and letters meant cheaper messages. These days, many people find text speak convenient and cool, and it is creeping into less informal types of writing. See some examples of text speak in the box.

b4	before
ruok?	_____
cul8r	_____
xlnt	_____
gr8	_____
2nite	_____

B Group work Read these opinions about text speak. Which one do you most agree with? Discuss your opinions about text speak with the group.

I try not to use text speak – except when I'm online or texting, of course – because it's annoying. I think people who use it in schoolwork and formal emails look idiotic and immature. —Raphael	I really feel old when my kids – and even my wife! – write to me using text speak. Nevertheless, I know that language always evolves. Just think of the difference between our English and Shakespeare's! —Rob
Txt spk is gr8! It's much easier and quicker, and u can use it for email, taking notes in class, and even in some homework assignments. —Wendy	People are free to use text speak if they think it's more convenient – after all, it's a free country. But I do hope it remains an alternative style, and that grammar is maintained. —Su-jin

LESSON B ▶ Natural language

1 What's correct language? (STARTING POINT)

Learning aim: Discuss correctness in language and see subject-verb agreement with quantifiers in context (10–15 minutes)

A
- Books closed. Ask Ss to say if they think writing in English is easier than speaking in English. Ask them if they worry about making mistakes in English or if they think it is more important just to be understood.
- Books open. Explain the task. Read the statements aloud. Check that Ss understand the following vocabulary.

> **Vocabulary**
> **majority** the largest amount of a whole
> **slang** informal, nonstandard words and phrases
> **has the right** is allowed
> **minority** the smallest amount of a whole

- Ss work individually to complete the activity.

B Pair work
- Explain the task. Read the example answer aloud.
- Ss work in pairs to do the activity.
- Have Ss share their partner's opinions with the class.

2 Text speak (DISCUSSION)

Learning aim: Talk about text speak (15–20 minutes)

A Pair work
- Books closed. Ask Ss what *text speak* is and if they ever use it.
- Books open. Explain the task. Read the text aloud.
- Ss work in pairs to complete the activity.
- Go over answers with the class.

Answers
b4 = before
ruok? = Are you OK?
cul8r = See you later.
xlnt = excellent
gr8 = great
2nite = tonight

- Ask Ss if they know any other text speak. Write their answers on the board.

> **Optional activity:** *Text speak* (10–15 minutes)
> **Ss write their own text speak.**
> - Ss work in pairs to write a message using text speak. The message could be about something they did yesterday or what they will do on the weekend, or Ss can use their imaginations and pretend they are on vacation and writing to a friend. Tell them to use as much text speak as possible.
> - Have pairs exchange messages and read them.

B Group work
- Explain the task. Read the opinions aloud. Answer any questions about vocabulary.
- Ss work individually to choose the opinion they most agree with. Then Ss work in groups to discuss their opinions.
- Have a S from each group report on the group's discussion to the class.

💡 To help Ss participate in this exercise, download the Fresh Idea *Face up, face down* from the Teacher Support Site.

3 Subject-verb agreement with quantifiers (GRAMMAR)

Learning aim: Practice using subject-verb agreement with quantifiers (20–25 minutes)

> **Grammar notes**
>
> Generally, when a collective noun refers to a single, impersonal unit, a singular pronoun is used to refer to it.
> *My baseball team has a lot of great players on it.*
>
> When a collective noun refers to a group of various individuals, a plural pronoun is used.
> *My baseball team is great. They are all my friends.*
>
> Some other examples of collective nouns are *audience, class, couple, crowd, family, group, team.*

- Books closed. Write on the board:
    1. *Each person in the class _____ (be) very nice.*
    2. *Half of my classmates _____ (be) from Japan.*

  Read the sentences aloud and ask Ss to fill in the blanks. Ask them why they think the verb should be singular or plural. (Answers: Sentence 1: *is* (singular); Sentence 2: *are* (plural). In sentence 1, the verb is singular because it agrees with the singular subject noun *each person*. In sentence 2, the verb is plural because it agrees with the plural subject noun *half of my classmates*.)
- Books open. Discuss the information in the grammar box and read the example sentences.

A

- Have Ss look at the Starting Point on page 84 again. Explain the task and read the questions aloud.
- Go over answers with the class.

> **Answers**
>
> There are <u>plenty of</u> people with foreign accents who <u>speak</u> English well. (plural verb)
>
> <u>All varieties of</u> English <u>are</u> equally valid. (plural verb)

B

- Explain the task and go over the example with the class. Ss work individually to complete the sentences.
- Ss work in pairs to compare their answers. Go over answers with the class.

> **Answers**
>
> 1. agree
> 2. attend
> 3. speaks
> 4. are
> 5. use / uses
> 6. is
> 7. contains
> 8. is

C Group work

- Explain the task. Read the beginning of each sentence aloud. Answer any questions about vocabulary. Have one pair of Ss read the example conversation to the class.
- Ss work individually to complete the sentences.
- Ss work in groups to discuss their answers.
- Have a S from each group report on the group's discussion to the class.

> **Possible answers**
>
> 1. Lots of the slang people use these days comes from words they hear in popular music.
> 2. The majority of people my age don't / doesn't care about proper grammar.
> 3. Some of the language older people use has a richer vocabulary.
> 4. None of my friends corrects / correct my English.
> 5. Most of the news anchors you see on TV are very well spoken.
> 6. Every one of my teachers assigns / assign homework.

3 GRAMMAR

Subject-verb agreement with quantifiers

All (of), a lot of, lots of, plenty of, some (of), most (of), and fractions take a singular verb if the noun they modify is uncountable or singular. They take a plural verb if the noun they modify is plural.
A lot of advanced **grammar is** complicated.
Most people don't need to write well.
Three-quarters of email **messages contain** grammar errors.

Each of, every one of, none of, and collective nouns, such as *majority (of)* and *minority (of),* typically take a singular verb, but often take a plural verb after a plural noun in informal speech.
None of us has / have the right to correct other people's grammar.
The **majority of** teenagers **use / uses** too much slang.
A **minority of** my friends **care / cares** about speaking correctly.

Everyone, someone, anyone, no one, each + noun, and *every* + noun are followed by a singular verb.
Every variety **is** correct.
No one expects email to be correct.

GRAMMAR PLUS see page 125

A Look at the Starting Point on page 84 again. Can you find other quantifiers? Are they followed by a singular or plural verb?

B Complete these sentences with the correct form of the verb in parentheses. Use the simple present.

1. A lot of people _____agree_____ (agree) that spelling and grammar shouldn't change.
2. All of the students in my class _____ (attend) English club meetings.
3. Most of the faculty at school _____ (speak) at least three languages.
4. A quarter of my classmates _____ (be) going to study abroad next semester.
5. The majority of people _____ (use) text speak in their emails.
6. None of the information in the email _____ (be) correct.
7. Every letter I receive usually _____ (contain) one or two spelling mistakes.
8. Over four-fifths of the world population _____ (be) able to read and write.

C Group work Complete these sentences with information about how people use language in different situations. Then discuss your answers.

1. Lots of the slang people use these days . . .
2. The majority of people my age . . .
3. Some of the language older people use . . .
4. None of my friends . . .
5. Most of the news anchors you see on TV . . .
6. Every one of my teachers . . .

"Lots of the slang people use these days comes from words they hear in popular music."

"That's true. In hip-hop slang, 'crib' means home, and 'bling' means flashy jewelry."

LESSON B / Natural language

4 VOCABULARY
A way with words

A The expressions on the left can be used to comment on the way people speak. Match them with their definitions on the right.

1. have a sharp tongue ____
2. have a way with words ____
3. stick to the point ____
4. talk around a point ____
5. talk behind someone's back ____
6. talk someone into something ____
7. talk someone's ear off ____
8. love to hear oneself talk ____

a. talk about something without addressing it directly
b. enjoy talking even if nobody is paying attention
c. talk about a person without him or her knowing
d. continue talking about a main idea
e. talk in a bitter, critical way
f. talk until the other person is tired of listening
g. convince a person to do something
h. have a talent for speaking

B Pair work Use expressions from above to comment on these people and the way they are speaking.

1 | Klaus
"I wouldn't say I dislike the book, or at least I don't think so. I guess it's hard to say."

2 | Risa
"Why don't you want to go? Come on! It'll be fun, and it's cheap. I'll even drive!"

3 | Sandra
"Just be quiet! You don't know what you're talking about, so stop wasting my time!"

4 | Philip
"Diane got an F on her test. She tried to put it away quickly, but I saw it anyway!"

VOCABULARY PLUS see page 139

5 LISTENING & SPEAKING
Assert yourself!

A Listen to three one-sided conversations. Write the number of the conversation next to the correct description.

____ a. One person is talking the other person's ear off.
____ b. One person is trying to talk the other person into doing something.
____ c. One person isn't sticking to the point.

B Listen again. Which expressions do you hear used in the conversations? Write the number of the conversation next to the correct expression.

____ a. Could I say something?
____ b. Thanks for asking, but . . .
____ c. I just wanted to say . . .
____ d. That's nice, but we really need to . . .
____ e. That's really nice of you, but . . .
____ f. Getting back to what we were talking about . . .

C Pair work Prepare a conversation similar to those from the listening. Use the expressions in part B. Then perform the scene for the class.

4 A way with words (VOCABULARY)

Learning aim: Learn and practice using idioms related to use of language (10–15 minutes)

A
- Books closed. Ask Ss if they remember what an idiom is. (Answer: an expression or group of words whose meaning is different from the meanings of the individual words) Ask Ss to say any idioms they already know and write them on the board.
- Books open. Explain the task. Tell Ss that the numbered expressions in the left-hand column are idioms. Read the expressions and definitions aloud. Answer any questions about vocabulary.
- Ss work individually to complete the task. Go over answers with the class.

Answers			
1. e	3. d	5. c	7. f
2. h	4. a	6. g	8. b

B Pair work
- Explain the task. Read the texts aloud. Answer any questions about vocabulary.
- Ss work in pairs to comment on each person using the expressions from part A.
- Go over answers with the class.

Answers
1. Klaus: talk around a point
2. Risa: talk someone into something
3. Sandra: have a sharp tongue
4. Philip: talk behind someone's back

5 Assert yourself! (LISTENING & SPEAKING)

Learning aim: Develop skills in listening for gist and details (20–25 minutes)

A 🔊 [CD 3, Track 10]
- Explain the task. Read the descriptions aloud.
- Play the recording once as Ss listen. Play the recording again while Ss number the descriptions. Replay as many times as needed. Ss listen and check their answers.
- Ss work in pairs to compare their answers. Go over answers with the class.

Answers
a. 2   b. 3   c. 1

Audio script: See page T-174.

B 🔊 [CD 3, Track 11]
- Read the expressions aloud. Explain that Ss will listen again and write the number of the conversation each expression appears in.
- Play the recording once as Ss listen. Play the recording again while Ss write the correct numbers. Replay as many times as needed. Ss listen and check their answers.
- Go over answers with the class.

Answers
a. 2   b. 3   c. 2   d. 1   e. 3   f. 1

Audio script: See page T-174.

C Pair work
- Explain the task. Ss work in pairs. If necessary, suggest the following scenarios:
  1. Friend A is talking Friend B's ear off about the crowded transportation and traffic in the city. Friend B is trying to occasionally interrupt and express an opinion or two.
  2. Two friends are planning a birthday party. Friend A keeps talking about other things and won't stick to the point. Friend B keeps reminding Friend A to concentrate on the party.
  3. Friend A is trying to talk Friend B into doing something dangerous, for example, skydiving. Friend B keeps politely refusing and explaining why he or she isn't interested.
- Have pairs choose a scenario, write a conversation, and practice it. Make sure they use expressions from part B.
- Have pairs perform their scene for the class.

6 English varieties (READING)

Learning aim: Develop skills in understanding vocabulary in context, making inferences, and giving a personal reaction to a reading (25–30 minutes)

A Pair work

- Books closed. Ask Ss which countries have English as their main language or have a high percentage of their population who can speak it. (Possible answers: the United States, the United Kingdom, Australia, New Zealand, Canada, Antigua, Bahamas, Botswana, Fiji, India, Israel, Kenya, Malawi, Nigeria, Pakistan, the Philippines, the Virgin Islands, South Africa, etc.)
- Ask Ss if they have heard native speakers from different English-language-speaking countries speak English in person, in movies, or on the Internet. Ask Ss if they can hear a difference in accent or idioms and if they think one country's English is easier to understand than another's.
- Books open. Explain the task. Read the title of the article aloud. Ask Ss to define *abroad*. (Answer: in or to a foreign country)
- Ss work in pairs to discuss the question.
- Have Ss read the article silently. Check that Ss understand the following vocabulary.

> **Vocabulary**
>
> **convenience store** a store that sells many everyday items and is open 24 hours or late into the evening
>
> **muster** produce
>
> **converse** have a conversation
>
> **credibility** qualities someone has that make people respect or admire them
>
> **mere** only
>
> **extended (tourist)** (a tourist) staying a long time
>
> **fool** make people believe something that is not true
>
> **belong** feel you are part of a group
>
> **common ground** something that people can agree on
>
> **the same on paper** the same in theory, but not in real life
>
> **on the ground** in the country where the language is spoken (in this context)

- Have pairs compare their ideas to the author's.
- Go over the answer with the class.

> **Possible answer**
>
> I think the quote means that while England and the United States are separated physically, the variety of English is also different and is, therefore, something else that distinguishes the countries from each other.

B

- Explain the task. Ss work individually to answer the question. Then Ss work in pairs or groups to compare and discuss their answers.
- Go over answers with the class.

> **Answers**
>
> 3, 4

C Group work

- Explain the task. Read the questions aloud.
- Ss work in groups to discuss the questions.
- Ask groups to share their ideas with the class. To make sure that reporting to the class goes smoothly, groups can choose one or two members to report their ideas. Have Ss review their ideas with their own group at the end of the task to see if the group agrees with the information they will be presenting.
- As a final class discussion, ask Ss for some examples of the differences between British and American English. Have them explain whether or not they think the differences are significant.

> **Optional activity:** *Fill in the blanks* (15 minutes)
>
> **Ss write a cloze exercise.**
>
> - Ss work in pairs to write three or four sentences about the article, leaving a word or two blank.
>   Example: *There can be many _____ in the same language spoken in two countries*.
>   Make sure Ss understand that they shouldn't copy sentences directly from the article; they should write about the article in their own words.
> - Tell Ss to close their books. Have pairs exchange sentences and fill in the blanks. Then have them check each other's answers.

For more practice with group presentations, download the Worksheet **10.2 Persuasive presentation** from the Teacher Support Site.

Do your students need more practice?	
Assign . . .	for more practice in . . .
Grammar Plus 10B	Grammar
Vocabulary Plus 10B	Vocabulary
Online Vocabulary Accelerator 10B	Vocabulary
Workbook Lesson B	Grammar, Vocabulary, Reading
Online Workbook Lesson B	Grammar, Vocabulary, Reading, Listening

6 READING
English varieties

A **Pair work** Read the quote in the first line of the article. What do you think it means? Then read the article to compare your ideas to the author's.

SLANG Abroad

George Bernard Shaw said, "England and America are two countries separated by a common language." I never really understood the meaning of this quote until a friend and I stopped at a London convenience store. We had some trash to throw away, so I, in as polite a manner as I could muster, asked the clerk for a trash can. Then I asked him again, thinking he didn't hear me. And then I asked again, only this time while speaking the international language (loudly and slowly while pointing to the object I wanted to throw away). After this horribly rude display, he politely asked me what a trash can was. So I told him it was a place for my garbage. I guess this weak explanation worked. The clerk then produced a small trash can from behind the counter and in the most you-must-not-be-from-around-here tone he could muster said, "rubbish bin."

Different names for objects, however, are not the main problem. Anyone can learn a language. But to really be a speaker of the language, you need to understand its idioms and its slang. There is a distinct difference between someone who learned a language in a classroom and someone who is a native speaker. Using slang proves that the speaker has been in a country long enough to learn it, and that offers a benefit greater than just being able to converse on a casual level. It allows the two speakers to get much closer much more quickly.

Eventually, after living somewhere for a while you pick up a few things, and this new language education gives a credibility that just pronouncing a city address cannot. It shows a belonging and membership in the club of permanent residents and that one is not just a mere extended tourist. I know it sounds superficial, that by being able to understand words that may or may not be in a dictionary, we can fool people into thinking we belong, but it isn't. What knowing and using slang shows is a basic understanding of a culture. It offers both members of the conversation a common ground.

And that's the point. Britain and America are two countries separated by a common language, but then again so are Mexico and Spain, Brazil and Portugal, and France and Haiti. While these countries' languages may all seem the same on paper, they're not. Really learning the languages can only be done on the ground. And once that learning is done, something far greater is achieved than just not sounding like a fool.

Source: "Slang Abroad," by Ben Falk, *The Daily Colonial*

B Which of these statements would the author probably agree with? Compare and discuss your answers.

1. It's impossible for anyone learning a foreign language to ever sound like a native speaker.
2. Studying books about slang is an effective way to learn how it's used.
3. Despite how connected the world is, slang and idioms remain very local.
4. Really learning a language means knowing how people actually use it.

C **Group work** Discuss these questions. Then share your answers with the class.

1. Do you agree with the author's idea that one can only really learn a language by living in a country where it's spoken? Why or why not?
2. Have you or anyone you know ever had any experiences like the one in the first paragraph? What happened? Do you think such misunderstandings are common?

11 EXCEPTIONAL PEOPLE
LESSON A ▶ High achievers

1 STARTING POINT
They've had an impact!

A Read about the exceptional people below. Have you heard of any of them? What sort of impact have they had on other people?

MAHATMA GANDHI

(1869–1948) Gandhi was a great political and spiritual leader in India. Although he was educated in England, Gandhi is best remembered for his struggle for Indian independence, which had far-reaching effects. His epoch-making victories through peaceful means later inspired other great leaders, like Martin Luther King Jr. and Aung San Suu Kyi.

NATALIA VODIANOVA

(1982–) Born in Russia, this blue-eyed, brown-haired beauty was working at a fruit stand by age 11. At 17, she moved to Paris and soon after signed with a well-known modeling agency. She was well received and quickly became a popular fashion model. A kind-hearted superstar, she created the Naked Heart Foundation to build playgrounds for underprivileged children in Russia.

ANDRE AGASSI

(1970–) Andre Agassi's hard-driving father always planned to make him a tennis star. Intensely coached, he was practicing with pros by age five. During his career, Agassi won every important tournament at least once and earned over 100 million dollars. Now retired but socially engaged, he built a free school for youth in one of Las Vegas's poorest neighborhoods.

B Group work Think of people who have had an impact on the world. Discuss their achievements, and then choose the person who has had the biggest impact.

2 DISCUSSION
Exceptional values

A Group work Think about the people you talked about in the Starting Point. What values do you think were most important to each of them? Why?

"I think Gandhi valued patience. He had patience with people and patience to achieve his goal through nonviolent measures."

B Look at this list of life values. Choose the three that are the most important in your life. If your top values aren't here, add them to the list.

- ☐ achievement
- ☐ compassion
- ☐ cooperation
- ☐ creativity
- ☐ environmentalism
- ☐ health
- ☐ independence
- ☐ responsibility
- ☐ spirituality
- ☐ wealth
- ☐ _____
- ☐ _____

C Group work Explain your choices to the members of your group. Then make a list of the three life values that are the most important to your group as a whole.

11 EXCEPTIONAL PEOPLE
LESSON A ▶ High achievers

> In this unit, Ss use compound adjectives and superlative compound adjectives to talk about the qualities of role models and heroes.

1 They've had an impact! (STARTING POINT)

Learning aim: Discuss exceptional people and see compound adjectives in context (10–15 minutes)

A

- Books closed. Ask Ss to think about important achievements that have taken place in the world or in their country during their lifetime. Tell Ss that these achievements can be of any kind (e.g., political, medical, technological, artistic, philanthropic, etc.). Give Ss time to think of ideas and then write the achievements on the board. Ask: *Which achievements are the most important?* Circle the top five. (Leave these on the board for Exercise 1B.)

- Ask Ss to think about the person or people responsible for these achievements. Ask Ss to identify the qualities that these people probably have in common (e.g., intelligent, independent, hardworking, brave). Write the qualities on the board. (Leave these on the board for Exercise 2.)

- Books open. Focus Ss' attention on the three pictures and ask them if they know anything about the three people. Make three columns on the board, one for each person. Write the information that Ss call out in the appropriate column.

- Explain the task and read the questions aloud. Have Ss read the descriptions silently to themselves. Check that Ss understand the following vocabulary.

> **Vocabulary**
> **epoch-making** causing historical changes
> **means** ways or methods
> **underprivileged** not having enough money, food, educational opportunities, or other basic resources
> **hard-driving** forcing someone to work hard to achieve something
> **socially engaged** participating in activities or issues in one's community or society

- Give Ss time to think about their answers to the questions. Discuss answers as a class.

B Group work

- Explain the task. Ss work in groups to do the activity. Remind Ss to refer to the achievements written on the board in part A.

- Have a S from each group report on the group's discussion to the class.

2 Exceptional values (DISCUSSION)

Learning aim: Talk about the values of exceptional people (15–20 minutes)

A Group work

- Explain the task. Read the questions and the example answer aloud.

- Give Ss time to think about their answers. Remind Ss to refer back to the qualities written on the board in Exercise 1A. Then Ss work in groups to discuss their ideas.

B

- Explain the task. Read the list of life values aloud. Answer any questions about vocabulary.

- Ss work individually to complete the activity.

C Group work

- Explain the task. Ss work in groups to do the activity.

- Have a S from each group read their list to the class.

> **Optional activity:** *Class debate* (15–20 minutes)
> Ss have a class debate.
> - Write on the board:
>   *Caring for the environment is the single most important life value we have today.*
> - Divide the class into two groups: A and B. Tell group A to think of as many reasons as they can in favor of the statement. Tell group B to think of as many reasons as they can against the statement.
> - Give Ss time to think of reasons individually. Then have them discuss their answers with their group.
> - Have each group take turns presenting their ideas to the class.

3 Compound adjectives (GRAMMAR)

Learning aim: Practice using compound adjectives (20–25 minutes)

> **Grammar notes**
> Compound adjectives usually cannot be separated into a noun + be + adjective construction, even though it might seem like it would mean the same thing.
> Correct: *He is a very absent-minded professor.*
> Incorrect: *His mind is very absent.*
>
> Some compound adjectives that can be separated are *kind-hearted, cold-hearted, blue-eyed* (or any other color), and *brown-haired* (or any other color).

- Books closed. Write on the board:

  No one likes him. He is a cold-hearted man.

  Ask Ss to identify the adjective. (Answer: cold-hearted) Ask them why it is different from other adjectives. (Answer: It is two words together.) Ask Ss what they think it means. (Answer: having no sympathy or concern for other people)

- Books open. Discuss the information in the grammar box and read the example sentences.

A

- Have Ss look at the Starting Point on page 88 again. Explain the task and read the questions aloud. Go over answers with the class.

> **Answers**
> Pattern a:
> blue-eyed, brown-haired, kind-hearted
> Pattern b:
> best remembered, well-known, well received, underprivileged, intensely coached, socially engaged
> Pattern c:
> far-reaching, epoch-making, hard-driving

B

- Explain the task. Read the sentences and the example answer aloud.
- Ss work individually to complete the activity.
- Go over answers with the class.

> **Answers**
> 1. Roger Federer is a <u>well-known</u> athlete.
> 2. The play was <u>well received</u> by most theater critics.
> 3. Many charities are set up to help <u>underprivileged</u> children.
> 4. The <u>kind-hearted</u> celebrity gave money to the homeless.
> 5. The work of Gandhi had <u>far-reaching</u> effects.
> 6. The <u>blue-eyed</u> child was adopted by a celebrity.

4 Compound adjectives related to the body (VOCABULARY)

Learning aim: Learn and practice using compound adjectives related to the body (10–15 minutes)

A

- Explain the task. Read the words and synonyms aloud.
- Ss work individually to complete the activity.
- Go over answers with the class.

> **Answers**
> 1. empty-headed
> 2. hotheaded / hot-blooded
> 3. cold-hearted / hard-hearted / cold-blooded
> 4. openhearted / warm-hearted / soft-hearted
> 5. hardheaded
> 6. open-minded
> 7. narrow-minded
> 8. absent-minded
> 9. coolheaded
> 10. warm-hearted / soft-hearted

B Pair work

- Explain the task. Read the example answer aloud.
- Ss work in pairs to do the activity.
- Have Ss share their partner's answers with the class.

For more practice with vocabulary, download the Worksheet **11.1 In your opinion** from the Teacher Support Site.

T-89 UNIT 11 Exceptional people

3 GRAMMAR

Compound adjectives

Compound adjectives are modifying phrases made up of two or more words. They can be joined by a hyphen, appear as a single word, or appear as two separate words. Always check a dictionary before using compound adjectives in writing.

Three common patterns for compound adjectives in English are:

a. adjective + noun + -ed *(absent-minded, high-spirited, long-winded, soft-hearted)*
When preceding a noun, these compounds are usually written with a hyphen unless they are one word.

b. adverb + past participle *(much-loved, well-dressed, highly acclaimed, widely respected)*
Compounds with adverbs ending in *-ly* are never hyphenated.
Other adverbs are usually hyphenated before but not after the noun.

c. adjective, adverb, or noun + present participle *(easygoing, forward-thinking, thought-provoking)*
When preceding a noun, these compounds are usually written with a hyphen unless they are one word.

GRAMMAR PLUS see page 126

A Look at the Starting Point on page 88 again. Can you find more compound adjectives? Which patterns from the grammar box do they follow?

B Rewrite these sentences using the compound adjectives from the Starting Point to replace the words in boldface. Sometimes more than one answer is possible.

1. Roger Federer is an athlete **everybody knows**.
   Roger Federer is a well-known athlete.
2. The play was **praised** by most theater critics.
3. Many charities are set up to help children **who are poor**.
4. The **very generous** celebrity gave money to the homeless.
5. The work of Gandhi had effects **that reached around the world**.
6. The child **with blue eyes** was adopted by a celebrity.

4 VOCABULARY

Compound adjectives related to the body

A Combine the words from both boxes to create compound adjectives and match them with their synonyms below. Sometimes more than one answer is possible.

| absent | cool | hard | narrow | soft | blooded | hearted |
| cold | empty | hot | open | warm | headed | minded |

1. silly and brainless *empty-headed*
2. quick to anger _____
3. uncaring or unkind _____
4. sweet and loving _____
5. stubborn and unyielding _____
6. tolerant and unbiased _____
7. intolerant and disapproving _____
8. forgetful _____
9. calm and unexcitable _____
10. friendly and kind _____

B Pair work Use the compound adjectives in part A and others you can create to describe exceptional people or characters from movies, television, or books.

"Sherlock Holmes is an open-minded detective who uses his powers of observation to catch cold-blooded killers."

VOCABULARY PLUS see page 140

LESSON A High achievers 89

5 LISTENING
Do you want to be a high achiever?

A Listen to a speaker talk about the qualities of high achievers. Choose the four qualities he talks about.

	Suggestion		Suggestion
☐ lifelong learning		☐ positive attitude	
☐ high self-esteem		☐ risk-taking	
☐ responsibility		☐ creativity	

B Listen again. What does the speaker suggest people do in order to build the four qualities of high achievers? Write the suggestions in the chart.

6 DISCUSSION
Winning words

A Pair work Read these quotations from high achievers. Can you restate these quotations in your own words?

a 
Mark Zuckerberg
entrepreneur
"The biggest risk is not taking any risk."

b 
Gloria Estefan
singer
"You don't have to give up who you are to be successful just because you're different."

c 
Donald Trump
businessman and TV personality
"If you're going to be thinking anyway, you might as well think big!"

d 
Andrea Jung
businesswoman
"If you feel like it's difficult to change, you will probably have a harder time succeeding."

e 
Laird Hamilton
surfer and model
"Make sure your worst enemy doesn't live between your own two ears."

Useful expressions

Describing what something means
What this means to me is that . . .
My understanding of this is that . . .
I interpret this to mean . . .

B Group work Which of the quotations in part A might be useful for the following kinds of people? Do you know any other sayings or quotations that might be helpful?

1. someone who wants to get rich in business
2. someone who wants success but worries about how much work or time it will take
3. someone who wants to study abroad but is afraid of not fitting in somewhere new
4. someone who is only working part-time and putting off starting a real career
5. someone who is hesitant to register for a class because of self-doubt

UNIT 11 Exceptional people

5 Do you want to be a high achiever? (LISTENING)

Learning aim: Develop skills in listening for the main ideas and details (15–20 minutes)

A [CD 3, Track 12]

- Explain the task. Read the qualities aloud. Check that Ss understand the following vocabulary.

> **Vocabulary**
>
> **comfort zone** life situations that are familiar and safe
>
> **no pain, no gain** a common saying that means "to achieve anything in life, you have to work hard"

- Play the recording as Ss choose the four qualities. Replay as many times as needed.
- Ss work in pairs to compare answers. Go over answers with the class.

> **Answers**
>
> lifelong learning, responsibility, risk-taking, creativity

Audio script: See page T-175.

B [CD 3, Track 13]

- Read the question aloud. Explain that Ss will listen again for the speaker's suggestions.
- Play the recording once as Ss listen. Play the recording again as Ss write the suggestions in the chart. Replay as many times as needed. Ss listen and check their answers.
- Ss work in pairs to compare answers. Go over answers with the class.

> **Answers**
>
> lifelong learning: absorb information through books, blogs, videos, and social media sites; take courses
>
> responsibility: don't blame others for your failures; don't use difficult situations as excuses
>
> risk-taking: try something you are afraid to do; go out of your comfort zone
>
> creativity: brainstorm solutions for a problem; keep a creativity journal

Audio script: See page T-175.

6 Winning words (DISCUSSION)

Learning aim: Talk about quotations from high achievers (15–20 minutes)

A Pair work

- Focus Ss' attention on the pictures and names. Ask Ss what they know about each person.
- Explain the task. Read the quotations aloud. Answer any questions about vocabulary. Point out the Useful Expressions box. Give an example of how to use each phrase.
- Give Ss time to think individually about their answers. Then Ss work in pairs to compare their answers.
- Have Ss share their answers with the class.

> **Possible answers**
>
> a. It is risky not to try to do new things.
> b. You don't have to be like everyone else to be a successful person.
> c. You should always think big, that is, in a more ambitious way.
> d. If doing things a different way than you're used to is difficult for you, it will probably be hard for you to succeed.
> e. Don't let your own thoughts and ideas stop you from doing something.

B Group work

- Explain the task. Read the list of descriptions aloud. Answer any questions about vocabulary.
- Ss work in groups to do the activity.
- Have a S from each group report on the group's answers to the class.

> **Possible answers**
>
> 1. c, a
> 2. d, e
> 3. a, b, d, e
> 4. d, e
> 5. a, d, e

> **Optional activity:** *More quotes* (15–20 minutes)
>
> Ss paraphrase more quotations.
>
> - Write on the board:
>
>   *"Try not to become a man of success but rather to become a man of value."* Albert Einstein (1875–1955)
>
>   *"Life is what happens to you while you're busy making other plans."* John Lennon (1940–1980)
>
>   *"Never bend your head. Hold it high. Look the world straight in the eye."* Helen Keller (1880–1968)
>
> - Ask Ss to say anything they know about each famous person.
> - Ss work in pairs to paraphrase the quotations. Have pairs share their answers with the class.
> - Alternatively, ask Ss to write their favorite quotations on the board and then paraphrase them for the class.

UNIT 11 Exceptional people

7 Biographical profile (WRITING)

Learning aim: Write a biographical profile
(40–50 minutes)

A

- Books closed. Have a brief class discussion about biographies. Ask: *Do you like to read biographies? What kind of information is usually included in a biography?*
- Books open. Tell Ss to read the information in the box at the top of the page. Ask: *What is in the thesis statement of a biographical profile?* (Answer: what makes the person interesting or special) *How are paragraphs arranged?* (Answer: usually in chronological order)
- Explain to Ss that in a biographical profile, the first paragraph should state your thesis, and the following paragraphs should be about important events in the person's life, organized in chronological order.
- Explain the task. Have Ss read the essay silently to themselves. Check that Ss understand the following vocabulary.

> **Vocabulary**
>
> **rejected** not accepted
>
> **if you don't know . . . you must be from another planet** a common expression that means "You must know about . . . because it is so well known that everyone knows about it"
>
> **genius** a person who has extraordinary abilities or intelligence
>
> **social security** money provided by the government for people who are old, disabled, or retired

- Ss work individually to number the paragraphs in the correct order.
- Go over answers with the class. Have Ss say what information helped them put the paragraphs in order.

> **Answers**
> 4, 2, 1, 3

B

- Explain the writing task. If necessary, give Ss time to research the person as homework and bring their notes and list of key events to the next class.
- Ss work individually to write their profiles.
- Go around the class and help as needed.

C Pair work

- Explain the task. Ss work in pairs to exchange profiles and take turns answering the questions.
- Go around the class and help as needed. Encourage Ss to ask and answer follow-up questions.

Do your students need more practice?	
Assign . . .	for more practice in . . .
Grammar Plus 11A	Grammar
Vocabulary Plus 11A	Vocabulary
Online Vocabulary Accelerator 11A	Vocabulary
Workbook Lesson A	Grammar, Vocabulary, Writing
Online Workbook Lesson A	Grammar, Vocabulary, Writing

7 WRITING
Biographical profile

> A biographical profile usually begins with an introduction that includes a thesis statement about what makes the person interesting or special. The subsequent paragraphs are then usually arranged in chronological order.

A The paragraphs in this biographical profile about J. K. Rowling have been scrambled. Read the composition and put the paragraphs in order.

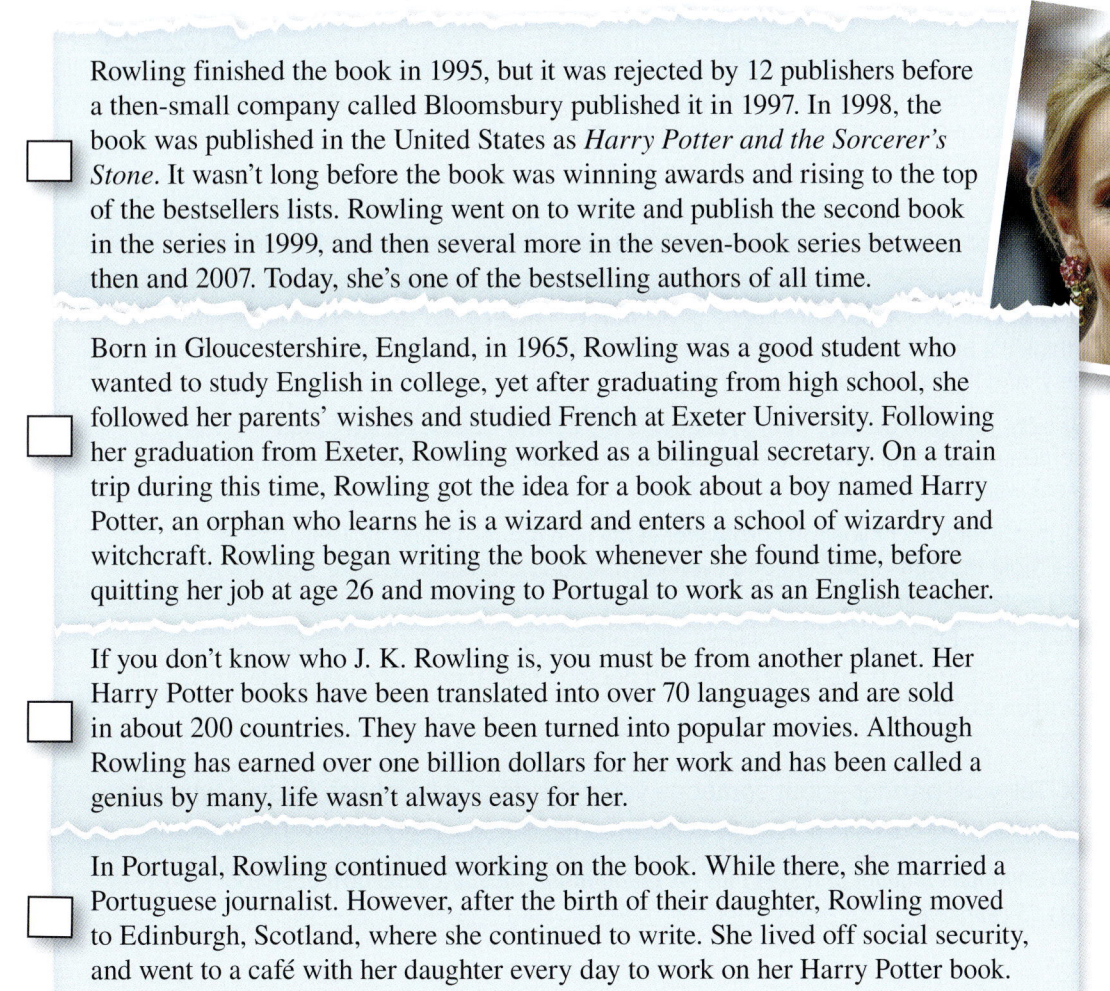

☐ Rowling finished the book in 1995, but it was rejected by 12 publishers before a then-small company called Bloomsbury published it in 1997. In 1998, the book was published in the United States as *Harry Potter and the Sorcerer's Stone*. It wasn't long before the book was winning awards and rising to the top of the bestsellers lists. Rowling went on to write and publish the second book in the series in 1999, and then several more in the seven-book series between then and 2007. Today, she's one of the bestselling authors of all time.

☐ Born in Gloucestershire, England, in 1965, Rowling was a good student who wanted to study English in college, yet after graduating from high school, she followed her parents' wishes and studied French at Exeter University. Following her graduation from Exeter, Rowling worked as a bilingual secretary. On a train trip during this time, Rowling got the idea for a book about a boy named Harry Potter, an orphan who learns he is a wizard and enters a school of wizardry and witchcraft. Rowling began writing the book whenever she found time, before quitting her job at age 26 and moving to Portugal to work as an English teacher.

☐ If you don't know who J. K. Rowling is, you must be from another planet. Her Harry Potter books have been translated into over 70 languages and are sold in about 200 countries. They have been turned into popular movies. Although Rowling has earned over one billion dollars for her work and has been called a genius by many, life wasn't always easy for her.

☐ In Portugal, Rowling continued working on the book. While there, she married a Portuguese journalist. However, after the birth of their daughter, Rowling moved to Edinburgh, Scotland, where she continued to write. She lived off social security, and went to a café with her daughter every day to work on her Harry Potter book.

B Choose a famous person you know a lot about. Make notes and list key events from this person's life in chronological order. Then use your notes to write a biographical profile.

C Pair work Exchange profiles with a partner, and answer these questions.

1. Does your partner's profile begin with an introduction and include a thesis statement?
2. Is the information in the profile arranged in chronological order?
3. Can you suggest any improvements to make the profile more interesting or effective?
4. What else would you like to know about the person your partner wrote about?

LESSON A High achievers

LESSON B ▶ People we admire

1 STARTING POINT
Role models

A Read these online posts about role models. What life values are reflected in each post?

Open Up! YOUR SPACE TO SHARE FEELINGS AND IDEAS

Up for Discussion: Tell us about the people you respect and admire. **+ new post**

RobertD They may not be the smartest or the best-looking people in the world, but I'd say my friends are the people I most admire. We stick together and watch out for each other – and learn a lot from each other, too.

Alena92 I've always looked up to my father. He's the hardest-working and the least narrow-minded man I know. He's always taught me that hard work is the surest way to be successful.

OwnDrummer I'm not sure I have a role model. I mostly like to do my own thing. I think it's because I'm not the most easily impressed person when I meet someone new, and I'm pretty slow to trust people.

Sporty_girl One person I really respect is my soccer coach. He's a tough competitor, and he's the best-trained soccer player I know. He's also one of the most warm-hearted.

Thoughtful2 My philosophy professor is my role model, definitely. Her class is the most thought-provoking one I've ever attended. Someday, I'd like to be as well respected as she is.

Amber334 I've always wanted to be more like my sister Tonya. While I tend to worry a lot, Tonya is the most easygoing person in our family. She never lets little problems bother her.

B Pair work Tell your partner about someone you consider a role model. Explain why you respect and admire that person. Your partner will then tell the class about the person.

"Bruno has an enormous amount of respect for his grandfather. He started his own business when he was 18 years old . . ."

2 LISTENING
People who make a difference

🔊 **A** Listen to Luisa talk about her grandmother and Chu Lan talk about his tennis coach. How do Luisa and Chu Lan feel about the people they are describing?

🔊 **B** Listen again. In what ways did these people influence Luisa and Chu Lan? Write two ways for each.

	How did Luisa's grandmother influence her?	How did Chu Lan's coach influence him?
1.		
2.		

LESSON B ▶ People we admire

1 Role models (STARTING POINT)

Learning aim: Discuss role models and see superlative compound adjectives in context (10–15 minutes)

A

- Books closed. Ask Ss to define *role model*. (Answer: a person whose behavior is imitated by others because it's admirable) Ask Ss if they think it is important to have role models.
- Books open. Explain the task. Read the posts aloud. Check that Ss understand the following vocabulary.

> **Vocabulary**
> **open up** say what you honestly think
> **stick together** support and help each other

- Ss work individually to answer the question.
- Go over answers with the class.

> **Possible answers**
> RobertD: friendship
> Alena92: hard work, open-mindedness
> OwnDrummer: independent thinking
> Sporty_girl: kindness, professionalism
> Thoughtful2: intellectual curiosity, respect
> Amber334: confidence

B Pair work

- Explain the task. Read the example answer aloud. Ss work in pairs to do the activity.
- Have Ss share their partner's answers with the class.

2 People who make a difference (LISTENING)

Learning aim: Develop skills in listening for gist and details (15–20 minutes)

A 🔊 **[CD 3, Track 14]**

- Explain the task. Read the question aloud to the class. Ask Ss to predict what kinds of things Luisa and Chu Lan will say. Check that Ss understand the following vocabulary.

> **Vocabulary**
> **think back on it** rethink more carefully about something that happened in the past

- Play the recording as Ss listen for the answers to the question. Replay as many times as needed. Ss listen and check their answers.
- Go over the answers with the class.

> **Possible answers**
> Luisa respects her grandmother and feels she is strong and very smart.
> Chu Lan feels grateful to his coach, and he feels like they were friends.

Audio script: See page T-175.

B 🔊 **[CD 3, Track 15]**

- Explain that Ss will listen again and answer the questions in the chart. Tell Ss to look at the chart and determine the information they need to complete it.
- Tell Ss to listen for the answers. Play the recording as Ss complete the chart. Replay as many times as needed. Ss listen and check their answers.
- Ss work in pairs to compare answers. Go over answers with the class.

> **Answers**
> How did Luisa's grandmother influence her?
> 1. She taught Luisa how to respect other people.
> 2. Her grandmother helped make the whole family very close.
>
> How did Chu Lan's coach influence him?
> 1. The coach's constant encouragement gave him lifelong confidence.
> 2. He helped him decide on a career in sports medicine.

Audio script: See page T-175.

UNIT 11 Exceptional people T-92

3 Superlative compound adjectives (GRAMMAR)

Learning aim: Practice using superlative compound adjectives (20–25 minutes)

> **Grammar notes**
> If one of the words in the compound adjective has an irregular superlative form (e.g., *good*, *bad*, *well*), the same irregular form is generally used in the superlative of the compound adjective.
>
> Superlative (single) adjectives:
> *He is a good writer.*
> *He is the best writer in our country.*
>
> Superlative compound adjectives:
> *He is a well-known writer.*
> *He is the best-known writer in our country.*

- Books closed. Write on the board:

  My grandfather is the most open-minded person I've ever known.

  Ask Ss to identify the adjective. (Answer: open-minded) Ask: *What is the function of the phrase* the most*?* (Answer: It makes the adjective a superlative.) Ask Ss how many people are being compared in the sentence. (Answer: more than two)

- Books open. Discuss the information in the grammar box and read the example sentences.

A

- Have Ss look at the Starting Point on page 92 again. Explain the task and read the question aloud.
- Go over answers with the class.

> **Answers**
> There are eight superlative compound adjectives:
> the best-looking
> the hardest-working
> the least narrow-minded
> the most easily impressed
> the best-trained
> the most warm-hearted
> the most thought-provoking
> the most easygoing

B

- Explain the task. Read the phrases and example answer aloud. Answer any questions about vocabulary. Ss work individually to complete the activity.
- Ss work in pairs to compare their answers. Go over answers with the class.

> **Answers**
> 1. the most awe-inspiring place
> 2. the most widely read book
> 3. the best-looking man
> 4. the most thirst-quenching beverage
> 5. the most highly developed mind
> 6. the most warm-hearted friend / the warmest-hearted friend
> 7. the most far-reaching plan / the farthest-reaching plan
> 8. the most thought-provoking novel
> 9. the best-defined project / the most well-defined project
> 10. the worst-intentioned person / the most badly intentioned person

C

- Explain the task. Read the phrases and the example answer aloud. Answer any questions about vocabulary.
- Ss work individually to complete the sentences. Then Ss work in pairs to compare answers.
- Go over answers with the class.

> **Possible answers**
> 1. The most awe-inspiring natural place I've ever been to is the Grand Canyon.
> 2. The most widely read magazine in the country is probably *National Geographic*.
> 3. In my opinion, the best-looking actor in the world is Robert Pattinson.
> 4. On a hot day, the most thirst-quenching drink is iced tea.
> 5. The most thought-provoking movie I've ever seen is *Les Misérables*.
> 6. The warmest-hearted / the most warm-hearted person I know is my mother.
> 7. The best-looking leader my country has ever had was John F. Kennedy.

UNIT 11 Exceptional people

3 GRAMMAR

Superlative compound adjectives

Superlative compound adjectives generally follow the same hyphenation rules as compound adjectives.

The superlative form of compound adjectives is most often formed by adding *the most* and *the least*. There is never a hyphen after *most* or *least*.
I'm not **the most easily impressed** person.
Tonya is **the most easygoing** person in our family.
He's **the least narrow-minded** man I know.

When the first word of a compound adjective is an adjective or adverb of one or sometimes two syllables, the superlative can also be formed by adding *the* and using the superlative form of the first word.
He is **the hardest-working** man I know.
They may not be the smartest or **the best-looking** people in the world.

Compound adjectives in their superlative form can also occur after the verb *be* without a noun.
Of all the men I know, he's **the hardest working**.

GRAMMAR PLUS see page 127

A Look at the Starting Point on page 92 again. How many superlative compound adjectives can you find?

B Rewrite these phrases using the superlative form of the compound adjective.

1. an awe-inspiring place
   the most awe-inspiring place
2. a widely read book
3. a good-looking man
4. a thirst-quenching beverage
5. a highly developed mind
6. a warm-hearted friend
7. a far-reaching plan
8. a thought-provoking novel
9. a well-defined project
10. a bad-intentioned person

C Complete these sentences with the superlative compound adjectives you wrote in part B and your own ideas. Share your answers with a partner.

1. . . . natural place I've ever been to is . . .
   The most awe-inspiring natural place I've ever been to is the Grand Canyon.
2. . . . magazine in the country is probably . . .
3. In my opinion, . . . actor / actress in the world is . . .
4. On a hot day, . . . drink is . . .
5. . . . movie I've ever seen is . . .
6. . . . person I know is . . .
7. . . . leader my country has ever had is / was . . .

LESSON B People we admire 93

4 VOCABULARY
Phrasal verbs

A Read the sentences below. Then match the phrasal verbs in boldface with their definitions.

a. take care of
b. defend or support
c. go see if someone is all right
d. rely on
e. confront
f. overcome
g. resemble (an older relative) in looks or character
h. achieve what is expected

___ 1. It's only natural for children to **look to** their parents for advice.

___ 2. Sometimes we need to **get through** difficulties in order to succeed.

___ 3. Before parents go to bed, they should **check on** their kids and see if they're OK.

___ 4. I expect my children to **look after** me when I reach old age.

___ 5. Parents need to teach their children to **face up to** their problems and solve them.

___ 6. When I argue with my sister, it seems like my parents **side with** her.

___ 7. The children of accomplished parents often find it difficult to **live up to** the high expectations people have for them.

___ 8. When it comes to finances, I **take after** my dad; he could never save money either.

B Pair work Discuss the sentences in part A with a partner. Comment on the statements, and talk about how they apply to your life.

"I find that the older I get, the more I look to my parents for advice."

VOCABULARY PLUS see page 140

5 DISCUSSION
Everyday heroism

A Pair work Read what Farah says about heroic behavior. What is her definition of a hero? Do you agree with the definition? Do you have other examples?

To me, heroes often aren't the most widely recognized people, and on the surface, their actions don't necessarily seem to be the most awe inspiring. A hero could be a parent who, after an exhausting day, helps a child with a difficult homework assignment. It could be a person on the street who picks up and returns something you didn't realize you'd dropped, someone who stops by to check on you when you're ill, someone who sides with you when you've been wronged, or someone who takes time out of a busy schedule to help you with a problem. A hero is not just a person who has the courage to take a risk; he or she is also a person who has the courage to always be kind to people no matter what they're going through.
Farah, 26

B Group work Discuss these situations. What would you do to make a difference?

a Your next-door neighbor fell and broke her leg. She lives by herself.

b The condition of your neighborhood park has deteriorated, and fewer and fewer people are using it.

c Children in a nearby low-income neighborhood seem to have few opportunities for academic success.

d A friend of yours has lost his or her job and can't seem to find another one.

"I would check on my neighbor from time to time and help her with some of her daily chores."

4 Phrasal verbs (VOCABULARY)

Learning aim: Learn and practice using phrasal verbs (10–15 minutes)

A
- Books closed. Ask Ss to define *phrasal verb*. (Answer: a verb plus a particle, such as *down*, *into*, *out*, or *up*; the meaning of a phrasal verb is different from the meaning of its parts) Ask Ss to call out some phrasal verbs they already know, and write them on the board.
- Books open. Explain the task. Read the definitions and the sentences with the phrasal verbs aloud. Answer any questions about vocabulary.
- Ss work individually to complete the activity. Go over answers with the class.

Answers			
1. d	3. c	5. e	7. h
2. f	4. a	6. b	8. g

B Pair work
- Explain the task. Read the example answer aloud.
- Ss work in pairs to comment on the sentences in part A.
- Have Ss share their partner's answers with the class.

5 Everyday heroism (DISCUSSION)

Learning aim: Talk about everyday heroes and practice the lesson vocabulary (15–20 minutes)

A Pair work
- Explain the task. Read the questions and text aloud. Answer any questions about vocabulary.
- Have Ss think about their answers individually. Ss work in pairs to compare their answers.
- Have Ss share their partner's answers with the class.

Answers

Her definition is someone who is kind to people no matter what they're going through.

Answers to the second and third questions will vary.

B Group work
- Explain the task. Read the situations aloud. Answer any questions about vocabulary.
- Ss work in groups to do the activity.
- Have a S from each group report on the group's answers to the class.

Possible answers
a. I would check on my neighbor from time to time and help her with some of her daily chores.
b. I would try to organize a community group to clean the park together and restore it.
c. I would volunteer to tutor.
d. I might help my friend do a job search.

Optional activity: *My hero* (15–20 minutes)

Ss discuss heroes.
- Ss work in groups to choose one modern-day hero. Tell Ss to think of reasons why the person is a hero and what they admire about the person.
- Have one S from each group tell the class the hero they chose and why. Make a chart on the board with the name of each hero. Ask a S from each group to write their reasons in the chart.
- Have the class choose one hero from the chart. If Ss can't agree, have the class vote on one hero.

To help Ss with the discussion in this exercise, download the Fresh Idea *Can I add something here?* from the Teacher Support Site.

6 A champion for women in Africa (READING)

Learning aim: Develop skills in understanding vocabulary in context, reading for specific information, making inferences, and giving a personal reaction to a reading (25–30 minutes)

A Pair work

- Books closed. Ask Ss what *NGOs* are and what they do. (Answer: *NGO* stands for *nongovernmental organization*. They are private institutions that are independent from the government. They usually work to make positive changes in a country or a particular area.)
- Books open. Explain the task. Read the title of the article aloud. Ask Ss to define *social entrepreneur*. (Answer: someone who creates an organization to help with or focus on social issues)
- Ss work in pairs to discuss the question. Go over the answer with the class.

> **Possible answer**
> UNICEF – helps educate and feed underprivileged and impoverished children

- Have Ss read the article silently to themselves. Check that Ss understand the following vocabulary.

> **Vocabulary**
>
> **dogged** persistent
>
> **can't be done-ers** people who say that something isn't possible
>
> **beneficiaries** people who receive help, money, or support from a person or group
>
> **never take your eye off the ball** a common expression that comes from sports meaning "don't become distracted by other influences, and keep your main goal as your priority"
>
> **gut feeling** a spontaneous, emotional response to something; a feeling that is not necessarily logical or well thought out, but feels like the right thing to do anyway

B

- Explain the task. Ss work individually to complete the activity.
- Go over answers with the class.

> **Answers**
> 1. T   2. NG   3. NG   4. F   5. T   6. T

> **Optional activity:** *Fill in the blanks* (15 minutes)
> **Ss write a cloze exercise.**
> - Ss work in pairs to write three or four sentences about the article, leaving a word or two blank.
>   Example: *Ann Cotton, a _____ _____, makes a big difference in women's lives.*
>   Make sure Ss understand that they shouldn't copy sentences directly from the article; they should write about the article in their own words.
> - Tell Ss to close their books. Have pairs exchange sentences and fill in the blanks. Then have them check each other's answers.

C Group work

- Explain the task. Read the questions aloud.
- Ss work in groups to discuss the questions.
- Ask groups to share their ideas with the class.

> **Possible answers**
> 1. It is successful because she listened to people's problems before trying to help them. She was successful at getting donors to give money because they could see the program was working. Camfed has attracted and retained many outstanding people to work for the organization. Many people who received help from Camfed and who were transformed through education now head programs.
> *Answers to the second question will vary.*
>
> 2. Answers will vary.

For an alternative reading text or extra practice, download the Worksheet **11.2 Humanitarian** from the Teacher Support Site.

Do your students need more practice?	
Assign . . .	for more practice in . . .
Grammar Plus 11B	Grammar
Vocabulary Plus 11B	Vocabulary
Online Vocabulary Accelerator 11B	Vocabulary
Workbook Lesson B	Grammar, Vocabulary, Reading
Online Workbook Lesson B	Grammar, Vocabulary, Reading, Listening

UNIT 11 Exceptional people

6 READING
A champion for women in Africa

A **Pair work** Do you know any nongovernmental organizations (NGOs)? Discuss some of the ways they are making a change. Then read the article.

ANN COTTON, SOCIAL ENTREPRENEUR

The following is an interview with Ann Cotton, founder and chief executive of the Campaign for Female Education (Camfed), an NGO whose programs invest in the education of girls and young women and have benefited over two million children in the poorest areas of Africa.

How do you define a social entrepreneur? Someone who witnesses the pain and struggle in the lives of others and is compelled to act and to work with them.

What skills are needed to be a social entrepreneur? You need to be absolutely dogged. You need to listen to the people experiencing the problems, and their ideas need to crowd out the words of the "can't be done-ers."

How did your work as a former teacher and head of children's assessment help in setting up Camfed? There will always be children who don't fit the institution and whose sense of exclusion is reinforced day by day. Their experience shaped my approach to children and young people in Africa.

How did you learn how to run a successful charity? I learned by doing, and from others who were encouraging and generous in their help. I belonged to a community of activists that was inspirational.

How did you manage the growth of Camfed from supporting 32 girls, with £2,000 raised from selling your homemade cakes, to a £3,000,000 NGO? Lucy Lake [currently chief executive officer] and I built the whole model from the grassroots up. Donors could see it was working and began to get behind us in increasing numbers. We attract and retain outstanding individuals. In Africa, the early beneficiaries head the programs – young women who share a background of rural poverty, transformation through education, and the courage to bring about change.

What has been the key to the success of Camfed? Never take your eye off the ball. Always remember that you and everyone on the team are the servant of the cause – in our case, girls' education and young women's leadership in Africa.

What advice would you give tomorrow's social entrepreneurs? Be greedy for social change, and your life will be endlessly enriched. The only failure lies in not trying, or giving up.

What is the best piece of management advice you have received? Have faith in your intuition and listen to your gut feeling.

Source: "Leading Questions," interview by Alison Benjamin, *The Guardian*

B Are these statements about the reading true (*T*), false (*F*), or is the information not given (*NG*) in the interview? Write the correct letters.

____ 1. According to Ann Cotton, a social entrepreneur feels driven to help those who suffer in life.

____ 2. Ann Cotton's experience of being excluded in school has guided her approach to setting up Camfed.

____ 3. Today, Camfed continues to fund its programs through cake sales.

____ 4. Camfed's programs are run only by the most highly trained experts in management.

____ 5. Camfed's cause is to educate young women in Africa and encourage them to become leaders.

____ 6. Ann Cotton thinks managers should trust their instincts.

C **Group work** Discuss these questions with your group.

1. How does Ann Cotton explain the success of Camfed? Which of the factors mentioned do you think were the most important?

2. Do you think Ann Cotton is an exceptional individual, or could anyone have done what she did? Explain your answer.

12 BUSINESS MATTERS

LESSON A ▶ Entrepreneurs

1 STARTING POINT
Success stories

A Match these descriptions of successful companies with the company name.

___ 1. The Body Shop   ___ 2. Google   ___ 3. Sanrio

a. Larry Page and **Sergey Brin** started this innovative company in a dorm room at Stanford University. They didn't get along at first, and had they been unable to work together, the most widely used Internet search engine might never have been created. Should you ask about their company's goal, they'll probably smile and tell you it's to organize all of the world's information in order to make it accessible and useful.

b. Should you want to buy natural skin and hair care products, this company offers over 1,200 choices. **Anita Roddick** started the company to support her family. Had she been wealthy, she might not have gone into business. These stores communicate a message about human rights and environmental issues. The company is famous for its fair trade practices in impoverished communities.

c. In 1960, **Shintaro Tsuji** created a line of character-branded lifestyle products centered around gift-giving occasions. However, had this Tokyo-based company not created Hello Kitty, it wouldn't have become nearly so successful. Hello Kitty goods are in demand all over the world. They include purses, wastebaskets, pads and pens, erasers, cell phone holders, and much, much more.

B Pair work Discuss these questions.

1. What might be some reasons for the success of these companies?
2. Can you think of other successful companies? What do they offer?

2 LISTENING
Unsuccessful endeavors

A Group work Brainstorm some of the factors that can make a new business fail.

B Listen to two people discuss their unsuccessful attempts to start a business. What types of business did they try to get into? Why did they choose those types? Complete the chart.

	Type of business	Reason for choosing it
1.		
2.		

C Listen again. Write the main reasons why each attempt failed.

1. _____
2. _____

96   UNIT 12   Business matters

12 BUSINESS MATTERS
LESSON A ▶ Entrepreneurs

> In this unit, Ss use subject-verb inversion in conditional sentences and adverb clauses of condition to talk about business and jobs.

1 Success stories (STARTING POINT)

Learning aim: Discuss successful companies and see subject-verb inversion in context (10–15 minutes)

A
- Books closed. Ask Ss to call out names of successful companies or brand names that are very popular. Write them on the board.
- Books open. Explain the task. Read the company names and descriptions aloud.
- Ss work individually to complete the activity.
- Go over answers with the class.

Answers		
1. b	2. a	3. c

B Pair work
- Explain the task. Read the questions aloud. Ss work in pairs to discuss the questions.
- Have pairs share their answers with the class.

2 Unsuccessful endeavors (LISTENING)

Learning aim: Develop skills in listening for gist and details (20–25 minutes)

A Group work
- Books closed. Ask Ss if they can think of any businesses that have failed.
- Books open. Explain the task. Ss work in groups to brainstorm some factors.
- Have a S from each group share the group's answers with the class.

Possible answers
The market was too small for the product or service.
It wasn't well-advertised.
There wasn't enough money to run the business.
There was a poor economy at the time.

B 🔊 [CD 3, Track 16]
- Explain the task. Tell Ss to look at the chart and determine the information they need to complete it. Check that Ss understand the following vocabulary.

Vocabulary
residential an area with only homes – no businesses or offices
bad sign something that suggests an unpleasant event or result could occur
keep track of maintain up-to-date information about

- Play the recording. Ss listen for the answers and complete the chart. Replay as many times as needed. Ss listen and check their answers.
- Ss work in pairs to compare answers. Go over answers with the class.

Answers
1. Type of business: restaurant
   Reason: She always loved cooking.
2. Type of business: develop and sell an app
   Reason: He heard you could get rich and didn't need much money to start.

Audio script: See page T-175.

C 🔊 [CD 3, Track 17]
- Explain that Ss will listen again for the reasons each business failed.
- Play the recording once as Ss listen for the reasons. Play the recording again while Ss write their answers. Replay as many times as needed. Ss listen and check their answers.
- Go over answers with the class.

Answers
1. didn't go slowly; not enough regular customers; poor location; had to charge high prices
2. couldn't think of any good ideas for apps that hadn't been done already

Audio script: See page T-175.

UNIT 12   Business matters   T-96

3 Subject-verb inversion in conditional sentences (GRAMMAR)

Learning aim: Practice using subject-verb inversion in conditional sentences (20–25 minutes)

> **Grammar notes**
>
> In past conditional sentences, the event in the *if* clause did not happen. These sentences state what is contrary to the fact.
>
> The fact:
> *It wasn't a nice day. We didn't have a good time.*
>
> Conditional sentence:
> *If it had been a nice day, we would have had a good time.*

- Books closed. Write on the board:

  If he had studied more, his grade would have been better.

  Ask: *Did he study a lot?* (Answer: no) *Did he do well on the test?* (Answer: no)

- Write on the board:

  Had he studied more, his grade would have been better.

  Ask: *Is this sentence different in meaning from the first?* (Answer: no) Ask Ss how the sentence is different. (Answer: The subject and verb have been inverted, and *if* is not included.)

- Books open. Discuss the information in the grammar box and read the example sentences.

A

- Have Ss look at the Starting Point on page 96 again. Explain the task and read the question aloud.
- Go over answers with the class.

> **Answers**
>
> Paragraph a:
> *Should you ask about their company's goal, they'll probably smile . . .*
>
> Paragraph b:
> *Had she been wealthy, she might not have gone into business.*

B

- Explain the task. Read the sentences and the example answer aloud. Answer any questions about vocabulary.
- Ss work individually to complete the activity. Then Ss work in pairs to compare answers.
- Go over answers with the class.

> **Possible answers**
>
> 1. Had that company taken the competition into consideration, it wouldn't have gone out of business.
> 2. Had that fast-food chain offered healthy options, its sales might not be down.
> 3. Had Terry developed a serious business plan, she wouldn't have missed a number of opportunities.
> 4. Had I not decided to go to business school, I might not have started my own business.
> 5. Should the government encourage international business, the economy might not slow down.
> 6. Had my friends and I known enough about the potential of the Internet, we would have started an online business.
> 7. Had I not known it would take 10 years to pay off my college loans, I might not have chosen an affordable school.
> 8. Had I not thought my friend's business idea would fail, I might have lent her some money.

C Pair work

- Explain the task. Read the beginning of each sentence aloud.
- Ss work individually to complete the sentences. Then Ss work in pairs to share their answers.
- Have Ss share their partner's answers with the class.

UNIT 12 Business matters

3 GRAMMAR

Subject-verb inversion in conditional sentences

In past unreal conditional sentences, people sometimes replace *if* by inverting the subject and the auxiliary *had*. This occurs mainly in more formal speech and writing.
If they **had been** unable to work together, the search engine **might never have been** created.
Had they **been** unable to work together, the search engine **might never have been** created.

The same construction is possible for negative sentences. Notice that negative forms are not contracted and *not* is separated from *had* in these sentences.
If this company **hadn't created** Hello Kitty, it **wouldn't have become** nearly so successful.
Had this company **not created** Hello Kitty, it **wouldn't have become** nearly so successful.

In present and future real conditionals, people often replace *if* by putting *should* at the beginning of the sentence. Note that this use of *should* does not express obligation.
If you **want** to buy natural skin care products, this company offers over 1,200 choices.
Should you **want** to buy natural skin care products, this company offers over 1,200 choices.

GRAMMAR PLUS *see page 128*

A Look at the Starting Point on page 96 again. Can you find other conditional sentences with subject-verb inversion?

B Combine these pairs of sentences using conditional clauses and subject-verb inversion. Then compare with a partner. Sometimes more than one answer is possible.

1. That company didn't take the competition into consideration. It went out of business.
   Had that company taken the competition into consideration, it wouldn't have gone out of business.

2. That fast-food chain hasn't offered any healthy food options. Its sales are down.

3. Terry didn't develop a serious business plan. She missed a number of opportunities.

4. I decided to go to business school. I started my own business.

5. The government doesn't encourage international business. The economy is slowing down.

6. My friends and I didn't know enough about the potential of the Internet. We didn't start an online business.

7. I knew it would take 10 years to pay off my college loans. I chose an affordable school.

8. I thought my friend's business idea would fail. I didn't lend her any money.

C **Pair work** Complete these sentences with your own information, and share them with a partner.

1. Had I saved more money when I was younger, . . .
2. Should all the students in the class start a small business, . . .
3. Had I not decided to take this English course, . . .
4. Had I followed my parents' advice, I would have . . .
5. Should I have the opportunity to start a business, I might . . .
6. Had I known five years ago what I know now, I'd probably . . .

LESSON A Entrepreneurs

4 VOCABULARY
Prepositions following *work*

A The expressions on the left are composed of *work* and a preposition. Match them with their definitions on the right.

1. work **against** your interests ____
2. work **around** a problem ____
3. work **for** a boss ____
4. work **toward** a goal ____
5. work **off** a debt ____
6. work **on** a task ____

a. be employed by
b. apply effort to
c. make it harder (for someone) to achieve something
d. work while avoiding (a difficulty)
e. work in order to achieve
f. work in order to eliminate

B Complete each statement with the correct preposition.

1. Entrepreneurs don't waste time trying to solve insolvable problems; they work _____ them.
2. Inexperience can work _____ young people looking for jobs.
3. Workers are happier when they work _____ a variety of projects, not just the same one.
4. My uncle lent me $4,000 to buy a car, but he's letting me work _____ part of the loan by painting his house.

VOCABULARY PLUS see page 141

5 DISCUSSION
Too good to be true?

A Read these advertising messages for different job opportunities. Which do you find the most believable? Which do you find the least? Why?

1 Break into the fashion industry! Our classes are your first step to working toward your goal of becoming a glamorous fashion model.

2 Start your career in real estate. You can buy houses for as little as $2,000 and resell them for a huge profit with our real-estate buying program.

3 Get paid for your time on social networking sites. Earn thousands every month just for posting comments!

4 How would you like to get paid just for going shopping? Does it sound too good to be true? It's not. Ask us how!

5 Invest like a professional. Send us $50 for information on how to make millions in the stock market.

Useful expressions

Expressing suspicion
That's a little hard to believe.
It sounds fishy to me.
It sounds too good to be true.

"In my opinion, the most believable one is number three. I read that companies pay people to write positive posts about their products. The one I found hardest to believe is . . ."

B **Group work** Discuss the questions with your group.

1. What would probably happen if you replied to an ad like one of those above?
2. What are some other examples of hard-to-believe advertisements?
3. Who do you think is attracted to these types of messages? Why?

4 Prepositions following *work* (VOCABULARY)

Learning aim: Learn and practice using expressions composed of *work* and a preposition (10–15 minutes)

A

- Explain the task. Read the expressions aloud. Answer any questions about vocabulary.
- Ss work individually to complete the activity.
- Go over answers with the class.

Answers		
1. c	3. a	5. f
2. d	4. e	6. b

B

- Explain the task. Ss work individually to complete the activity. Then Ss work in pairs to compare their answers.
- Go over answers with the class.

Answers			
1. around	2. against	3. on	4. off

5 Too good to be true? (DISCUSSION)

Learning aim: Talk about job opportunities (15–20 minutes)

A

- Books closed. Ask Ss what *too good to be true* means. (Answer: something that seems so good that you can't believe it's actually possible)
- Books open. Explain the task. Read the messages and example answer aloud. Answer any questions about vocabulary.
- Point out the Useful Expressions box. Give an example of how to use each expression.
- Ss work individually to think of answers to the questions. Discuss Ss' opinions as a class.

B Group work

- Explain the task. Read the questions aloud. Answer any questions about vocabulary.
- Ss work in groups to do the activity.
- Have a S from each group report on the group's answers to the class.

Optional activity: *My business* (15–20 minutes)

Ss plan a business.

- Ss work in groups. Tell Ss to agree on a business that they would like to start. Tell them they have $250,000 to start their business.
- Have each group choose a secretary to record their business expenditures. If necessary, brainstorm the types of expenditures a business would have (e.g., rent, decorating, supplies, staff, etc.) as a class.
- Have a S from each group tell the class about the group's business plan.

For more practice discussing this topic, download the Worksheet *12.1 Why did they succeed . . . or not?* from the Teacher Support Site.

UNIT 12 Business matters

6 Formal letters (WRITING)

Learning aim: Write a formal letter using five parts (40–50 minutes)

A

- Books closed. Ask Ss when someone might write a formal letter. Write their answers on the board. Ask Ss to describe the format of a formal letter. Block out the format of an imaginary formal letter on the board (no content is necessary).
- Books open. Tell Ss to read the information in the box at the top of the page and the box with the five parts of a formal letter. Ask: *Do formal letters include personal information?* (Answer: no) *What are the five parts of a formal letter?* (Answer: heading, inside address, greeting, body, and closing)
- Explain to Ss that in a formal letter, each paragraph should be brief, to the point, and only about one idea.
- Explain the task. Have Ss read the letter silently to themselves.
- Have Ss label the letter with the five parts listed in the box.
- Go over answers with the class. Have Ss say what information is in each part.

Answers

1 (heading):
335 Henry St.
New York, NY 10002
July 10, 2014

2 (inside address):
Mr. Jonathan Hayes, Director
Institute for Study Abroad
1472 Park Avenue
Summit, NJ 07091

3 (greeting):
Dear Mr. Hayes:

4 (body):
I am writing to request . . . I look forward to receiving the information.

5 (closing):
Sincerely,
Donna Malnick

B

- Explain the writing task. Ss work individually to write their letters. Remind Ss to include all five parts of a formal letter.
- Go around the class and help as needed.
- Ss work in pairs to exchange letters and take turns suggesting improvements.
- Go around the class and help as needed. Encourage Ss to ask and answer follow-up questions about the letter and ask about anything they don't understand.

Do your students need more practice?	
Assign . . .	for more practice in . . .
Grammar Plus 12A	Grammar
Vocabulary Plus 12A	Vocabulary
Online Vocabulary Accelerator 12A	Vocabulary
Workbook Lesson A	Grammar, Vocabulary, Writing
Online Workbook Lesson A	Grammar, Vocabulary, Writing

6 WRITING
Formal letters

Formal letters don't include personal information that is irrelevant to the topic. Unlike personal letters, formal letters tend to avoid contractions and idioms.

A Read this formal letter. Then label the five parts listed in the box.

1. The **heading** includes your address and the date. It typically goes in the top left corner. If you use letterhead stationery with an address, only the date is added.
2. The **inside address** is below the heading. It contains the addressee's name, title (if you know it), and address.
3. For the **greeting**, you should write "Dear" and "Mr." or "Ms." along with the person's family name. If you don't have a specific person to contact, write "Dear Sir or Madam." The greeting is usually followed by a colon (:).
4. The **body** of the letter follows. The first paragraph is used to state the reason for the letter. The paragraphs that follow should each focus on only one point. The letter generally concludes by thanking the reader in some way.
5. The **closing** includes a closing phrase, your signature, and your name and title (if you have one).

---

1 — (335 Henry St.
New York, NY 10002
July 10, 2014)

DM
DONNA MALNICK

Mr. Jonathan Hayes, Director
Institute for Study Abroad
1472 Park Avenue
Summit, NJ 07091

Dear Mr. Hayes:

I am writing to request more information concerning your study abroad programs. Your programs sound extremely interesting, and I hope to participate in one of them next year. Your Study Abroad in Paris program sounds particularly fascinating.

I would like to sign up for the Paris program beginning in June. I'm still trying to decide whether to choose the homestay option or the dormitory option. Would it be possible to send me further information about those two choices in order to help me make a decision?

I realize that all the spaces in your Paris program may already be filled. In that case, my second choice would be the Study Abroad in Toulouse program. My third choice would be your Study Abroad in Strasbourg program.

Thank you very much for your help. I look forward to receiving the information.

Sincerely,

Donna Malnick
Donna Malnick

B Imagine that you are interested in learning more about a study program. Write your formal letter to the program director expressing interest and requesting information. Include all five parts of a formal letter.

LESSON A Entrepreneurs 99

LESSON B ▶ The new worker

1 STARTING POINT
Attitudes at work

A What kinds of working conditions would you like at your job? Choose the statements you agree with.

What are you looking for in a JOB?

1. I would be happier and more productive if my workspace were neat and organized.
2. I would take almost any job provided that there were opportunities to learn.
3. I wouldn't care about a high salary if a job allowed me to balance my work, family, and social life.
4. I wouldn't mind working in an office, assuming that I had the freedom to be creative.
5. If the company I worked for dealt fairly with me, I would be loyal to it.
6. I would only take a job on the condition that it offered long-term security.
7. I would quit a job that required me to be dishonest, whether or not it were high paying.
8. Supposing I had the choice, I would prefer to work with a group rather than by myself.

B **Group work** Compare your answers with the members of your group. How are you different? Do you think you would make a harmonious group of co-workers?

2 DISCUSSION
The dream job

A Look at this checklist of considerations in choosing a job. Add two more items to the list. Then choose the three items that are the most important to you.

The ideal job . . .
- ☐ allows me to travel often.
- ☐ offers me a high salary.
- ☐ isn't stressful at all.
- ☐ doesn't require long hours.
- ☐ gives me the freedom to be creative.
- ☐ has a flexible schedule.
- ☐ lets me wear casual clothes.
- ☐ has an excellent health plan and benefits.
- ☐ has lots of opportunity for advancement.
- ☐ is close to my home or school.
- ☐ _____.
- ☐ _____.

B **Pair work** Share your ideas with a partner. Explain and compare your choices.

"For me, the ideal job should have a flexible schedule so that I always have time for family and a social life . . ."

UNIT 12 Business matters

LESSON B ▶ *The new worker*

1 Attitudes at work (STARTING POINT)

Learning aim: Discuss working conditions and see adverb clauses of condition in context (10–15 minutes)

A
- Books closed. Ask Ss to brainstorm the kinds of jobs they would like and what it is about the jobs that appeals to them. Write their ideas on the board.
- Books open. Explain the task. Read the statements aloud. Check that Ss understand the following vocabulary.

> **Vocabulary**
>
> **workspace** a person's office, cubicle, or desk
>
> **loyal** committed to a person, company, or organization
>
> **long-term security** not having to worry about losing your job or job benefits; feeling that you will have your job for a long time

- Have Ss choose the statements they agree with.

B Group work
- Explain the task and read the questions aloud. Make sure Ss understand what *harmonious* means. (Answer: working together productively without conflict)
- Ss work in groups to do the activity.
- Have a S from each group report on the group's discussion to the class.

2 The dream job (DISCUSSION)

Learning aim: Talk about dream jobs (15–20 minutes)

A
- Books closed. Ask Ss what they think *dream job* means. (Answer: the job you would have if you could choose any job in the world)
- Books open. Explain the task. Read the checklist aloud. Answer any questions about vocabulary.
- Ss work individually to choose their answers and add two more items of their own. Brainstorm possible items to add as a class, if necessary.

B Pair work
- Explain the task. Read the example answer aloud.
- Ss work in pairs to do the activity. Remind them to give reasons for their choices.
- Have Ss share their partner's choices and reasons with the class.
- As Ss share their choices, write their answers on the board. Then have the class vote on which one is the single most important aspect of a job.

> **Optional activity:** *Job match* (15–20 minutes)
>
> **Ss play the role of job counselor.**
>
> - Ss work in groups to talk about their answers for Exercise 1A and Exercise 2A. Tell groups that it is their job to recommend an ideal job for each group member based on their answers. Encourage group members to ask the job seeker follow-up questions to make an ideal match. If necessary, brainstorm different jobs, including more unusual jobs, as a class.
> - Have Ss tell the class the job that was chosen for them and why, and if they agree with the choice.

For more practice discussing this topic, download the Worksheet *12.2 Hot jobs* from the Teacher Support Site.

3 Adverb clauses of condition (GRAMMAR)

Learning aim: Practice using adverb clauses of condition (15–20 minutes)

> **Grammar notes**
> Instead of beginning with *if*, conditional clauses may begin with the following expressions: *assuming (that)*, *on the condition (that)*, *provided (that)*, *supposing (that)*, and *whether or not*.
> These expressions modify the main clause in the sentence.

- Books closed. Write on the board:

  I would work in a large, busy company provided that I had my own private office.

  Ask Ss to identify the main clause and the conditional clause. (Answer: *I would work in a large, busy company* = main clause; *provided that I had my own private office* = conditional clause) Ask Ss to describe the relationship between the two clauses. (Answer: The conditional clause expresses a condition of the main clause.)

- Books open. Discuss the information in the grammar box and read the example sentences.

A

- Have Ss look at the Starting Point on page 100 again. Explain the task and read the question aloud. Go over answers with the class.

> **Possible answers**
> 1. I would be happier and more productive <u>provided that</u> my workspace were neat and organized.
> 3. I wouldn't care about a high salary <u>on the condition that</u> a job allowed me to balance my work, family, and social life.
> 5. <u>Provided that</u> the company I worked for dealt fairly with me, I would be loyal to it.

B

- Explain the task. Ss work individually to complete the activity.
- Ss work in pairs to compare their answers. Go over answers with the class.

> **Answers**
> 1. e   2. a   3. b   4. f   5. c   6. d

C Pair work

- Explain the task. Read the beginning of each sentence and the example answer aloud. Answer any questions about vocabulary.
- Ss work individually to complete the sentences with their own information. Then Ss work in pairs to discuss their answers.
- Go over answers with the class.

> **Possible answers**
> 1. I would enjoy managing an office, assuming I had responsible people working for me.
> 2. Provided a company paid for my commute, I would be willing to live in another city.
> 3. Whether or not I have enough money in the bank, I'm going to start my own business.
> 4. I would take a reduction in salary on the condition that my boss did, too.
> 5. Supposing that I couldn't find a job, I'd be willing to relocate to another city.
> 6. I would agree to work overtime, assuming that the bosses showed their appreciation in some way.
> 7. On the condition that I were guaranteed two weeks' vacation a year, I'd accept the job.

T-101   UNIT 12   Business matters

3 GRAMMAR

Adverb clauses of condition

Conditional sentences do not necessarily use *if*. The following expressions are also used. The tense agreement in the clauses is the same as in conditional sentences with *if*.

Provided (*that*) and *on the condition* (*that*) introduce a condition on which another situation depends.
I would take almost any job **provided that** there were opportunities to learn.
I would only take a job **on the condition that** it offered long-term security.

Whether or not introduces a condition that does not influence another situation.
I would quit a job that required me to be dishonest, **whether or not** it were high paying.

Assuming (*that*) introduces an assumption upon which another condition depends.
I wouldn't mind working in an office, **assuming that** I had the freedom to be creative.

Supposing (*that*) introduces a possible condition that could influence another situation.
Supposing I had the choice, I would prefer to work with a group rather than by myself.

GRAMMAR PLUS *see page 129*

A Look at the Starting Point on page 100 again. Can you replace the sentences with *if* with another expression?

B Match the items to make logical sentences.

1. Whether or not you have a clear job description, ____
2. Assuming that you have an original idea, ____
3. On the condition that I didn't have to be away for more than two or three days, ____
4. Provided that I could find extra time, ____
5. Supposing a close friend wanted to start a business with you, ____
6. Whether or not I actually get the job, ____

a. you might be able to start a successful business.
b. I would be willing to travel on business.
c. would you jump at the opportunity?
d. I felt the interview process was a valuable experience.
e. you need to be flexible and cooperative.
f. I'd like to do some volunteer work.

C **Pair work** Complete these sentences with your own information. Then discuss them with a partner.

1. I would enjoy managing an office, assuming . . .
   I had responsible people working for me.
2. Provided a company paid for my commute, I . . .
3. Whether or not I have enough money in the bank, I . . .
4. I would take a reduction in salary on the condition that . . .
5. Supposing that I couldn't find a job, I . . .
6. I would agree to work overtime, assuming that . . .
7. On the condition that I were guaranteed two weeks' vacation a year, . . .

LESSON B The new worker

4 VOCABULARY & SPEAKING
Qualities essential for success

A Choose three qualities that are important to working alone successfully and three that are important to working well with others. Write them in the chart.

A SUCCESSFUL WORKER NEEDS TO . . . .

- have good communication skills
- have initiative
- be trustworthy
- have leadership ability
- have influence
- have charisma
- have specialized training
- have self-discipline
- be innovative
- be adaptable
- be optimistic
- be conscientious

To work alone successfully, you need to	To work well with others, you need to . . . .
have initiative	

B **Pair work** Discuss the qualities you chose. Why do you think they're important?

"I feel you can work alone successfully, provided you have initiative."

"I totally agree. You need to have a lot of initiative because you don't have a boss to tell you what to do."

VOCABULARY PLUS see page 141

5 LISTENING
Can you really learn that?

A Listen to three people who participated in workshops for their jobs. What type of workshop did each person attend?

1. Anne: _____ 2. Thomas: _____ 3. Paulina: _____

B Listen again. What did each person learn from his or her workshop experience?

Anne: _____

Thomas: _____

Paulina: _____

C **Pair work** Would you like to take part in such workshops? Why or why not? Discuss your reasons.

102 UNIT 12 Business matters

4 Qualities essential for success (VOCABULARY & SPEAKING)

Learning aim: Learn and practice using vocabulary for talking about working alone and with others (15–20 minutes)

A

- Focus Ss' attention on the picture. Ask them to describe what is happening. Elicit words and phrases such as: *working together, cooperating, collaborating,* and *working as a team*.
- Explain the task. Read the qualities aloud. Answer any questions about vocabulary.
- Ss work individually to complete the activity. Go over answers with the class.

> **Possible answers**
>
> To work alone successfully, you need to:
> have initiative, be trustworthy, have specialized training, have self-discipline, be innovative, be optimistic, be conscientious
>
> To work well with others, you need to:
> be trustworthy, have leadership ability, have influence, have charisma, have good communication skills, have specialized training, be adaptable, be optimistic, be conscientious

B Pair work

- Explain the task. Have one pair of Ss read the example conversation to the class.
- Ss work in pairs to discuss their answers.
- Have Ss share their partner's answers with the class.

5 Can you really learn that? (LISTENING)

Learning aim: Develop skills in listening for the main ideas and details (20–25 minutes)

A 🔊 [CD 3, Track 18]

- Explain the task. Read the question aloud. Check that Ss understand the following vocabulary.

> **Vocabulary**
>
> **funny** strange
>
> **ground rules** the basic guidelines for a situation
>
> **objective** based on facts and not influenced by personal feelings
>
> **addressing** identifying and talking about
>
> **tackle** try to solve or overcome a problem
>
> **put yourself in someone else's shoes** try to imagine what it is like to be in someone else's situation

- Tell Ss to listen for the workshops the speakers mention. Play the recording once as Ss listen. Play the recording again while Ss write their answers. Replay as many times as needed. Ss listen and check their answers.
- Go over answers with the class.

> **Answers**
>
> 1. Anne: communication workshop
> 2. Thomas: problem-solving workshop
> 3. Paulina: role-playing workshop

Audio script: See page T-176.

B 🔊 [CD 3, Track 19]

- Explain that Ss will listen again for what each person learned from their workshop experience.
- Play the recording once as Ss listen. Play the recording again while Ss write their answers. Replay as many times as needed. Ss listen and check their answers.
- Go over answers with the class.

> **Answers**
>
> Anne learned not to interrupt people; not to take things too personally; to criticize ideas, not people; and to respect differences.
>
> Thomas learned the benefits of working as a group to solve problems.
>
> Paulina learned how to put herself in other people's shoes to better understand their needs.

Audio script: See page T-176.

C Pair work

- Explain the task. Read the questions aloud. Ss work in pairs to do the activity.
- Have Ss share their partner's answers with the class.

6 Working with others (READING)

Learning aim: Develop skills in understanding vocabulary in context, and giving a personal reaction to a reading (25–30 minutes)

A Pair work

- Books closed. Ask Ss what *temperament* means. (Answer: the part of someone's character that affects behavior and moods – e.g., happy, angry, calm) Ask a few Ss to describe their own temperaments. Write their answers on the board.
- Books open. Explain the task. Have Ss read the article silently to themselves. Check that Ss understand the following vocabulary.

Vocabulary

diversity different types

authority the power and responsibility to make decisions for the whole group

autonomy freedom to make your own decisions

impulsive tending to do things without thinking beforehand

strive work hard to achieve a goal

integrity commitment to moral values

- Ss work individually to list three categories that their friends would fit into. Then have Ss work in pairs to discuss their answers.

B

- Explain the task. Ss work individually to complete the activity.
- Go over answers with the class.

Answers
1. e   2. c   3. g   4. a   5. b   6. d   7. f

Optional activity: *Fill in the blanks* (15–20 minutes)

Ss write a cloze exercise.

- Ss work in pairs to write three or four sentences about the article, leaving a word or two blank.
  Example: *It is important to have _____ on a team of co-workers*.
  Make sure Ss understand that they shouldn't copy sentences directly from the article; they should write about the article in their own words.
- Tell Ss to close their books. Have pairs exchange sentences and fill in the blanks. Then have them check each other's answers.

Optional activity: *Vocabulary* (15–20 minutes)

Ss practice the vocabulary from the reading.

- Have Ss look at the article again. Tell them to write down any words that they did not know before.
- Ask Ss to call out their words and write them on the board. As a class, write definitions for each word.
- Have Ss write a sentence using each word. Make sure they write sentences that show they understand the meaning of the word.
- Ask Ss to read their sentences to the class.

C Group work

- Explain the task. Read the questions aloud.
- Ss work in groups to discuss the questions.
- Ask groups to share their ideas with the class. To make sure that reporting to the class goes smoothly, groups can choose one or two members to report their ideas. Have Ss review their ideas with their own group at the end of the task to see if the group agrees with the information they will be presenting.

To help Ss with the reading, download the Fresh Idea *Instant messaging* from the Teacher Support Site.

Do your students need more practice?	
Assign . . .	for more practice in . . .
Grammar Plus 12B	Grammar
Vocabulary Plus 12B	Vocabulary
Online Vocabulary Accelerator 12B	Vocabulary
Workbook Lesson B	Grammar, Vocabulary, Reading
Online Workbook Lesson B	Grammar, Vocabulary, Reading, Listening

6 READING
Working with others

A Pair work Do your friends tend to have similar values and temperaments? Read the article and make a list of three categories that your friends would fit into.

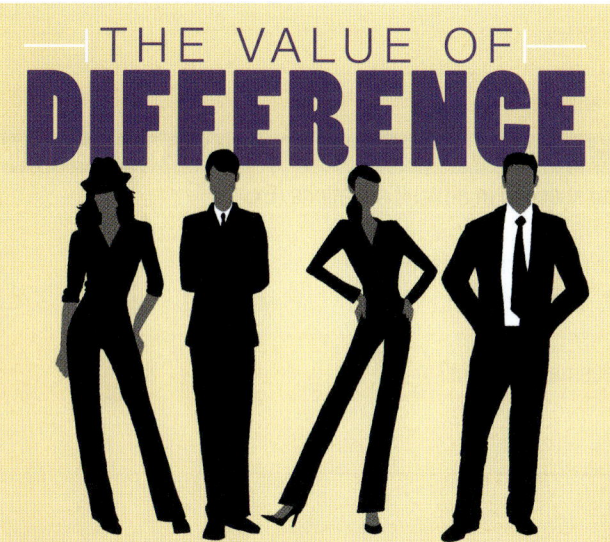

THE VALUE OF DIFFERENCE

Every person is unique. We work with many people who are different from us. It is important to realize that differences are good and to appreciate that not all people are like us. On a team, the strengths of one worker can overcome the weaknesses of another. The balance created by such variety makes a team stronger.

There are three basic ways that people differ from one another: values, temperament, and individual diversity (gender, age, etc.).

Values are the importance that we give to ideas, things, or people. While our values may be quite different, organizational behavior expert Stephen Robbins suggests that people fall into one of three general categories:

Traditionalists: People in this category value hard work, doing things the way they've always been done, loyalty to the organization, and the authority of leaders.

Humanists: People in this category value quality of life, autonomy, loyalty to self, and leaders who are attentive to workers' needs.

Pragmatists: People in this category value success, achievement, loyalty to career, and leaders who reward people for hard work.

Another important way in which people differ is temperament. Your temperament is the distinctive way you think, feel, and react to the world. All of us have our own individual temperament. However, experts have found that it is easier to understand the differences in temperament by classifying people into four categories:

Optimists: People with this temperament must be free and not tied down. They're impulsive, they enjoy the immediate, and they like working with things. The optimist is generous and cheerful and enjoys action for action's sake.

Realists: People with this temperament like to belong to groups. They have a strong sense of obligation and are committed to society's standards. The realist is serious, likes order, and finds traditions important.

Futurists: People with this temperament like to control things and are also self-critical. They strive for excellence and live for work. The futurist focuses on the future and is highly creative.

Idealists: People with this temperament want to know the meaning of things. They appreciate others and get along well with people of all temperaments. The idealist is romantic, writes fluently, and values integrity.

Source: *Job Savvy: How to Be a Success at Work*, by LaVerne Ludden

B Match the categories from the article with the descriptions.

1. traditionalist ____
2. humanist ____
3. pragmatist ____
4. optimist ____
5. realist ____
6. futurist ____
7. idealist ____

a. generous and cheerful; enjoys action for action's sake
b. serious and likes order; has a strong sense of obligation
c. values quality of life; attentive to workers' needs
d. strives for excellence; focuses on the future
e. values doing things the way they've always been done
f. romantic; writes fluently; values integrity
g. values loyalty to career, success, and achievement

C Group work Discuss these questions. Then share your answers with the class.

1. How would you categorize your own values and temperament? Give examples.
2. Which category of people would you prefer to work with on a challenging project? Explain.

LESSON B The new worker 103

COMMUNICATION REVIEW
UNITS 10–12

✓ SELF-ASSESSMENT

How well can you do these things? Choose the best answer.

I can . . .	Very well	OK	A little
▸ Take part in a discussion about what people have to do to succeed in difficult situations (Ex. 1)	☐	☐	☐
▸ Understand a lecture about language learning (Ex. 2)	☐	☐	☐
▸ Describe people's personal qualities and give reasons for my descriptions (Ex. 3)	☐	☐	☐
▸ Describe and evaluate my own personal qualities (Ex. 4)	☐	☐	☐

Now do the corresponding exercises. Was your assessment correct?

1 SPEAKING
Speaking tips

A **Pair work** What would each person have to do to succeed? Think of several conditions that would work for each situation.

1. Mary has been asked to give a formal talk on a topic she knows little about.
2. Julia has been asked to give a short speech at a friend's wedding.
3. Hal is too timid to join in the group's conversation after class.
4. Tom had some bad experiences at job interviews, and now he gets really nervous before them.

B **Group work** Discuss your ideas with another pair. Do you have similar suggestions?

"Providing Mary spends time reading about the topic, she shouldn't have a problem."
"That's true, assuming she has time to do plenty of research and rehearse first."

2 LISTENING
Good language learners

🔊 **A** Listen to a lecture about good language learning. Who is the lecture for? Choose the correct answer.

☐ a. people who are learning another language
☐ b. people who are going to travel abroad
☐ c. people who want to be language teachers

🔊 **B** Listen again. Choose the compound adjectives that are used to describe good language learners.

☐ 1. highly motivated   ☐ 4. pattern-seeking   ☐ 7. well-known
☐ 2. forward-thinking   ☐ 5. open-minded   ☐ 8. self-aware
☐ 3. risk-taking   ☐ 6. well-organized   ☐ 9. widely recognized

Units 10-12
COMMUNICATION REVIEW

> Ss assess how well they have learned the communication skills in Units 10–12.

✓ Self-assessment

Review aim: Ss assess how well they have learned the material in Units 10–12 (10–15 minutes)

- Books closed. List or elicit from Ss the language and topics covered in Units 10–12.
- Books open. Explain the task. Read the list of skills aloud.
- Ss work individually to do the assessment.
- Tell Ss they will review their assessment after doing the activities in this unit.

1 Speaking tips (SPEAKING)

Review aim: Give advice on speaking and practice adverb clauses of condition (15–20 minutes)

A Pair work
- Explain the task. Read the situations aloud.
- Ss work in pairs to take turns giving advice about each situation. Make sure Ss use adverb clauses of condition. Give some examples to the class first, if necessary.

B Group work
- Explain the task. Have one pair of Ss read the example conversation to the class.
- Put pairs together and have Ss work in groups to discuss their advice from part A.
- Have a S from each group report on the group's discussion to the class.
- Have the class vote on the best advice for each situation.

2 Good language learners (LISTENING)

Review aim: Develop skills in listening for gist and details (20–25 minutes)

A 🔊 [CD 3, Track 20]
- Explain the task. Tell Ss to look at the list of possible answers. Check that Ss understand the following vocabulary.

> **Vocabulary**
> **show of hands** a vote accomplished by counting the raised hands of people in a group
> **inquisitive** curious
> **link up** connect
> **implications** probable effects

- Tell Ss to listen for the answer to the question. Play the recording once as Ss listen. Play the recording again while Ss choose the correct answer. Replay as many times as needed. Ss listen and check their answers.
- Go over the answer with the class.

> **Answer**
> c. people who want to be language teachers

Audio script: See page T-176.

B 🔊 [CD 3, Track 21]
- Explain that Ss will listen again and choose the compound adjectives that are used to describe good language learners. Read the compound adjectives aloud.
- Play the recording while Ss choose the compound adjectives. Replay as many times as needed.
- Ss work in pairs to compare answers. Go over answers with the class.

> **Answers**
> 1, 3, 4, 5, 6, 8

Audio script: See page T-176.

- To review the grammar, make copies of the audio script and have Ss work in pairs to underline all the examples of superlative compound adjectives, adverb clauses of condition, and discourse markers they can find.

3 The most and the best (DISCUSSION)

Review aim: Discuss personal qualities and practice using superlative compound adjectives (20–25 minutes)

A
- Explain the task. Focus Ss' attention on the beginning of each sentence. Read the example answer aloud.
- Ss work individually to complete the sentences. Make sure they include reasons for their answers.
- Ss work in pairs to compare answers.
- Have Ss share their partner's answers with the class.

B Pair work
- Explain the task. Have Ss say the superlative form of each compound adjective. (Answers: 1. the best-looking; 2. the most thought-provoking; 3. the most widely respected; 4. the most kind-hearted / the kindest-hearted)
- Ss work in pairs to discuss who they both would choose for each compound adjective and to write sentences.
- Have pairs share their answers with the class.

> **Optional activity:** *Class poll* **(15–20 minutes)**
> Ss vote for their favorites.
> - Write Ss' answers from part B on the board. Have Ss give reasons for their answers.
> - Ask the class to vote for the person they feel is the best example for each compound adjective.

4 Personal qualities (SPEAKING)

Review aim: Talk about personal traits and practice using character adjectives (15–20 minutes)

A
- Explain the task. Read the question and the descriptions aloud. Ask Ss to define *charismatic*, *people person*, *optimistic*, *confident*, and *adapting*.
- Give Ss time to think individually about their answers to the question.
- Have Ss share their answers with the class.

B Pair work
- Explain the task. Read the list of qualities and the example answer aloud. If necessary, brainstorm follow-up questions Ss could ask their partner.
- Ss work in pairs to do the activity.
- Have Ss share their partner's answers with the class.

> **Optional activity:** *I wish I . . .* **(10–15 minutes)**
> Ss discuss desired personal qualities.
> - Ss work in groups to talk about which personal qualities they wish they had and why.
> - Have a S from each group report on the group's answers to the class.

✓ Have Ss look at their answers to the self-assessment at the beginning of this review unit. As a class, discuss which skills were easy and which were more difficult and why.

3 DISCUSSION
The most and the best

A Complete the sentences with your own information. Add reasons for your opinions, and compare with a partner.

1. One of the most open-minded people in my family is . . .
2. I imagine that a lot of the most hardworking people . . .
3. The most forward-thinking person I've ever met is . . .
4. The majority of my friends would agree that the best-dressed celebrities include . . .
5. The most easygoing person I've ever known is . . .
6. Some of the most well-informed people I can think of are . . .

"One of the most open-minded people in my family is my uncle John. He's always willing to go to new places and try new things."

B Pair work Who are some people you both admire? Use the superlative form of these compound adjectives to write sentences about them. Give reasons.

1. good-looking
2. thought-provoking
3. widely respected
4. kind-hearted

4 SPEAKING
Personal qualities

A Which of these people is most similar to you, and which is least similar?

Rita: "I've been told that I'm a charismatic person. The truth is that I'm a people person, and I'm not afraid to share my ideas with others."

Su Lyn: "I'm very optimistic. I try to look at the good side of things, and I'm always confident that even the worst situations will turn out to be fine."

Alberto: "I've lived in three different countries and have attended six different schools. Yet I've never had problems adapting to new situations."

B Pair work Which of these are your strongest qualities? Which do you feel are most necessary to realize your own personal and professional goals?

- adaptability
- charisma
- conscientiousness
- determination
- honesty
- initiative
- optimism
- self-confidence
- self-control

"I think I'm very adaptable. Since I'd like to be an actor, and the work is unpredictable, I think that's an important quality."

GRAMMAR PLUS

1A Phrasal verbs

> **Additional phrasal verbs**
> **Separable:** call off, count out, cut off, get across, hand over, pass up, take back
> **Inseparable:** go over, hang around, live up to, look after, pick on, run out of, touch on
> **Intransitive:** catch on, come along, come over, fall apart, show up, turn out
>
> **Certain intransitive two-word phrasal verbs, when followed by a preposition, can then take an object.**
>
> back down (from)   cut back (on)   drop out (of)   give in (to)
> catch up (to)   cut down (on)   get along (with)   give up (on)
> check out (of)   drop in (on)   get away (with)   look back (on)
>
> When confronted with an argument, Mark never **backs down**.
> Mark never **backs down from** an argument.

1 Underline the phrasal verb in each sentence. Is the verb separable (S) or inseparable (I)? Is it transitive (T) or intransitive (NT)? Write the correct letters.

_S, T_ 1. The referees <u>called</u> the soccer match <u>off</u> due to heavy rain.

____ 2. Jessica asked me to come over to her house for dinner.

____ 3. Sometimes I find it hard to live up to my parents' expectations.

____ 4. Sally insulted me yesterday, but today she took back her remark.

____ 5. When entertaining, there's nothing worse than running out of food at your party.

____ 6. When Jim gave me the chance to share his apartment, I couldn't pass up the opportunity.

2 Complete the sentences with intransitive phrasal verbs and a preposition from the grammar box. Be sure to use the correct form of the verb.

1. When my grandfather and I go jogging together, I sometimes need to stop and wait for him to ____*catch up to*____ me.

2. I didn't want to try bungee jumping, but I finally _____ the pressure from my friends and tried it. It was fun!

3. Even when you fail, a true friend will never _____ you.

4. My friends and I are trying to _____ the money we spend, so on Fridays we just watch TV at my house.

5. Mia's father is successful, even though he _____ college.

6. There's a long line of people waiting to _____ the hotel.

7. I insist on honesty; I won't let anyone _____ lying to me.

1B Gerund and infinitive constructions

The verbs *forget*, *mean*, and *regret* can be followed by either an infinitive or a gerund. However, the meaning is significantly different in each case.

Forget followed by an infinitive refers to something you didn't actually do. *Forget* followed by a gerund refers to an action that you in fact did earlier.
Marcello **forgot to meet** his best friend at the train station.
Marcello never **forgot meeting** his favorite actor.

Mean followed by an infinitive means "intend." In this case, *mean* is usually used in the negative or in the past tense. *Mean* followed by a gerund means "involve or necessitate."
I **meant to visit** Sheila while I was in Hawaii, but I didn't have the chance.
Inviting Emile to the party **means inviting** Eva, too. She'd be so insulted if we didn't.

Regret followed by infinitives such as *inform*, *announce*, and *say* is a polite way of introducing bad news in official communication. *Regret* followed by a gerund means "be sorry for/about."
The corporation **regrets to inform** you that all job vacancies have been filled.
Donna really **regretted missing** her best friend's wedding.

Be + adjective expressions are often followed by an infinitive.
be amazed   be determined   be happy   be lucky
be ashamed   be eager   be hesitant   be ready

Be + adjective + preposition and verb + preposition expressions are often followed by a gerund.
be bored with   be convinced of   be good at   be used to   be worried about
apologize for   complain about   object to   participate in   take part in   think of

1 Choose the correct form of the verb.

1. Manny forgot *to do* / (*doing*) his homework for English class because he had completed it over a month ago.
2. Mina didn't mean *to frighten* / *frightening* the baby with the doll.
3. Though she didn't have much, Wendy never regretted *to spend* / *spending* money on her friends.
4. I always forget *to call* / *calling* my parents, and they get really mad at me.
5. Attending my high school reunion means *to see* / *seeing* old friends as well as people I didn't like very much.
6. We regret *to announce* / *announcing* that Flight 54 has been delayed.

2 Complete the sentences with the infinitive or gerund form of the verb in parentheses.

1. Gil is really eager ___to rekindle___ (rekindle) his relationship with Lana.
2. I've been worried about _____ (meet) my new college roommate.
3. I think you're really lucky _____ (have) so many close friends.
4. Have you thought of _____ (send) an e-card instead of mailing a card?
5. I'm ashamed _____ (say) that my college roommate and I never reconnected.
6. I would like to apologize for _____ (rehash) all these old issues.

UNIT 1 Grammar Plus 107

2A Review of verb patterns

Here are some verbs that are used with each pattern.

a. verb + infinitive
afford, fail, hasten, learn, prepare, proceed, seek, strive
I really **strive to wear** the latest styles and trends.

b. verb + object + infinitive
advise, allow, authorize, cause, convince, encourage, instruct, permit, persuade, urge
The salesperson **convinced me to buy** a dress I knew I didn't need.

c. verb + gerund
can't help, can't see, can't stand, enjoy, get through, keep on, (not) mind, miss, postpone, risk
I **can't see paying** high prices for clothes that will be out of style in a year.

d. verb + object + preposition + gerund/noun
blame (for), dissuade (from), forgive (for), interest (in), keep (from), suspect (of), thank (for)
Can I **interest you in going** on a shopping spree with me?

1 Label the words in boldface in the text below with the correct verb pattern above.

A famous saying goes, "Clothes make the man." My mother used to say that to me because I was a sloppy dresser, and she (1) _b_ **urged me to look** my best. She'd coax me to dress better, but nothing could (2) ____ **keep me from wearing** jeans. At my high school, students never (3) ____ **failed to wear** jeans to school, and my mother always sighed and tried to (4) ____ **dissuade me from leaving** the house in my old, torn jeans. On my graduation from high school, my parents gave me my first suit and (5) ____ **advised me to** "**dress** for success."

Since then, I've changed quite a bit. I really (6) ____ **enjoy dressing** fashionably. I can (7) ____ **afford to wear** stylish slacks and shirts, with well-polished shoes. It's funny, but I (8) ____ **don't miss wearing** jeans one bit.

2 Complete the sentences by putting the words in parentheses in the correct order and by choosing the correct verb form. Write the letter of the pattern from the grammar box next to each sentence.

_d_ 1. I _forgave my sister for giving away_ my old laptop. (my sister / forgive / give away / for)

____ 2. I never _____ more for quality clothes. (mind / pay)

____ 3. Harold _____ his jacket last week. (allow / wear / me)

____ 4. Shirley _____ her dry cleaning for another week. (pick up / postpone)

____ 5. Lydia's dad _____ him a necktie for Father's Day. (get / her / thank / for)

____ 6. The man stole the sneakers, and then _____ them in the mall. (wear / proceeded)

2B Cleft sentences with *what*

> To emphasize the whole sentence rather than just the part following the main verb, use a cleft sentence with *what* and a form of the verb *do*.
> I try to project a positive attitude.
> **What I try to project is** a positive attitude. *(emphasizes* a positive attitude*)*
> **What I do is** try to project a positive attitude. *(emphasizes the whole sentence)*
>
> She complained to the waiter about the quality of the food.
> **What she complained about to the waiter was** the quality of the food.
> **What she did was** complain to the waiter about the quality of the food.
>
> Cleft structures can include expressions like *the reason why, the thing that, the place where,* and *the person who.* These structures are typically used with the verb *be*.
> I'm wearing sunglasses to protect my eyes.
> **The reason why** I'm wearing sunglasses **is** to protect my eyes.
>
> I do all my shopping at the mall.
> **The place where** I do all my shopping **is** (at) the mall.

1 Rewrite these sentences as cleft sentences with *what* to emphasize the whole sentence.

1. The candidate showed the voters he was a trustworthy man.
   What the candidate did was show the voters he was a trustworthy man.
2. My mother shouldn't have made me wear my sister's old clothes.
3. I'm going to send all my shirts out to be dry-cleaned.
4. My friends call me at work all the time.
5. My father judges people too much by their appearance.
6. Employees should carry ID cards at all times.
7. Eleanor wore her mother's wedding dress at her own wedding.
8. Martin spilled spaghetti sauce on his shirt.
9. Sam bought a whole new wardrobe.
10. Mary is going to wear her diamond necklace to the party.

2 Rewrite these sentences as cleft sentences by starting them with the expressions in parentheses.

1. I'm wearing a tie to impress my boss. (the reason why)
   The reason why I'm wearing a tie is to impress my boss.
2. I lost my watch in the park. (the place where)
3. The office dress code changed last Friday. (the day when)
4. My dog wears a sweater because his fur is short. (the reason why)
5. I remember the intense expression on his face. (the thing that)
6. Lori keeps her jewelry under her bed. (the place where)

UNIT 2 Grammar Plus 109

3A Indefinite and definite articles

> In completely general statements with uncountable nouns, do not use an article before the noun. However, *the* is required when the noun is made more specific by a modifying phrase following it.
> **Ethics** is becoming an important part of the field of genetics.
> **The ethics of cloning** should be addressed by experts in the field.
>
> **Image** is an important part of success.
> **The image she projected** did not serve her well in court.
>
> **With certain exceptions, do not use *the* before:**
> countries (exceptions: *the Philippines, the United Arab Emirates, the United Kingdom, the United States*)
> streets and cities (exception: *the Hague*)
> individual lakes, bays, islands, continents, mountain peaks (exception: *the Matterhorn*)
>
> **Do use *the* before:**
> rivers, oceans, seas, gulfs, mountain ranges, peninsulas, deserts, forests

1 Do the nouns in these sentences require a definite article? Write *the*, or *X* if none is needed.

1. A large number of oil wells have been drilled in **the** Gulf of Mexico.
2. There is no room for ____ frivolity when discussing ____ safety of nuclear power.
3. ____ United States utilizes more genetically modified food than ____ Europe does.
4. You shouldn't expect ____ confidentiality when you upload anything to the Internet.
5. In a moment, our experimental driverless vehicle will turn right on ____ Elm Street.
6. Many people do not believe that ____ rights of animals should be protected.
7. A global warming monitoring station is located on top of ____ Mount Rutherford.
8. I think ____ human error is to blame for the majority of aircraft accidents.

2 Review the rules for articles on page 19. Then fill in the blanks with a definite article, an indefinite article, or *X* if none is needed. Sometimes more than one answer is possible.

(1) **X** Energy seems to be on everyone's mind these days. (2) ____ people are worried because they know that petroleum reserves are not infinite. It's also alarming that (3) ____ temperature of the earth seems to be rising year by year. Many scientists blame (4) ____ warming of the earth on (5) ____ burning of petroleum-based fuels.

However, there is no reason to give up (6) ____ hope, as (7) ____ alternatives are available. One example is (8) ____ wind farm, a collection of wind turbines that turn wind energy into electric power. Another example is (9) ____ hydroelectric facilities, which change (10) ____ energy created by moving water into electric power. (11) ____ hydroelectric facility on (12) ____ Paraná River in Brazil generates about 20 percent of the power used in the country. A final example is (13) ____ solar power. It is one of (14) ____ cleanest sources of energy and is attracting (15) ____ attention as well. Many countries, including (16) ____ United Arab Emirates, (17) ____ Spain, and (18) ____ India have built large solar power plants.

Lastly, it's important that we all conserve energy. Take (19) ____ moment to shut off and unplug any electrical items when you leave (20) ____ room.

UNIT 3 Grammar Plus

3B -ing clauses

When -ing clauses begin a sentence, the agent of the -ing clause must be the subject of the main clause that follows.
Incorrect: Trying hard to fix my computer, ~~the dog~~ kept staring at me.
(The agent of the -ing clause seems to be the dog.)
Correct: Trying hard to fix my computer, I noticed the dog staring at me.
(The agent of the -ing clause and the subject of the main clause are the same.)

Incorrect: Doing yard work, ~~his clothes~~ got very dirty.
(The agent of the -ing clause seems to be his clothes.)
Correct: Doing yard work, he got dirt all over his clothes.
(The agent of the -ing clause and the subject of the main clause are the same.)

In addition to starting a sentence, -ing clauses can also follow these expressions:
have a good time   have an easy time   have fun   spend time
have a hard time   have difficulty   have problems   waste time

1 Choose the main clause that makes sense with the -ing clause.

1. Making strange noises, _b_
   a. I knew that my computer would crash.
   b. my computer stopped working.

2. Being technophiles, ____
   a. we're never afraid to try new gadgets.
   b. the latest gadgets always interest us.

3. Talking on her cell phone, ____
   a. the car went right through a red light.
   b. Pam didn't pay attention to her driving.

4. Quickly closing her laptop, ____
   a. Meg accidentally spilled her coffee.
   b. Meg's coffee was accidentally spilled.

5. Having studied robotics at school, ____
   a. they could explain how the robot worked.
   b. the robot was no mystery to them.

2 Combine these sentences using an expression from the grammar box to start the sentence.

1. I played video games all day Saturday. I had a good time.
   I had a good time playing video games all day Saturday.

2. My brother was shopping for cars. He had a hard time.

3. Fred constantly checks his social networking pages. He wastes a lot of time.

4. I'm attending the big technology expo next week. I'm going to have fun.

5. Nash is having difficulty. He's trying to comprehend the concept of DNA storage.

6. Norah was writing a genetic technology lecture. She spent a lot of time on it.

7. The guard used the video surveillance camera to identify the intruder. He had an easy time.

8. We were trying to follow what the scientist was saying. We were having problems.

4A Reporting clauses

> In reporting clauses, verbs such as *admit*, *agree*, *announce*, *comment*, *complain*, *confess*, *disclose*, *explain*, *inform*, and *reveal* are frequently followed by an indirect object. In this case, *that* should be retained for clarity.
> Several people **agreed with me that** logic, not superstition, is the best way to make decisions.
> Max **explained to the teacher that** a black cat never means bad luck in his country.
>
> The following nouns are also often used in reporting clauses. Here, too, *that* is helpful in making the meaning clear and should be retained.
>
> | accusation | assertion | comment | explanation | response |
> |---|---|---|---|---|
> | argument | claim | decision | remark | suggestion |
>
> Bill made the **assertion that** he'd have no luck at all if it weren't for bad luck.
> Liliana repeated her **argument that** only foolish people believe in magic.
> The class rejected Niran's **suggestion that** we cancel class on Friday the 13th.

1 Using the words in parentheses, rewrite these sentences with reporting clauses in the simple past.

1. He had an irrational fear of spiders. (Luis / admit / his friend)
   Luis admitted to his friend that he had an irrational fear of spiders.

2. Some people really are luckier than others. (Min / agree / me)

3. There are too many pigeons in the park. (many people / complain / park staff)

4. He had spent his father's lucky dollar on candy. (Marco / confess / his mother)

5. It's bad luck to step on a crack in the sidewalk. (Marcie / explain / her little sister)

6. The day he met his wife was the luckiest day of his life. (Felix / announce / his wedding guests)

2 Combine the sentences using a reporting clause with one of the nouns from the grammar box.

1. Kim accused Anna of being a superstitious person. Anna didn't agree.
   Anna didn't agree with Kim's accusation that she was a superstitious person.

2. Gianna argues that everything happens for a reason. Many people disagree.

3. Leslie asserted that superstition is based in fear. Carlos didn't understand.

4. Jae-woo decided that a trip to Las Vegas was what he needed. We were surprised.

5. Ernesto commented that hard work is more important than luck. Lily repeated what he said.

6. Hiroshi claimed he had won the chess game thanks to beginner's luck. Sandra didn't believe him.

7. Patrick remarked that Tanya probably shouldn't push her luck. Tanya ignored what he said.

8. Mr. Wang responded that actions speak louder than words. I understood him.

4B Reporting clauses in the passive

> **The following verbs can be used in reporting clauses in the passive.**
> announce   deny   maintain   reveal   suggest
> confirm   estimate   observe   rumor   understand
>
> **Reporting clauses in the passive are commonly used with a variety of structures.**
> **Simple present:** It **is suggested** that passengers report anything suspicious to the driver.
> **Simple past:** It **was** flatly **denied** that a nuclear submarine had been lost in the Arctic Ocean.
> **Present perfect:** It **has been estimated** that the construction of Stonehenge took over 20 million hours.
> **Past perfect:** It **had been rumored** that a monster was living in the lake.
> **With modals:** It **couldn't be denied** that many mysteries elude scientific understanding.
> **With past modals:** It **should have been confirmed** that the flight would be delayed.
>
> **Reporting clauses in the passive are used in written and formal English and are not common in conversation.**

1 Add a reporting clause in the passive with *it* to these statements. Use the verb and the suggested structure in parentheses.

1. The lost city of Atlantis had been discovered on April Fool's Day, 1980. (announce, simple past)
   It was announced that the lost city of Atlantis had been discovered on April Fool's Day, 1980.

2. A fast-food restaurant discontinued a favorite hamburger as a publicity stunt. (reveal, present perfect)

3. Some people have a higher level of intuition than others. (understand, simple present)

4. Crop circles, patterns created by flattening crops, are a clever hoax. (can't deny, present modal)

5. The moon's pull on the earth affects the ocean tides. (maintain, simple present)

6. The politician was deceiving the nation. (should reveal, past modal)

7. A positive attitude was an important part of his cure. (observe, simple past)

8. One out of ten people falls for Internet scams every year. (estimate, past perfect)

2 Rewrite these statements with a reporting clause in the passive with *it*.

1. An unknown source maintains that the Loch Ness Monster has been sighted several times.
   It is maintained that the Loch Ness Monster has been sighted several times.

2. Archeologists have revealed that the ancient residents of Easter Island likely painted their statues.

3. Officials should have observed that there was a mysterious substance on the train floor.

4. People can't deny that ancient civilizations possessed knowledge lost to us today.

5. A newspaper has confirmed that a pack of 400 wolves was terrifying a town in Siberia.

6. The authorities have announced that 10 people on the ship got sick.

5A Sentence adverbs

> To express the speaker's attitude about the entire sentence, sentence adverbs are most often located at the beginning of the sentence and set off by a comma.
> **Predictably**, the hero of the movie won the heart of the girl.
>
> Sentence adverbs can be used in place of longer clauses that modify a sentence.
> **People were amazed that** the movie sold 26 million tickets on its opening weekend.
> **Amazingly**, the movie sold 26 million tickets on its opening weekend.
>
> **Nobody was surprised that** the sequel was also extremely popular.
> **Not surprisingly**, the sequel was also extremely popular.
>
> The following conjunctive adverbs link a sentence with a preceding idea.
> accordingly   consequently   hence   indeed   meanwhile   otherwise   thus
>
> The coming attractions ended and the movie began; **accordingly**, the audience fell silent.

1 Rewrite the sentences using sentence adverbs to replace the boldfaced words.

1. **It's apparent to me that** movies with clichéd storylines are still very popular.
   Apparently, movies with clichéd storylines are still very popular.

2. **It's fortunate that** there were good movies available on the 13-hour plane ride.

3. **I'm being honest when I say that** I just don't care for love stories, no matter how moving they may be.

4. **Nobody can question the fact that** many historical movies present an incorrect view of history.

5. **It was bad luck that** Carol's computer froze while she was streaming that movie.

6. **In essence**, that movie is a tale of good versus evil.

7. **If it fulfills its potential**, the Internet could be the first place all new movies are shown.

8. **It's obvious to me that** you are only pretending to have seen the movie.

9. **I'm being serious when I say that** if a movie is based on a book, always read the book first.

2 Complete the sentences with a conjunctive adverb from the grammar box. Sometimes more than one answer is possible.

1. A growing number of students are watching the movie rather than reading the assigned book. _Consequently_ , there has been a decrease in the reading skills of graduating seniors.

2. At the Mainstreet Theater, you sit in front of a table to watch the movie. _____, you are served by waiters who take your order and walk between the rows.

3. Moviegoers are prohibited from texting and talking during the movie; _____, anyone who violates that policy will be asked to leave.

4. The most popular movie stars demand extremely high salaries; _____ the cost of producing movies with "big names" has risen.

5. It's recommended that you buy tickets in advance; _____, you might not get a seat.

5B Such . . . that and so . . . that

In written English, *so* and *such* are most often followed by a *that* clause. However, in conversation, *so* and *such* are frequently used alone to express emphatic stress.
The host on that game show is **so** funny!
That actress plays her role **so** convincingly!
The writers of that new sitcom show **such** originality!
That was **such** a great documentary!

So much, *so little*, *so many*, and *so few* can also be used without a *that* clause and for emphatic stress.
There are **so many** reality TV shows these days!
That game show gives away **so much** money!

In conversation, *much* and *little* can be used as adverbs following *so*.
Why do you watch TV **so much**? *(much = "frequently")*
That actor is featured **so little** that I sometimes forget he's on the show. *(little = "infrequently")*

Much, *little*, *many*, and *few* can also serve as pronouns for nouns.
TV can be bad for your health. I sometimes watch so **much** (TV) my eyes hurt.
He needs more free time. He has so **little** (free time) he can't keep up with the latest TV shows.
I don't watch soap operas anymore. I've seen so **many** (soap operas) that I'm tired of them.
TV news requires reporters, but there are so **few** (reporters) that many stories aren't covered.

1 Complete these sentences with *so*, *such*, *so much*, *so little*, *so many*, or *so few*.

1. You should see the Beyoncé documentary. It's _____**so**_____ interesting!
2. It's a good night for watching TV. There are _____ new shows on!
3. Ed spent _____ money on that TV that he can't afford a stand.
4. Turn off that program right now! I've never heard _____ language!
5. _____ TV shows interest Jon that he rarely watches TV.
6. Shelby works long hours. He has _____ time for TV.

2 Complete the text with *so*, *such*, *so much*, *so little*, *so many*, or *so few*.

I've spent (1) _____**such**_____ a lot of time watching reality TV that I guess I'm sort of an expert. There are (2) _____ genres of reality TV shows that it's confusing, and the list of individual shows is (3) _____ long nobody can remember them all.
A very popular one is about fishermen in Alaska. Those guys catch (4) _____ seafood they fill up the boat! They catch a lot of viewers, too, with consistently high ratings and more than a few important awards. One low-rated show is about home renovations. In fact, (5) _____ people watch it that it's going to be canceled. My favorite is about pet cloning. It's quite popular. However, it's (6) _____ a strange show that I'm really surprised (7) _____ people like it.
I'm really glad there are channels dedicated entirely to reality TV. Honestly, I have (8) _____ interest in other TV genres that reality TV is all I watch!

6A Double comparatives

These structures are commonly used in double comparatives.

The + more / less + clause
The more I listen to classical music, the more I appreciate it.

The + comparative form of adjective + clause
The more romantic a song is, the less my brother wants to listen to it.

The + comparative form of adverb + clause
The louder Mario plays his stereo, the more his neighbors complain.

The + more / less / fewer + noun / gerund + clause
The more dancing you do, the more natural you'll feel on the dance floor.

Short double comparatives without verbs are common in conversation. Many of them end in *the better*.
The more, the merrier!
The bigger, the better!
The sooner, the better!

1 Fill in the blanks to create appropriate double comparatives. For comparatives with adjectives or adverbs, more than one answer is possible.

1. Ricky seems to play his music loud in his car in order to get attention.
   ___*The louder*___ the music is, ___*the more*___ people turn their heads.

2. This song is so catchy! _____ I listen to it, _____ I like it.

3. The price of concert tickets has really gone up. And, _____ the performer is, _____ the ticket is.

4. I love soothing background music. _____ the music is, _____ stress I feel.

5. They play music at the baseball game to get the fans excited. _____ the music plays, _____ the fans yell.

6. Practice makes perfect. _____ you practice, _____ you will become.

7. Even age won't slow that performer down. _____ she gets, _____ performances she gives.

2 Complete each conversation with one of the short double comparatives without verbs from the grammar box.

1. A: When should we officially end this meeting?
   B: _____!

2. A: How many people do you think we should invite to the party?
   B: _____!

3. A: What would you like your new house to be like?
   B: _____!

116 UNIT 6 Grammar Plus

6B Will and would for habits and general truths

> *Used to* and *would* are both used to express habits in the past.
> Before he became a big star, Mark **used to** play music on the street for money.
> Before he became a big star, Mark **would** play music on the street for money.
>
> However, *would* cannot be used with stative verbs such as *be*, *have*, *like*, *live*, *love*, *mean*, and *own*.
> **Correct:** When I was young, I **used to** have a clarinet.
> **Incorrect:** When I was young, I ~~would~~ have a clarinet.

1 Complete the sentences using *would* wherever possible. If *would* is not possible, use *used to*.

1. Before Elvis made it big, he ____would____ sing with his family on the front porch of his house in Tupelo, Mississippi.

2. I _____ own a violin that my uncle gave me for my birthday. I don't know where it is now.

3. Since the young Beethoven loved nature, he _____ take long walks along the banks of the Rhine River.

4. That performer _____ be washed up, but he has since made a remarkable comeback.

5. Before he was discovered by a Hollywood talent scout, that singer _____ regularly announce local sports events on the radio.

6. Café La Fortuna in New York City, where John Lennon _____ like to have coffee and read the newspaper, closed down in 2008.

7. In the 1990s, Pavarotti _____ perform as part of The Three Tenors with José Carreras and Plácido Domingo.

8. In high school, Madonna _____ love to dance and _____ always get excellent grades.

9. Although my family wasn't wealthy, we _____ own a concert-quality grand piano.

2 Complete the paragraph using the correct form of the verb in parentheses. Use *would* or *will* for habits and general truths wherever possible.

Music has played an important role in my life since I was very young. When I was a boy, our family (1) ___would sit___ (sit) on the green lawn in the center of town on Saturday nights listening to the town band. Between songs, I (2) _____ (like) to talk to the musicians about their instruments, which fascinated me. I (3) _____ (ask) them if I could play their trumpets and clarinets, and they (4) _____ (say) no in as gentle a way as they could. Who could have imagined that I would become an instrument maker? I've got my own family now. On warm Saturdays, I (5) _____ (take) them down to the center of town to listen to the town band. And, every time we go, my own son (6) _____ (bother) the musicians with questions and requests. After all, like father, like son!

7A Optional and required relative pronouns

> When the relative pronoun is the complement (or object) of a preposition, *whom* is required (not *who*).
> No one can live on that land now except indigenous people **to whom** special permits have been given.
>
> Similarly, *which* is required (not *that*) when the preposition precedes the relative pronoun.
> My parents' generation stood for certain principles **against which** my generation has rebelled.
>
> The relative pronoun *whose* is not only used for people. It can also represent animals or things. This relative pronoun is required.
> There are some new fitness classes **whose** purpose is to provide safe exercise for the elderly.

1 Complete the sentences with *whom*, *which*, or *whose*.

1. Junk food advertisements are particularly effective in influencing the buying patterns of the young people to ____*whom*____ they are aimed.

2. "Where is society heading?" is a difficult question, the answer to _____ I don't think anybody really knows.

3. That insurance company currently offers low-cost health plans to people _____ workplace doesn't offer any.

4. I'd like to join the debate about the future of international travel, but I'm afraid it's a subject about _____ I know almost nothing.

5. Improper or insufficient education is the root of intolerance. The world would change for the better if we understood the people against _____ we have prejudices.

6. My parents owned a fully detached house with a big yard. Unfortunately, my friends and I are all apartment dwellers for _____ owning such a house just isn't possible.

2 Review the rules for pronouns on page 55. Complete the text with the appropriate relative pronouns. Sometimes more than one answer is possible.

I once read a story about a little boy (1) __*who / that*__ received an insect – a large beetle – for his birthday. Frustrated by the insect's frantic movements, the boy turned it over and over looking for a switch (2) _____ could turn it off. Clearly, this was a boy (3) _____ understanding of animals and the natural world was extremely limited. The result was a boy for (4) _____ a living thing was indistinguishable from a toy.

Parents should expose their children to nature from a young age. There is a farm not far from the city to (5) _____ hundreds of families go every weekend. There, city kids (6) _____ might not otherwise have had the chance are able to see, and even to touch, a wide variety of living things. By encountering animals (7) _____ are real, not just pictures, children learn the important lesson that these are living creatures (8) _____ are worthy of respect, just like us.

7B As if, as though, as, the way, and like

> When *as* introduces a clause expressing a comparison, subject-verb inversion can occur in affirmative sentences.
> **With *do*:** Marissa has a lot of trouble accepting change, **as does Trina**.
> **With auxiliary verbs:** Mitt has coped well with changes at work, **as have his co-workers**.
> **With modals:** Grandma would tell us stories of the old days, **as would Grandpa**.
> **With *be*:** Marcel is wary of technology, **as is his whole family**.
>
> When both clauses have the same subject, *as if* and *as though* clauses with adjectives or past participles are frequently shortened by removing the subject and *be*.
> Bill is talking about quitting his job, **as though (he were)** single and carefree.
> Marvin sat motionless in front of his new media center, **as if (he were)** glued to the chair.
>
> Notice that we use a past form of a verb after *as if* and *as though* when these phrases are followed by a hypothetical or unreal situation.
> Bill is talking about quitting his job **as though** he **were** carefree. *(He has responsibilities.)*
> Some young people replace their gadgets every year **as if** they **had** all the money in the world.

1 Combine these sentences using a clause expressing comparison with *as*. Use subject-verb inversion.

1. The students at my new school welcomed me warmly. The teachers welcomed me, too.
   The students at my new school welcomed me warmly, as did the teachers.

2. Moving to Spain will bring about many changes in my life. Getting a new job will, too.

3. Clarissa is enjoying retirement. Her husband is also enjoying it.

4. Claudia went to a traditional Chinese opera last night. Jim went, too.

5. The teachers' union is supporting a four-day workweek. The transit workers' union is supporting this as well.

6. I've given up my car and am taking public transportation now. Several of my co-workers are taking public transportation, too.

7. I can cope well with changes. My wife can cope well with changes, too.

8. Amber believes that it is often foolish to resist change. Josh also believes that it is often foolish to do so.

2 Rewrite the sentences, shortening the longer clauses and lengthening the shorter clauses. Follow the model in the grammar box.

1. Guests in the theater felt a strange sensation, as if transported back in time.
   Guests in the theater felt a strange sensation, as if they had been transported back in time.

2. That family lives without electricity, as though they were trapped in the 1800s.

3. The music sounded great on my new sound system, as if it were played by a live band.

4. That kid's clothes looked too big for him, as though borrowed from an older brother.

5. My grandmother looks odd in that photo, as if she were annoyed.

UNIT 7 Grammar Plus 119

8A Placement of direct and indirect objects

> The following verbs are commonly used with both a direct and indirect object.
> bring   hand   order   pay   serve
> give   make   owe   promise   throw
>
> When the direct object is a pronoun, it goes before the indirect object.
> When the indirect object is a pronoun, it can go before or after the direct object.
> The boss owes **it to Sid**. (it = *direct object*)
> The boss owes **him a month's salary**. (him = *indirect object*)
> The boss owes **a month's salary to him**. (him = *indirect object*)
>
> When both objects are pronouns, only one pattern is possible:
> direct object + *to / for* + indirect object.
> The boss owes **it to him**.
> The boss ordered **it for him**.

1 Complete the sentences using the words in parentheses. Write each sentence in two different ways.

1. Finally, the waiter brought . . . (our dinners / us)
   Finally, the waiter brought us our dinners.
   Finally, the waiter brought our dinners to us.

2. After an hour of searching, the clerk gave . . . (a suitable pair of shoes / me)

3. At that café, they won't serve . . . (your meal / you) unless you pay for it in advance.

4. I didn't have any cash, so I handed . . . (my credit card / the clerk)

5. The potter at that shop promised . . . (a beautiful vase / my mother)

6. While they were swimming, their father ordered . . . (lunch / them)

7. I don't have any more cash, but I can pay . . . (the rest / you) tomorrow.

8. At the baseball game, the vendor threw . . . (a bag of peanuts / him)

2 Rewrite the following sentences in as many ways as possible using pronouns in place of the nouns in boldface.

1. The clerk gave **Maria the wrong blouse**.
   The clerk gave her the wrong blouse. / The clerk gave the wrong blouse to her. / The clerk gave it to Maria. / The clerk gave it to her.

2. The salesman sold **his last vacuum** to **John**.

3. That company still owes **Michael one week's pay**.

4. The real estate agent didn't mention **the leaky roof** to **the customers**.

5. The travel guide found **two wonderful antique shops** for **the tourists**.

6. Thomas reminded Daniel that he had promised **a diamond ring** to **Liz**.

7. The hotel chef made **my mother an omelet**.

8. After the receipt was printed, the clerk handed **Eleanor a pen**.

8B Verbs in the subjunctive

> The following verbs can be followed by a *that* clause with a subjunctive verb.
> advise   beg   require   stipulate
> ask   prefer   specify   vote
>
> He **advised that** his students **be** on time.
> Our store policy clearly **stipulates that** all sales associates **report** to work by 8:30 A.M.
>
> **The negative subjunctive is formed with *not* and the base form of the verb.**
> The advertising executive's contract required that he **not receive** a bonus that year.
>
> **The passive form of the subjunctive is formed by *be* + past participle.**
> The sponsors asked that their product **be featured** prominently in the movie.
> The manufacturers preferred that their shaving cream **not be endorsed** by misbehaving stars.

1 Complete the sentences using an active or passive subjunctive form of the verbs in the box. Verbs may be used more than once.

| broadcast | not contain | give | prevent | remove | not send |

1. The return policy stipulated that customers ___be given___ cash refunds for returned items.

2. A new guideline advises that telemarketers _____ from calling after 8:00 P.M.

3. It is required that an advertisement _____ any false information.

4. Parents begged that companies _____ from advertising candy on children's TV shows.

5. The contract clearly specifies that the station _____ our ads 24 hours a day.

6. The customer repeatedly asked that she _____ a free sample of the perfume.

7. I would prefer that companies _____ me spam e-mail of any kind.

8. We voted that those billboards blocking the town's ocean view _____.

2 Complete the sentences with an appropriate form of the verb in parentheses. Use the subjunctive when possible.

1. It's clear that the time devoted to commercials on TV ___has increased___ (increase) over the past 10 years.

2. She advised that pressure _____ (apply) to companies that engage in false advertising.

3. I learned that my neighbor _____ (be) a stealth marketer.

4. The store required that each customer _____ (open) his or her bag for inspection.

5. He specified that this advertisement _____ (place) in this month's issue.

6. The actress begged that she _____ (not cast) in such a low-budget commercial.

7. I discovered that my sister _____ (be) addicted to shopping.

UNIT 8 Grammar Plus 121

9A *Whenever* and *wherever* contrasted with *when* and *where*

> If *whenever*, *wherever*, *when*, and *where* are followed by subject + *be* + adjective / past participle, the subject and *be* are often deleted. This occurs mainly in formal speech and writing.
> Pet owners must take their pets to the vet **whenever / when** ~~taking them is~~ **advisable**.
> Laws concerning the welfare of helper animals should be enforced **wherever / where applicable**.
>
> *Whenever* and *wherever* can have the meaning "no matter when / where."
> A: My dog doesn't like it when I give her a bath at night.
> B: Mine doesn't like it **whenever** I give him a bath!
>
> *Whenever* and *wherever* can also have the meaning "although I don't know when / where."
> We'll have to get together on his birthday, **whenever** that is!
> Their dog was found in a park outside of Hicksville, **wherever** that is!
>
> *Whenever* and *wherever* are rarely used following the focus adverbs *even*, *just*, *right*, and *only*. *When* and *where* are often used instead.
> My cats show me affection **even when** I'm in a bad mood.
> Elephants will survive in the wild **only where** they are protected from illegal hunting.

1 Shorten the sentences by crossing out the subject and the form of *be* in the adverbial clause.

1. Pets need to be given attention every day, not just when ~~giving them attention is~~ convenient.

2. Dog owners are expected to use leashes to walk their dogs where using those items is required by law.

3. My veterinarian suggested that I buy Barkies brand dog food when Barkies brand is available.

4. Whenever disciplining them is appropriate, owners of intelligent animals must be prepared to discipline their pets.

5. Exotic animals may not be kept as pets wherever keeping such pets is prohibited by law.

2 Review the grammar rules on page 71. Complete the sentences with *when*, *whenever*, *where*, or *wherever*. Sometimes more than one answer is possible.

1. _When_____ my dog ran out of the yard this morning, I called his name, but he kept on running.

2. _____ somebody walks past my house, my dog growls at him or her.

3. The insect looked so much like a leaf that I didn't notice it even _____ I looked right at it.

4. _____ we used to live, the landlord would let tenants have as many pets as they wanted.

5. The sign says that this parrot is from the Kakamega Forest, _____ that is!

6. Over the course of the year, _____ I visited her apartment, she seemed to have added another cat. By spring, she had at least five.

9B Noun clauses with *whoever* and *whatever*

> In formal speech and writing, *whoever* is used for the subject and *whomever* is used for the object of a clause. *Whomever* is rare in conversation.
> **Whoever** wants a unique experience should try scuba diving in a coral reef.
> I'll take **whomever** the instructor chooses for my rock-climbing partner.
>
> When referring to a known and limited group of items, *whichever* can be used to mean "whatever one" or "whatever ones."
> For your birthday, I'll pay for kayaking or skydiving lessons. You can choose **whichever** you want.
> I've packed three kinds of sandwiches for the picnic. Your friends can have **whichever** they want.

1 Complete the sentences with *whoever* or *whomever*.

1. I'm eating lunch outdoors today. ___Whoever___ wants to eat with me is welcome.
2. Access to this beach is strictly limited to residents and _____ they invite.
3. I believe urban environments without a significant presence of nature are unhealthy for _____ they surround.
4. _____ lives in that house must love the sun – it's made almost entirely of glass.
5. Some doctors say that spending more time in natural sunlight can be one source of relief for _____ winter depression afflicts.
6. _____ thinks that our city parks are just a waste of space has certainly lost touch with nature.
7. The manager position at the eco-resort will be filled by _____ the board of directors selects.

2 Fill in the blanks with *whoever*, *whatever*, or *whichever*.

Here's an idea for (1) ___whoever___ is feeling out of touch with nature. Why not enroll in a nature adventure program at a NaturVenture camp?

NaturVenture camps are convenient. Campers don't need to bring anything to our camps, because they can obtain (2) _____ they need from the camp stores. There's also a great selection of locations. There are four NaturVenture camps: on a river, in the forest, in the desert, and in the mountains.

In all four locations, we know how to get people in touch with nature! Our expert guides teach campers (3) _____ they want to know about kayaking, horseback riding, rock climbing, and many other outdoor activities. At our camps, we always keep safety in mind. Our trained medical staff is always on hand to assist (4) _____ might need help. The food is great, too. (5) _____ our chefs prepare always gets plenty of compliments.

Campers can choose (6) _____ of our four camps interests them. We offer one-week or two-week programs, so campers can choose (7) _____ suits their schedules and their budgets. And remember – there is a 10 percent discount for (8) _____ enrolls online. Sign up today!

10A Overview of passives

> **The passive voice with a modal can be used in short answers.**
> A: Why wasn't that author awarded the Nobel Prize for literature?
> B: I don't know, but he **should have been**. *(He should have been awarded the Nobel Prize for literature.)*
>
> The verb *get* can also serve as an auxiliary to form the passive voice. It is less formal and primarily used in spoken English. *Get* always indicates a change (with a meaning close to *become*), while *be* can indicate an unchanging state or a dynamic one.
> Larry and Natalie **got married** in 2006. *(Their wedding occurred in 2006.)*
> Larry and Natalie **were married** in 2006 when they went to Greece. *(Their wedding may have occurred before 2006.)*
>
> The verb *get* is also commonly used in expressions such as *get acquainted, get arrested, get dressed, get excited, get married,* and *get scared.*

1 Complete the short answers with the appropriate modal in the passive voice. Sometimes more than one answer is possible.

1. A: Will that Shakespeare class be offered next semester, too?
   B: Oh, yes. I'm absolutely sure that it ___*will be*___.

2. A: Should text speak be used in essays by some students?
   B: Actually, I think it _____.

3. A: Could English be overtaken as the main international language someday?
   B: Well, in my opinion, it _____.

4. A: Was the television turned off when we went to bed?
   B: No, it wasn't, but it _____.

5. A: Would our class have been canceled if the teacher had been sick?
   B: Yes, it _____. Thank goodness she's not sick!

6. A: Do you think fluency in English can be achieved in five years?
   B: I'm pretty sure it _____, but you'd have to study and practice diligently.

2 Complete the sentences with the correct form of *be* or *get*.

1. While I was reading a book in the bathtub, I heard someone knocking, so I quickly ___*got*___ dressed and answered the door.

2. Sam and Al had never met, so I gave them a few minutes to _____ acquainted.

3. Martin Luther King Jr. _____ remembered for his contribution to advancing civil rights for African Americans in the United States.

4. When she saw my father carrying her birthday gift, all of a sudden, my little sister _____ really excited and started jumping up and down.

5. I've never tried that language-learning method myself, but I know that it _____ designed by a famous professor.

10B Subject-verb agreement with quantifiers

A (*large / small / great*) *number of* always modifies a plural noun. The resulting expression takes a plural verb.
A (large) number of students in my English class **were** absent on Friday.

When certain collective nouns, such as *majority* or *minority*, act as a whole unit or a single group, they take a singular verb.
All students can express their opinions, but **the majority rules**.
In the United States, **Spanish speakers** constitute a linguistic **minority** that **is** growing rapidly.

Majority and *minority* are followed by the plural form of *be* when the complement is a plural noun.
If you ask my father about young people today, he'll tell you that **the majority are slackers**.
Of people who are concerned with using language correctly, only **a small minority are linguists**.

1 Review the rules for quantifiers on page 85. Choose the correct form of the verb. If both forms are possible, choose both.

1. A minority of American English speakers (*understand*) / (*understands*) Australian slang.
2. A great number of my friends *has / have* sharp tongues.
3. My students can't write without spell check. The majority *isn't / aren't* great spellers.
4. In the parliament, the newly elected majority *is / are* ready to make some changes.
5. A number of hip-hop expressions *has / have* been added to dictionaries.
6. A majority of my friends *has / have* a way with words.
7. There are times when a minority *speak / speaks* louder than a majority.
8. A number of languages *is / are* spoken in India.

2 Complete these sentences with the singular or plural simple present form of the verb in parentheses.

1. Each person _____*finds*_____ (find) the level of formality he or she is comfortable with.
2. No one _____ (know) the exact number of words in the English language.
3. Most of my friends _____ (speak) English fluently.
4. None of the linking verbs _____ (be) normally used in the passive voice.
5. A lot of people _____ (go) abroad to practice English.
6. A recent report indicated that about one-fourth of American high school students _____ (not graduate).
7. Plenty of my friends _____ (like) to send each other text messages.
8. Every language _____ (have) formal and less formal registers.
9. Every one of my in-laws _____ (talk) my ear off on the phone.
10. All fluent speakers _____ (need) to have an understanding of idiomatic language.

11A Compound adjectives

The following compound adjectives follow the pattern: noun + past participle.
awestruck   frostbitten   handwritten   homemade   store-bought   waterlogged
bloodstained   handmade   heartbroken   moth-eaten   sunburned   windswept

The following compound adjectives are found written as one word in many dictionaries.
airborne   barefooted   downhearted   lightweight   painstaking
airsick   daylong   hardheaded   newfound   seaworthy

In the comparative form of compound adjectives, *more* and *less* are not followed by hyphens.
a more forward-looking plan   a less easygoing person   a more highly trained applicant

1 Use one-word adjectives from the grammar box to rewrite the sentences.

1. The flight attendant helped the passengers who felt sick on the airplane.
   The flight attendant helped the airsick passengers.

2. We attended a meeting that lasted from 9:00 in the morning to 6:00 in the evening.

3. The passengers boarded the vessel that was worthy of making an ocean voyage.

4. The sailors stopped at an island that had only recently been discovered.

5. The star was overwhelmed by the fans who showed their admiration for her.

6. Jason caught a virus that was carried through the air.

2 Combine the words from both boxes to create compound adjectives and complete the sentences. Check a dictionary for meaning and hyphen use.

| forward | hand | home | tender | broken | hearted | made | winded |
| frost | heart | long | widely | bitten | thinking | respected | written |

1. The short __handwritten__ message on this photo of Marilyn Monroe makes it very valuable.

2. Because of his great experience in international affairs, the president is _____ in political circles.

3. The audience understood that they wouldn't be able to leave for a while; the speaker had a reputation for being _____.

4. Emma's boyfriend was exceptional. She was _____ when he moved away.

5. My grandmother would never serve anything store-bought. Her cakes and cookies were all _____.

6. Our country needs a more _____ leader, one who can prepare us for crises before they occur.

7. The _____ celebrity was well known for helping any needy person who contacted her.

8. The arctic explorers wore protective gear so that their hands and feet didn't get _____.

11B Superlative compound adjectives

The following adjectives and adverbs have irregular comparative and superlative forms. They are frequently used in comparative and superlative compound adjectives.

Adjective	Comparative	Superlative
good	better	best
bad	worse	worst
far	farther / further	farthest / furthest

Adverb	Comparative	Superlative
well	better	best
badly	worse	worst
little	less (lesser)	least
much	more	most
far	farther / further	farthest / furthest

As with other superlative adjectives, the article *the* is not used when the noun is preceded by a possessive.

Venezuela's **best-known** poet will be reading one of his works at the public library this week.

1 Write sentences as in the example using the information and the superlative form of the comparative adjective. Sometimes more than one answer is possible.

1. Charlize Theron is / good-looking actress / I've ever seen
   Charlize Theron is the best-looking actress I've ever seen.

2. My company president is / well-dressed executive / I've ever worked for

3. Last year, I went on one of / badly planned vacations / I've ever taken

4. Our chief of police is / little-appreciated public servant / our town has ever had

5. Mr. Fredericks is / well-loved teacher / our class has ever had

6. That player is / bad-tempered guy / our basketball team has ever hired

7. Professor Vargas is / much-honored academic / our college has ever invited to speak

8. That movie was filmed at / far-flung location / the studio has ever used

2 Write sentences using the superlative form of the compound adjective. Be careful to use hyphens and *the* correctly.

1. That company's (lightweight) camera is the Photoflash X25.
   That company's most lightweight camera is the Photoflash X25.
   That company's lightest-weight camera is the Photoflash X25.

2. My uncle's face looks (awestruck) in the photograph on the right.

3. Henry was (broad-minded) when it came to questions of cultural difference.

4. I take after my father, who is (hardheaded) man I know.

5. Joyce is quite smart, but she's not (well-read) person in the world.

6. To me, Japan's (awe-inspiring) sight is probably Mount Fuji.

7. Perhaps (widely recognized) actress from Malaysia is Michelle Yeoh.

8. One of the (low-lying) countries in Europe is Holland.

12A Subject-verb inversion in conditional sentences

> When present or future real conditionals are expressed with *should* at the beginning of the sentence, the base form of the verb is used.
> **If** you're looking for a competent employee, Ted is your man.
> **Should** you **be** looking for a competent employee, Ted is your man.
>
> Subject-verb inversion in conditional sentences occurs rarely with *could* and *might*, usually in literary or archaic contexts, and often with adverbs such as *but* or *just*.
> **Could** he **but** win her love, the world would be his.
> **Might** I **just** see my country once more, my heart would find peace.
>
> In formal situations, people sometimes replace *if* by putting the past subjunctive *were* at the beginning of unreal conditional sentences.
> **If** she **found** enough investors, she could form a startup company.
> **Were** she **to find** enough investors, she could form a startup company.
>
> **If** she **had been** wealthy, she might not have gone into business.
> **Were** she **to have been** wealthy, she might not have gone into business.

1 Rewrite these sentences using *should* at the beginning of the sentence and the base form of the verb.

1. If Sven goes into business for himself, I'm sure he'll do very well.
   Should Sven go into business for himself, I'm sure he'll do very well.
2. If Annie gets a raise, she'll be able to pay her college debts.
3. If Shin is sick tomorrow, would you be able to work in his place?
4. If you find yourself swamped by work, hire an assistant.
5. If a business is set up in a good location, customers will naturally come.
6. If a problem arises, you need to find a way to work around it.
7. If there's a chance of failure, I'd rather not take the risk.
8. If there's a lot of demand for a product, the price naturally rises.

2 Review the grammar rules on page 97 and in the grammar box. Then rewrite the sentences using subject-verb inversion.

1. If you asked him, he'd tell you the secret of his success.
   Were you to ask him, he'd tell you the secret of his success.
2. If the board approved the measure, the president would surely not veto it.
3. If his boss hadn't been working against him, Jake would have been promoted.
4. If I had looked at my calendar, I would have known about the meeting.
5. If I could just win the gold medal, I'd be happier than the richest man.
6. If we received adequate funding, our program could be a great success.
7. If they were aware of the risk, they would quickly patent their idea.
8. If Tamara hadn't spoken out, the boss would have ignored her.

12B Adverb clauses of condition

> *In the event (that)* and *(just) in case* also introduce a condition on which another situation depends. *In the event (that)* is more formal.
> **In the event that** a replacement cannot be found, you'll have to take on extra responsibilities.
> Here's a number to call **just in case** the copy machine breaks down.
>
> *Whether or not* is used instead of *if* to introduce a condition on which another situation depends. *Or not* is placed directly after *whether* or at the end of the clause.
> **Whether or not** it involves travel, I'm going to have to take this job.
> **Whether** it involves travel **or not**, I'm going to have to take this job.
>
> *Even if* introduces a condition which, if it is true, doesn't affect the outcome of a situation. It is frequently used with *still*.
> I'm (**still**) going to call in sick tomorrow **even if** I'm not actually sick.
>
> *If only* introduces a condition that the speaker strongly wishes to be true.
> **If only** I had known about that job opening, I would have applied for it immediately.

1 Match the clauses to make logical conditional sentences.

1. If only I hadn't insulted my boss, _e_
2. Whether you feel happy inside or not, ___
3. Even if you have great leadership skills, ___
4. Just in case you didn't get the memo, ___
5. If only I could wear casual clothes to work, ___
6. Whether or not the schedule is flexible, ___
7. Even if my company offers me a raise, ___
8. In the event that the manager retires, ___

a. here's a copy for your files.
b. I wouldn't have to spend so much money on suits.
c. you'll likely be promoted to fill her position.
d. I'm still going to take a job with another firm.
e. I'm sure he wouldn't have fired me.
f. the manager wants you to smile for the customers.
g. you can't be forced to work more than 40 hours a week.
h. you still have to earn the workers' respect.

2 Choose the expression that best completes the sentence.

1. (*Just in case*) / *If only* I have to go on a business trip this week, I've kept my schedule open.
2. *Even if* / *Assuming that* the weather is nice, this weekend's company picnic should be fun.
3. *In the event that* / *Whether or not* I receive training, I'm still not confident in my abilities.
4. *Even if* / *If only* I were in charge of hiring people, I'd give everybody a pay raise.
5. *Provided that* / *Just in case* employees do what is required, salaries are increased every year.

VOCABULARY PLUS

1A Adjectives and verbs to describe friendship

Use the verb or adjective form from each pair in the box to complete the conversations.

admire	clash	empathize	endure	harmonize
admirable	clashing	empathetic	enduring	harmonious

1. A: My dad has been friends with Ahmet since they were roommates in college, and they still get together once a month.
   B: I really _____*admire*_____ that! They must get along really well!

2. A: Teresa listens to her friends when they have problems and makes a real effort to understand their feelings.
   B: It sounds like she's _____. In my opinion, that's an admirable quality.

3. A: Whenever I'm with Jake, we get into a fight about something ridiculous.
   B: It's too bad you two always _____. Some friends bring out the worst in us.

4. A: My parents get along really well. On the rare occasion they have an issue, they try to discuss it rationally and reach a fair compromise.
   B: It's good they have a _____ relationship. They must be great role models.

5. A: Some psychologists think that only people with similar personalities form strong, long-lasting friendships.
   B: I'm not sure I agree. I can think of lots of people with different personalities who have _____ friendships. Look at us! We've been friends for over 20 years.

1B *re-* verbs

Use the correct form of five more verbs from the box to replace the underlined mistakes.

| rebuild | recall | reconnect | redefine | rehash | rekindle | replace | resurface |

1. Emil and Lydia attended the same school many years ago. Recently, they found each other on a social networking site and <u>replaced</u> their friendship. _____*rekindled*_____

2. We hadn't seen Ian in class for days and were getting worried. He finally <u>rehashed</u> this morning and said he'd been called away to a family emergency. _____

3. If I can't <u>reconnect</u> the last time I saw a friend, I can usually find that information by using the calendar function on my tablet. _____

4. It's annoying when Jack <u>resurfaces</u> the same old arguments. He repeats the same points over and over again, hoping that we'll finally agree with him. _____

5. Rachel and Yumi had a huge argument and stopped speaking to each other. Now, they've both apologized and are trying to <u>recall</u> their damaged friendship. _____

6. Smartphones let us send texts and photos, locate friends, and update our status on social networking sites. They've <u>rebuilt</u> how we communicate. _____

2A Adjectives to describe style

Cross out the word or phrase that does not fit the meaning of the sentence.

1. Fashion design students are up on the latest trends and always look so *chic / stylish / ~~sloppy~~*.

2. The fashion photographer has a low opinion of people who always wear old jeans and T-shirts no matter the occasion. He thinks they're *frumpy / sloppy / elegant*.

3. The top women executives in that corporation favor beautifully tailored jackets and dresses. They all have *a classic / a quirky / an elegant* look.

4. On some airlines, the flight attendants wear well-designed uniforms that are functional yet *fashionable / retro / chic*.

5. The lawyers in my firm generally wear conservative suits to work, but on weekends, they often wear *functional / trendy / flashy* clothes to company parties.

6. The band members wear vintage jackets, ripped black jeans, and red sneakers. They're trying to achieve a look that's *stuffy / funky / quirky*.

2B Adjectives to describe outward appearance

Choose the correct words to complete the conversations.

1. **A:** I was watching that new British drama on TV last night. My favorite character is the college professor. He seems intelligent and looks (dignified) / innocent in his dark suit and neatly trimmed beard.

   B: I saw that show, too. I really like the psychologist. You can tell by his friendly, open personality that he's really *intense / trustworthy*.

   A: One character I dislike is the opera singer. She's always sneaking around and looks quite *sinister / sympathetic* in her dark sunglasses and black scarf.

2. **A:** Did you see the portraits at the exhibit? That general has a reputation as a great leader, but looked almost too confident in that photo. He seemed *arrogant / intellectual*.

   B: I agree. Did you see the photo of the fashion model? I think of her as being sophisticated, but in that photo, she looked sweet and *smug / innocent*.

   A: The photographer definitely has a knack for capturing personalities. I loved his shot of the artist who lives alone on a mountain. I thought she looked pretty *eccentric / sympathetic* hiking in that quirky hat and long dress.

3A Adjectives to discuss technology-related issues

Choose the best words to complete the text.

Technology does amazing things to improve our lives, but there are some things that we should keep in mind. We love all the cool things our smartphones can do, but do you think it's (1) *unethical / hazardous / (prudent)* to upgrade our phones every six months just to get a few more features? Aren't there more worthwhile ways to spend our money? Also, phones are made of plastic, metal, chemicals, and other potentially (2) *audacious / confidential / hazardous* materials, so we have to recycle or dispose of old devices carefully.

Another concern is electronic banking. It's certainly convenient to pay bills online, but many people worry about keeping financial information (3) *confidential / problematic / unethical*. It seems like no matter how complex our passwords are, (4) *frivolous / audacious / confidential* hackers are always able to break into our accounts – and they rarely get caught. We should track down these (5) *unethical / prudent / frivolous* tech wizards and hire them to be our security experts!

3B Collocations to express different attitudes

Combine words from the boxes to complete the sentences. Some of the prepositions are used more than once.

| aware | fed up | intimidated | knowledgeable | leery | reliant |

| about | by | of | on | with |

1. As a security expert, Mia is *knowledgeable about* using fingerprint and facial recognition systems instead of passwords.

2. Ryan is observant and notices things that most of us would miss. When he walks around our city, he's highly _____ surveillance cameras that record people's activities.

3. My father-in-law is skeptical about most things and is especially _____ people who offer get-rich-quick schemes. He prefers to make money by working hard and making prudent investments.

4. Jana is in her 80s now and has become increasingly _____ her daughters to help around the house and drive her to appointments.

5. The teenagers I know think most advertising is annoying and are becoming really _____ pop-up ads appearing on their smartphones all the time.

6. Our manager criticizes our work and often loses his temper. We sometimes feel _____ him, but we're not sure how to improve the situation.

4A Expressions with *luck*

Use the phrases in the box to correct the underlined mistakes in the sentences.

bad luck	no such luck	the best of luck
beginner's luck	pushing his luck	the luck of the draw

1. As soon as Mei finished writing her paper, her computer crashed, and she lost all her work. That was <u>beginner's luck</u>! ___**bad luck**___

2. It's dangerous for Todd to ride his motorcycle without a helmet. He hasn't had an accident yet, but he's <u>out of luck</u>. _____

3. Nico will start his new job at the engineering firm tomorrow. I wished him <u>the luck of the draw</u>. _____

4. Our favorite band was playing at the Village Jazz Club. I had hoped to get tickets, but <u>best of luck</u>. The performance was completely sold out. _____

5. Did you hear about the woman who bought a valuable antique vase for five cents at her first online auction? That was truly a case of <u>pushing her luck</u>! _____

6. Jeff had to move to a new apartment this month. By coincidence, there was an apartment available where his best friend lives. Talk about <u>no such luck</u>! _____

4B Adjectives to describe truth and fabrication

Choose the correct words to complete the conversation.

Marla: Why are you reading that silly magazine? You know that most of those stories are (1) *conceivable /* (*dubious*) */ credible* at best.

Chad: But I enjoy making fun of the articles! Look at this crazy story about a man who saw an upside-down rainbow. Everyone knows that a rainbow's arc is at the top. It sounds pretty (2) *fishy / plausible / conceivable* to me.

Marla: Well, actually, I recently read in a science journal that an upside-down rainbow can occur. There's even a scientific name for it. So I think that story is (3) *iffy / misleading / well-founded* after all.

Chad: Really? Well, OK, here's a story about glowing green mushrooms. It's reported that if you put one on a newspaper in a dark room, it would give off so much light that you could read the words! This story sounds (4) *credible / phony / convincing* to me. I've never heard of anything like that.

Marla: But jellyfish and fireflies give off light, so why do you think it's (5) *far-fetched / convincing / misleading* for mushrooms to glow?

Chad: Well, I haven't see any (6) *fishy / convincing / dubious* evidence that glowing plants exist. But now that you say that, it does make me wonder.

Marla: Yeah, maybe that "silly magazine" isn't so silly!

5A Adjectives to describe movies

Cross out the word that does not fit the meaning of each sentence.

> **Here are today's film reviews from our Big City Critic:**
>
> *Mystery of the Purple Fox* is set in a beautiful forest, and the actors are very talented. Unfortunately, it was easy to guess how the movie would end in the first five minutes because the story was (1) *riveting / predictable / formulaic*. This director's work in the past has been (2) *clichéd / inspiring / engrossing*, so I was disappointed to see such (3) *predictable / touching / mediocre* work in this film.
>
> *Glacier Meltdown* is a documentary about how icebergs are melting at an alarming rate, causing the world's sea levels to rise. It was (4) *engrossing / riveting / formulaic* to see the gorgeous ice formations, but it was depressing to learn how quickly they are disappearing. It was (5) *inspiring / mediocre / moving* to watch the scientists endure dangerous conditions and severe weather as they examined the glaciers.

5B Types of TV programs

Choose the true statement for each sentence.

1. This season's most popular show has a complicated plot and characters that are always facing romantic problems and personal disasters.
   - ☐ a. This season's most popular show is a sketch comedy show.
   - ☐ b. This season's most popular show is a sports program.
   - ☐ c. This season's most popular show is a soap opera.

2. This new program features fashion stylists who pick out clothing for celebrities for important events. Viewers get to see them in action as they work.
   - ☐ a. The stylists are participants on a game show.
   - ☐ b. The stylists are stars of a reality TV show.
   - ☐ c. The stylists are hosts on a talk show.

3. The star of this show is a chef who demonstrates how to prepare exotic dishes from all over the world.
   - ☐ a. The chef stars in a sitcom about a restaurant.
   - ☐ b. The chef prepares unusual dishes on a cooking show.
   - ☐ c. The chef gives reports about food on a news program.

4. This show features animated characters. Dee the Dinosaur is the smart one. Fritz the Frog is silly and funny.
   - ☐ a. Dee and Fritz are characters in a cartoon.
   - ☐ b. Dee and Fritz are reality TV stars.
   - ☐ c. Dee and Fritz are the subjects of a documentary.

6A Collocations to describe music

Use the best two phrases from each box to complete the conversations.

| an exhilarating tempo | the mellow sounds | the monotonous beat |

Ann: I really enjoy listening to hip-hop music. I think it has
(1) _an exhilarating tempo_.

Ben: Call me old-fashioned, but I actually prefer
(2) _____ of slow jazz.

| a catchy tune | a frenetic pace | a soothing rhythm |

Liz: When I work, I usually have classical music playing in the background. It has (3) _____ that helps me stay calm.

Rob: I need to feel energized when I work, so I listen to rap. It has (4) _____ that keeps me going.

| a catchy tune | a haunting melody | an exhilarating tempo |

Ted: I enjoy songs that are pleasant and easy to remember. There's something very satisfying about singing along with (5) _____.

Jen: Oddly enough, I prefer evocative music that sounds sad. Folk music often has (6) _____ that is hard to forget.

6B Idioms used in the entertainment industry

Match the correct words to complete the sentences.

1. Vanessa is a talented young actress who's auditioning to get her first part in a movie. She's trying to be __d__.

2. My favorite band retired years ago, but I just heard it's making ____. The band is playing at Music Hall next month.

3. If you're starting out as a comedian and want to get ____, you should try out your material in comedy clubs.

4. Maya's first song was at the top of the charts last year. She's working hard on new music because she doesn't want to be ____.

5. That blues guitarist used to be a popular musician. Unfortunately, he's not getting any club dates, and he seems to be ____.

6. To succeed as a dancer, you usually have to pay ____ in the chorus line and work hard for years before you're noticed.

7. That actor is ____ on the new television series. The network just signed him to a huge multi-year contract.

a. a one-hit wonder
b. a comeback
c. washed up
d. discovered
e. your foot in the door
f. your dues
g. a big hit

7A Prefixes to create antonyms

Cross out the word that does not fit the meaning of each sentence.

1. A: Today I saw a driver in a car at a stoplight. He was texting, talking on a cell phone, and had his laptop open – all at once!
   B: Unfortunately, that seems to be a common practice these days. It seems *indecisive* / *illogical* / *irresponsible* to me.

2. A: My sister really surprised me the other day. She actually picked up her clothes from the floor and cleaned our room!
   B: I used to think she was pretty *irresponsible* / *immature* / *intolerant*, but I guess she's changing.

3. A: My nephew hasn't even tried to get a job since he graduated. He lives with his parents, doesn't pay rent, and stays out all night.
   B: Wow, he sounds like an *inconsiderate* / *immature* / *inconsistent* person. It must be hard on your aunt and uncle. Maybe he'd be motivated if they made him pay rent.

4. A: A recent article said that it's becoming common for people to be expected to work extremely long hours in some professions.
   B: Yes, I've heard that lawyers often work past midnight to prepare for big trials. It's considered *indecisive* / *irresponsible* / *improper* to leave the office before being completely prepared.

7B Collocations with *change*

Correct the underlined mistake in each sentence. Write the correct form of a word or phrase from the box.

| anticipate | bring about | cope with | go through | welcome |

1. Some people get into financial trouble because they use their credit cards all the time and are unable to make their payments. Then they have to anticipate serious lifestyle changes to pay off their debt. ___go through___

2. The mayor is admired for consistently initiating action to improve the city. He is always looking for ways to cope with change. _____

3. A few longtime residents want everything in their neighborhood to stay the same. They're not the type of people to resist changes. _____

4. The company plans to provide more on-the-job training. The director avoids this change will lead to a more knowledgeable and productive staff. _____

5. During the last recession, some people were unemployed for several months. They welcomed some difficult changes by relying on their families for support. _____

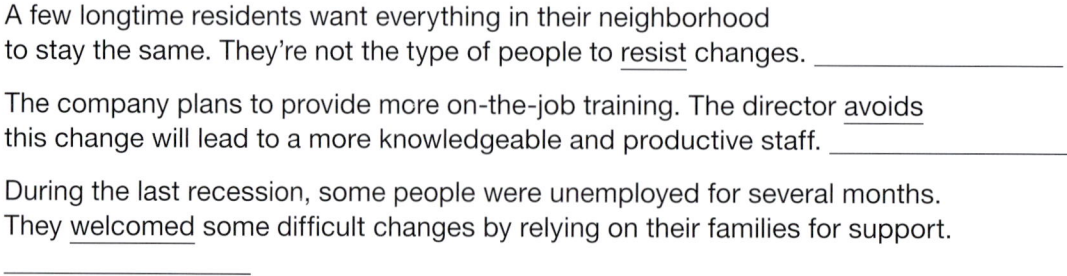

8A Expressions to discuss shopping

Use the correct form of the expressions from the box to complete the text.

| make an impulse buy | be a compulsive shopper | go over her credit limit |
| go window-shopping | have buyer's remorse | be a bargain hunter |

Did you ever notice how people have different shopping styles? My mom has always been price conscious and (1) __is a bargain hunter__. Whenever there's a sale, she combs through everything, looking for the lowest prices. On the other hand, my friend Maggie doesn't even look at price tags and buys everything in sight. She just can't control her urge to shop. She definitely (2) _____. She often spends more than the bank allows on her charge cards, but doesn't worry about (3) _____. Now, my sister Shelly has a totally different shopping style. She drives me insane because she never buys anything. She prefers to (4) _____, just peering at the displays of the latest fashions. Crazy, right? As for me, I have to admit that at times, I have the urge to go on a shopping spree. Shopping is all about having fun. I certainly don't plan to buy three pairs of shoes, but all of a sudden, there they are in my shopping bag! OK, I admit to (5) _____ every once in a while. But I confess that I (6) _____ on occasion and end up returning things. There's only so much room in my closets!

8B Marketing strategies

Read the situations. Then choose the correct ending to make a true sentence.

1. That actress made a commercial for a new floral perfume. She makes a point of saying that she wears it in real life. The perfume maker . . .
   - ☐ a. is offering a comparative-marketing program.
   - ☐ b. must think a celebrity endorsement will increase sales.

2. Every time the main character on that sitcom has breakfast, viewers can clearly see the product name on the box of cereal on the table. That cereal company . . .
   - ☐ a. is using a product-placement strategy.
   - ☐ b. is offering free samples.

3. The credit card company gives points every time shoppers use their card. Many customers keep the card for a long time to earn points. The credit card company retains its customers by using . . .
   - ☐ a. a loyalty program.
   - ☐ b. coupon codes.

4. When consumers searched for smartphone features and prices, one brand kept popping up. As part of its marketing strategy, the smartphone company is using . . .
   - ☐ a. word-of-mouth marketing.
   - ☐ b. search-engine marketing.

9A Physical features of animals

Choose the correct words to complete the conversation.

Ahn: I've been studying how animals defend themselves. It's fascinating how a bird can use its (1) *feathers / fangs /* (beak) to fight off predators.

Phil: Birds can be fierce, especially if they're protecting their nests.

Ahn: Speaking of fierce, when I was hiking last week, I ran across a herd of wild mountain goats. Two male goats were in a battle, using their (2) *horns / scales / gills* and (3) *claws / hooves / tusks*.

Phil: Goats are considered to be smart, and they are amazing climbers. What other animals have you studied?

Ahn: Last year, I spent time at an ocean research facility to study dolphins.

Phil: Oh, my eight-year-old son has been fascinated by them lately. Someone told him that dolphins didn't have (4) *fins / scales / tails* and didn't breathe through (5) *gills / paws / wings*, and he was really puzzled – "Why not, if they live in the ocean?" When I explained that dolphins are mammals, and not fish, he was amazed. Now he reads every dolphin book he can find.

Ahn: Hey, maybe he'll want to study animals someday, like I do!

9B Nature-related idioms

Replace the underlined phrases with the correct idioms from the list.

| a breath of fresh air | as clear as mud | set in stone | under the weather |
| a drop in the ocean | a walk in the park | the tip of the iceberg | up in the air |

1. They're going to open the new nature preserve to the public sometime soon, though the exact date is still <u>not decided on</u>. __up in the air__

2. I know my own effort to reduce carbon pollution by driving an electric car is just <u>a small thing</u>, but I like to know I'm doing something to help. _____

3. I've been feeling <u>unwell</u> for days now. I should really see my doctor. _____

4. A politician helping clean up the park is <u>something new and exciting</u>! I wish more public officials would help the community. _____

5. His explanation of the new environmental law was <u>extremely confusing</u>. I still have no idea of what it's about! _____

6. People are cutting down trees illegally, but I'm sure that's just <u>a small part of the problem</u>. There are bound to be more problems than that. _____

7. I was nervous about presenting my research to the Conservation Board, but in the end it was <u>really easy</u>. They were such good listeners! _____

8. The timetable for the conference is <u>unchangeable</u>. There's no way we can reschedule. _____

10A Discourse markers

Cross out the discourse marker that does not fit the meaning of the sentence.

Greetings, jobseekers!

Do job interviews make you nervous? I used to feel that way, too, but not anymore. My advice is to be prepared for the interview. (1) *Furthermore* / *To begin* / *First of all*, do some research on the company you will interview with, so you can talk about the company in an informed way during the interview. Learn about its business goals, products and services, and financial health. (2) *Next* / *Nevertheless* / *Second*, anticipate the questions the interviewer may ask you – and think of good answers! (3) *Yet* / *In addition* / *Furthermore*, it's a good idea to jot down your own questions about job responsibilities and opportunities for growth. At this point, you may feel totally ready for your interview. (4) *Likewise* / *Yet* / *Nevertheless*, there's one more step you should take: role-play an interview with a trusted friend or relative. That will increase your ability to communicate with self-assurance. (5) *In conclusion* / *To sum up* / *Similarly*, it may feel like all this preparation is a lot of work, but it'll be worth it when you walk confidently into that interview room.

10B Idioms related to the use of language

Complete the sentence about each situation using an expression from the box. Use the correct form of the verbs and pronouns.

| have a sharp tongue | stick to the point | talk behind someone's back |
| have a way with words | talk around a point | talk someone's ear off |

1. Last night, Jessica called Mei Ling and discussed her personal problems for three hours. Mei Ling didn't know how to get her friend off the phone!

   Mei Ling thought that Jessica was _talking her ear off_.

2. Tom began his presentation by talking about oil drilling in Alaska. Then suddenly, he changed the subject to farming methods in China. The audience seemed a little confused.

   Tom needed to _____.

3. My uncle often criticizes my cousin about his grades, his choice of friends, and how little he helps around the house. I think sometimes my uncle is a little harsh.

   My uncle can sometimes _____.

4. Ron is one of those salespeople who can talk his customers into buying anything! I once saw him convince a guy to spend half his salary on a ring for his girlfriend.

   Ron certainly _____.

5. When Pat has to discuss a thorny issue with a friend, she never addresses the problem directly. People get frustrated because she won't say what's really bothering her.

   Pat has to stop _____.

6. After we left the party, Josh started complaining about how unfriendly Anna was. I told him that it was unfair to talk about someone who wasn't there to defend herself.

   I wanted Josh to stop _____.

11A Compound adjectives related to the body

Choose the true statement for each sentence.

1. To be effective during a crisis, it's a good idea not to get overly emotional.
   - ☐ a. You should remain coolheaded even during a crisis.
   - ☐ b. You should be cold-hearted even during a crisis.

2. People should be willing to consider different points of view, no matter how extreme.
   - ☐ a. People should be absent-minded about different points of view.
   - ☐ b. People should be open-minded about different points of view.

3. Some people can be stubborn about doing things their own way and rarely compromise.
   - ☐ a. People who can't make compromises are hard-hearted and poor team players.
   - ☐ b. People who can't make compromises are hard-headed and poor team players.

4. Mammals maintain a fairly constant body temperature, regardless of their environment.
   - ☐ a. Mammals are warm-blooded creatures.
   - ☐ b. Mammals are warm-hearted creatures.

5. Some folks have little tolerance for people who have different beliefs or ideas.
   - ☐ a. It's unfortunate that some folks are so empty-headed about others.
   - ☐ b. It's unfortunate that some folks are so narrow-minded about others.

11B Phrasal verbs

Choose the correct words to complete the conversation.

Amy: I have to fly home this weekend to (1) *take after / (check on)* my grandparents. They don't like to admit it, but they can use a little help around the house these days.

Luke: You go home a lot, don't you? That's great that you (2) *look after / look to* your grandparents!

Amy: Well, I feel compelled to (3) *get through / live up to* my responsibilities. Besides, my grandparents took such good care of me as a child. Now it's my turn!

Luke: It sounds like you (4) *take after / side with* your grandparents! They must be excellent role models for you and your brothers.

Amy: Unfortunately, my younger brother Ethan is having a hard time at school. I'm going to talk with him this weekend. He needs to (5) *face up to / live up to* his problems. I think I'll remind him about the challenges our grandparents faced when they were young, and how they were still able to finish college.

Luke: I'm sure that you'll help him (6) *get through / look to* this difficult period.

12A Prepositions following *work*

Complete the conversations with the words from the box. Use the correct form of the verbs.

work against   work around   work for   work off   work toward

1. A: We've been discussing this issue with the manufacturer for months. The engineers are getting close to figuring out a way to make the batteries last longer.
   B: That's great! Sounds like you're __working toward__ a solution.

2. A: We don't have enough staff to finish the analysis on time. We've asked management for help, but they can't hire any new people right now.
   B: That's too bad! It seems like your bosses are _____ you.

3. A: My parents lent me a lot of money, and I don't know how to pay them back.
   B: Do they need help around their house? Maybe you could _____ some of your debt by doing yard work, cleaning the garage, and things like that.

4. A: Our firm has offices in Beijing and New York. Sometimes it's tricky to juggle the time zones, especially when we're trying to schedule meetings.
   B: Having colleagues in different locations can be a challenge, but hopefully you'll find a way to _____ that problem.

5. A: My last boss was extremely demanding. I learned a lot from her, but it was tough working 80 hours a week! If she was in the office, we had to be there, too.
   B: Sounds like a valuable learning experience. In the future, I hope you get to _____ a manager with a more balanced approach to life!

12B Expressions related to success in the workplace

Choose the best words to complete the email.

Hello Mark,

Thank you for agreeing to write the job description for our new position. Here are my thoughts on what to include when you write it. Since this is an entrepreneurial company, we should put a high priority on finding someone who has original ideas and (1) *(is innovative)* / *has charisma* / *has influence*. We need a person who (2) *has specialized training* / *has initiative* / *has influence* and doesn't wait to be told what to do. In addition, since our company works in close-knit teams, the new hire should (3) *have good communication skills* / *have self-discipline* / *be optimistic* and be good at explaining ideas. We also want a candidate who (4) *has specialized training* / *is conscientious* / *has leadership ability* and can inspire others to do their best work. Finally, since we deal with a lot of internal and external change, the person we hire must (5) *be adaptable* / *be trustworthy* / *be conscientious* and able to cope with some degree of uncertainty.

I look forward to reading the job description.

Regards,

Laura

Grammar Plus ANSWER KEY

Unit 1

LESSON A
Exercise 1
1. called off; S, T
2. come over; I, NT
3. live up to; I, T
4. took back; S, T
5. running out of; I, T
6. pass up; S, T

Exercise 2
1. catch up to
2. gave in to
3. give up on
4. cut back on
5. dropped out of
6. check out of
7. get away with

LESSON B
Exercise 1
1. doing
2. to frighten
3. spending
4. to call
5. seeing
6. to announce

Exercise 2
1. to rekindle
2. meeting
3. to have
4. sending
5. to say
6. rehashing

Unit 2

LESSON A
Exercise 1
1. b 2. d 3. a 4. d 5. b 6. c 7. a 8. c

Exercise 2
1. d; forgave my sister for giving away
2. c; mind paying
3. b; allowed me to wear
4. c; postponed picking up
5. d; thanked her for getting
6. a; proceeded to wear

LESSON B
Exercise 1
1. What the candidate did was show the voters he was a trustworthy man.
2. What my mother shouldn't have done was make me wear my sister's old clothes.
3. What I'm going to do is send all my shirts out to be dry-cleaned.
4. What my friends do is call me at work all the time.
5. What my father does is judge people too much by their appearance.
6. What employees should do is carry ID cards at all times.
7. What Eleanor did was wear her mother's wedding dress at her own wedding.
8. What Martin did was spill spaghetti sauce on his shirt.
9. What Sam did was buy a whole new wardrobe.
10. What Mary's going to do is wear her diamond necklace to the party.

Exercise 2
1. The reason why I'm wearing a tie is to impress my boss.
2. The place where I lost my watch is (in) the park.
3. The day when the office dress code changed was last Friday.
4. The reason why my dog wears a sweater is because his fur is short.
5. The thing that I remember is the intense expression on his face.
6. The place where Lori keeps her jewelry is under her bed.

Unit 3

LESSON A

Exercise 1
1. the
2. X, the
3. The, X
4. X
5. X
6. the
7. X
8. X

Exercise 2
1. X
2. X
3. the
4. the
5. the
6. X
7. X
8. a / the
9. X
10. X / the
11. A
12. the
13. X
14. the
15. X
16. the
17. X
18. X
19. a
20. a / the

LESSON B

Exercise 1
1. b   2. a   3. b   4. a   5. a

Exercise 2
1. I had a good time playing video games all day Saturday.
2. My brother had a hard time shopping for cars.
3. Fred wastes a lot of time constantly checking his social networking pages.
4. I'm going to have fun attending the big technology expo next week.
5. Nash is having difficulty trying to comprehend the concept of DNA storage.
6. Norah spent a lot of time writing a genetic technology lecture.
7. The guard had an easy time using the video surveillance camera to identify the intruder.
8. We were having problems trying to follow what the scientist was saying.

Unit 4

LESSON A

Exercise 1
1. Luis admitted to his friend that he had an irrational fear of spiders.
2. Min agreed with me that some people really are luckier than others.
3. Many people complained to the park staff that there are / were too many pigeons in the park.
4. Marco confessed to his mother that he had spent his father's lucky dollar on candy.
5. Marcie explained to her little sister that it is / was bad luck to step on a crack in the sidewalk.
6. Felix announced to his wedding guests that the day he met his wife was the luckiest day of his life.

Exercise 2
1. Anna didn't agree with Kim's accusation that she was a superstitious person.
2. Many people disagree with Gianna's argument that everything happens for a reason.
3. Carlos didn't understand Leslie's assertion that superstition is based in fear.
4. We were surprised by Jae-woo's decision that a trip to Las Vegas was what he needed.
5. Lily repeated Ernesto's comment that hard work is more important than luck.
6. Sandra didn't believe Hiroshi's claim that he had won the chess game thanks to beginner's luck.
7. Tanya ignored Patrick's remark that she probably shouldn't push her luck.
8. I understood Mr. Wang's response that actions speak louder than words.

LESSON B

Exercise 1
1. It was announced that the lost city of Atlantis had been discovered on April Fool's Day, 1980.
2. It has been revealed that a fast-food restaurant discontinued a favorite hamburger as a publicity stunt.
3. It is understood that some people have a higher level of intuition than others.
4. It can't be denied that crop circles, patterns created by flattening crops, are a clever hoax.
5. It is maintained that the moon's pull on the earth affects the ocean tides.
6. It should have been revealed that the politician was deceiving the nation.
7. It was observed that a positive attitude was an important part of his cure.
8. It had been estimated that one out of ten people falls for Internet scams every year.

Exercise 2
1. It is maintained that the Loch Ness Monster has been sighted several times.
2. It has been revealed that the ancient residents of Easter Island likely painted their statues.
3. It should have been observed that there was a mysterious substance on the train floor.
4. It can't be denied that ancient civilizations possessed knowledge lost to us today.
5. It has been confirmed that a pack of 400 wolves was terrifying a town in Siberia.
6. It has been announced that 10 people on the ship got sick.

Unit 5

LESSON A
Exercise 1

1. <u>Apparently</u>, movies with clichéd story lines are still very popular.
2. <u>Fortunately</u>, there were good movies available on the 13-hour plane ride.
3. <u>Honestly</u>, I just don't care for love stories, no matter how moving they may be.
4. <u>Unquestionably</u>, many historical movies present an incorrect view of history.
5. <u>Unfortunately</u>, Carol's computer froze while she was streaming that movie.
6. <u>Essentially</u>, that movie is a tale of good versus evil.
7. <u>Potentially</u>, the Internet could be the first place all new movies are shown.
8. <u>Obviously</u>, you are only pretending to have seen the movie.
9. <u>Seriously</u>, if a movie is based on a book, always read the book first.

Exercise 2

1. Consequently
2. Meanwhile
3. thus / accordingly / hence / consequently / indeed
4. consequently / hence / thus / accordingly
5. otherwise

LESSON B
Exercise 1

1. so
2. so many
3. so much
4. such
5. So few
6. so little

Exercise 2

1. such
2. so many
3. so
4. so much
5. so few
6. such
7. so many
8. so little

Unit 6

LESSON A
Exercise 1

Possible answers

1. The louder, the more
2. The more, the more
3. the more popular, the more expensive
4. The more soothing, the less
5. The louder, the louder
6. The more, the better
7. The older, the better

Exercise 2

1. The sooner, the better
2. The more, the merrier
3. The bigger, the better

LESSON B
Exercise 1

1. would
2. used to
3. would
4. used to
5. would
6. used to
7. would
8. used to, would
9. used to

Exercise 2

1. would sit
2. used to like
3. would ask
4. would say
5. will take
6. will bother

Unit 7

LESSON A
Exercise 1
1. whom
2. which
3. whose
4. which
5. whom
6. whom

Exercise 2
1. who / that
2. that / which
3. whose
4. whom
5. which
6. who / that
7. that / which
8. that

LESSON B
Exercise 1
1. The students at my new school welcomed me warmly, as did the teachers.
2. Moving to Spain will bring about many changes in my life, as will getting a new job.
3. Clarissa is enjoying retirement, as is her husband.
4. Claudia went to a traditional Chinese opera last night, as did Jim.
5. The teachers' union is supporting a four-day workweek, as is the transit workers' union.
6. I've given up my car and am taking public transportation now, as are several of my co-workers.
7. I can cope well with changes, as can my wife.
8. Amber believes that it is often foolish to resist change, as does Josh.

Exercise 2
1. Guests in the theater felt a strange sensation, as if they had been transported back in time.
2. That family lives without electricity, as though trapped in the 1800s.
3. The music sounded great on my new sound system, as if played by a live band.
4. That kid's clothes looked too big for him, as though they were borrowed from an older brother.
5. My grandmother looks odd in that photo, as if annoyed.

Unit 8

LESSON A
Exercise 1
1. Finally, the waiter brought us our dinners / our dinners to us.
2. After an hour of searching, the clerk gave a suitable pair of shoes to me / me a suitable pair of shoes.
3. At that café, they won't serve you your meal / your meal to you unless you pay for it in advance.
4. I didn't have any cash, so I handed the clerk my credit card / my credit card to the clerk.
5. The potter at that shop promised my mother a beautiful vase / a beautiful vase to my mother.
6. While they were swimming, their father ordered them lunch / lunch for them.
7. I don't have any more cash, but I can pay you the rest / the rest to you tomorrow.
8. At the baseball game, the vendor threw him a bag of peanuts / a bag of peanuts to him.

Exercise 2
1. The clerk gave her the wrong blouse / the wrong blouse to her / it to Maria / it to her.
2. The salesman sold it to John / his last vacuum to him / John his last vacuum.
3. That company still owes him one week's pay / one week's pay to him.
4. The real estate agent didn't mention it to them / it to the customers / the leaky roof to them.
5. The travel guide found two wonderful antique shops for them / them two wonderful antique shops / some for them / some for the tourists.
6. Thomas reminded Daniel that he had promised her a diamond ring / a diamond ring to her / one to her / one to Liz.
7. The hotel chef made her an omelet / an omelet for her / one for her / her one / it for her.
8. After the receipt was printed, the clerk handed her a pen / it to her / a pen to her / one to her / her one.

LESSON B
Exercise 1
1. be given
2. be prevented
3. not contain
4. be prevented
5. broadcast
6. be given
7. not send
8. be removed

Exercise 2
1. has increased
2. be applied
3. was
4. open
5. be placed
6. not be cast
7. is / was

Unit 9

LESSON A
Exercise 1

1. Pets need to be given attention every day, not just when ~~giving them attention is~~ convenient.
2. Dog owners are expected to use leashes to walk their dogs where ~~using those items is~~ required by law.
3. My veterinarian suggested that I buy Barkies brand dog food when ~~Barkies brand is~~ available.
4. Whenever ~~disciplining them is~~ appropriate, owners of intelligent animals must be prepared to discipline their pets.
5. Exotic animals may not be kept as pets wherever ~~keeping such pets is~~ prohibited by law.

Exercise 2

1. When
2. Whenever / When
3. when
4. Where
5. wherever
6. whenever / when

LESSON B
Exercise 1

1. Whoever
2. whomever
3. whomever
4. Whoever
5. whomever
6. Whoever
7. whomever

Exercise 2

1. whoever
2. whatever
3. whatever
4. whoever
5. Whatever
6. whichever
7. whichever
8. whoever

Unit 10

LESSON A
Exercise 1

1. will be
2. should be / shouldn't be
3. could be / couldn't be / might be
4. should have been
5. would have
6. could be

Exercise 2

1. got   2. get   3. is   4. got   5. was

LESSON B
Exercise 1

1. understand / understands
2. have
3. aren't
4. is
5. have
6. has / have
7. speaks
8. are

Exercise 2

1. finds
2. knows
3. speak
4. are / is
5. go
6. don't graduate
7. like
8. has
9. talks / talk
10. need

T-146   Grammar Plus answer key

Unit 11

LESSON A
Exercise 1
1. The flight attendant helped the airsick passengers.
2. We attended a daylong meeting.
3. The passengers boarded the seaworthy vessel.
4. The sailors stopped at a newfound island.
5. The star was overwhelmed by the awestruck fans.
6. Jason caught an airborne virus.

Exercise 2
1. handwritten
2. widely respected
3. long-winded
4. heartbroken
5. homemade
6. forward-thinking
7. tenderhearted
8. frostbitten

LESSON B
Exercise 1
1. Charlize Theron is the best-looking actress I've ever seen.
2. My company president is the best-dressed / most well-dressed executive I've ever worked for.
3. Last year, I went on one of the worst-planned vacations I've ever taken.
4. Our chief of police is the least-appreciated public servant our town has ever had.
5. Mr. Fredericks is the best-loved / most well-loved teacher our class has ever had.
6. That player is the worst-tempered / most bad-tempered guy our basketball team has ever hired.
7. Professor Vargas is the most-honored academic our college has ever invited to speak.
8. That movie was filmed at the farthest-flung / most far-flung location the studio has ever used.

Exercise 2
1. That company's most lightweight / lightest-weight camera is the Photoflash X25.
2. My uncle's face looks the most awestruck in the photograph on the right.
3. Henry was the most broad-minded / broadest-minded when it came to questions of cultural difference.
4. I take after my father, who is the hardest-headed / most hardheaded man I know.
5. Joyce is quite smart, but she's not the best-read / most well-read person in the world.
6. To me, Japan's most awe-inspiring sight is probably Mount Fuji.
7. Perhaps the most widely recognized actress from Malaysia is Michelle Yeoh.
8. One of the lowest-lying / most low-lying countries in Europe is Holland.

Unit 12

LESSON A
Exercise 1
1. <u>Should Sven go into business for himself</u>, I'm sure he'll do very well.
2. <u>Should Annie get a raise</u>, she'll be able to pay her college debts.
3. <u>Should Shin be sick tomorrow</u>, would you be able to work in his place?
4. <u>Should you find yourself swamped by work</u>, hire an assistant.
5. <u>Should a business be set up in a good location</u>, customers will naturally come.
6. <u>Should a problem arise</u>, you need to find a way to work around it.
7. <u>Should there be a chance of failure</u>, I'd rather not take the risk.
8. <u>Should there be a lot of demand for a product</u>, the price naturally rises.

Exercise 2
1. <u>Were you to ask him</u>, he'd tell you the secret of his success.
2. <u>Were the board to approve the measure</u>, the president would surely not veto it.
3. <u>Had his boss not been working against him</u>, Jake would have been promoted.
4. <u>Had I looked at my calendar</u>, I would have known about the meeting.
5. <u>Could I but just win the gold medal</u>, I'd be happier than the richest man.
6. <u>Were we to receive adequate funding</u>, our program could be a great success.
7. <u>Were they to be aware of the risk</u>, they would quickly patent their idea.
8. <u>Had Tamara not spoken out</u>, the boss would have ignored her.

LESSON B
Exercise 1
1. e 2. f 3. h 4. a 5. b 6. g 7. d 8. c

Exercise 2
1. Just in case
2. Assuming that
3. Whether or not
4. If only
5. Provided that

Vocabulary Plus ANSWER KEY

Unit 1

LESSON A
1. admire
2. empathetic
3. clash
4. harmonious
5. enduring

LESSON B
1. rekindled
2. resurfaced
3. recall
4. rehashes
5. rebuild
6. redefined

Unit 2

LESSON A
1. sloppy
2. elegant
3. a quirky
4. retro
5. functional
6. stuffy

LESSON B
1. A: dignified
   B: trustworthy
   A: sinister
2. A: arrogant
   B: innocent
   A: eccentric

Unit 3

LESSON A
1. prudent
2. hazardous
3. confidential
4. audacious
5. unethical

LESSON B
1. knowledgeable about
2. aware of
3. leery of
4. reliant on
5. fed up with
6. intimidated by

Unit 4

LESSON A
1. bad luck
2. pushing his luck
3. the best of luck
4. no such luck
5. beginner's luck
6. the luck of the draw

LESSON B
1. dubious
2. fishy
3. well-founded
4. phony
5. far-fetched
6. convincing

Unit 5

LESSON A
1. riveting
2. clichéd
3. touching
4. formulaic
5. mediocre

LESSON B
1. c
2. b
3. b
4. a

Unit 6

LESSON A
1. an exhilarating tempo
2. the mellow sounds
3. a soothing rhythm
4. a frenetic pace
5. a catchy tune
6. a haunting melody

LESSON B
1. d
2. b
3. e
4. a
5. c
6. f
7. g

Unit 7

LESSON A
1. indecisive
2. intolerant
3. inconsistent
4. indecisive

LESSON B
1. go through
2. bring about
3. welcome
4. anticipates
5. coped with

Unit 8

LESSON A
1. is a bargain hunter
2. is a compulsive shopper
3. going over her credit limit
4. go window-shopping
5. making an impulse buy
6. have buyer's remorse

LESSON B
1. b
2. a
3. a
4. b

Unit 9

LESSON A
1. beak
2. horns
3. hooves
4. scales
5. gills

LESSON B
1. up in the air
2. a drop in the ocean
3. under the weather
4. a breath of fresh air
5. as clear as mud
6. the tip of the iceberg
7. a walk in the park
8. set in stone

Unit 10

LESSON A
1. Furthermore
2. Nevertheless
3. Yet
4. Likewise
5. Similarly

LESSON B
1. talking her ear off
2. stick to the point
3. have a sharp tongue
4. has a way with words
5. talking around a point
6. talking behind her / Anna's back

Unit 11

LESSON A
1. a
2. b
3. b
4. a
5. b

LESSON B
1. check on
2. look after
3. live up to
4. take after
5. face up to
6. get through

Unit 12

LESSON A
1. working toward
2. working against
3. work off
4. work around
5. work for

LESSON B
1. is innovative
2. has initiative
3. have good communication skills
4. has leadership ability
5. be adaptable

Unit 1 LANGUAGE SUMMARY

Vocabulary

Adjectives
Describing friendship
admirable
beneficial
clashing
empathetic
enduring
harmonious

Verbs
Describing friendship
admire
benefit
clash
empathize
endure
harmonize

Verbs with prefix -re
rebuild
recall
reconnect
redefine
rehash
rekindle
replace
resurface

Additional vocabulary
connection
extroverted
face-to-face
interaction
introverted
social media
virtual

Useful expressions

Expressing opinions
I have to say that . . .
In my opinion, . . .
Personally, I (don't) think . . .
The way I see it, . . .

Disagreeing politely
I see what you mean, but . . .
I see your point, but . . .
I'm not sure I agree.
Do you think so?

Agreeing on importance
And let's not forget . . .
Well, I think it's important . . .
Yeah, that's true, but even more important is . . .
You're right . . . is also quite important.

Unit 2 LANGUAGE SUMMARY

Vocabulary

Adjectives
Describing styles
chic
classic
conservative
elegant
fashionable
flashy
formal
frumpy
functional
funky
quirky
retro
sloppy
stuffy
stylish
trendy

Adjectives
Describing outward appearance
arrogant
dignified
eccentric
innocent
intellectual
intense
sinister
smug
sympathetic
trustworthy

Additional vocabulary
acknowledge
apology
assumption
overcome
perceive
reassure
recover
self-deprecating

Unit 3 LANGUAGE SUMMARY

Vocabulary

Adjectives
Describing issues related to technology
audacious
confidential
frivolous
hazardous
problematic
prudent
unethical

Expressions
Expressing attitude
aware of
crazy about
curious about
familiar with
fed up with
grateful for
intimidated by
knowledgeable about
leery of
reliant on
sick of
suspicious of

Additional vocabulary
ban
boredom
expectation
experiment
offline
struggle
succumb
transform

Useful expressions

Expressing caution and confidence
I have every confidence that . . .
I'm a bit leery of . . .
I'm all for . . .
You should think twice about . . .

Unit 4 LANGUAGE SUMMARY

Vocabulary

Expressions

Expressions with luck
bad luck
beginner's luck
best of luck
luck of the draw
no such luck
out of luck
push your luck

Adjectives

Describing truths or fabrication
believable
conceivable
convincing
credible
dubious
far-fetched
fishy
iffy
misleading
phony
plausible
well-founded

Additional vocabulary

boost
effectiveness
enhance
good luck charm
jinx
mindset
ritual
trigger

Useful expressions

Reporting something surprising
Believe it or not, . . .
Did you hear what happened?
Get this – . . .

Unit 5 LANGUAGE SUMMARY

Vocabulary

Adjectives

Describing movies
clichéd
engrossing
formulaic
inspiring
mediocre
moving
predictable
riveting
touching

Nouns

Types of TV programs
cartoon
cooking show
documentary
drama series
game show
news program
reality TV show
sitcom (situational comedy)
sketch comedy show
soap opera
sports program
talk show

Additional vocabulary

attempt
capture
feature-length film
film clip
footage
star (v)
time capsule

Useful expressions

Suggesting improvements
I think what it needs is . . .
It might be better if you . . .
It'd be even better if . . .
You might want to . . .

Unit 6 LANGUAGE SUMMARY

Vocabulary

Adjectives
Describing music
catchy
evocative
exhilarating
frenetic
haunting
mellow
monotonous
soothing

Expressions
Idioms used in the entertainment industry
be a big hit
be a has-been
be a one-hit wonder
be discovered
be washed up
break into the business
get your big break
get your foot in the door
make a comeback
make a name for yourself
make it big
pay your dues

Additional vocabulary
astonishing
bootleg copy
construction worker
long-forgotten
popularity
release
reputation
reveal

Useful expressions

Asking about opinions
Are you into . . . ?
How do you feel about . . . ?
What do you think of/about . . . ?

Unit 7 LANGUAGE SUMMARY

Vocabulary

Adjectives

Antonyms with prefixes
illogical
immature
improper
inconsiderate
inconsistent
indecisive
intolerant
irresponsible

Verbs

Collocations with change
anticipate a change
avoid a change
bring about a change
cope with a change
go through a change
resist a change
welcome a change

Additional vocabulary

advocate
consumption
deprivation
phenomenon
poverty
precious
re-evaluate
valuable
widespread

Useful expressions

Asking for more specific information
In what way(s)?
What makes you say that?
Why do you think that?

Unit 8 LANGUAGE SUMMARY

Vocabulary

Expressions
Describing shopping experiences
be a bargain hunter
be a compulsive shopper
bid on an item
go on a shopping spree
go over your credit limit
go window-shopping
have buyer's remorse
make an impulse buy

Nouns
Marketing strategies
a celebrity endorsement
comparative marketing
coupon codes
a free sample
a loyalty program
product placement
search-engine marketing
word-of-mouth marketing

Additional vocabulary
amplify
clandestine
covert
hyperconnected
peddle
persuasive
pervasive
unsuspecting

Useful expressions

Asking for advice
What do you think I should do?
What would you do if you were in my position?
What would you do if you were me?

Unit 9 LANGUAGE SUMMARY

Vocabulary

Nouns
Physical features of animals
beaks
claws
fangs
feathers
fins
fur
gills
hooves
horns
paws
scales
tails
tusks
wings

Expressions
Nature-related idioms
a breath of fresh air
a drop in the ocean
a walk in the park
as clear as mud
set in stone
the tip of the iceberg
under the weather
up in the air

Additional vocabulary
amiable
dump
field (v)
infiltrate
park ranger
therapeutic
unnerved
vexed
year-round
yield

Unit 10 LANGUAGE SUMMARY

Vocabulary

Adverbs
Discourse markers
first / second / third
first of all
furthermore
in addition
in conclusion
likewise
nevertheless
next
similarly
to begin
to sum up
yet

Expressions
Idioms related to the use of language
have a sharp tongue
have a way with words
love to hear oneself talk
stick to the point
talk around a point
talk behind someone's back
talk someone into something
talk someone's ear off

Additional vocabulary
belonging
casual
common ground
credibility
muster
superficial

Unit 11 LANGUAGE SUMMARY

Vocabulary

Adjectives
Compound adjectives related to the body
absent-minded
cold-blooded
cold-hearted
coolheaded
empty-headed
hard-hearted
hardheaded
hot-blooded
hotheaded
narrow-minded
open-minded
openhearted
soft-hearted
warm-blooded
warm-hearted

Verbs
Phrasal verbs
check on
face up to
get through
live up to
look after
look to
side with
take after

Additional vocabulary
beneficiary
compel
dogged
enriched
gut feeling
intuition
NGO (nongovernmental organization)
social entrepreneur

Useful expressions

Describing what something means
I interpret this to mean . . .
My understanding of this is that . . .
What this means to me is that . . .

Unit 12 LANGUAGE SUMMARY

Vocabulary

Verbs
Prepositions following **work**
work against
work around
work for
work off
work on
work toward

Expressions
Essential qualities for success in the workplace
be adaptable
be conscientious
be innovative
be optimistic
be trustworthy
have charisma
have good communication skills
have influence
have initiative
have leadership ability
have self-discipline
have specialized training

Additional vocabulary
autonomy
diversity
futurist
humanist
idealist
integrity
loyalty
optimist
pragmatist
realist
self-critical
temperament
traditionalist

Useful expressions

Expressing suspicion
It sounds fishy to me.
It sounds too good to be true.
That's a little hard to believe.

Student's Book AUDIO SCRIPTS

1 RELATIONSHIPS

LESSON A, Ex. 2 [p. 2, CD 1 Tracks 2 and 3]

Professor Roth: All right, class . . . um, how was everyone's weekend? Did anyone get together with a friend? Yes, Jessica, what did you do?

Jessica: Um, well, nothing much, really. Some of my girlfriends and I went out for lunch. We pretty much sat at a café and talked.

Professor Roth: Uh-huh. What about?

Jessica: Um, you know, about nothing . . . and everything! Um, let's see, about my sister's new baby, and about when she could go back to work, and, you know, who should take care of the baby. Things like that.

Professor Roth: OK! Now, what about the guys? Any of you get together with a friend?

George: Uh, well, a . . . a buddy and I went to a ballgame.

Professor Roth: OK. What did you talk about?

George: Uh . . . the game? I mean, you know, when we're at the game we, you know, talk about the players and what's going on in the game and . . .

Professor Roth: Nothing else?

George: Well, not really. I mean, were we supposed to talk about something?

Professor Roth: Perfect! Do you know what just happened, class? Jessica and George have just demonstrated for us the basic idea of today's lecture – that friendship between women is different from friendship between men.

This is an idea put forward by Deborah Tannen in her book, *You Just Don't Understand: Women and Men in Conversation*, and that's what I'd like to talk about today.

Now, Deborah Tannen is an author and linguist who has written about the relationships between men and women and why they often don't understand one another.

According to Tannen, when a woman talks with a man, she often feels as though he isn't really listening or that they aren't really having a conversation, right? And a man often doesn't understand what the woman really wants from him. "What's her point?" he wonders. "Where is this conversation going?" How many of you feel that this sounds familiar? OK, most of you.

Well, Tannen points out that we can understand this difference in communication better when we examine how men and women view friendship.

OK. For a woman, her best friend is someone she can be close with and talk to. They talk in detail about everyday events in their lives. They share feelings and secrets. Talking gives women a chance to better understand their world – and themselves.

For a man, talking is generally more straightforward. It's about giving and getting facts. Men generally don't base their friendships on talking but on doing – getting together with buddies, playing sports, or going places. Men will often put down a woman's need to talk with her close friend about a subject in great detail. They don't understand how women can put up with such long conversations.

OK, so, who here agrees with Tannen's ideas?

LESSON B, Ex. 2 [p. 6, CD 1 Tracks 4 and 5]

Dena: It's really crazy how Kate and I became friends. I guess it was about two years ago now. I was on a plane, flying from New York to Los Angeles for work. Anyway, I noticed that the woman sitting next to me was reading the same book as me, so we started talking. She told me her name was Kate, and that she was going to her college roommate's wedding in Monterey. We had a great conversation and talked the entire trip – seven hours!

But, unfortunately, the flight had been delayed in New York by bad weather, and when we got to L.A., Kate found out she'd missed her connecting flight to Monterey. So, I invited her to stay with me in my hotel in L.A., but the airline had already promised to give her a room at a hotel near the airport, and she had to catch a really early flight the next day. We talked and talked until the hotel shuttle bus came, but as her bus drove away, I realized that I had completely forgotten to get her email, telephone number, or anything! Ugh. I felt bad because I would have liked to hang out with her back in New York. We had a lot in common.

Well, three months later, my roommate had a bunch of people over for a party one Thursday evening. I started talking to this woman, Samantha. She told me she had just gotten married a few months ago in Monterey. I remembered Kate had said she was going to a wedding in Monterey, so I then asked her if she'd had a roommate in college named Kate. She was very surprised and said that she had. Then I told her all about meeting Kate on the plane to L.A. So, to make a long story short, Samantha called Kate up right away, and Kate came over to the party. It was so exciting to see her again, and we're all good friends now.

2 CLOTHES AND APPEARANCE

LESSON A, Ex. 5 [p. 12, CD 1 Tracks 6 and 7]

1. Mark
Well, back in my high school days, in the early 90s, I was really into rock and alternative music. I saw the band Nirvana, and they were totally awesome. After that, I started to do the grunge thing – ripped jeans, checked flannel shirts, and a wool cap. But grunge didn't really stay popular very long, and after a couple of years, I got into rap and hip-hop. It was really the rap artists who finally inspired me to wear baggy jeans, oversized T-shirts, hooded sweatshirts, and, of course, my baseball cap – you know, a more urban style! Yeah, I think it was in the mid-90s when I went to my first hip-hop concert. After that, I completely gave up my grunge style.

2. Shelby

Growing up, my mom always dressed me in very conservative clothes. I never had a problem with it until, um, I think when I started high school. Right around that time, I began to feel that my clothes were really boring and stuffy. I started asking my mom to buy me more stylish things, but she always said no. It was so frustrating! Well, when I was old enough, I finally bought the clothes *I* liked – and I went for a total goth look. I wore long black dresses, heavy black boots, dark makeup . . . My mother really hated it, but I guess I wanted to make a statement. Now that I'm in college, I just wear comfortable, fun clothes – mostly long flowing floral skirts and dresses and long tunics. I guess you would call it the bohemian look.

3. Carlos

Well, I was really into sports in high school, and I was always wearing sweatpants, a jogging suit, or jerseys with numbers on them. I didn't have much time for fashion. I guess I had a sporty look. But nowadays, you'll almost always see me in light-colored slacks, a nice polo shirt, and maybe a sweater when it's cold. A lot of people call it the preppy look. I don't see any need to change it. It worked for me in college, and it works for me now. It's a classic look. Naturally, I'll put on something formal if I'm going to a wedding or a special event, and when I plan to do something athletic, then, of course, I wear sports clothes.

LESSON B, Ex. 2 [p. 14, CD 1 Tracks 8 and 9]

1. Gabriela

People say, you know, that personality is more important than appearance. But honestly, when you meet someone, you don't *see* their personality, you see how they look. The way people dress, for example, can tell you a lot about them. Later, you know, after you've talked to someone for a while, that's when you get to know their personality, . . . but that takes time. But an impression, . . . you form one of those right away. Well, I do anyway.

2. Joon

Well, in a social setting – a party, club, a restaurant, something like that – I like to look at a person's face. Uh, but in a business setting, it's somewhat different. It's more people's overall appearance that matters. I like to see how people appear to others, how they interact, how they present themselves to people. You know, I think it's actually – I like to see their level of confidence. I . . . I think confidence is what's important to me.

3. Alice

Um, when I meet new people, uh . . . I guess it's their eyes. They have to be big, kind, and . . . um . . . interesting. Uh, I really don't care about clothing or hair color, or anything like that.

3 SCIENCE AND TECHNOLOGY

LESSON A, Ex. 2 [p. 18, CD 1 Tracks 10 and 11]

Tim: Hello, and welcome to *Eyes on Tech*, a show that brings you the cutting edge of today's technology. I'm your host, Tim Arnold. Today, I'm taking a ride with our technology editor, Crystal Morton, in a car with . . . no driver!

Crystal: That's right, Tim. It's a little frightening, isn't it?

Tim: I have to admit it is, a little.

Crystal: Well, don't worry, Tim. Everyone's nervous at first. You'll get used to it.

Tim: But driverless car technology is safe, isn't it?

Crystal: Well, it's actually still in development, so I'm not sure anyone can say it's perfectly safe because there might be problems the developers haven't encountered yet. But the cars are equipped with lots of laser scanners, radar, and cameras for safe navigation. Some experts even say that if the whole country switched to driverless cars, the number of traffic accidents would fall dramatically.

Tim: Wow! That would be great!

Crystal: Wouldn't it, though? And another benefit would be the amount of money saved on road construction, as it would no longer be necessary to make roads "human-proof" with lights, guardrails, safety signs, and the like.

Tim: That would be a plus. It sounds like everyone would benefit from driverless cars.

Crystal: Well, not everyone. Businesses that profit from auto accidents, for instance, would lose hundreds of billions of dollars. Gas stations would also feel a negative impact with a drop in sales. Driverless cars usually choose more efficient routes than humans, and they get good gas mileage because of the way they're designed.

Tim: I can see how that wouldn't be advantageous for the gas companies, but it would certainly be a benefit for consumers. Now, what about professional drivers? If driverless car technology really caught on, there'd be no more need for taxi drivers, truck drivers, bus drivers . . .

Crystal: There's no question that a lot of changes would occur in the economy. The worldwide changes that could happen are difficult to imagine. But they'll likely take place slowly and steadily over time, so the impact won't be such a shock.

Tim: It's really incredible. Um, how about parking, though? Sometimes parking spaces are nearly impossible to find, especially in the city. Would there be special garages reserved for driverless cars somewhere?

Crystal: No, and there wouldn't have to be. Planners envision that driverless cars would often be shared by multiple users. As soon as one dropped you off at your destination, it would then go and pick up another person. This would result in fewer cars on the road, less traffic congestion, and plenty of parking spots!

Tim: Wow, never having to worry about parking would be great. But I imagine repairs could be quite a headache. I would think that not many people are qualified to repair such complex technology.

Crystal: That's very true. Repairs on the navigation systems require skills that the average auto repairman just doesn't have at this point.

Tim: Well, I see we're just about out of time. This has certainly been a smooth ride, hasn't it, Crystal?

Crystal: It certainly has. It makes me want to thank the driver . . . but, of course, there isn't one!

Tim: Thanks for riding with us! If you'd like to learn more about driverless car technology, visit . . .

LESSON B, Ex. 2 [p. 22, CD 1 Tracks 12 and 13]

Comedian: Oh-ho-ho-ho, the convenience of technology, right? A swipe here, a touch there, and – *zing* – life is easier! Not so fast . . . Honestly, technology is sometimes just one big *in*convenience! Take, for instance, that useful tool, autocorrect. It fixes our grammar and spelling so that we don't have to spend all that time consulting dictionaries and such. And it helps us write those perfect texts our favorite English teacher would be *so* proud of. What could be better, right? Wrong! I don't know about yours, but the thing my autocorrect loves to do is . . . *over*correct! Just the other day, I was writing a cover letter to Mr. Coffel. Not your everyday last name, so I carefully typed C-O-F-F-E-L. What I didn't notice was that my ever-so-helpful autocorrect changed it to "Mr. *Coffee*!" So my perfect cover letter now started: "Dear Mr. Coffee" . . . Guess who didn't get an interview for that job . . .

And then there's voice recognition. I talk, and my phone types. Easy, right? Well, it would be easy *if* my phone actually recognized what I'm saying! But it doesn't *understand* me! Get this . . . I was in the mood to go out last Saturday, so I told my phone, "Find Megan." No problem, her number came up right away. Then I said, "Hi, there! I'd really like to go out for a romantic dinner with you. Where should we go? Send text." *Zing*! My text rocketed through space. And Megan immediately wrote back wanting to go out with me, right? Wrong again! Because what Megan received was this *lovely* message, "I'd really like to go out for a romantic dinner with *Sue*. Where should we go?" I don't even know a woman named Sue, but Megan wouldn't give me a chance to explain! So, you can guess again . . . Yep, Megan and I did *not* go out for that dinner.

So, that brings me to another so-called *useful* tool, autofill. You just type the start of a name, and the computer or smartphone automatically fills in the rest. Convenient, right? Wrong again! I don't know about your phones, but mine *never* fills in the right information! Remember my dateless Saturday night? Well, instead of feeling sorry for myself, I decided to invite my friend Drew to dinner. Of course, I decided *not* to send a text using voice recognition after my problem with Megan. So, I did it the *safe* way . . . I typed in his name. D–R . . . and the phone filled in the rest. Great! Then I typed, "Hey, let's go out to dinner. Westside Café. 8:00. I'll pay!" He texted back immediately, "I'm in! Thanks!" Perfect! So, I headed out, got on the subway. When I got off the subway, I noticed 10 other friends had texted me saying they could come. What? Well, instead of filling in Drew's number, my phone had filled in "Drama Club," a group contact I have with all the numbers of my Drama Club friends. All 20 people in the group got the message, and 10 actually showed up! Guess who bought dinner for 10 friends.

Ah, yes, the convenient world of technology – a swipe here, a touch there, auto this, auto that, and this guy has no job interview, no Megan, and no money!

1-3 COMMUNICATION REVIEW

Ex. 1 [p. 26, CD 1 Tracks 14 and 15]

Lucy: Hi, Karla, what are you up to?

Karla: Hey, Lucy. I'm on this social networking site, and I'm trying to reconnect with people from high school. I've started organizing our 25-year class reunion. It's less than six months away. I really can't keep putting it off. You're coming, right?

Lucy: Of course. So, how's it going?

Karla: Well, I ran into a couple of problems at first, but now I've figured out how to use the site. It's really easy. It's got a neat search feature you can use to find people who went to a specific school in certain years. I've already created a profile for the reunion, and I've connected with quite a few people from our class. You can see some of their names and pictures here on the screen.

Lucy: Are you asking everybody from our class?

Karla: Oh, yes. I think I should. Why?

Lucy: There were some personality clashes, remember?

Karla: How could I forget?

Lucy: Well, they could resurface, that's all I'm saying.

Karla: I know. But 25 years is a long time. I think it'll be OK. In fact, I think it'll be amazing to reconnect with all these people we haven't seen in years. And with this search function, I'm pretty sure I'll be able to find almost everybody's contact information. It's really incredible how some people have changed. Just look at this guy. Do you know who that is?

Lucy: Wait. Don't tell me. Is that . . . Is that Andrew? Oh! He looks so stuffy now!

Karla: I know, I know! Back in school he was always Mr. Preppy.

Lucy: Personally, I was never crazy about his style. And I think he was more like Mr. Arrogant, and, you know, he still looks pretty smug. Look what he's wearing. Where did he get that suit?

Karla: Lucy!

Lucy: I'm sorry, but people like that bring out the worst in me. I got sick of him always putting everyone else down.

Karla: I know. Me, too, actually. You know this one, right?

Lucy: Hey! Is that Renée?

Karla: Yes, it is. She hasn't changed much, has she?

Lucy: No. She looks just as bohemian now as she did back in school. She always was a quirky dresser. It's a nice look. I always admired her – she wasn't afraid to be herself. Her profile says she's an artist.

Karla: And do you remember this guy?

Lucy: He looks really familiar. Hmm. No, I'm not sure.

Karla: It's Mike.

Lucy: Mike? Wow, he's looking very formal these days. He used to really hate getting dressed up for anything, even graduation, remember?

T-166 Student's Book audio scripts

Karla: Oh, yeah . . .

Lucy: This is so cool, Karla. You've done a good job finding everyone.

Karla: Well, I haven't found everyone yet, so let me get back to that.

4 SUPERSTITIONS AND BELIEFS

LESSON A, Ex. 5 [p. 30, CD 1 Tracks 16 and 17]

1.

Woman 1: Ah-choo! Ah-choo! Ugh! Excuse me.

Man: Bless you!

Woman 2: Bless you!

Woman 1: Thanks! Ugh! These allergies are so annoying. You all must be tired of saying, "Bless you."

Woman 2: No, that's all right. But isn't it funny how we automatically do that when someone sneezes? It's some kind of superstition, isn't it?

Man: Yes. You know, a long time ago, it was commonly thought that when people sneezed, their heart stopped beating. You would bless them as a way to ensure the return of life or to encourage their heart to continue beating.

Woman 1: Well, uh, you know, thanks, but it's really just my allergies!

2.

Mom: Oh, no! Oh, I can't believe I dropped that mirror. What bad luck!

Son: Don't worry, Mom. I'll pick it up for you.

Mom: Oh, thanks. But, you know, I can just hear my grandmother's voice saying, "Now you're in for seven years of bad luck."

Son: Why would she say that?

Mom: Oh, you know. She was very superstitious. She believed that once a mirror is broken, you can't see yourself as a whole person in it, so something really bad is going to happen to you.

Son: Yeah, but why . . . why seven years of bad luck?

Mom: Well, I guess a long time ago, people thought it took seven years for the body to repair itself. So, I guess it would take seven years to fix a "broken" body.

Son: Seven years is a really long time. I guess I'm glad I didn't break that mirror.

Mom: Oh!

Son: Mom, I'm only kidding! I mean, you don't really believe that somebody . . .

3.

Man: Don't bother going in to see Mr. Wilson right now. He's in a *really* bad mood today.

Woman: Oh, no, he probably got up on the wrong side of the bed.

Man: What do you mean by that?

Woman: You never heard that expression?

Man: No.

Woman: Well, you know, it's an old superstition from when some people believed that the right side was good and the left side was bad.

Man: Why did they believe that?

Woman: I don't know. I guess since most people are right-handed, they felt like being left-handed was suspicious.

Man: Well, don't tell that to Mr. Wilson.

Woman: Why?

Man: He's left-handed!

LESSON B, Ex. 4 [p. 34, CD 1 Tracks 18 and 19]

Tonya: Hi, Sam!

Sam: Hi, Tonya! How was your journalism class today?

Tonya: Oh, it was so interesting. Dr. Wagner spoke about journalistic hoaxes. A lot of them were like harmless April Fools' pranks, done just for fun, but some were meant to make a point. And some of the hoaxes really took people in and scared them.

Sam: Oh, how well I know that! I experienced a frightening journalistic hoax in Belgium firsthand when I was a student there.

Tonya: In Belgium? Dr. Wagner didn't mention anything about a hoax in Belgium. What happened?

Sam: Well, it was the middle of December. We were watching TV when it was reported that the Dutch-speaking part of Belgium had declared independence.

Tonya: You mean, it had become a separate country?

Sam: Well, that's what the guy on TV said, anyway. He seemed perfectly credible, and we all thought he was, you know, trustworthy. I mean, there's always been some tension between the north and south of Belgium. And the report even showed King Albert II and Queen Paola getting on a plane as if they were leaving the country.

Tonya: That must have been scary.

Sam: Oh, definitely. People were frantic. Thousands of viewers called the TV station trying to find out what happened, and so many people went to their website that it crashed.

Tonya: Wow, people were really in a panic, huh?

Sam: Yeah, but get this. It was all phony, just a hoax cooked up by the TV station. After about a half hour, they put up a message saying, "This is fiction," but it was too late – the damage had already been done.

Tonya: So, why did they do it?

Sam: The station claimed to have broadcast the phony story to call attention to the political and economic issues between the north and the south. The story was so believable that some foreign ambassadors in Brussels called authorities to find out what was going on.

Tonya: Gosh, what an incredible hoax!

Sam: It really was, but eventually things calmed down. But even the head of news at the TV station admitted that the hoax had scared more people than they had expected.

Tonya: Wow, what an amazing experience. I can't wait to tell my class about it tomorrow!

5 MOVIES AND TELEVISION

LESSON A, Ex. 4 [p. 38, CD 2 Tracks 2 and 3]

1. Heather
In my opinion, a good storyline is essential. Movies in this genre often have simple plots that are, quite frankly, predictable. When I see this kind of movie, I want interesting, and even surprising, things to happen.

Of course, humor is also a key element, but I think it's important that the humorous situations and the relationships between the characters are realistic – they have to be believable *and* funny. Too many times, when a love story is combined with humor, the movie becomes far-fetched. The situations may be funny, but they don't reflect things that really happen in life – well, not in *my* life at least.

I also think that the best movies in this genre appeal to both men and women. Ideally, these movies should be perfect for a good "date night," but more often than not, they only appeal to women . . .

2. Josh
For me, the first thing is that a movie in this genre needs to appeal to all ages – not just kids. And I think that sophisticated humor and well-thought-out stories can help make these movies engaging for children and adults.

Second, a good film makes me forget that I'm not watching real people or seeing real objects. I know they can do a lot of that through quality computer graphics, but I think a dynamic plot, an attractive setting, and interesting characters are just as important . . .

But the most important thing to me is the talent. They have to get talented people for the voices of the characters. The voices need to give the characters personality so that they are, you know, credible and don't come across as one-dimensional or phony. I mean, isn't that the reason why so many famous actors get cast as voices for these types of movies?

3. Felipe
I think that having outstanding special effects is an important part of this genre. It's one of the main reasons people go see these movies. Although we know that the events can't happen in real life, we want to feel like they could!

Uh, and the realness . . . the realness of the characters is important. I think it works best when the characters react to impossible situations in realistic ways. It makes us care about what happens to them.

And, uh, I also think that behind all good movies in this genre lies a talented director. A good director gets the most out of the actors and ensures the special effects are convincing to make a truly engrossing film.

4. Dana
Obviously, the singing and dancing need to be good in this genre. So a cast of talented actors is extremely important in my opinion – they need to be able to sing, dance, *and* act. Not every actor can do all that.

Another key feature for me is the soundtrack. The songs need to drive the plot, but they also need to be pleasurable and memorable. What I'm trying to say is that we should enjoy the music for the music itself. I mean, we should want to listen to it again . . . even when we're not watching the movie.

And finally, I also think this type of movie needs some sort of conflict to make it interesting. The characters need to face a problem, have an argument, or something like that. It can't just be all song and dance and happy times.

LESSON B, Ex. 4 [p. 42, CD 2 Tracks 4 and 5]

Alice: Good morning.

Pete: Hi, Alice.

Ellen: Hi, guys.

Rick: Good morning, everyone. OK, I hope you've had time to think of some fantastic ideas for new shows. The network is counting on us to come up with some winners. So, let's start with your basic ideas and brainstorm from there. Pete, why don't you go first?

Pete: OK. Well, I was thinking about a new sitcom called *Café People*. Sitcoms about quirky groups of friends seem to work, so I'm thinking maybe a show about a group of college graduates. They all have aspirations to pursue "big careers," but in the meantime, they have jobs that they aren't crazy about.

Rick: Like what?

Pete: Um, well, for example, one could be a guy who's stuck working in a pet shop. His real dream is to be a music producer, but things never seem to go his way. There should be two or three other main characters like him, each with a different aspiration and working in a different place.

Rick: OK, I see . . . But, Pete, how will these people interact if they're working in different places?

Pete: Oh, that's where the café comes in – it's where they meet to discuss their offbeat experiences at their different jobs.

Rick: A café, huh. Well, this basic sitcom pattern has been very successful before, but it's not quite what the network is looking for right now. Most of our current viewers seem to be interested in something less . . . predictable. I appreciate your ideas, Pete, but I'm afraid we'll have to go for something less formulaic. Let's hear another idea.

Alice: I'll go next. My idea is for a new type of cooking show called *Serve Yourself!* It'd be aimed at people in their late teens and early twenties, like college students, who have to cook for themselves but don't have the time, the money, or the desire to do so. The recipes would be simple and inexpensive, but they'd also be healthy and taste great.

Rick: Uh-huh . . . But I feel like it needs something, Alice. Any ideas, guys?

Pete: Hmm . . . Maybe the cooking could take place on a set that looks like a dormitory room, you know, in a little kitchenette or something.

Rick: Excellent idea, Pete!

Alice: Oh, and I just had a thought! We make the show available online. You know, podcasts people could download so they can follow along in their kitchens.

Rick: Now you're cooking, Alice! OK. This one is a go. The online aspect is just what our viewers want, and the how-to approach should be a big hit. OK, Ellen, you're on.

Ellen: OK, here's my idea . . . a reality TV show that focuses on language learning.

Rick: Mmm . . . language learning? . . . It sounds a little academic for a TV show.

Ellen: No, wait, listen . . . I'm calling it *New Borders*. Here's the basic idea: Several people are given a month to learn a foreign language. Then we fly them to a country where the language is spoken and capture their adventures.

Pete: So . . . if they studied French, you'd drop them off in France?

Ellen: Yeah, or maybe even somewhere more exotic, like Madagascar.

Rick: Now, *that* sounds intriguing. But it might be better if we could include some kind of competition. How could we work that in?

Alice: Maybe contestants could be judged on how successfully they accomplish certain things. You know, whether they're able to order a meal, get to a certain destination in the country, that kind of thing.

Rick: *That* sounds more like what the network is looking for. And most of our viewers are interested in traveling and learning about other cultures, so that should be a win.

Wow! Great job, team! Two potential concepts in one morning. Ha, that's an accomplishment. How about we break for lunch and brainstorm some more ideas this afternoon?

6 MUSICIANS AND MUSIC

LESSON A, Ex. 2 [p. 44, CD 2 Tracks 6 and 7]

Lisa: Hey, Adam! Check out this new music site I found!

Adam: Let me see . . . Hey, there's some cool stuff here. They have such a huge selection!

Lisa: I know. Awesome, isn't it? And you can listen to all of it before you buy . . .

Adam: Yeah. Look, they've got 80s pop, 90s pop . . . Let's check out the 80s pop.

Lisa: No way. My father listens to that all the time, and I'm sick of it. The less I hear of that, the better.

Adam: Oh, well, OK. Um, what about this reggae tune?

Lisa: Go for it!

Adam: What do you think?

Lisa: I'm not crazy about it.

Adam: Me, neither. I'm not into it at all. Why don't you pick one now?

Lisa: OK, let's see. What's this? Bluegrass?

Adam: Oh, yeah, bluegrass. I think that's some kind of country music.

Lisa: Well, here goes . . . Wow, that's sort of cool. I kind of like it.

Adam: You do? I guess it's kind of interesting, but it's a little weird. Anyway, let's move on. How about this one? It's a new hip-hop single.

Lisa: That sounds good.

Adam: Here goes.

Lisa: Oh, yeah! That's amazing!

Adam: I love it.

LESSON B, Ex. 4 [p. 50, CD 2 Tracks 8 and 9]

Theresa: Hi, Paul!

Paul: Oh, hi, Theresa.

Theresa: What's wrong? I mean, is everything OK?

Paul: Oh, well, since you asked . . . I've been getting pretty frustrated lately. You know, I took a year off from college to try to break into the music business, but I just, um, I can't seem to get my foot in the door, you know?

Theresa: Oh, don't be frustrated, Paul!

Paul: It's hard not to be. You know, I've posted quite a few videos of my music online, but they're definitely not creating enough buzz. And my parents are starting to bug me about going back to school.

Theresa: I can understand your parents' concerns, and I think you should respect that. But it's *your* life, Paul, not your parents'. You should tell them that you need a little more time.

Paul: It's not that easy, especially when I'm feeling so down about myself – I've been even doubting my ability lately.

Theresa: Don't doubt yourself, Paul. You're so talented! You have to take yourself seriously. If you don't, nobody else will.

Paul: I know you're right, but I don't know what else to do. Maybe I need a new image.

Theresa: Oh, I don't think so. My advice is just to look confident! The music world is very competitive, and you just can't afford to look like you don't have enough self-confidence. You have to project a confident image no matter how you feel inside.

Paul: I know you're right, but like you said, it's *so* competitive. Maybe I should just –

Theresa: But there are success stories! Take my cousin Ted, for example. He's a successful musician now, but for years, he only had small gigs, hardly made any money, and simply felt like a failure.

Paul: See, that's what I mean . . .

Theresa: But the thing is, he never gave up. He just kept at it, and then one night some people in the music business heard him play. They liked what they heard, and they stayed to talk to him after the show. And that was the beginning of his recording career!

Paul: Hmm . . . really?

Theresa: Yes, really! So you see, even if you fail sometimes, you've got to keep going. I mean, don't give up, OK?

Paul: Hey, you know, it's good to hear stories like that. It makes me feel a little more hopeful. Thanks, Theresa.

Theresa: Don't mention it. Now, why don't you play me your new song?

Paul: Sure!

4–6 COMMUNICATION REVIEW

Ex. 3 [p. 53, CD 2 Tracks 10 and 11]

Interviewer: And next, tonight I'll be talking to Jeffrey Steinhart, theater critic for the *Chronicle*. Hello, and welcome to *Backstage*, Jeffrey.

Jeffrey: Thanks very much, Anna. It's good to be here.

Interviewer: So, you're going to tell us about superstitions in the acting profession. Some people say that it is one of the most superstitious professions in the world. Is that true?

Jeffrey: Well, clearly there are actors who aren't superstitious, but there are certainly a lot of superstitions connected to theaters all over the world. There are a few possible explanations for why this might be.

The first, really, is historical. In the past, many of the people who criticized theaters and acting argued that playing a role – pretending to be another person – was wrong. So actors were looked down on in some societies, and I think that the more this happened, the more they felt cut off from society.

Not surprisingly, they developed their own "society" or community. But, obviously, actors move around, they travel, so the theater buildings become "home," and the superstitions are the same wherever the theater is.

Interviewer: I see. Can you give us some examples of superstitions in the theater?

Jeffrey: Well, cats are very welcome in theaters, especially black cats. There is, clearly, a practical reason for this: You don't want mice running around nibbling the costumes.

But there's more to it than that. Some actors claim that it is bad luck to wear a costume unless a cat has slept on it. I remember one actor who would leave his costume out on a chair before the opening night, hoping a cat would fall asleep on it.

Interviewer: Really?

Jeffrey: Absolutely. And some American theaters will raise the curtain and begin the play 13 minutes after the hour to make sure that they're lucky with the audience.

Interviewer: Black cats? The number 13? Those are usually considered *bad* luck!

Jeffrey: That's right. I think it's another way of saying, "We're different."

Interviewer: Right. And what about certain plays being considered unlucky? Could you tell us more about that?

Jeffrey: Ah, of course, Shakespeare's *Macbeth*. Many actors believe that it is bad luck to even say the name of the play in a theater building, so they call it "the Scottish play," or sometimes just "that play." If an actor accidentally says "Macbeth," he or she will leave the room immediately, go outside, and turn around three times to the right, then knock on the door and ask permission to come back in. This goes back to the first performance in London in 1606!

Interviewer: That's interesting. Is "that play" still considered unlucky?

Jeffrey: Well, some think it is, but it has also done very well on Broadway, so those actors probably think it's lucky!

7 CHANGING TIMES

LESSON A, Ex. 5 [p. 56, CD 2 Tracks 12 and 13]

Speaker: Welcome, everyone. I really appreciate you all taking time out of your busy day to attend this presentation.

As stated in the invitation, the topic is "Accommodating Generation Y in the Workplace." Let me begin with a little background information. You may be familiar with the term "Generation X." For my purposes, Generation X means the group of people born starting in the late 1960s up until about 1980. I think most of the managers in this room fall in that category, right?

I thought so . . . So, what about Generation Y? Well, roughly speaking, Generation Y covers all people born between around 1980 and 2000. Most of our staff is now Generation Y, and this will, of course, be true for some time.

However, our management style has been slow in catching up with this trend. We're still basically a Generation X style management team – and we've got to change to focus on the needs of Generation Y employees. To assist you in transitioning your departments, upper management has developed a three-point plan.

First, you've all become accustomed to managing Gen X-ers, who like a clear dividing line between private life and work life. Generation Y-ers, on the other hand, are often more flexible and tolerant when balancing work and private life. Therefore, we're introducing a new corporate social networking website for corporate communications of all kinds – available 24/7 – to give employees more flexibility. Information on how to create an account and suggestions on how to make the best use of this system will be sent to everyone shortly.

Our second point may directly affect your management style. The Gen X-ers you've come to know so well often want to be left alone to do their work. They're often happiest with a hands-off type of boss – and that's fine. Now, the expectations that Gen Y-ers have of a boss and colleagues are *a little* different. They want to regularly share their opinions and ideas with their managers and supervisors, and they want and value work-related comments and advice from them. To meet this need and open lines of communication between staff and management, we will be asking all managers to make themselves available one hour per week to speak with staff informally – listening to employees' concerns and offering advice and feedback.

Lastly, our Generation X employees have always been focused on their own job security and financial security, and that's a responsible thing to do. Generation Y, however, is more volunteer-minded and known for wanting to help others. And that's not a bad thing, either. We want to encourage this spirit of volunteerism, and that's why we're beginning a community outreach program. Any employee who wants to volunteer in the community for a worthwhile local cause will get up to 14 hours a year of paid time off to do just that. Our Gen Y staffers should be excited about this opportunity, and we hope others will get involved, too.

One final note: While we're instituting these changes to better meet the needs of our Generation Y employees, please don't be inconsiderate of the feelings of your Generation X staff. Reassure them that none of the new programs will require any extra time or work from them, but welcome them to take part if they want to.

Well, that concludes my presentation. Now I'd like to open it up to questions . . .

LESSON B, Ex. 2 [p. 58, CD 2 Tracks 14 and 15]

Mr. Turner: Yes?

Jody: Uh, hello. Mr. Turner? I'm Jody.

Mr. Turner: Oh, hi, Jody. I've been expecting you. Come on in and have a seat.

Jody: Thanks.

Mr. Turner: Well, then . . . you're interested in volunteering for Houses for All?

Jody: Well, I think I am. I guess that's what I'm hoping to make a decision about after talking to you today. I'm looking for a positive change in my life, and I'm hoping Houses for All could be it.

Mr. Turner: It may be, Jody. Let me give you a little background information about Houses for All. As you know, we're a nonprofit organization that builds houses for families who need them. We're funded by donations, and all of our builders are unpaid volunteers. We go to several countries around the world, and we ask that volunteers cover their own airfare back and forth to the country they are assigned to.

Jody: Oh, OK. I'll have to give that some thought. I wouldn't want the price of a plane ticket to stand in my way, but I'm not sure if I can afford it.

Mr. Turner: I can understand that.

Jody: On the other hand, I do think that participating in your program will help me get a good job in the future. My friends say that employers really notice when people have Houses for All on their résumés.

Mr. Turner: Yes, well, that's certainly true. I think it's because people who have experienced our program gain a new faith in themselves, a kind of confidence that sets them apart from the average job applicant.

Jody: You know, a teacher once told me that a little more confidence would really help me. That would really be beneficial.

Mr. Turner: Good. Now, are you aware that volunteers are required to give us a one-year commitment? That means a full year abroad, with no trips back, not even on holidays. Not everyone is ready for that.

Jody: Actually, the length of the stay is no problem for me. I'd be fine with staying there for a full year. One of the things I hope to get out of the program is a broader and more global way of looking at things, and I know a change like that takes time.

Mr. Turner: Well, that's certainly an admirable goal. But keep in mind that culture shock has been an issue for many program participants.

Jody: I've heard about it, but I can't believe I would be affected. The only thing I really have to watch out for is what I eat. I have some allergies to nuts and other things that can be a real problem if I'm not careful.

Mr. Turner: Hmm. I'm afraid it would be up to you to avoid anything you can't eat. It's not something *we* can really control.

Jody: Sure, I understand. Now, you said volunteers are involved in building homes, but my experience in that area is pretty limited.

Mr. Turner: Not to worry. That's actually true of most of our new volunteers. We have a complete training program to give you all the skills you need.

Jody: That's a bit of a relief. I'm not very good with my hands, but I do like challenges and will do my best to learn the necessary skills.

Mr. Turner: Well, Jody, it seems to me as if you have the kind of attitude that Houses for All looks for in its volunteers. If you decide to apply, please feel free to give me a call if you have any more questions.

Jody: Thanks so much, Mr. Turner! I will.

8 CONSUMER CULTURE

LESSON A, Ex. 2 [p. 62, CD 2 Tracks 16 and 17]

1. Ben
I definitely prefer shopping online because even if one retailer doesn't have what I want, it's likely that another retailer is going to have it. I rarely have to worry about things being completely sold out anymore.

And nothing can compare to the Internet in terms of selection. I love being able to buy things from anywhere in the country – or anywhere in the world! Of course, the farther away the store, the more I have to pay for shipping, which I have to admit is one drawback. It can be quite expensive sometimes. But I usually get a really good price because I'm able to compare prices so easily online – some websites even do it for you.

Basically, it's a great way to shop, except for having to wait for delivery. That can be unpredictable, which bothers me, since I'm . . . I'm kind of an impatient person, I guess.

2. Anna

When it comes to shopping for clothes, I'm *not* an online shopper. I really need to try clothes on before I buy them to make sure they fit right. I've had some bad experiences buying clothes online, and in some cases, ended up having to return them.

And I really appreciate the personal touch of attentive sales staff that you get in a store. Some have a lot of experience and can be really helpful.

Of course, not everything about shopping in stores is perfect. For example, some of the stores I like can get incredibly crowded during big sales, which is really annoying. And when a store doesn't have what I need, I have to go somewhere else, which wastes a lot of time.

That said, I still prefer shopping in stores because a shopping trip is usually social for me – a way to go out with friends and have fun.

LESSON B, Ex. 2 [p. 66, CD 2 Tracks 18 and 19]

1.

Mary: Bill, are you sure you're not too tired to keep working on our project?

Bill: I *am* tired, but we have two more ads to write before our presentation in 10 hours. What can I do?

Mary: Here, Bill, try some Healthy Go. Just one glass of this fantastic energy drink has the same amount of vitamins and minerals as 12 different fruits and vegetables.

Bill: But this looks just like tomato juice!

Mary: Try it!

Bill: OK . . . Wow! I see what you mean. I feel so much better – energized!

Mary: Good! Now we're sure to get our presentation done on time!

2.

Hailey: Hi, Laura! What a surprise! Won't you come in?

Laura: Hi, Hailey! And hello to you, too, Mittens! Oh! Mittens is getting thin, isn't she!

Hailey: Yes, I'm afraid so. She just isn't eating like she used to.

Laura: What are you feeding her?

Hailey: Oh, you know, whatever cat food is on sale.

Laura: You should try Meow Chow. It's a little more expensive than the other brands, but it's organic, so it's made only with pure, high-quality ingredients. Nothing artificial is ever added. And cats seem to really like it!

Hailey: OK, Laura. I'll give it a try! . . .

* * *

Hailey: Hi, Laura!

Laura: Hi, Hailey! And hello to you, too, Mittens. Oh, Hailey, doesn't she look beautiful!

Hailey: She's got her appetite back, and she's eating well again – thanks to you!

Laura: You mean, thanks to Meow Chow!

3.

Jake: Argh, Sonia's party has started by now. I can't believe we got lost. Has the map loaded on your phone yet?

Erik: No! I'm still waiting for it to come up. Sometimes it takes a really long time, especially out here in the country. In fact, I don't think I'm even getting a connection right now.

Jake: Don't tell me you're still using that same old phone service!

Erik: I'm afraid so. I just can't afford to upgrade to a better service.

Announcer: Tired of your slow phone? Afraid of paying too much for a reliable, high-speed connection? Then a Budget Talk smartphone is just what you need. Our research shows that a Budget Talk connection is 10 times faster than the average connection. What's more, Budget Talk guarantees you a fast, reliable connection, even in rural areas.

Enrolling in a Budget Talk service plan is simple. And we'll even give you a Budget Talk smartphone absolutely free, just for signing up.

Do you have the need for speed? Then sign up for a Budget Talk service plan today.

9 NATURE

LESSON A, Ex. 2 [p. 70, CD 3 Tracks 2 and 3]

1.

Helping Hands is an organization that trains monkeys to aid quadriplegics – people who are unable to use their arms or legs. These animals are able to perform easy but necessary tasks, such as turning electric switches on and off, fetching objects, and picking things up off the floor. They can even be taught to scratch an itch on someone's nose. How are they trained? The young monkeys are placed with foster families who love them, take care of them, and prepare them for their roles as helpers. When the monkeys are adults, they go back to the organization for more advanced training. Once the monkeys are placed with a quadriplegic, they can be helpful for many years.

2.

These days, many nursing homes are discovering the powerful impact that animals, such as dogs, can have on their elderly residents. Owners bring in healthy dogs with good dispositions for weekly visits. Residents look forward to their arrival, often smiling and showing a true interest in the animals. They make more of an effort to walk or move their wheelchairs over to the dogs to pet them. This probably has a lot to do with the fact that dogs give everyone their attention, not caring about age, looks, or ability to speak. For some residents, it may spark fond memories of pets. The owners of the dogs also benefit from the experience. They see the happiness that volunteering their pets brings.

LESSON B, Ex. 2 [p. 74, CD 3 Tracks 4 and 5]

Gil Sanders: Hello, Mr. Morales. I'm Gil Sanders, from *Nature's Way Magazine*.

Mr. Morales: Nice to meet you, Gil. And welcome to the Eco-Harmony Resort. Did you have any trouble finding my office?

Gil Sanders: Well, I certainly didn't expect it to be way up here in the treetops!

Mr. Morales: Well, the architects believed that, as the manager of the resort, I really should be in touch with nature as much as possible.

Gil Sanders: Well, it certainly is an impressive structure.

Mr. Morales: Isn't it, though? It rises 50 meters, right up into the rain forest canopy – the treetops, as you say. All of the resort's buildings were designed so that guests really feel as if they're part of the rain forest, part of nature. It's just one of the features that make our resort so special.

Gil Sanders: You really do get a spectacular view up here. And there seem to be birds and other animals everywhere!

Mr. Morales: That's because the resort doesn't have any fences or barriers to keep them out. It was designed to create an environment where humans and animals live together in harmony.

Gil Sanders: That sounds like a difficult balance to maintain. It seems to me that some guests might be frightened by such close contact with wildlife, and others might accidentally harm the animals.

Mr. Morales: You're right. And to avoid just those things, we have an orientation program to help guests understand the wildlife. Some of our nature guides, who have lived and worked in the rain forest most of their lives, educate our guests on the dos and don'ts of living around animals – which may be unfamiliar to them. We don't want guests feeling anxious around the animals, when one of the main reasons people come here is to relax.

Gil Sanders: Relax, yes. I understand the resort has a world-class spa.

Mr. Morales: Oh yes. We have become quite famous for our massage treatments, which use skin products derived from plants that are only found here in the rain forest.

Gil Sanders: So, there seem to be plenty of options for people who want to come here for relaxation.

Mr. Morales: Yes, but there's plenty of excitement here, too. For example, we have a number of eco-friendly zip lines set up on the mountainside. You can see them if you look right over there.

Gil Sanders: *Eco*-friendly zip lines?

Mr. Morales: Yeah, zip lines. You know, long cables that people hook themselves to, and then slide along, above the trees.

Gil Sanders: Oh, sorry. I know what zip lines are, but I've never heard of "eco-friendly" ones.

Mr. Morales: Well, ours are considered eco-friendly because we made sure they don't disturb any wildlife or damage any trees. Also, the zip lines don't use any electricity or emit any fumes into the environment. They're really a lot of fun, and they make you understand how the rain forest birds must feel as you zoom over the trees. They give you a bird's eye view, so to speak!

Gil Sanders: Wow, I'll have to try that.

Mr. Morales: You'll love it. Oh! I see it's nearly 2:30! Alba, one of our guides, is going to show you around the resort. After the tour, she'll bring you back here, and you and I can have a more formal interview.

Gil Sanders: Sounds good. Thank you, Mr. Morales. I'm getting a better sense of the resort already.

7–9 COMMUNICATION REVIEW

Ex. 4 [p. 79, CD 3 Tracks 6 and 7]

Host: Welcome to *Pet Expert*. Today on the show we have Dr. Amanda Benson with us. Welcome to the show, Dr. Benson.

Amanda: Thanks, Matt. It's nice to be here.

Host: Now, your specialty area is the African grey parrot. What can you tell us about this bird?

Amanda: Well, first, I'd like to talk a bit about who should have a parrot, cover some of the basics of caring for an African grey, and answer some frequently asked questions.

Host: Great. But first, *I* have a question: Is owning an African grey parrot illegal?

Amanda: No, but it *is* illegal to import or buy *wild* birds. So it's important to buy from a reputable breeder who has bred the bird in captivity.

Host: All right. So, who should have an African grey as a pet?

Amanda: The short answer is whoever has the time, space, and interest to take care of a highly intelligent creature. Uh, an exception is people who have asthma. Greys groom their feathers with a dust that's similar to talcum powder. This may cause problems for people with asthma. Families with children should be aware that while greys make interesting and affectionate pets, they can be unpredictable. They have very strong beaks and have been known to bite.

Host: You said these are intelligent birds?

Amanda: African greys are *extremely* intelligent and become bored quite easily. It's absolutely vital that they have stimulation and physical interaction.

Host: Do they need time outside the cage every day?

Amanda: Yes. Most experts agree that three hours a day is vital. They *can* stay out all day, as long as they're supervised. Oh, and they also need toys in their cages – bells, ropes, and ladders are very popular. And there are some excellent videos you can get, which provide the sounds of other birds as well as visual stimulation for the parrots.

Host: Videos? For birds?

Amanda: Absolutely. These don't replace human interaction with your bird, but you can put a video on continuous play when you're out of the house, for example. Greys need stimulation. For that reason, the cage should be located where the bird can see what's going on in the household. A light corner of the living room is a good spot.

Host: What about teaching parrots to talk?

Amanda: It can be very rewarding and a lot of fun. There's been some amazing research done on African greys. In fact, it seems as if they are capable of real, meaningful communication.

Host: Amazing! And what do parrots eat?

Amanda: Fruit, vegetables, nuts – a varied diet. Some birds are quite fussy; others will eat whatever you give them. It's important not to give them avocados, though. Avocados can make a parrot very sick or even kill it.

Host: How long do African greys live?

Amanda: 40 to 50 years is not uncommon.

Host: Oh, wow! That's a long-term commitment.

Amanda: It sure is! People should think carefully before buying an African grey.

Host: Well, thank you very much, Dr. Benson. And thanks to all . . .

10 LANGUAGE

LESSON A, Ex. 5 [p. 82, CD 3 Tracks 8 and 9]

To begin, let me say that making a presentation is often a source of anxiety for many people. They usually rank it as one of the things they least want to do. It's been said that some people fear public speaking more than death! But it doesn't have to be that way. Here are some tips to make your next presentation go smoothly.

First, as a presenter, you need to consider your audience – the people who will be listening to you. Keep in mind what they want to hear from you. It's important to remember that your presentation is for *them*, not for some other imaginary audience.

Second, let me stress that you need to create an outline. The outline contains the ideas you need for your introduction as well as the main point of your presentation and, finally, your conclusion. Keep it clear and simple without too many details.

With your outline in hand, it's time to practice your presentation. You might choose to practice in front of a mirror, with a friend, or you might record it and listen to it after. Practice will make you more confident.

Next, let's talk about giving the actual presentation. Humor can be very useful at the beginning of a presentation, as it puts the audience at ease and gets them on your side. So, if you can, you should start with a joke or funny story.

Posture is very important. Don't stand up there like a stick, holding on to the table or podium with both hands. Try to look relaxed and natural, even if you're feeling a little nervous. Eye contact is also very important, but keep in mind that you shouldn't stare at any one person or area for too long. Keep moving your eyes slowly around the room from person to person. Your voice should sound friendly and natural, and

should be expressive rather than flat.

After your presentation is complete, always welcome questions from the audience. However, too many questions from one person can be tedious for the audience, so ask those enthusiastic questioners to speak with you afterwards, one-on-one.

In conclusion, some preparation, practice, and following the right steps should give you enough confidence to stay calm for your next presentation – and not fear it.

LESSON B, Ex. 5 [p. 86, CD 3 Tracks 10 and 11]

1.

Husband: Honey, it says here on our credit card bill that someone spent $1,000 on a health club and spa membership. Was that you?

Wife: Yes, dear, I did. Fitness is so important to me, and plus, it's a family membership, so you and the kids can use it, too!

Husband: That's nice, but we really need to save money. And there are so many less expensive health club options. I think you should cancel the membership.

Wife: Oh, that reminds me. Have you contacted the dentist yet to cancel your appointment for next week? Since we're going on vacation, you won't be able to make it. I'm really looking forward to our trip, aren't you?

Husband: Yes, of course, but getting back to what we were talking about, don't you think it would be wise for us to cancel the health club membership?

Wife: Well, I suppose I do tend to spend too much. I know how you worry about money, and I don't mean to make you angry. Sometimes I think I just can't do anything right. I don't know how you put up with all my . . .

Husband: Never mind, honey, that's OK. Let's talk again after our vacation.

Wife: OK, dear. Well, I'm off to the health club. I want to look my best for our vacation!

2.

Father: This looks like a good spot, Son. I've got a feeling that this is where the fish are! Put down the anchor. Careful! I don't want you falling out of the boat!

Son: OK, Dad.

Father: Here's your fishing rod, Son. Ahhh! It's great to be out here fishing, just nature and us, isn't it? Since the beginning of civilization, it's been the same story. Humans and their struggle to find food – the struggle for survival!

Son: Uh, Dad?

Father: Oh, I know, Son. You're a little young to understand. When you get to be my age, you start to look at life a little differently. You start to see the big picture and . . .

Son: Uh, Dad, uh, could I say something, Dad?

Father: You don't have to say anything, Son. I understand. You're glad I took you on this fishing trip, you're happy to be with your old dad in this beautiful place, and . . .

Son: I just wanted to say that there's a hole in the boat.

Father: A hole in the boat? Why didn't you tell me? Quick, start the engine! Let's get back to dry land!

3.

Donna: Hello?

Jen: Hi, Donna!

Donna: Hi, Jen! I was just thinking of calling you!

Jen: Really? What a coincidence! Well, anyway, I'm calling for a very special reason. This Friday evening, I'm planning a party at my house. It's my birthday, and I'm inviting about 30 friends over. Would you like to come?

Donna: Oh, thanks for asking, Jen, but I'm afraid I can't make it.

Jen: Can't make it? What do you mean? It's going to be such a great party! I've hired a caterer and a band – everything's going to be first class! Is it transportation? I'd be happy to pick you up.

Donna: That's really nice of you, but that's not the reason I can't come.

Jen: Well, what is the reason, then?

Donna: Well, Friday is *my* birthday, too, and I'm having a party at my house! In fact, I was planning to invite you!

11 EXCEPTIONAL PEOPLE

LESSON A, Ex. 5 [p. 90, CD 3 Tracks 12 and 13]

Speaker: Do you want to be a high achiever?

Crowd: Yes!

Speaker: Then you're going to have to think like a high achiever! Are you ready to change the way you think?

Crowd: Yes!

Speaker: Are you willing to change the way you do things?

Crowd: Yes!

Speaker: Ha, then it sounds like you're ready to be high achievers!

The first thing you've got to keep in mind is that life is a constant process of learning. The secret of any kind of success is education. And we're all able to take in much more information than we think we can. People who aim to be high achievers can take advantage of this in a number of ways. For example, no matter what you're trying to achieve, make sure to absorb information about it every day. Read books, magazines, blogs. Watch videos, exchange information on social media sites. Do whatever you can to increase your knowledge in your chosen field. And, whenever they're available, take courses that will build your knowledge in the area you're interested in.

In conversations with many high achievers over the years, I've come to understand that high achievers always accept total responsibility for their situation. In order to develop this quality in yourself, practice not blaming other people for your failures. Also, try not using difficult situations as excuses. High achievers know that the keys to success are always in their hands and that it's *their* responsibility to use them.

Now we come to the quality of high achievers that I think many people have the most trouble developing in themselves. I'm talking about the vital quality of being a risk taker. Now, if you're already willing to take risks, that's great. If not, you can start by going after opportunities that are a little risky. Think of something you've always wanted but were afraid to try for. Then, go for it – even if you're going out of your comfort zone. Remember: No pain, no gain!

Creativity is another quality that all high achievers share. Creativity involves trying to think about things in new and different ways. The next time you're faced with a difficult problem, brainstorm as many possible solutions as you can. You'll find that the first solutions you think of are rarely the best ones, while the last ones tend to be the most creative. Another great idea is to start a creativity journal. During the week, jot down those creative ideas you'd otherwise just forget. Then, at the end of the week, go over them and see which ones you can use . . .

Now, everyone, it's time to break into work groups to practice some of the ideas we've learned. I want all of you to take . . .

LESSON B, Ex. 2 [p. 92, CD 3 Tracks 14 and 15]

1. Luisa
Who influenced me the most? Oh, that's an easy one. That would be my mother's mother, my grandma. She came to live with us after my grandfather died, so she was always around while I was growing up. She did a great job helping my mother and father, and also us kids. She was such a strong woman, and very smart, too, you know? It's hard to explain, but she was kind of like the "glue" of the family; she somehow, without saying it directly, managed to communicate to us the importance of family, of staying close as a family. Another thing she used to teach us was respect – respect for our parents, for her, but also respect for all people. When I think back on it, I feel that my grandmother was really an amazing woman.

2. Chu Lan
Let's see . . . If I had to choose the person whose example made the biggest difference in my life, it would have to be my high school tennis coach, Mr. Wade. I'm so grateful for all of his help and advice. In fact, everyone on the tennis team appreciated Mr. Wade. His constant encouragement really gave us confidence – you know, the kind of confidence that you keep your whole life. He had a way of convincing you that there was nothing you couldn't do. And he was incredibly patient and easygoing. We all felt like he was more than just a coach – we felt he was one of our friends. And even though I didn't have the talent to actually become a professional tennis player, Mr. Wade spent a lot of time helping me think about my future and finally decide to pursue a career in sports medicine.

12 BUSINESS MATTERS

LESSON A, Ex. 2 [p. 96, CD 3 Tracks 16 and 17]

1.
I always dreamed of working for myself and opening my own restaurant. I always loved cooking. So, when it came time for college, I knew that the Cooking Institute was definitely the place for me. And when I graduated, I couldn't wait to get started.

Well, that was probably my first mistake. I didn't go slowly. I picked a building for my restaurant that had a lot of charm, but it was in a residential neighborhood where parking was really difficult. I didn't have enough regular customers because people didn't really drive by and see it. At first, I thought it was great to not have any competition. Had I realized then that other restaurants in the area were necessary to create more business, I would have known it was a bad sign.

My other mistake was that I wanted to serve only the best and use organic food and exotic ingredients. Well, the problem with that was I had to charge a lot for the food. That didn't help business either. Had I known then what I know now, I'm sure I wouldn't have failed.

2.

In college, I heard about students who had gotten rich by developing and selling apps. It was an attractive idea – you don't need much money to start, and I certainly didn't have much. But I didn't really have any computer programming skills either. But then I learned about software you can use to create apps even if you don't know much about programming. I got one of these programs and tried it out. It was so simple! Now I just needed a new idea for an app.

One evening I sat down to brainstorm with friends. We checked each of our ideas online to make sure they were original. First, we thought of an app that tells you what movies are playing in theaters, but there were already several apps for that. Then we thought of an app that locates coffee shops near where you are. There was already an app for that, too. How about an app to check your eyesight? An app to keep track of the food in your refrigerator? An app to see what hairstyle would look good on you? There were apps for all of those things! We brainstormed for hours and couldn't come up with a single new idea, so . . . we finally just gave up.

But I'm glad I tried. If I hadn't searched the Internet that day, I wouldn't know about all of the cool apps out there!

LESSON B, Ex. 5 [p. 102, CD 3 Tracks 18 and 19]

1. Anne
I attended a workshop on how to communicate better with the people I work with. It's funny because the leader set up ground rules right away and wrote them on the board. Some people laughed and said they felt like they were in kindergarten. The rules were pretty basic. Don't interrupt other people when they're talking. Don't take things too personally. Criticize ideas, not people. And respect differences. We could see during the workshop how those little rules kept things flowing much more smoothly. I've found that I've been remembering them at work, too.

2. Thomas
OK, well, last week I went to a workshop on how to solve problems by working in small groups. The workshop coordinator started off by breaking the class into groups of six. Each group chose a leader, a recorder, and a spokesperson. We all had to discuss a problem and brainstorm ideas. The leader didn't make decisions . . . she just made sure that everyone spoke. The recorder wrote an objective summary of the group's conclusions. Then the spokesperson reported our results to the rest of the workshop and answered any questions. We all learned the benefit of addressing work-related problems as a group and joining together to come up with a solution. I think this system is definitely better than trying to tackle a problem separately. It's less stressful, and sharing different ideas helps you come to an interesting solution sometimes.

3. Paulina
Well, I attended a role-playing workshop in the store where I work. All the managers and salespeople got together and took turns pretending to do the other person's job as well as playing the part of the customer. The leader would give us a scenario, like "An angry customer tells the salesclerk that he wants to speak to the manager." Well, that's a common one! Well, anyway, we would role-play the situation for five minutes and then analyze it. You know, it was actually very interesting to put yourself in someone else's shoes. It helps you to better understand the needs and concerns of your fellow workers, supervisors, and customers.

10-12 COMMUNICATION REVIEW

Ex. 2 [p. 104, CD 3 Tracks 20 and 21]

Professor: Good morning, everyone. This is the first of three sessions we'll have on the topic of "The Good Language Learner."

All of you should have been sent the course work. I hope everyone has had a chance to print out the notes for today and that you've all had time to do the reading.

How many of you have the notes and have done the reading? Show of hands? Everyone's done that? Ah, good, then at least you'll all know what I'm talking about even if I don't.

OK, so first, let's brainstorm some of your ideas about the characteristics of good language learners. I'm interested in hearing about your own experiences and opinions, as well as what you've read.

All right, Helen, why don't you get us started?

Helen: OK, well, to begin, I think the majority of successful language learners are highly motivated.

Professor: Good, fine. What else?

Helen: I think they need to be willing to take risks and to generally be inquisitive.

Professor: Good. Highly motivated, risk-taking . . . why do you think risk taking is important?

Helen: Not being afraid to make mistakes means that you're actually going to be using the language more, I think. You're kind of experimenting, looking for patterns.

Professor: OK, pattern seeking. Interesting. Anyone else have some ideas? Uh, Charlie?

Charlie: I think being open-minded is essential.

Professor: Open-minded. Why would that be important, do you think?

Charlie: Well, I think it kind of goes along with pattern seeking, looking for ways things link up, whether or not the patterns are similar in your first language. It's kind of like creative problem solving.

Actually, I think good language learners need to be a little experimental. I guess that goes along with risk taking. They're willing to live with not knowing what everything means and how everything works.

Professor: OK. Do you think that there are strategies that learners need to have in place to actually use this information? Maxine?

Maxine: I think a lot of good language learners develop their own systems for recording and remembering, um, vocabulary, for example. Being well organized and self-aware are important.

As *you* say, all successful learners have to be able to make use of the information they get.

Charlie: Do you think most people learn a language more easily in a classroom or by just picking it up?

Professor: It depends on the person. And, of course, it depends on how much language learners are exposed to.

OK, to sum up, provided there is plenty of exposure to the language and that the learner has at least some of these characteristics and strategies, language learning will take place whether or not it's in a classroom.

Let's go on now to look at what the implications are for the language-teaching classroom. I want you to turn to your textbooks . . .

Workbook ANSWER KEY

1 RELATIONSHIPS

LESSON A • The best of friends

1 Grammar

Separable: cheer (me) up, bring out (the best), puts (me) down, turn (her) down

Inseparable: come by, run into, open up, do without

Three-word verbs: stand up for

Intransitive: drift apart

2 Vocabulary

1. clash
2. admirable
3. harmonize
4. enduring
5. benefited
6. empathetic

3 Grammar

1. stand up for
2. cheer her up
3. turned him down
4. do without
5. ran into
6. drifted apart

4 Grammar

Answers will vary.

5 Writing

A 1. Be a person that your friend can trust.
   Know when to give advice and when to keep silent.
   Pay attention to what your friend thinks and feels.

   2. Join clubs and other organizations related to your interests or hobbies.
   Sign up for a class, such as painting or cooking.
   Participate in community service activities, such as working with the elderly.

   3. Keep in touch through social media, video calls, and email.
   Get together and travel whenever possible.
   Send cards and presents for special occasions, such as birthdays and holidays.

B *Answers will vary.*

C *Answers will vary.*

LESSON B • Make new friends, but keep the old . . .

1 Grammar

1. Circle: tend to be, plan to start
   Underline: considering starting
2. Circle: tend to be
   Underline: appreciate spending, enjoy sharing
3. Circle: intend to start
   Underline: enjoy biking, suggest starting, considering entering

2 Grammar

Answers to the questions will vary.

1. to borrow
2. practicing
3. to go out
4. to be invited
5. hanging out / to hang out
6. going
7. talking / to talk

3 Vocabulary

1. rekindled
2. replace
3. rebuild
4. recall
5. redefined
6. rehash
7. resurfaced
8. reconnecting

4 Grammar

Possible answers

1. We should plan to take a walk somewhere nice.
2. I would suggest relaxing at a cozy café.
3. We should consider going to a club so we can dance.
4. You might prefer to get / getting tickets to a concert so we can hear some live music.

5 Reading

A 1. spurs
   2. lean
   3. nagging
   4. a clear nod to
   5. predisposed to
   6. tend and befriend

B 2, 3, 5

T-178 Workbook answer key

2 CLOTHES AND APPEARANCE

LESSON A • *The way we dress*

1 Grammar
1. i
2. g
3. d
4. e
5. h
6. b
7. c
8. f
9. a

2 Vocabulary
1. stylish
2. chic
3. conservative
4. stuffy
5. sloppy
6. retro
7. functional
8. trendy

3 Grammar
1. to impress
2. to put
3. to look
4. buying
5. to avoid
6. spending
7. to donate
8. to feel

4 Grammar
Answers will vary.

5 Writing
A Thesis statement 1:
There are many reasons for getting dressed up.

Thesis statement 2:
I feel that young people need to reject the pressure to dress stylishly.

B *Answers will vary.*

C *Answers will vary.*

D *Answers will vary.*

LESSON B • *How we appear to others*

1 Grammar
What I noticed first was the three inches he grew.

What struck me most about him was how grown up he sounded.

What I realized at the end of the visit was that I have a really terrific brother!

2 Grammar
Possible answers

1. what I noticed first was how relaxed and friendly she seems
2. what I liked best was her eyes
3. what struck me was what she did with her hair
4. what I admired was her beautiful voice

3 Vocabulary
1. eccentric
2. sinister
3. arrogant
4. sympathetic
5. trustworthy
6. intense
7. intellectual
8. dignified

4 Grammar
Answers will vary.

5 Reading
A
1. willing to listen, engaged in conversation
2. willing to listen, not engaged in conversation
3. not willing to listen, engaged in conversation
4. not willing to listen, not engaged in conversation

B
1. fugitive
2. reflective
3. responsive
4. combative

3 SCIENCE AND TECHNOLOGY

LESSON A • *Good science, bad science*

1 Grammar

1. For some people, using an abacus is an alternative to using <u>a</u> calculator.
2. <u>The</u> abacus is the earliest form of mechanical computing.
3. *Correct as is.*
4. It consists of wires strung across <u>a</u> wooden frame.
5. . . . On <u>the</u> wires are beads, which represent units.
6. *Correct as is.*
7. <u>A</u> skilled operator can make calculations on it very quickly.

2 Vocabulary

1. frivolous
2. problematic
3. confidential
4. hazardous
5. unethical
6. audacious
7. prudent

3 Grammar

1. the
2. X
3. an / the
4. the
5. a
6. a
7. X
8. a
9. X / the
10. X / the
11. an
12. a

4 Grammar

Answers will vary.

5 Writing

A *Possible answers*

Paragraph 1: One day in the not-so-distant future, small robotic spaceships will search the inner solar system mapping asteroids and determining which to harvest.

Paragraph 2: Robotically controlled factories built on asteroids will turn space rock water into rocket fuel and asteroid metals into everything needed for space-based manufacturing.

Paragraph 3: . . . big investors are already taking such ideas seriously enough to put substantial money into asteroid mining and space exploration companies.

By locating manufacturing facilities and rocket fueling stations on asteroids already in space, costs will be reduced and long journeys into space will become possible.

Paragraph 4: . . . most of the technology needed to mine asteroids and build orbital factories doesn't exist yet.

Still, early investors and the companies they're investing in believe they will be successful and that along the way the asteroid-mining technologies they develop will help bring about a new age.

B 1. There is a great deal of serious interest in mining asteroids for their valuable resources.
2. Asteroid mining could lead to a new era of space exploration and colonization.

C *Answers will vary.*

LESSON B • *Technology and you*

1 Grammar

1. different time, reason
2. reason
3. same time
4. different time, reason
5. different time, reason
6. same time
7. different time, reason

2 Grammar

Possible answers

1. Lily broke her digital camera taking a picture. / Taking a picture, Lily broke her digital camera.
2. Having watched a show about alternative energy, Diego bought an electric car.
3. Being a resourceful person, Bella built her own computer.
4. Having injured his arm, Dan received a bone scan.
5. Celia is in her car listening to satellite radio.
6. Being an eco-conscious person, Ken always recycles his old electronics.

3 Vocabulary

1. c
2. f
3. a
4. h
5. g
6. e
7. d
8. b

4 Grammar

Answers will vary.

5 Reading

A unsurprisingly common

B 1. a   2. b   3. b   4. a

4 SUPERSTITIONS AND BELIEFS

LESSON A • *Superstitions*

1 Vocabulary
1. e   2. f   3. d   4. c   5. a   6. g   7. b

2 Grammar
When someone asserts that you can see . . .

. . . they'll sometimes admit that they can't find . . .

And if people argue that you can badly hurt . . .

Others have claimed that it's true . . .

However, experts agree that there's really no need . . .

. . . and they report that a dropped coin could not reach . . .

Do you ever doubt that we, as humans, have . . .

. . . some scientists explain that many other senses are . . .

3 Grammar
1. As a child, I believed (that) a monster was living under my bed.
2. To keep the monster away, I felt (that) I had to adjust the covers over me.
3. I assumed (that) my teddy bear would help me.
4. I doubted (that) my parents would believe me.

4 Grammar
Possible answers
1. Anna would explain that Friday the 13th is just like any other day.
2. Luke would admit that he keeps a lucky charm with him during important games.
3. Farah would argue that it's hard to prove whether the superstitions are true or not, but perhaps some are true.

5 Writing
A   1. c   2. b   3. f   4. d

B   *Answers will vary.*

LESSON B • *Believe it or not*

1 Grammar
It was said that the Martians were attacking . . .

. . . it was announced that the Martians were dying.

. . . it is generally claimed that many people believed it . . .

. . . and it was reported that there was widespread panic . . .

It has been suggested that Welles's broadcast offers . . .

2 Vocabulary
1. misleading   5. believable
2. convincing   6. conceivable
3. well-founded   7. dubious
4. iffy   8. credible

3 Grammar
1. It is estimated (that) more than two billion people use the Internet.
2. It is reported (that) fingernails grow faster on the hand that you use the most.
3. It is said (that) the oldest living tree on earth is nearly 5,000 years old.
4. It is believed (that) in a baby's first year of life, parents lose between 400 and 750 hours of sleep.
5. It is explained that items like plastic cups and bags take between 500 and 1,000 years to break down.
6. It is claimed (that) about 100 hairs fall from a person's head each day.

4 Grammar
1. It is said (that) 15 minutes of exercise per day may extend your life by three years.
2. It is reported (that) the average American child watches 20,000 commercials each year.
3. It is suggested that traditional treatments such as acupuncture are effective.
4. It is claimed (that) a cure for certain types of cancer will be found soon.
5. It is believed (that) some animals can predict earthquakes.

5 Reading
A
1. in 1995
2. millions of people
3. Verifying and debunking rumors, ridiculous claims, and email chain letters.

B   1. NG   2. NG   3. F   4. T   5. NG

5 MOVIES AND TELEVISION

LESSON A • *Movies*

1 Vocabulary

1. riveting
2. formulaic
3. mediocre
4. touching
5. engrossing
6. inspiring

2 Grammar

1. The writer <u>clearly</u> did his research and interviewed many people who knew her.
2. <u>Apparently</u> in May, but there will be a private viewing in April.
3. <u>Supposedly</u>, the director used footage of certain people without asking permission, and now there's a lawsuit.
4. The director <u>probably</u> thinks he doesn't need to try very hard any more after so many successful movies.
5. <u>Obviously</u>, you really like that kind of movie.
6. Yes, but <u>unquestionably</u>, there's a lot of deep emotion in them as well.

Certainty: clearly, obviously, unquestionably
Less certainty: apparently, supposedly
Possibility and probability: probably

3 Grammar

Possible answers

1. Apparently, that famous Dutch actor is going to direct a movie. / That famous Dutch actor is apparently going to direct a movie.
2. Some movie studios are frankly not interested in good acting as much as extreme action. / Frankly, some movie studios are not interested in good acting as much as extreme action.
3. This is definitely a magazine for anyone with a very strong interest in cinema.
4. There would probably be more interest in historical movies if they received more publicity.
5. Because of a lack of funding, there will potentially be fewer independent films made this year.

4 Grammar

Answers will vary.

5 Writing

A *Answers will vary.*
B *Answers will vary.*

LESSON B • *Television*

1 Grammar

1. such
2. so little
3. so
4. such
5. so much
6. so many
7. so few

2 Vocabulary

1. game show
2. soap opera
3. news program
4. sports program
5. talk show
6. documentary
7. cartoon
8. sitcom
9. cooking show
10. sketch comedy show

3 Grammar

Possible answers

1. TV is so engrossing to some children (that) they want to watch it all the time.
2. Soap operas are so addictive (that) many people watch them every day.
3. Nature documentaries are such fascinating programs (that) I watch as many of them as I can.
4. News programs can be so superficial (that) little information can be learned from them.
5. Reality TV shows are so inexpensive to produce (that) TV networks schedule them every night.
6. Some stars of TV drama series are such good actors (that) they are successful in movies, too.

4 Grammar

Answers will vary.

5 Reading

A
1. prosecutors
2. strike
3. forensic tests
4. empirical
5. juries

B
1. Yes
2. No
3. No
4. Yes

6 MUSICIANS AND MUSIC

LESSON A • *A world of music*

1 Grammar
1. more
2. harder
3. more
4. faster
5. less
6. better

2 Grammar
1. more
2. better
3. less
4. longer
5. sooner

3 Vocabulary
Answers will vary.

4 Grammar
Answers will vary.

5 Writing

A *Possible answers*

Live music:

You listen with many other people.

You can't adjust the volume.

You can listen only when musicians are playing on stage.

Recorded music:

You can't see the musicians while you listen.

You can adjust the volume.

You can listen to a song over and over.

You can listen to music in any order you'd like.

You can turn off or skip songs you don't like.

Live music and recorded music:

Sometimes you hear music you don't like.

You can sing along with your favorite songs.

You can hear music by well-known artists.

You can listen to any kind of music you're in the mood for.

B *Answers will vary.*

C *Answers will vary.*

LESSON B • *Getting your big break*

1 Vocabulary
1. pay
2. make
3. be
4. break
5. got
6. get
7. be
8. make

2 Grammar
1. would listen
2. will practice
3. will go
4. won't spend / will not spend
5. would turn up
6. would listen

3 Grammar
1. When the band comes onstage, the crowd <u>will</u> scream.
2. Before the band got popular, it <u>would</u> never sell out a concert in such a short time.
3. *Correct as is.*
4. *Correct as is.*
5. In the past, the band <u>would</u> play only hard rock songs.
6. Although the band used to sign autographs after a show, these days, security guards <u>will</u> not let fans backstage.

4 Grammar
Answers will vary.

5 Reading

A having to do with the nervous system

B 1. Yes   2. Yes   3. No   4. No   5. Yes

7 CHANGING TIMES

LESSON A • *Lifestyles in transition*

1 Grammar

1. that
2. that
3. which
4. that
5. who
6. that
7. which
8. whose

2 Grammar

1. O; Physical fitness is an important goal that a lot of people try to achieve.
2. R; Many people who / that find the time to work out regularly at a gym stay fit.
3. O; For the best results, it's important to find a gym (that / which) you like.
4. R; It may be a good idea to hire a trainer who / that can work with you privately.
5. R; Your trainer can give you advice that / which can help you avoid injuries.
6. O; If you get bored at the gym, try bringing some music (that / which) you can listen to while you exercise.

3 Vocabulary

1. indecisive
2. immature
3. illogical
4. consistent
5. inconsiderate
6. responsible

4 Grammar

Answers will vary.

5 Writing

A
1. I feel it is very important for families to have regular meals together.
2. The focus of the second paragraph is how they decided on the days to have dinner together.
3. The focus of the third paragraph is how the family dinners went.
4. The idea of having regular family meals together, which seemed difficult at first, has brought about many positive changes in our lives.

B *Answers will vary.*

C *Answers will vary.*

LESSON B • *A change for the better*

1 Grammar

1. like
2. as if
3. as though
4. as
5. the way
6. As
7. as if
8. Like

2 Vocabulary

1. e   2. b   3. f   4. d   5. c   6. a

3 Grammar

Possible answers

1. He feels as if he has lost a family tradition.
2. She feels the way she did when she began school and made many new friends.
3. She feels as though she is becoming less close to her grandmother.
4. He feels like he has found an exciting new career.

4 Grammar

Answers will vary.

5 Reading

A
1. outbreaks
2. epidemiology
3. analogy
4. contagious

B 1, 2, 5

8 CONSUMER CULTURE

LESSON A • *What's new on the market?*

1 Grammar

1. Some stores offer their ⟨customers⟩ frequent-buyer rewards as incentives to return.
2. Advertising is useful because it gives ⟨us⟩ information about improved products.
3. The salesperson recommended the latest headphones to ⟨me⟩.
4. Someone had to explain the new printer to ⟨Daniel⟩.
5. This GPS must have cost ⟨you⟩ a lot of money.
6. You should return those boots to ⟨the store⟩ if they're not comfortable.
7. Online auction sites offer ⟨collectors⟩ a great way to find the things they want.
8. I don't shop online often because I like to ask ⟨salespeople⟩ questions in person.

2 Grammar

1. The salesperson showed the woman the latest tablets.
2. The salesperson recommended the GS5 model to the woman.
3. He described the main features to her.
4. The woman asked him the price.
5. The salesperson told her the price.
6. She said nothing to him for a moment. / For a moment, she said nothing to him.
7. The salesperson offered her a discount.
8. She gave the money to the salesperson.

3 Grammar

Possible answers

1. Mai should return the book to the store and get one she doesn't have.
2. Kate and Ray should lend Pam some money.
3. Ian should teach his sister Thai.
4. Jessica should recommend Luigi's to her father.
5. Max should mention the problem to his friend.

4 Vocabulary

Possible answers

1. Both Monica and Emil love to go window-shopping.
2. Jeremy seems to be a compulsive shopper.
3. Mark is a real bargain hunter.
4. Anne and her mother went on a shopping spree.
5. Jen has a case of buyer's remorse.
6. Eric went over his credit limit.

5 Writing

A 1. a, b   2. a, c   3. b, c

B *Answers will vary.*

C *Answers will vary.*

LESSON B • *Consumer awareness*

1 Grammar

I saw the sales flier for your supermarket, and I felt it was imperative that I write you. All the food on sale this week is snack food or other highly processed foods. Although I buy these foods occasionally, I suggest that local and organic foods be on sale, too. It's crucial that people have the chance to buy affordable local foods, and I recommend that your supermarket start offering these items at better prices. I also propose that you offer a larger selection of fresh fruits and vegetables. Many people don't buy fresh foods because they are not easily available. I think it's essential that your customers get the chance to incorporate these foods into their meals.

2 Grammar

1. It is important that people learn how to block offensive ads on their devices.
2. It is vital that a health-conscious person eat fast food only once or twice a month.
3. It is essential that parents read reviews before their children see a movie.
4. We insist that the government prevent students from dropping out of school.

3 Grammar

Answers will vary.

4 Vocabulary

Answers will vary.

5 Reading

A hearing, sight, smell

B 1. c   2. a   3. b

9 NATURE

LESSON A • *Animals in our lives*

1 Grammar

1. wherever
2. whenever
3. whenever; wherever
4. Where
5. When

2 Grammar

1. Whenever I'm around a cat, I start sneezing. / I start sneezing whenever I'm around a cat.
2. Wherever I looked, there were amazing plants and animals. / There were amazing plants and animals wherever I looked.
3. She looks like that whenever she sees a bird outside. / Whenever she sees a bird outside, she looks like that.
4. Whenever I see fish swimming, I feel calm. / I feel calm whenever I see fish swimming.

3 Vocabulary

1. feather
2. tail
3. fangs
4. horns
5. beak
6. paws
7. fin
8. hooves
9. tusks
10. gills
11. wing
12. claws

4 Grammar

Answers will vary.

5 Writing

A
1. a. Yes   b. Yes   c. No   d. No
2. a. No   b. Yes   c. Yes   d. No
3. a. Yes   b. Yes   c. No   d. Yes

B *Answers will vary.*

C *Answers will vary.*

LESSON B • *In touch with nature*

1 Grammar

1. Whoever
2. whatever
3. whatever
4. whoever
5. whatever
6. Whoever

2 Vocabulary

1. as clear as mud
2. under the weather
3. a breath of fresh air
4. the tip of the iceberg
5. a walk in the park
6. set in stone
7. up in the air
8. a drop in the ocean

3 Grammar

Answers will vary.

4 Grammar

Answers will vary.

5 Reading

A
1. It's well known by Bosnian children.
2. "A Fairy Tale Comes True"; It's a Balkan fairy tale but it turned into reality for one poor family.

B
a. 4   d. x   g. 7
b. 3   e. 5   h. x
c. 6   f. 1   i. 2

10 LANGUAGE

LESSON A • Communication skills

1 Grammar

1. was giving
2. was introduced
3. should have been displayed
4. dropped
5. wasn't working
6. might have been saved
7. has praised

2 Grammar

1. The players were thanked after the soccer team won the championship.
2. I have been told that I have good presentation skills.
3. Foreign languages should be taught beginning in elementary school.
4. A new prize is being awarded to the best debate team.
5. The best-selling author is going to be interviewed on TV tonight.

3 Vocabulary

1. To begin / First of all, welcome to our seminar, "Giving Your Best Presentation."
2. In addition / Furthermore, many of us get very nervous just thinking about presenting . . .
3. First of all / To begin, outline your ideas carefully.
4. Nevertheless / Yet, don't depend too much on pictures and charts . . .
5. Likewise / Similarly, give yourself plenty of time to become familiar . . .
6. Next, practice the presentation a couple of times . . .
7. To sum up / In conclusion, preparation, practice, and confidence are the keys . . .

4 Grammar

Answers will vary.

5 Writing

A 1. Most students would benefit from training on how and where to find reliable information online.

Learning how to successfully do research online is as important to future studies and careers as learning subjects such as math and history is.

Many students need guidance to learn how to distinguish trustworthy sources from unreliable ones.

2. Most students in the twenty-first century already have the necessary skills to do online research or can learn these skills on their own.

The Internet is changing rapidly, and the skills students learn today may no longer be relevant in the near future.

Class time should be used for teaching more complex content and skills.

B Answers will vary.

LESSON B • Natural language

1 Grammar

| 1. were | 3. are | 5. share | 7. comes |
| 2. uses | 4. is | 6. needs | 8. put / puts |

2 Grammar

1. A majority of the students needs / need to know the language to get a better job.
2. All of the students want to be able to speak the language when they travel.
3. A minority of the students has / have to study the language because it's a required subject.
4. None of the students need / needs to be able to read literature in the language.
5. Half of the students study the language because they enjoy it.

3 Vocabulary

1. has a way with words
2. talk behind your back
3. talking my ear off
4. has a sharp tongue
5. stick to the point
6. loves to hear himself talk
7. talk me into something

4 Grammar

Answers will vary.

5 Reading

A
1. conceptualize   4. sole
2. surveys   5. mark
3. mind-bending   6. aboriginal

B 1. T   2. F   3. NG   4. T

11 EXCEPTIONAL PEOPLE

LESSON A • High achievers

1 Vocabulary
1. coolheaded
2. absent-minded
3. warm-hearted
4. empty-headed
5. hardheaded
6. open-minded
7. narrow-minded
8. cold-hearted

2 Grammar
Possible answers
1. The famous conductor is <u>widely recognized</u>.
2. In my opinion, the politician's speech was <u>long-winded</u>.
3. Nicole is a <u>curly-haired, brown-eyed</u> model.
4. Alyssa is an <u>easygoing</u> boss. She lets employees choose their hours.
5. Maxwell's is not a <u>well-known</u> restaurant.
6. Dr. Kendall's lectures are <u>thought-provoking</u>.
7. Katy made a good impression at the interview because she was so <u>well dressed</u>.

3 Grammar
Answers will vary.

4 Writing
A 1. 1939 2. 15 years 3. 1958
B a. 6 b. 1 c. 2
C *Answers will vary.*

LESSON B • People we admire

1 Grammar
Without a doubt, my <u>most fondly remembered</u> teacher is Mr. Hill, my college French professor. He was <u>the most kind-hearted</u> man, and he always showed concern for his students. He went out of his way to make us feel comfortable in class, so we never felt too nervous or anxious to participate. He was <u>the hardest-working</u> teacher I've ever had, and he would always come up with creative ways to help us understand <u>the most difficult</u> lessons. Mr. Hill truly loved French culture, so the cultural lessons were <u>the most thought-provoking</u> of all my classes. He made me feel that I was looking through a window into another world, and he made me want to be a part of that world. I'm afraid I don't remember much French now – it's not <u>the most easily retained</u> language, especially if you don't use it often – but I did learn how great a teacher can be and how rewarding it can be to learn about another culture.

2 Grammar
1. the most thought-provoking
2. the greatest-tasting
3. the most heartbreakingly convincing
4. the most widely downloaded
5. the most warm-hearted person
6. the most breathtakingly beautiful

3 Vocabulary
1. to
2. through
3. with
4. after
5. after
6. to
7. on
8. to

4 Grammar
Answers will vary.

5 Reading
A 2, 5, 6
B 1, 3, 5

12 BUSINESS MATTERS

LESSON A • *Entrepreneurs*

1 Vocabulary

1. for
2. off
3. against
4. around
5. on
6. toward

2 Grammar

1. Yes
2. Yes
3. Yes
4. No
5. Yes
6. No
7. Yes
8. Yes

3 Grammar

Possible answers

1. <u>Had</u> the woman <u>not answered the ad</u>, she'd never have become a veterinary assistant.
2. <u>Had</u> the couple <u>not gotten the cat</u>, they wouldn't have had so many kittens at home.
3. <u>Had</u> the man <u>not entered the speech contest</u>, he wouldn't have won first prize.
4. <u>Had</u> the woman <u>not taken the class</u>, she wouldn't have started her own business.
5. <u>Had</u> the man <u>not taken a number</u>, he would never have been served.
6. <u>Had</u> the woman <u>not seen the sale sign</u>, she wouldn't have bought her new laptop.

4 Writing

A Sentences that do not belong:

It is very kind of you to read this letter.

In fact, you have probably never had a candidate as qualified as I am!

None of my current colleagues wants me to leave.

B *Answers will vary.*

C *Answers will vary.*

LESSON B • *The new worker*

1 Grammar

1. Assuming that
2. Whether or not
3. Provided that
4. Supposing that
5. Whether or not

2 Grammar

Possible answers

1. I would probably accept it, too, provided that the benefits were also good.
2. On the condition that I didn't live too far away, I wouldn't mind commuting to work.
3. I would go a year without a raise, assuming that I had a chance of promotion later.
4. Supposing that the company were reorganizing and everyone were changing position, I would accept a demotion.
5. I wouldn't speak up against my boss, whether or not I disagreed with her.
6. I agree it's OK to lend a family member money to start a business provided that they were able to prove they could repay it.

3 Grammar

Answers will vary.

4 Vocabulary

Answers will vary.

5 Reading

A 1. 20 percent 2. None

B *Possible answers*

1. Engaged employees are significantly more productive, drive higher customer satisfaction, and outperform less engaged workers.
2. The four core needs are physical, emotional, mental, and spiritual.
3. Office environments should be safe, comfortable, and appealing to work in. In addition, they should include a range of physical spaces, offer healthy, high quality food at low prices, create places for employees to rest and renew, and provide a well-equipped gym.
4. Employees not only receive regular feedback but also have the chance to provide feedback to their supervisors.

Workbook answer key   T-189

1 DO OPPOSITES ATTRACT?

Before you watch

A What do people need to have in common for a harmonious relationship? Choose the three most important things partners should share in your opinion.

- ☐ cultural background
- ☐ past experiences
- ☐ religion
- ☐ hobbies/interests
- ☐ personality type
- ☐ tastes in books and movies
- ☐ outlook on life
- ☐ political views
- ☐ values

B **Pair work** Compare and discuss your choices in part A. Then decide upon the most important thing people should have in common. Share your choice with the class. Give reasons and examples to support your opinion.

A: We think the most important thing people should have in common is their values. If your values are different, it can affect a lot of areas in your life, like your future plans or how you raise your family.

While you watch

A Take notes to answer the questions in your own words.

1. What do experts think people need to look for in friendships and love relationships?
   _____

2. What may the differences that are attractive at first cause a couple to do later on?
   _____

3. Why is it harder for people with opposite personalities to form a relationship?
   _____

B Write the letter of the correct video character to complete each sentence. Use each letter twice.

a. The good girl
b. The laid-back artist 
c. The outgoing boyfriend 
d. The type-A businesswoman 

1. ____ should find someone with relaxed energy.
2. ____ is not a good match for a shy partner.
3. ____ may be better off dating a businessperson.
4. ____ would enjoy being with a highly social person.
5. ____ is preferred by the laid-back artist but is not a good match for one.
6. ____ may tend to fall for the rebel.
7. ____ may feel a businessperson has traits that are helpful.
8. ____ will have a harmonious relationship with a nice person.

T-190 Video activity worksheets   Photocopiable © Cambridge University Press 2015

C Choose the correct answer according to information in the video.

1. Research shows that people may admire _____.
   a. people like them
   b. expert opinions
   c. people who have skills they lack

2. We need to date people whose _____ are similar to our own.
   a. experiences and values
   b. personality and attitudes
   c. religious and political beliefs

3. People on dating websites usually decide to go out with people who _____ them.
   a. complement
   b. are similar to
   c. are the opposite of

4. If you end up dating someone who is your opposite, you should _____.
   a. remember to reconnect after arguments
   b. say good-bye
   c. examine the differences in attitude and personality

5. Differences in views on things like politics and movies are usually differences in _____.
   a. attitude
   b. personality
   c. values

6. Once opposite personalities clash, it may be harder for them to _____.
   a. reconnect with each other
   b. rehash old times
   c. share relaxed energy

After you watch

A **Pair work** The video states that there is a big difference between opposite attitudes and opposite personalities in relationships. Look at the personal aspects in *Before you watch* part A. Write *A* next to those related to attitude and *P* next to those related to personality. Discuss your choices.

B **Pair work** List the 10 most important things for you in a mate. Exchange lists and classify your partner's choices into traits relating to attitude, appearance, or personality. Then discuss the questions below.

1. Do you agree or disagree on the classifications?
2. Do you feel either list should be adjusted? If so, how and why?

A: The trait "likes sports" is an attitude, so it may not be very important.
B: I have to disagree. For me, sports are everything! If my partner didn't go to sporting events with me, he'd be very lonely!

2 ALL ABOUT FASHION

Before you watch

A Pair work Match the adjectives with the pictures. Then compare your answers. Did you choose the same images? Discuss your choices.

| conservative | flashy | futuristic | quirky |
| dignified | functional | over-the-top | sloppy |

1. _____
2. _____ 
3. _____  
4. _____ 
5. _____ 
6. _____ 
7. _____ 
8. _____ 

B Pair work Look at the styles in part A. Talk about your impression of each person based on what he or she is wearing.

A: I think number two looks elegant, but she may be a bit stuffy.
B: I agree. She looks like a person who might be nice but phony.

While you watch

A Choose the main topics discussed in the video.

☐ 1. self-expression
☐ 2. royalty
☐ 3. very large hats
☐ 4. youth culture
☐ 5. large necklaces
☐ 6. very high shoes
☐ 7. Egyptian eye makeup
☐ 8. bikinis
☐ 9. shopping
☐ 10. sweatshirts
☐ 11. retro looks
☐ 12. quirky combinations

T-192 Video activity worksheets

B Write *T* (true) or *F* (false). Then correct the false statements with a partner.

___ 1. Clothing has only recently become important to people.
___ 2. People dress for self-expression and are often inspired to dress like famous people.
___ 3. When we think of over-the-top seventeenth-century fashions, we tend to think of Queen Elizabeth.
___ 4. One of the biggest influences on fashion since the 1960s has been comfort.
___ 5. High shoes were invented to make people feel taller.
___ 6. The heavy eye makeup Egyptians wore served a functional purpose.
___ 7. In the future, we probably won't be permitted to choose what to wear.

C Choose the correct answers according to the information in the video.

1. Our clothing tends to tell the world _____.
   a. how we think   b. what our job is like   c. who we think we are

2. Fashion has been about self-expression _____.
   a. for about 3,000 years   b. since King Louis XIV   c. since the 1960s

3. Men were encouraged to wear powdered wigs _____.
   a. because the king did   b. because they wanted to be king   c. to cover their bald spots

4. An aspect of 1960s youth culture is that people decided to _____.
   a. dress more like celebrities   b. be comfortable   c. create their own styles

5. Usually the latest trend is a look that rebels against _____.
   a. revealing the body   b. the established look   c. sloppy looks

6. After a frumpy style has been around a while, the next look will probably be _____.
   a. quirky   b. futuristic   c. dignified

After you watch

A The video points out that the following things have been behind creating fashions. Give an example of a fashion item created for each reason.

1. People we look up to: _____
   _____

2. Comfort: _____
   _____

3. Necessity: _____
   _____

B Group work Discuss your answers to part A. What are the group's best examples? Share them with the class.

C Writing What is the biggest influence on your fashion choices? Why is it important to you? Write a paragraph explaining your view.

VIDEO ACTIVITIES

3 PAST AND FUTURE PREDICTIONS

Before you watch

Pair work What will the world be like 100 years from now? What new things will we have? What will we do differently? What will stay the same? Discuss the questions for each category. Then write your predictions.

1. Travel

   _____
   _____
   _____

2. Technology

   _____
   _____
   _____

3. Health

   _____
   _____
   _____

4. Education

   _____
   _____
   _____

5. (Other area / Your choice) _____

   _____
   _____
   _____

While you watch

A Write *T* (true) or *F* (false). Then correct the false statements with a partner.

____ 1. Very few predictions for the future that were made 100 years ago were accurate.

____ 2. Predictions that came true included the invention of certain types of communication and travel.

____ 3. Predictions that didn't come true included certain changes to education and special medical advancements.

____ 4. Two of the predictions that were somewhat true were about travel and communication.

____ 5. The modern-day people in the video make very different predictions for the future than the people of 100 years ago.

____ 6. Four of the modern-day people make predictions about transportation.

B Complete the predictions made in the past that were mentioned in the video.

1. People thought telephones would be _____.
2. They predicted that we would be able to communicate worldwide using _____.
3. They thought we would tour the country driving _____.
4. They suggested that we would clean our homes automatically using _____.
5. They thought that a college education would be _____.
6. They believed we would have killed all the _____.
7. They were certain we would have put an end to _____.
8. They thought we would get our shopping delivered by _____.
9. They thought students would learn because of _____ connected to their heads.

C Write the letter of the correct phrase to complete each sentence.

   a. cars will drive themselves
   b. people will choose their dreams
   c. there won't be any cars
   d. robots will do all the work
   e. people won't get sick anymore
   f. we will have flying cars

1. Joshua predicts that in the future ____.
2. Bao thinks that ____.
3. Yasmin expects that ____.
4. Mike thinks that ____.
5. Patricia believes ____.
6. Shane predicts that ____.

After you watch

A **Pair work** Look at your partner's predictions from *Before you watch*. How are they the same or different from the ones at the end of the video? How likely do you think they are to come true? Rate the predictions from 0 (very unlikely) to 10 (very likely).

B **Group work** Compare your predictions from part A. Choose a favorite prediction for each category and present it to the class. Do they think it will come true? Why or why not?

C **Writing** Write a paragraph about the three technological advances made in the last 100 years that you consider the most important. Give facts, reasons, and examples to support your opinion.

4 SUPERSTITIONS AROUND THE WORLD

Before you watch

A Pair work Answer the questions about common superstitions. Then interview a partner about his or her beliefs. Discuss your answers.

Do you . . .	Me Yes	Me No	My partner Yes	My partner No
1. believe the number 4 is unlucky?	☐	☐	☐	☐
2. believe the number 13 is unlucky?	☐	☐	☐	☐
3. assume black cats are good or bad luck?	☐	☐	☐	☐
4. carry a rabbit's foot for luck?	☐	☐	☐	☐
5. avoid walking under ladders?	☐	☐	☐	☐
6. avoid writing your name with red pen?	☐	☐	☐	☐
7. cross your fingers for good luck?	☐	☐	☐	☐
8. think breaking a mirror is unlucky?	☐	☐	☐	☐
9. think that an itchy palm means you will lose or gain money?	☐	☐	☐	☐

B Pair work Can you think of any other superstitions? Make a list and share it with the class.

While you watch

A Choose the superstitions that you hear mentioned in the video.

☐ 1. wearing red for good luck
☐ 2. crossing fingers for luck
☐ 3. the thirteenth floor of tall buildings
☐ 4. Loki the Norse god of evil
☐ 5. the number 7 being lucky
☐ 6. tossing a coin in a fountain
☐ 7. leaving chopsticks in a bowl of rice
☐ 8. dumping coconuts off a boat
☐ 9. leaving shoes overturned
☐ 10. walking under ladders

B Choose the correct answers according to the information in the video.

1. Most cultures have _____ ideas about luck.
   a. very different   b. very similar   c. several

2. The origin of number 13 as being unlucky may originate from _____.
   a. historians   b. the ancient Persians   c. tall buildings

3. Many superstitions are related to a fear of _____.
   a. ladders   b. death   c. rats

4. In some places, _____ is considered bad luck.
   a. how you eat   b. serving rice   c. placing certain eating utensils incorrectly

5. Some superstitions are based upon _____.
   a. real situations   b. travel restrictions   c. the style of objects

6. In Hawaii, there is a practice of dumping bananas off a boat as it is _____.
   a. arriving at the shore   b. sailing at sea   c. leaving the shore

C Take notes to answer the questions in your own words. Then compare answers with a partner.

1. Name three superstitions that are considered lucky.
   _____
   _____
   _____

2. What are three possible origins for the fear of the number 13?
   _____
   _____
   _____

3. Why is the number 4 considered unlucky in some places?
   _____

4. What is the reason for the Hawaiian superstition of dumping bananas off a boat?
   _____

After you watch

A **Pair work** The video mentions some reasons behind superstitions. List three superstitions and possible reasons behind them. You can make the reasons up, but try to make them believable.

1. Superstition: _____
   Reason: _____

2. Superstition: _____
   Reason: _____

3. Superstition: _____
   Reason: _____

B **Group work** Which reasons from part A seem the most convincing? The most unbelievable? Share your most believable reasons for the superstitions with the class. Which group's reasons are the best?

C **Writing** Do you think superstitions and good luck charms actually influence outcomes in life? Write a paragraph about your opinion. Give reasons and examples to support your view.

5 MEET THE DIRECTOR

Before you watch

A Which of these steps involved in making a movie do you think would be difficult to do? Which would be easier to do? Which do you think you might enjoy doing? Complete the chart.

	Difficult	Easier	I might enjoy doing
1. coming up with a good idea for the movie	☐	☐	☐
2. writing the script	☐	☐	☐
3. finding actors	☐	☐	☐
4. financing the movie	☐	☐	☐
5. shooting the movie	☐	☐	☐
6. directing the movie	☐	☐	☐
7. getting the movie into theaters	☐	☐	☐

B **Pair work** Compare your answers in part A. How similar or different are your choices? What are the reasons behind them?

While you watch

A Number the steps for making the movie *Rot* from 1 to 7 in the order the director mentions them.

____ using crowdfunding to get money for the movie

____ trying to raise money for the movie by showing people the unfinished script

____ more and more people connecting with the film idea

____ scouting locations and talking to people

____ paying for part of the movie with his own money

____ having small ideas that connected with a number of other ideas

____ putting the movie in film festivals

B Choose the correct answers according to the information in the video.

1. The director knew he had to make the movie when _____ .
   a. the ideas connected
   b. he realized it had a great metaphor
   c. everyone said it was a strong, moving idea

2. The director was _____ as he was writing the first draft of the script.
   a. scouting locations and trying to raise money
   b. asking studios for money
   c. living in a cabin

3. One challenge a new director faces is getting _____ .
   a. support from family and friends
   b. funding for a movie
   c. good ideas to connect

4. The director found it surprising that so many people _____ .
   a. thought the movie sounded cool
   b. helped pay for an unknown movie
   c. were making inexpensive movies

5. By putting his movie in as many film festivals as possible, the director hopes to _____ .
   a. encourage studios to make his next movie
   b. get his message across
   c. win lots of awards

6. One problem for new filmmakers nowadays is that _____ .
   a. there are not a lot of good ideas left
   b. people donate smaller amounts of money
   c. it is harder to get noticed

C Match the underlined words with the items to which they are referring.

a. the movie	d. the first ideas for the movie
b. get a movie noticed	e. the main character
c. the first draft of the script	f. universal themes

____ 1. "I wanted it to be touching."
____ 2. "... but I wanted to do them in a more original way ..."
____ 3. "... some of them go back over a year ago ..."
____ 4. "... I thought that was a great metaphor for just what's going on with him ..."
____ 5. "So I would give it to people, and at this point it probably wasn't that good ..."
____ 6. "But I feel that with the right idea and the right story, there's no reason why you can't do it."

After you watch

A Pair work Answer the questions and discuss the video. Then share your discussion with the class.

1. What things did you learn about making a movie as a new director?
2. What information from the video did you find the most interesting or surprising? Why?

B Pair work The video shows a few clips from the movie. Based on those clips, how do you think the story goes? Take turns summarizing your ideas about the story.

C Writing Crowdfunding is now being used to fund movies, art projects, travel plans, and special products. What would you like to raise money to do? Write a paragraph explaining your idea and why people might connect with it.

6 HILLARY REYNOLDS BAND

Before you watch

Pair work What do you think life is like for a new band that has not signed with a record label? Discuss the questions.

1. What kinds of tasks would a band have to do themselves if they have no agent or manager?
2. Where are the best venues for a new band to play?
3. What kinds of songs should a band play to catch people's attention?
4. How important are social media and the Internet in becoming successful today?

A: Without a manager or agent, there would be a lot of things a band would have to do.

B: Yeah, like book their own shows, talk to music producers, and maybe even manage the money.

While you watch

A Choose the best answers according to the information in the video.

1. What is one way the Hillary Reynolds Band describes their music?
   a. acoustic folk
   b. pop acoustic
   c. indie-folk

2. What is one challenge the band faces right now?
   a. They cannot get enough studio time.
   b. They have to book everything themselves.
   c. Their upcoming tour was canceled.

3. How does the band write and arrange songs?
   a. Hillary writes all their songs.
   b. The band collaborates on all their songs.
   c. Their songwriting processes are varied.

4. How does the band get people to listen to their music?
   a. They make sure a lot of people hear them.
   b. They do cold calls to make contacts.
   c. They play cover songs to get people's attention.

5. What does the band enjoy hearing most from their fans?
   a. that they were able to find them on social media
   b. that a song has made them feel good
   c. that they heard them on the radio somewhere

6. What does the band think it takes to be successful in the music business?
   a. hard work and passion
   b. passion and a good agent
   c. a good agent and love for the business

7. What are the band's hopes for the future?
   a. to get their songs on mainstream radio
   b. to meet more people in the music industry
   c. to continue playing music for people

B Write *T* (true) or *F* (false). Then correct the false statements with a partner.

____ 1. The Hillary Reynolds Band met at the Berklee College of Music.

____ 2. The band combines catchy pop melodies with electric instruments.

____ 3. Trevor plays the mandolin, Jeff plays the ukulele, Hillary plays the cello, and Chris plays the upright bass.

____ 4. Sometimes Hillary and the band write an entire song in one session.

____ 5. According to the band, a big résumé makes it easier to get more high-profile gigs.

____ 6. The band enjoys making music but also hopes that they will sign with a major label and become really famous.

C Who says it? Write *H* for Hillary, *T* for Trevor, or *J* for Jeff.

| Hillary | Trevor | Jeff |

____ 1. ". . . so we try to use those kinds of instruments and those kinds of sounds and textures to get across pop songwriting."

____ 2. "Most signed artists have a whole team of people that are dedicated to making the 'machine' work."

____ 3. "And that is what makes our songwriting so complex and so . . . so great."

____ 4. "And I think the more we play covers, the more they are willing to give our original songs a chance."

____ 5. "In the past, we would make a lot of cold calls because we wouldn't have a lot of contacts around the country . . ."

____ 6. ". . . bands would define success, by signing with a major label, becoming really famous . . ."

After you watch

A In the video, the band gives their opinions about what bands can do to be successful. What is your opinion on the following points related to this topic?

1. Does playing cover songs make a band more popular? Why or why not?
2. What does it take to be successful in the music business?
3. How would you define a successful band?

B **Pair work** Discuss your answers to part A. Then compare and contrast the Hillary Reynolds Band with a band that you think is successful. How are they the same? How are they different?

C **Group work** What does *success* mean in the entertainment industry in general? Choose a successful entertainer and describe why he or she has done well.

7 CHANGING GENDER ROLES

Before you watch

A Look at the jobs. Which are for men? Which are for women? Think of your first reaction and write *M* for men, *W* for women, or *B* for both.

___ 1. business leader   ___ 5. hairstylist   ___ 9. police officer
___ 2. doctor   ___ 6. homemaker   ___ 10. secretary
___ 3. engineer   ___ 7. lawyer   ___ 11. soldier
___ 4. farmer   ___ 8. nurse   ___ 12. teacher

B **Pair work** Do you agree or disagree on your choices? Discuss your answers and explain your opinions.

While you watch

A Choose the statement that best summarizes the main idea presented at these points in the video.

1.
 a. The gender roles of men and women in the past were not that diverse.
 b. For many centuries, gender roles in the home business were separated.
 c. Men and children worked on the farm and women worked in the home for many centuries.

2.
 a. The Industrial Revolution made people behave as though gender roles would not change.
 b. During the 200 years after the Industrial Revolution, gender roles went through a big change.
 c. In the twentieth century, gender roles went through a big change.

3.
 a. With further education, many women entered fields dominated by men.
 b. With women entering new fields, most men welcomed them.
 c. Some men welcome women in the workplace, but there are still some who resist them.

4.
 a. Children growing up today may not be able to decide what to do.
 b. Children who are growing up today may be able to choose any career they want.
 c. Attitudes and roles are likely to reverse for the new generation of children.

T-202   Video activity worksheets   Photocopiable © Cambridge University Press 2015

B Number the events from 1 to 8 in the order they are mentioned in the video.

____ Men left to fight in wars.
____ Men went to work in factories while women stayed home with the kids.
____ Women started to become doctors and business leaders.
____ Gender roles were similar, sharing work and having businesses at home.
____ Women started working in factories, offices, and stores.
____ More men started becoming teachers, nurses, and stay-at-home dads.
____ The Industrial Revolution created many jobs away from home.
____ Women sought further education.

C Take notes to answer the questions in your own words. Then compare answers with a partner.

1. How did many women feel after filling in for men during World Wars I and II?
   _____
   _____
   _____

2. What issues exist today for women who are in the same jobs as men?
   _____
   _____
   _____

3. What issues exist today for men whose jobs are considered feminine?
   _____
   _____
   _____

After you watch

A Pair work Ask and answer the questions about the video. Then share a summary of your discussion with the class.

1. What new things did you learn about gender roles?
2. What information did you find the most interesting or surprising? Why?

B Writing Do you think the jobs in *Before you watch* part A will always be associated with a gender, or might they change as the video infers? Write a paragraph explaining your opinion. Support your ideas with reasons and examples.

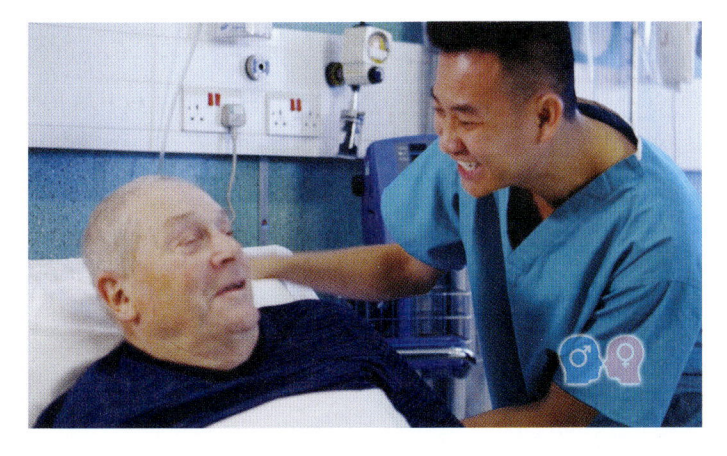

8 THE HISTORY OF ADVERTISING

Before you watch

A How many different ways to advertise can you think of? Write as many different types of advertising as you can (e.g., television commercials, magazine ads, mail, etc.).

_____
_____
_____
_____

B Pair work Compare your answers. Did your partner have any advertising media you didn't think of? Work together to think of other ways to advertise.

While you watch

A Watch the video and check your answers from *Before you watch* part A. How many of your answers are mentioned in the video? Watch again and write any types of advertising that you missed.

_____
_____
_____

B Choose the correct answers according to the information in the video.

1. Including online ads, it is estimated we see _____ of ads per day.
   a. hundreds   b. thousands   c. millions

2. Egyptian stone tablets may be considered a type of advertising because they _____.
   a. sold things from time to time   b. communicated messages   c. were a new medium

3. The first magazine was _____.
   a. a magazine for hairstylists   b. published in 1631   c. started in England

4. With direct marketing, advertising took the form of _____.
   a. recommending products in articles   b. sending postcards and catalogs   c. speaking to people individually

5. Billboards were useful to _____.
   a. advertise gas   b. promote radio ads   c. introduce television to the world

6. The invention of television _____ the most effective form of advertising.
   a. provided advertisers with   b. created infomercials as   c. entertained viewers with

7. The infomercial was created _____.
   a. in the 90s   b. 30 years after the first television commercial   c. when cell phones became popular

8. A possible future advertising medium mentioned is _____.
   a. dream commercials   b. infomercials on the moon   c. ads on glasses

T-204   Video activity worksheets   Photocopiable © Cambridge University Press 2015

C Choose the correct answers according to the information in the video.

	Newspaper	Mail	Television
1. This got a lot cheaper over time.	☐	☐	☐
2. This is one of the most effective forms of advertising.	☐	☐	☐
3. Advertising as we know it started with this.	☐	☐	☐
4. Magazine ads came after these ads.	☐	☐	☐
5. An ad for a watch is given as an example for this medium.	☐	☐	☐
6. Direct marketing was born in this medium.	☐	☐	☐

After you watch

A Think about the types of advertising you saw in the video. Which (if any) do you find enjoyable? Which (if any) do you find annoying? Make lists.

Enjoyable	Annoying

B **Pair work** Compare your lists from part A. Give reasons for your classifications. How similar or different are your views?

C **Group work** Discuss these questions. Then share your opinions with the class.

1. What are the positive and negative aspects of advertising? How does advertising help us? How might it be problematic?
2. What are some changes that could be made to improve advertising in general?
3. What are some other ways people might advertise in the future?

9 HUMANS AND ANIMALS

Before you watch

A Pair work At times, people compare human traits with animals, for example: *as quiet as a mouse*. Look at the adjectives and write the animal(s) you think are associated with them. Then add your own ideas.

1. courageous _____
2. hairy _____
3. slow _____
4. evil _____
5. busy _____
6. wise _____
7. my idea: _____
8. my idea: _____
9. my idea: _____

B Group work Compare your answers. Why might these comparisons be made? What characteristics tie these animals and human traits together?

While you watch

A Choose the statement that best summarizes the main idea presented at these points in the video.

1.
   a. When we have wanted animal companions, we have domesticated them.
   b. Wherever humans have wanted to go, animals have provided transportation.
   c. When we need help pulling things, animals are there.

2.
   a. When the earliest humans depicted their gods, it was usually an animal or part human and part animal.
   b. Whenever early humans depicted animals, they were really depicting humans.
   c. The earliest humans saw their gods when they looked to the skies.

3.
   a. Thousands of years ago, when humans described animals, they compared them to people.
   b. When different cultures describe humans, they usually compare humans to bears.
   c. Different cultures may use different descriptions, but we all compare humans to animals.

4.
   a. When we look at owls, we compare them to humans, too.
   b. When we tell stories, we often attribute human qualities to animals.
   c. Animal-like humans are common in entertainment media.

T-206   Video activity worksheets

Photocopiable © Cambridge University Press 2015

B Choose the correct answers according to the information in the video.

1. Through domestication, transportation, and survival, _____.
   a. humans have depicted animals as useful
   b. animals have become dependent on humans
   c. humans and animals have become strongly linked

2. The tradition of depicting gods as animals shows _____.
   a. that people saw gods all around them
   b. that all cultures are the same
   c. man's deep connection to animals

3. Early humans thought they saw _____.
   a. humans in animals
   b. animals in humans
   c. gods in some people

4. We use many phrases that _____.
   a. contrast human and animal behavior
   b. make fun of people by comparing them to animals
   c. use animals to describe the essence of a person

5. Cartoons and movies often show _____.
   a. animal attributes in humans
   b. interesting animal behavior
   c. animals with human qualities

C Match the animals with their associated human traits.

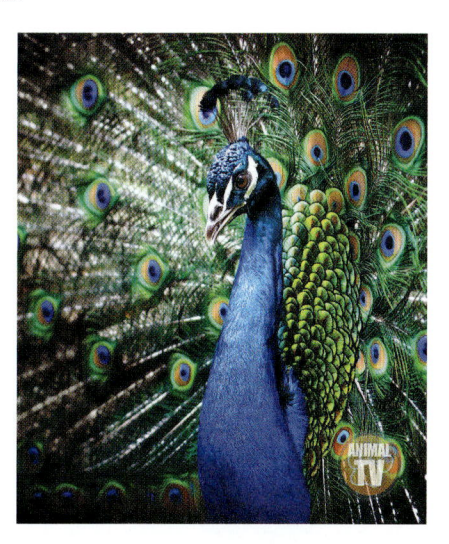

1. snake ____
2. lion ____
3. peacock ____
4. chicken ____
5. owl ____
6. bee ____
7. lamb ____
8. fox ____
9. gorilla ____
10. horse ____
11. kitten ____
12. snail ____

a. vain
b. wise
c. slow
d. sly
e. playful
f. courageous
g. scared
h. hungry
i. hairy
j. evil
k. busy
l. gentle

After you watch

A Compare your list of human–animal comparisons from *Before you watch* part A with the comparisons in the video. How similar or different are they?

B **Pair work** Review your comparisons from part A. Then think of famous people or characters with those traits. Share your choices with the class.

C **Group work** Discuss possible reasons why some animal comparisons may be different around the world. Consider the influences of culture, geography, and literature in shaping our perceptions of animals. Share your discussions with the class.

10 TIPS FOR BETTER PRESENTATIONS

Before you watch

A What do you know about making a good slide presentation? Take the quiz.
Write *T* (true) or *F* (false).

___ 1. It is better to stick only to the facts in a presentation and not tell stories, as they may divert listeners' attention.

___ 2. It is better to read your slides to make sure you get your information correct.

___ 3. If you are reading from a presentation, do not look at the screen the whole time. It can be distracting.

___ 4. It is best to put complete sentences and paragraphs on the screen to ensure you present all needed information.

___ 5. It is best to use a large dark font on a light background so that everyone can read your slides.

___ 6. Hand out any notes and presentation materials before you begin your talk so that people can follow along.

B **Pair work** Discuss your answers. Were most of your answers the same or different? Would you like to change any answers?

While you watch

A Who does each action while giving their presentation? Write *M* for the man or *W* for the woman. Then check your answers to *Before you watch* part A.

___ 1. uses storytelling to present information

___ 2. reads the presentation word for word

___ 3. talks in a conversational manner

___ 4. watches the slides during the presentation

___ 5. does not use bullet points

___ 6. does not put everything on the slides

___ 7. uses a small font

___ 8. does not give a handout until after the presentation ends

T-208 Video activity worksheets

B Write the letter of the correct phrase to complete each sentence.

> a. use bullet points
> b. try to tell a story
> c. post slide points one at a time
> d. watch the presenter
> e. look at the screen the whole time
> f. talk as if you were having a conversation
> g. give handouts at the end of the presentation
> h. use a large, dark font on a light background

1. The audience will find it more interesting if you ____ .
2. No one wants to hear you read, so ____ .
3. You take the focus off yourself if you ____ .
4. A successful presentation is when people ____ .
5. Because paragraphs on slides are hard to read, you need to ____ .
6. People who sit in the back will be able to read if you ____ .
7. The audience will get ahead of you if you don't ____ .
8. To encourage people to pay attention and not write while you are speaking, ____ .

C Choose the correct expressions to complete the statements according to the information in the video.

1. *Poor slideshows / Boring subjects* are the reason audiences dread watching presentations.
2. It is tedious for people to sit there while someone *talks as if having a conversation / reads exactly what is on the screen*.
3. A common problem during presentations is *looking only at the screen / talking too long about a subject*.
4. It is not necessary to *look at your slides at all / put your entire speech on the screen*.
5. In choosing to write the text for the slides, you should include *no more than three words / only the key words*.
6. It is a good idea to view your slides from the back of the room to check if *everyone can see you / your font is too small*.
7. Letting people know they will get a copy of the presentation discourages them from *taking their own notes / reading ahead on the slides*.

After you watch

A **Pair work** Which problems mentioned in the video have you or your partner seen or done in a presentation? How did it affect the presentation? Share your experiences with the class.

_____
_____
_____

B **Pair work** Think of three additional tips that could improve a presentation. Prepare a presentation about your tips.

1. _____
2. _____
3. _____

C **Group work** Take turns giving your presentation with another pair. Give each other tips to improve your presentation styles. Choose the best presenters and have them present the best ideas to the class.

11 ROLE MODELS

Before you watch

A Choose the top five qualities that first occur to you when you think of people who are role models.

- ☐ awe-inspiring
- ☐ coolheaded
- ☐ easygoing
- ☐ hard-driving
- ☐ highly acclaimed
- ☐ kind-hearted
- ☐ near-perfect
- ☐ open-minded
- ☐ outspoken
- ☐ positive-thinking
- ☐ well-known
- ☐ widely respected

B Pair work Select three qualities you both agree are typical of most role models. Share your opinions with the class and give reasons for your choices.

While you watch

Rachel   *Edgar*   *Sierra*   *Tim*

A Write *T* (true) or *F* (false). Then correct the false statements with a partner.

_____ 1. People are signing a pledge to share information about their role models.
_____ 2. At first, Edgar does not see the connection between being a coach and being a role model.
_____ 3. Rachel believes only celebrities can make good role models.
_____ 4. At first, Sierra thinks nurses make better role models than pediatricians.
_____ 5 Tim thinks Nelson Mandela was a great role model because he had an impact on a whole country.
_____ 6. Rachel thinks a role model should try to affect everyone in the world.

B Choose the correct names to make the statements true.

1. *Rachel / Edgar / Sierra / Tim* thinks you can't feel better if you feel sad.
2. *Rachel / Edgar / Sierra / Tim* is popular with the children that live near him.
3. *Rachel / Edgar / Sierra / Tim* points out that a positive attitude is a great thing to model.
4. *Rachel / Edgar / Sierra / Tim* makes entertainment products for children.
5. *Rachel / Edgar / Sierra / Tim* has a class project and talks to people on Saturdays.
6. *Rachel / Edgar / Sierra / Tim* is too self-critical and claims to be too hotheaded.
7. *Rachel / Edgar / Sierra / Tim* takes care of people for a living.
8. *Rachel / Edgar / Sierra / Tim* is eventually convinced that role models can be online, too.

C Who says it? Write *R* for Rachel, *E* for Edgar, *S* for Sierra, or *T* for Tim.

____ 1. "He made you want to work harder to live up to his expectations, you know."

____ 2. "It's not about being the most awe-inspiring person or even a near-perfect person."

____ 3. "Who's going to want to take after me?"

____ 4. "That's very thought provoking."

____ 5. "But I'll bet the way you interact with them could have far-reaching effects on their lives."

____ 6. "I try to always be the most positive-thinking person in the room."

____ 7. "You might be onto something."

____ 8. "But don't you actually have to meet people to be a role model?"

After you watch

A **Pair work** List five qualities Rachel demonstrates that make her a good role model. Then compare your list with a partner and give reasons for your choices.

1. _____
2. _____
3. _____
4. _____
5. _____

B Think about your own role model. List five qualities that make this person a good role model. Give reasons why these qualities are important.

1. _____
2. _____
3. _____
4. _____
5. _____

C **Writing** Write a paragraph about your own role model. Describe the person and write about at least three qualities that make him or her a good role model and why they are important.

12 JOB INTERVIEW DOS AND DON'TS

Before you watch

A What are some dos and don'ts for a job interview? List two or three items for each category.

Should do	Should not do
wear appropriate clothing	chew gum

B Pair work Compare your lists. Are your ideas the same or different? Discuss your thoughts and think of additional suggestions.

Additional DOs	Additional DON'Ts

While you watch

A Take notes to label each picture with the tips presented at or around these points in the video.

1.  _____
_____
_____

2.  _____
_____
_____

3.  _____
_____
_____

4.  _____
_____
_____

B Choose the correct answers according to the information in the video.

1. It's good to _____ and go over your notes to prepare for the interview.
   a. practice
   b. arrive early
   c. study the company

2. Staying calm and still helps you to _____ .
   a. have good posture
   b. seem confident
   c. maintain good eye contact

3. Had Steve not _____ , it might not have looked like he was interested in the job.
   a. asked intelligent questions
   b. mentioned the salary
   c. talked about the marketing director

4. One way Steve _____ was by mentioning the company's marketing region.
   a. acted confident
   b. did research
   c. demonstrated initiative

5. One reason Steve mentions he wants the job is because of _____ .
   a. his interest in the hardware industry
   b. the opportunities for advancement
   c. his feeling he is the right person for the job

C Take notes to answer the questions in your own words. Then compare your answers with a partner.

1. What three tips for keeping still and calm are mentioned in the video?

   _____
   _____
   _____

2. What three tips for "doing your homework" are mentioned in the video?

   _____
   _____
   _____

3. What is an example of a standard interview question in the video?

   _____
   _____

After you watch

A **Pair work** Which three suggestions from the video do you think are most important? Why? Discuss your opinions.

B **Pair work** Choose a job and think of details about a fictional or real company that offers the job. Prepare three questions and possible answers for a job interview with that company. Include at least one standard question.

	Question	Possible answer
1.		
2.		
3.		

C **Pair work** Use the questions and answers from part B to take turns role-playing a job interview. Offer helpful feedback about the interviewee's answers and performance.

1 DO OPPOSITES ATTRACT?

Story summary

"Do Opposites Attract?" explores the effects of personality and attitude on relationships. It is seen all the time in movies and on TV, but do opposites really bring out the best in each other? Experts say usually not. Although people may admire those whose skills and traits complement theirs, they need to date people who share their values, outlook on life, and experiences. What should someone do if they are dating a person who is opposite from them? Social scientists suggest they should consider if the differences that attracted them at first will cause them to clash and drift apart later. While differences in attitudes do not always affect a relationship, differences in personalities may make it much harder to empathize, reconcile after arguments, and handle compromises. In the end, experts suggest looking for someone with a similar personality.

Language summary

Grammar Phrasal verbs
Gerund and infinitive constructions

Vocabulary Adjectives and verbs to describe friendship
re- verbs

Before you watch page T-190

A

In this activity, Ss choose important things they think partners should share.

- **Preview the activity** Explain that Ss will watch a video about how opposites relate to one another in relationships. Direct Ss' attention to the list. Go over the instructions and read the items. Remind Ss they are giving their own opinions.
- **Do the activity** Have Ss choose the things they think are important for couples to share.

B Pair work

In this activity, Ss discuss their answers from part A.

- **Preview the activity** Have Ss read the instructions and the example answer. Tell them to review their own answers and then choose the most important thing partners should share. Remind Ss to support their opinion with reasons and examples.
- **Do the activity** Have pairs compare their answers and discuss their ideas. Help as needed.
- **Follow up** Have pairs briefly summarize their discussions for the class. Note the three most popular choices among Ss on the board.

While you watch pages T-190–191

A

In this activity, Ss answer general questions about the video in their own words.

- **Preview the activity** Go over the instructions. Have Ss read the questions.
- **Play the video** Have Ss take notes as they watch. Play the video again, if necessary. Allow time as needed for Ss to write their answers.

- **Check answers** Have Ss compare answers with a partner. Then go over the answers with the class.

Possible answers
1. We should look for people who are like us and who share our values, outlook on life, and experiences.
2. They may cause the people to clash and drift apart later on.
3. It's more difficult for opposite personalities to empathize with each other, reconnect after arguments, and handle compromises.

B

In this activity, Ss choose correct characters to complete sentences about the video.

- **Preview the activity** Go over the instructions. Have Ss read the statements.
- **Play the video** Have Ss write the letter for the correct character to complete each sentence. Remind Ss they will use each letter twice. Play the video again, if necessary.
- **Check answers** Go over the answers with the class.

Answers
1. b   2. c   3. d   4. c   5. d   6. a   7. b   8. a

- **Option** Have Ss complete the activity from memory, then play the video again to check the answers.

C

In this activity, Ss choose the correct information to complete sentences about the video.

- **Preview the activity** Go over the instructions. Have Ss read the sentences and answer options.
- **Play the video** Have Ss do the activity. Play the video again, if necessary.

- **Check answers** Go over the answers with the class.

Answers					
1. c	2. a	3. b	4. c	5. a	6. a

After you watch page T-191

A Pair work

In this activity, Ss categorize the personal aspects from *Before you watch* part A.

- **Preview the activity** Go over the instructions.
- **Do the activity** Have Ss look at the items in *Before you watch* part A and assign them to a category: attitude or personality. They then review and discuss their answers.

B Pair work

In this activity, Ss analyze and discuss a top 10 list of important relationship elements.

- **Preview the activity** Go over the instructions. Read the sample conversation with a volunteer.
- **Do the activity** Have pairs discuss their lists with each other as well as their answers to the questions. Have a few pairs share their ideas with the class. Is there a consensus among the class over the most important traits?
- **Option** Review the Ss' top choices listed on the board in *Before you watch* part B. Have the Ss' choices changed after watching the video? If so, have the class discuss why.

Project

A Write the script

In this activity, Ss write their own reaction video to "Do Opposites Attract?"

- **Preview the activity** Tell Ss they will work in small groups to make a video expressing their opinions about opposites in relationships. Ss will write a script and then act it out on camera. Explain that they will take turns speaking and operating the camera.
- **Brainstorm** Have the group brainstorm the idea for their video. First, what format will it be? A talk show with a host asking for the guest's opinions? A casual, scripted chat among friends? Opinions presented directly to the camera? A dating game show? Next, the group should brainstorm what they will talk about.

    Sample idea:

    Talk show
    - Prepared questions for the host:
        - How would you describe your personality? Does your ideal partner need to have similar attitudes or are different opinions OK?
        - What are some issues you and your partner must agree on? What issues are OK to disagree on?
        - Is being similar to each other more important for friendships or love relationships? Why?
    - Have the guests prepare their answers before shooting the video.

- **Outline** Have Ss make an outline of their script. They can use their own ideas or the following structure:
    - List the main ideas you will discuss.
    - Create the lines of dialog covering those ideas.
    - Check that the order of ideas flows well throughout the script and reorder as necessary.
- **Write the script** Have Ss write their scripts using their outlines. Have them read through their work as they go and revise as needed.
- **Check the script** Have Ss rehearse their scripts. Help as needed.

B Make and share the video

In this activity, Ss make and share their own reaction video about "Do Opposites Attract?"

- **Plan the video** Remind Ss that they will take turns speaking and operating the camera. Alternatively, Ss can set up the camera so they appear on-screen together to act out a situation.
- **Make the video** Have Ss make their videos.
- **Share the video** Ss share their videos with the class.
- **Option** Award prizes for the videos: best all-around, funniest, sweetest, etc. Be sure to give each group a prize.

2 ALL ABOUT FASHION

Story summary

"All About Fashion" talks about the history and causes behind fashion over the years. Fashion is not only about function; it is often about self-expression. People often look up to the wealthy, celebrities, and musicians for fashion inspiration. Historically, royalty such as France's King Louis XIV and England's Queen Elizabeth I have also influenced fashion. But since the 1960s, youth culture has become one of the biggest determiners of what is fashionable. Sometimes fashion starts out of comfort or wanting to look good, but at other times it comes out of necessity, such as wearing very high shoes to avoid stepping in mud or wearing eyeliner to block the sun's glare. Styles often come and go in cycles that are the opposite of the previous trend; for example, a sloppy look following an elegant trend or flashy fashions coming after conservative ones. Because of this, styles that were cool 30 years ago may come back as a retro look today. The only certain thing about fashion is that people will continue to express themselves through clothing.

Language summary

Grammar	Review of verb patterns	Vocabulary	Adjectives to describe style
	Cleft sentences with *what*		Adjectives to describe outward appearance

Before you watch page T-192

A Pair work

In this activity, Ss match adjectives to pictures of different fashion styles to preview the topic of the video.

- **Preview the activity** Explain that Ss will watch a video about fashion. Direct Ss' attention to the list of words and review vocabulary as needed. Go over the instructions.
- **Do the activity** Have Ss write the words under the pictures. Then have Ss compare answers and discuss their choices.
- **Check answers** Check the answers with the class.

Possible answers

1. sloppy	4. quirky	7. flashy
2. dignified	5. over-the-top	8. futuristic
3. functional	6. conservative	

B Pair work

In this activity, Ss discuss the fashion styles in part A.

- **Preview the activity** Have Ss read the instructions. Model the example conversation with a volunteer.
- **Do the activity** Have pairs discuss their opinions of the people wearing the different styles. Help as needed.
- **Follow up** Have pairs briefly summarize their discussions for the class.

While you watch pages T-192–193

A

In this activity, Ss listen for topics to get the gist of the video.

- **Preview the activity** Go over the instructions. Have Ss read the list of topics. Review vocabulary as needed.
- **Play the video** Have Ss choose the topics mentioned in the video. Play the video again, if necessary.
- **Check answers** Go over the answers with the class.

Answers

1, 2, 4, 6, 7, 11, 12

B

In this activity, Ss identify true and false statements about the video and correct the false items.

- **Preview the activity** Go over the instructions.
- **Play the video** Have Ss write *T* for true or *F* for false for each statement. Play the video again, if necessary. Allow time for Ss to revise the false statements.
- **Check answers** Go over the answers with the class.

Answers

1. F; Fashion has been a big part of the human experience for thousands of years.
2. T
3. T
4. F; One of the biggest influences on fashion since the 1960s has been youth culture.
5. F; High shoes were invented to prevent people from stepping in mud and animal waste in the streets.
6. T
7. F; In the future, as long as we are permitted to choose what to wear, we will express ourselves through clothing.

C

In this activity, Ss choose the correct information to complete sentences about the video.

- **Preview the activity** Go over the instructions. Have Ss read the sentences and answer options.
- **Play the video** Have Ss choose the correct answer to complete each sentence. Play the video again, if necessary.
- **Check answers** Go over the answers with the class.

Answers					
1. c	2. a	3. a	4. c	5. b	6. c

After you watch page T-193

A

In this activity, Ss give examples of fashion items created for specific reasons.

- **Preview the activity** Go over the instructions. Model an example for one of the reasons behind a fashion. Remind Ss that they are giving their own opinions.
- **Do the activity** Have Ss write their answers.

> **Possible answers**
>
> *People we look up to:* baggy pants that are very low (rappers); super high, interesting heels (Lady Gaga)
>
> *Comfort:* sneakers, sweatpants
>
> *Necessity:* warm winter coats, waterproof rain boots

B Group work

In this activity, Ss discuss and share their ideas from part A.

- **Preview the activity** Go over the instructions.
- **Do the activity** Ss discuss their answers to part A.

C Writing

In this activity, Ss write about influences on their own sense of fashion.

- **Preview the activity** Go over the instructions. Brainstorm a few ideas with the class.
- **Do the activity** Have Ss expand upon a paragraph outline to complete their writing. Remind them to use topic and supporting sentences and offer a conclusion.
- **Follow up** Have volunteers share their writing with the class.

Project

A Write the script

In this activity, Ss write their own video fashion report.

- **Preview the activity** Tell Ss they will work in small groups to make a video about fashion. Ss will write a script and then act it out on camera. Explain that they will take turns speaking and operating the camera.
- **Brainstorm** Have groups think about their approach to the fashion video. They can create a fashion show, give a report using magazine pictures, do a fashion advice interview/discussion, or capture a casual group discussion. Then have Ss make notes about the points they want to discuss, including style and trend descriptions and opinions about fashion.

    Sample idea:

    A fashion magazine report
    Ss find images from magazines and show them to the camera, pointing to the image while speaking.

    S1: I love this outfit. It looks like a style from the 1960s. The leather jacket and striped shirt are retro, like something Marlon Brando would have worn. They're also a little rebellious. This is a great look for going to a music concert. I think it's important to look cool at events like that.

- **Outline** Have Ss make an outline of their script. They can use their own ideas or the following structure:

  - Introduce and describe each fashion or style.
  - Describe the appearance of the clothing and person or the trend they are talking about.
  - Offer opinions on the style and possibly advice on wearing it.
  - Review the fashions discussed.

- **Write the script** Have Ss write their fashion reports using their outlines. Have them read through their work as they go and revise as needed.
- **Check the script** Have Ss rehearse their scripts. Help as needed.

B Make and share the video

In this activity, Ss make and share their own video fashion report.

- **Plan the video** Remind Ss that they will take turns speaking and operating the camera. Alternatively, Ss can set up the camera so they appear on-screen together to act out a situation.
- **Make the video** Have Ss make their videos.
- **Share the video** Ss share their videos with the class.
- **Option** Have a group discussion about the videos. Which video has the most unusual approach? Which is the most accurate in its assessment of fashion? Which is the most well made or well written?

3 PAST AND FUTURE PREDICTIONS

Story summary

"Past and Future Predictions" is a report that discusses predictions made in the past about technological advances that would occur 100 years in the future. It points out that some of the assumptions people made proved to be accurate (in terms of the capability) and predicted some of the technology available today, including wireless telephones (cell phones), using moving pictures to communicate with people all over the world (video chat), houses on wheels (RVs), and electric scrubbers to clean the house (automatic floor cleaners). It also mentions other predictions that simply didn't happen (e.g., free college education for everyone, elimination of mosquitoes, a cure for cancer). Finally, it talks about predictions that were only partly true. While there are no flying cars, some people do commute by airplane. People thought store purchases would arrive in homes through tubes, which they don't, but packages are delivered to our homes in a short time. People predicted that students' brains would be connected to machines to learn. This is not the case, but there are "wired" classrooms (classrooms using computers). The video then offers a few predictions for the next 100 years from interviews with people in the present day. Those people predict that in the future, robots will do all the work, all diseases will be cured, people will tell computers what they want to dream, cars will drive themselves, and, once again, that cars will fly.

Language summary

Grammar Indefinite and definite articles
 -ing clauses

Vocabulary Adjectives to discuss technology-related issues
 Collocations to express different attitudes

Before you watch page T-194

Pair work

In this activity, Ss discuss what they think the world will be like 100 years from now.

- **Preview the activity** Explain that Ss will watch a video about predictions for the future that people made 100 years ago. Go over the instructions and the categories. Point out that they can choose the topic for the last category.
- **Do the activity** Have pairs discuss the questions and categories and make predictions for the future.
- **Follow up** Have pairs share their ideas with the class. Write the class's top five predictions on the board.

While you watch pages T-194–195

A

In this activity, Ss identify true and false statements about the video and correct the false items.

- **Preview the activity** Go over the instructions. Have Ss look at the statements.
- **Play the video** Have Ss do the activity while they watch the video. Play the video again to allow Ss time to complete the activity, if necessary. Then have pairs discuss their answers and correct the false statements.
- **Check answers** Go over the answers with the class. Elicit corrections for the false statements.

Answers

1. F; Some of the predictions for the future that were made 100 years ago were remarkably accurate.
2. T
3. T
4. F; Predictions that were somewhat true were about travel, shopping, and education.
5. F; The modern-day people make very similar predictions to the people of 100 years ago.
6. F; Only three of the modern-day people make predictions about transportation.

B

In this activity, Ss write correct words to complete predictions in the video.

- **Preview the activity** Go over the instructions. Have Ss read the statements to preview them.
- **Play the video** Have Ss do the activity as they watch the first half of the video. Play the video again, if necessary.
- **Check answers** Go over the answers with the class.

Possible answers

1. wireless
2. moving pictures
3. houses on wheels
4. electric scrubbers
5. free for everyone
6. mosquitoes
7. cancer
8. tubes
9. wires

C

In this activity, Ss choose correct phrases to complete sentences about the video.

- **Preview the activity** Go over the instructions. Have Ss read the answer choices and statements.
- **Play the video** Have Ss answer from memory first. After Ss have completed the activity, play the second half of the video for them to check answers.
- **Check answers** Go over the answers with the class.

Answers					
1. d	2. e	3. b	4. c	5. a	6. f

After you watch page T-195

A Pair work

In this activity, pairs compare and rate their predictions.

- **Preview the activity** Go over the instructions.
- **Do the activity** Have pairs discuss their predictions and ratings.

B Group work

In this activity, small groups compare their predictions.

- **Preview the activity** Go over the instructions.
- **Do the activity** Have groups compare their predictions and choose one favorite prediction for each category. Then have the group say if they think it will or will not come true and why. Help as needed.
- **Follow up** Have groups share their ideas. Make notes on the board to choose the class's best predictions.

C Writing

In this activity, Ss write about technological advances made in the past 100 years.

- **Preview the activity** Go over the instructions. Hold a brief brainstorming session for the class about important technological advances made in the last 100 years, such as the cell phone, the computer, or the television. Make notes on the board.
- **Do the activity** Have Ss make a paragraph outline and then expand upon it to complete their writing.
- **Follow up** Have Ss share their writings with the class. Note the class's top five technological advances.

Project

A Write the script

In this activity, Ss write their own video about predictions.

- **Preview the activity** Tell Ss they will work individually to make their own video about predictions. Ss will write a script and then act it out on camera. Explain that they will then take turns speaking and operating the camera with another individual when filming.
- **Brainstorm** Brainstorm ideas with the class about topics the Ss can talk about and how they can approach making the video. Explain that Ss can make predictions, focus on predictions made in the past that have or have not come true, or base their video on their writing from *After you watch* part C.

  Sample idea:

  Inventions I'd like to see
  - *Invention 1:* a pill that gets you caught up on sleep; you can study or work more (80% sure this will happen)
  - *Invention 2:* a floating transportation pod that takes you where you want to go – warm, safe, and dry – without having to drive it. You just say where to go, and the pod floats you there. (95% sure this will happen)

- **Outline** Have Ss make outlines of their scripts. They can use their own ideas or the following structure:
  - Introduce the main concept of the video.
  - Present each invention, stating its purpose, how it will improve things, and how likely you think the item is. (May want to supplement with pictures or images.)
  - At the end, summarize the ideas and tell why you think they may come true.
- **Write the script** Have Ss write their scripts using their outlines. Have Ss read through their work and revise as needed.
- **Check the script** Have Ss rehearse their scripts. Help as needed.

B Make and share the video

In this activity, Ss make and share their own video about predictions.

- **Plan the video** Ss may want to have a classmate operate the camera for them.
- **Make the video** Have Ss make their videos.
- **Share the video** Ss share their videos with the class.
- **Option** Have a group discussion about the videos. Did anyone have the same ideas? How many people wrote about past inventions? Future inventions? Have Ss vote on which future predictions are most likely to come true or are the most interesting.

4 SUPERSTITIONS AROUND THE WORLD

Story summary

"Superstitions Around the World" explores global ideas about good and bad luck. Rabbit's feet, crossing one's fingers, *maneki-neko* (the Japanese waving cat statue), and four-leaf clovers are usually considered good luck. The number 13 is commonly considered unlucky, which may have its origins in Norse mythology, the Bible, or the Persian zodiac. In parts of Asia, the number 4 is unlucky because it sounds like the word for *death*, and chopsticks left standing straight up in a bowl are also considered bad luck. Some superstitions are practical in origin, like the Hawaiian practice of dumping bananas overboard when leaving shore to protect against stowaway animals like spiders and rats.

Language summary

Grammar   Reporting clauses
Reporting clauses in the passive

Vocabulary   Expressions with *luck*
Adjectives to describe truth and fabrication

Before you watch   page T-196

A Pair work

In this activity, Ss answer questions and interview a partner about superstitions.

- **Preview the activity** Explain that Ss will watch a video about superstitions. Direct Ss' attention to the superstition survey. Go over the instructions and do the first question as a model.
- **Do the activity** Allow time for Ss to complete the survey for themselves. Then have Ss interview their partners.

B Pair work

In this activity, Ss list other superstitions.

- **Preview the activity** Have Ss read the instructions.
- **Do the activity** Have pairs come up with other superstitions. Help as needed.
- **Follow up** Have pairs list their superstitions for the class. Make a list of the most commonly mentioned superstitions on the board.

While you watch   pages T-196–197

A

In this activity, Ss listen for topics to get the gist of the video.

- **Preview the activity** Go over the instructions. Have Ss read the superstitions.
- **Play the video** Have Ss choose the superstitions that are mentioned in the video as they watch. Play the video again, if necessary.
- **Check answers** Go over the answers with the class.

Answers
2, 3, 4, 7, 10

B

In this activity, Ss choose the correct information to complete sentences about the video.

- **Preview the activity** Go over the instructions. Have Ss read the sentences and answer options.
- **Play the video** Have Ss complete the sentences as you play the video. Play the video again, if necessary.
- **Check answers** Go over the answers with the class.

Answers
1. b   2. b   3. b   4. c   5. a   6. c

C

In this activity, Ss take notes to answer questions about the video in their own words.

- **Preview the activity** Go over the instructions. Have Ss read the questions.
- **Play the video** Have Ss take notes and then write the answers in their own words. Play the video again, if necessary. Have Ss compare their answers with a partner.
- **Check answers** Go over the answers with the class.

Possible answers
1. a rabbit's foot, crossing fingers, *maneki-neko* (cat statue), four-leaf clover
2. Loki the Norse God of Evil was the thirteenth guest at a banquet and caused a tragedy; Judas Iscariot was the thirteenth guest at Jesus's last supper; ancient Persians believed the sky would collapse after the twelfth zodiac sign had ruled the world
3. In Asia the word for four sounds like the word for death.
4. Dumping bananas may protect ships from being infested by rats and spiders.

After you watch page T-197

A Pair work

In this activity, Ss tell or make up reasons behind superstitions.

- **Preview the activity** Go over the instructions. Tell Ss to try to make their reasons believable. Give the following example, if necessary: *Walking under a ladder being bad luck is probably based on avoiding death. It could be dangerous if you knock the ladder over while someone is on it, or bumping it could cause something to fall on you, like a tool or paint can.*
- **Do the activity** Have Ss write their answers. Help as needed.

B Group work

In this activity, Ss discuss their ideas from part A.

- **Preview the activity** Go over the instructions.
- **Do the activity** Have pairs share their ideas with another pair. Then have pairs share their best, most believable ideas with the class. Have the class choose the most believable and most far-fetched ideas.

C Writing

In this activity, Ss write about superstitions.

- **Preview the activity** Go over the instructions. Brainstorm a few ideas to answer the question with the class by writing a topic sentence and a few supporting details or examples. Remind Ss they are giving their own opinions and supporting them.
- **Do the activity** Have Ss write about their opinion on superstitions. Help as needed.
- **Follow up** Have some Ss read their paragraphs to the class.

Project

A Write the script

In this activity, Ss write their own video about superstitions, beliefs, or sayings.

- **Preview the activity** Tell Ss they will work in small groups to make a video about superstitions, beliefs, or sayings. Ss will write a script and act it out on camera. Explain that they will take turns speaking and operating the camera.
- **Brainstorm** Have Ss think of interesting superstitions, beliefs, or sayings from their own or other cultures and families. Beliefs can include things like putting a plant in the correct corner of a room to bring money or an ache in one's knee meaning a storm is coming. Sayings can include things like "The way to a man's heart is through his stomach" or "No news is good news." Next, have them decide how they will present their information. Some possible ways might be as a group discussion, a conversation, acting out an event and giving an explanation, or a narrated documentary with photo support. Then have Ss make notes and possibly do research to get more information.

  Sample idea:
  Group discussion about family beliefs
  - *Description:* A group discusses beliefs of their elder relatives.
  - *Beliefs:* S1 reports on Grandmother A's belief: if she spills salt, she tosses some more salt over her shoulder. S2 reports on Grandmother B's belief: She says a picture falls off the wall when someone dies.
  - *Discussion:* Others in the group ask questions about meanings and report on similar beliefs in their families.

- **Outline** Have Ss make an outline of their script. They can use their own ideas or the following structure:
  - Introduce and categorize the topic (good luck, bad luck, sayings, etc.).
  - Report on what the concept is and in what context it is applied.
  - Speculate on what the concept means or where it comes from.
  - Relate ideas about meaning and make comparisons to same/similar ideas in other areas of the world.
- **Write the script** Have Ss write their scripts using their outlines. Have them read through their work as they go and revise as needed.
- **Check the script** Have Ss rehearse their scripts. Help as needed.

B Make and share the video

In this activity, Ss make and share their own video about superstitions, beliefs, or sayings.

- **Plan the video** Remind Ss that they will take turns speaking and operating the camera. Alternatively, Ss can set up the camera so they appear on-screen together to act out a situation.
- **Make the video** Have Ss make their videos.
- **Share the video** Ss share their videos with the class.
- **Option** Have a group discussion about the videos. Which video is the most interesting? Which superstitions, beliefs, or sayings are familiar? Do you think there are any other meanings or origins for the concepts than those mentioned in the videos?

5 MEET THE DIRECTOR

Story summary

"Meet the Director" is an interview with Ryan Bliss, director of *Rot*, a movie about a man dying from a flesh-eating disease who goes out to a remote cabin to reflect on his life. The director wanted to make a movie about lost love in an original way. He worked on the idea for over a year and eventually everything came together. As he started telling people about his idea, they all knew it was a very moving and powerful idea, so he felt he had to make the movie. The process of writing and funding the movie was not easy for Bliss. Unable to get funding from studios, Bliss spent his own money to create the first part of *Rot*. He then turned to crowdfunding to raise the rest of the money and was surprised when not only family and friends but also strangers donated money to his idea. He notes that crowdfunding has made it easier to get movies made for starting filmmakers but suggests that having a strong idea is still necessary to get noticed. Bliss next plans to put the movie in film festivals to get his name noticed and to get help funding his next movies.

Language summary

Grammar Sentence adverbs
Such . . . that and So . . . that

Vocabulary Adjectives to describe movies

Before you watch page T-198

A

In this activity, Ss examine the steps in making a movie to preview the video topic.

- **Preview the activity** Explain that Ss will watch an interview of a young movie director. Direct Ss' attention to the list of tasks when making a movie. Go over the instructions.
- **Do the activity** Have Ss evaluate the steps. Remind Ss that they are giving their own opinions.

B Pair work

In this activity, pairs discuss their answers from part A.

- **Preview the activity** Go over the instructions.
- **Do the activity** Have pairs discuss their answers to part A and note the reasons behind them.
- **Follow up** Have pairs share their discussions with the class.

While you watch pages T-198–199

A

In this activity, Ss identify the order of steps for making the movie as they are mentioned in the video.

- **Preview the activity** Go over the instructions. Have Ss look at the list of steps. Explain that Ss will number the steps in the order they are mentioned in the video.
- **Play the video** Have Ss do the activity while they watch the video. Play the video again to allow Ss time to complete the activity, if necessary.
- **Check answers** Go over the answers with the class.

Answers
5, 3, 6, 2, 4, 1, 7

B

In this activity, Ss choose the correct information to complete sentences about the video.

- **Preview the activity** Go over the instructions. Have Ss read the statements and answer choices. Point out they should answer according to the video.
- **Play the video** Have Ss do the activity as they watch the video. Play the video again, if necessary.
- **Check answers** Go over the answers with the class.

Answers
1. c   2. a   3. b   4. b   5. a   6. c

- **Option** Have Ss complete the activity from memory, then play the video again to check the answers.

C

In this activity, Ss match pronouns to what they are referencing in the video.

- **Preview the activity** Go over the instructions. Have Ss read the answer choices and statements.
- **Play the video** Have Ss do the activity. Play the video again, if necessary.
- **Check answers** Go over the answers with the class.

Answers
1. a   2. f   3. d   4. e   5. c   6. b

T-222 Video notes

After you watch page T-199

A Pair work

In this activity, pairs discuss what they learned and found interesting in the video.

- **Preview the activity** Go over the instructions.
- **Do the activity** Have pairs discuss their answers to the questions.
- **Follow up** Have pairs share their discussions with the class.

B Pair work

In this activity, pairs speculate on what they think the story of the movie mentioned in the video is about.

- **Preview the activity** Go over the instructions. Tell pairs they should use the clips they saw to piece together how they think the movie's storyline goes.
- **Do the activity** Have each pair write an outline for the movie's story. Help as needed.
- **Follow up** Have pairs share their ideas. Then have the class decide on the most likely final version.

C Writing

In this activity, Ss write about a project they would like to crowdfund.

- **Preview the activity** Go over the instructions. Hold a brief class brainstorming session about projects Ss would like to do if they had enough money. Encourage them to think freely and ask questions for further information.
- **Do the activity** Have Ss make a paragraph outline and then expand upon it to complete their writing.
- **Follow up** Have Ss share their writing with the class. Have the class choose the top three ideas they most connect with and would fund if they could.

Project

A Write the script

In this activity, Ss write their own video about a favorite movie or TV show.

- **Preview the activity** Tell Ss they will work in pairs to make a video about a favorite movie or TV show. Ss will write a script and then talk about it or act out scenes from it on camera.
- **Brainstorm** Brainstorm ideas with the class about favorite movies and TV shows and how Ss can approach making their video. Remind Ss that they can describe a movie or show, say what it is about, or describe anything they know about how it was made. They can also act out scenes if they like.

   Sample ideas:
   - *Idea 1:* Talk about a movie or TV show, explaining the storyline, the stars, and what people like and dislike about it
   - *Idea 2:* Present an idea for a movie or TV show and try to "sell" it to the audience to get funding
   - *Idea 3:* Act out scenes from a favorite movie or TV program; the class guesses which movie or program is being recreated

- **Outline** Have Ss make an outline of their script. They can use their own ideas or the following structure:

   Report on my favorite show
   - S1 introduces the show and basic idea and story.
   - S2 discusses actors on the show and how they handle its themes.
   - S1 talks about the critical acclaim for the show and why people like or don't like it.
   - S2 gives a summary of the show and why it was chosen.

- **Write the script** Have Ss write their scripts using their outlines. Have Ss read through their work and revise as needed.
- **Check the script** Have Ss rehearse their scripts. Help as needed.

B Make and share the video

Ss make and share their own video about a movie or TV show.

- **Plan the video** Remind Ss that they will take turns speaking and operating the camera. Alternatively, Ss can set up the camera so they appear on-screen together.
- **Make the video** Have Ss make their videos.
- **Share the video** Ss share their videos with the class.
- **Option** Have a group discussion about the videos. Have Ss say one thing they liked about each video. Then have them say one way they think each video could be improved.

6 HILLARY REYNOLDS BAND

Story summary

This video is an interview with the Boston-based musical group the Hillary Reynolds Band. The group is comprised of Hillary (mandolin), Trevor (cello), Jeff (ukulele), and Chris (acoustic upright bass). They describe their music as indie-folk or folk-pop, in which catchy pop melodies are played on acoustic folky instruments. As an unsigned band, they usually have to do everything themselves, from booking gigs to writing, arranging, and producing their own music. They also write their own songs, the process for which is varied. Sometimes writing is done by one person; other times, they all collaborate to write a song. Since they have been playing for a while, getting jobs has now become easier, and people contact them to give them work. Their fans reach out to them through all social media platforms, and the band loves to hear how their songs have touched people. When asked what it takes to be successful in the music business, they say it takes a lot of hard work and passion. In the end, their hope for the future is to be able to continue making music together and for their fans to be able to listen to their music and feel they know the band personally.

Language summary

Grammar Double comparatives
Will and *would* for habits and general truths

Vocabulary Collocations to describe music
Idioms used in the entertainment industry

Before you watch page T-200

Pair work

In this activity, Ss discuss what they think life is like for an unsigned band.

- **Preview the activity** Explain that Ss will watch a video about an unsigned band, which is a band that does not have record label support. Direct Ss' attention to the list of questions. Go over the instructions and the model discussion.
- **Do the activity** Have pairs discuss the questions. Help as needed.
- **Follow up** Have pairs share their ideas with the class. Ask questions to get Ss to support their opinions with further information.

While you watch pages T-200–201

A

In this activity, Ss choose the best answers to general questions about the video.

- **Preview the activity** Go over the instructions. Have Ss look at the questions and answer choices.
- **Play the video** Have Ss do the activity while they watch the video. Play the video again to allow Ss time to complete the activity, if necessary.
- **Check answers** Go over the answers with the class.

Answers
1. c   2. b   3. c   4. c   5. b   6. a   7. c

B

In this activity, Ss identify true and false statements about the video and correct the false items.

- **Preview the activity** Go over the instructions. Have Ss look at the list of statements.
- **Play the video** Have Ss do the activity while they watch the video. Then have pairs correct the false statements.
- **Check answers** Go over the answers with the class.

Answers
1. T
2. F; The band combines catchy pop melodies with acoustic instruments.
3. F; Trevor plays the cello. Hillary plays the mandolin.
4. T
5. T
6. F; The band enjoys making music and just wants to continue to make music together.

C

In this activity, Ss match quotes to the people who said them.

- **Preview the activity** Go over the instructions. Have Ss read the quotations.
- **Play the video** Have Ss answer from memory first. Then play the video for them to check answers.
- **Check answers** Go over the answers with the class.

Answers
1. T   2. H   3. H   4. T   5. J   6. T

After you watch page T-201

A

In this activity, Ss give their opinions about what bands can do to be successful.

- **Preview the activity** Go over the instructions. Explain that Ss will take notes on their answers.
- **Do the activity** Have Ss do the activity. Help as needed.

B Pair work

In this activity, pairs compare their answers from part A.

- **Preview the activity** Go over the instructions.
- **Do the activity** Have pairs compare their answers and then compare a successful band they know to the Hillary Reynolds Band. Help as needed.
- **Follow up** Have pairs share their answers with the class.

C Group work

In this activity, groups discuss what success in the entertainment industry means in general.

- **Preview the activity** Go over the instructions. Put the pairs from part B into groups of two pairs each.
- **Do the activity** Have groups discuss what makes an entertainer successful. Then have groups choose one entertainer (musician, actor, comedian, etc.) and describe the reasons for the person's success.
- **Follow up** Have groups share their ideas and discuss the people they chose. What are the class's top three entertainers? What are the top qualities people feel make them successful?

Project

A Write the script

In this activity, Ss write their own video about music.

- **Preview the activity** Tell Ss they will work in small groups to make a video about music. Explain that Ss will give a report on a band they know, either successful or unsigned. Ss will write a script and then act it out on camera.
- **Brainstorm** Review the questions from *While you watch* part A. These are some of the questions the band was asked in the video. Ss can use these questions as a starting point for their video. Brainstorm any other questions that Ss may want to use and how they can approach making the video.
- **Outline** Have Ss make an outline of their script. They can use their own ideas or the following structure:

    Shared report
    Each member of the group gives one or two pieces of information about a band or group.
    - Describe the band or group's style of music.
    - Describe challenges they presently face or have faced in the past.
    - Describe how they create their music.
    - Describe how they get gigs / where they play.
    - Talk about how they respond to and keep in contact with their fans.
    - Explain what their future may be.

- **Write the script** Have Ss write their scripts using their outlines. Have Ss read through their work and revise as needed.
- **Check the script** Have Ss rehearse their scripts. Help as needed.

B Make and share the video

In this activity, Ss make and share their own video about music.

- **Plan the video** Remind Ss that they will take turns speaking and operating the camera. Alternatively, Ss can set up the camera so they appear on-screen together to act out a situation.
- **Make the video** Have Ss make their videos.
- **Share the video** Ss share their videos with the class.
- **Option** Have a group discussion about the videos. Did any groups talk about the same band? Were there any similar answers to the questions? Which video styles worked best with the topic?

7 CHANGING GENDER ROLES

Story summary

"Changing Gender Roles" presents the history of changing roles of men and women at work. For many centuries, both men and women worked on the farm and in businesses at home. The Industrial Revolution brought about a major change as men started leaving home to work in factories while women stayed home with the children. When men went off to fight World War I and World War II, women filled in at factory and office jobs. After the war, no longer satisfied to return to their homes as if nothing had changed, many women sought education in typically masculine fields and became doctors and business leaders. Some men accepted this change and sought jobs in typically feminine fields, such as being teachers and homemakers. But other people resisted these changes, and some people today still can't cope with these changing roles. No one knows what will happen next, but it is certain the future will be full of more changes.

Language summary

Grammar Optional and required relative pronouns
As if, *as though*, *as*, *the way*, and *like*

Vocabulary Collocations with *change*

Before you watch page T-202

A

In this activity, Ss give their opinions on whether jobs are for men, women, or both.

- **Preview the activity** Explain that Ss will watch a video about men's and women's roles in society. Direct Ss' attention to the list of jobs. Go over the instructions.
- **Do the activity** Have Ss write *M* for men, *W* for women, or *B* for both depending on who they think usually does the job.

B Pair work

In this activity, Ss discuss their answers from part A.

- **Preview the activity** Have Ss read the instructions.
- **Do the activity** Have pairs compare answers and discuss their ideas about the jobs in part A.
- **Follow up** Have pairs briefly summarize their discussions for the class.

While you watch pages T-202–203

A

In this activity, Ss choose the best summary of the information in the video at a certain point.

- **Preview the activity** Go over the instructions. Have Ss look at the pictures and read the statements.
- **Play the video** Have Ss choose the sentence that best conveys the main point of the video for each image shown. Play the video again, if necessary.
- **Check answers** Go over the answers with the class.

Answers
1. a   2. c   3. a   4. b

B

In this activity, Ss identify the order of events as they are mentioned in the video.

- **Preview the activity** Go over the instructions. Have Ss read the statements.
- **Play the video** Play the video and have Ss number the statements in order. Pause the video or play it again as needed for Ss to complete the activity.
- **Check answers** Go over the answers with the class.

Answers
4, 3, 7, 1, 5, 8, 2, 6

C

In this activity, Ss take notes to answer questions about the video in their own words.

- **Preview the activity** Go over the instructions. Tell Ss they should use their own words to write notes to answer the questions.
- **Play the video** Have Ss do the activity. Play the video again, if necessary. Help as needed.
- **Check answers** Have pairs compare their answers. Go over the answers with the class.

Possible answers
1. They loved the new opportunities and felt freed from the home. They didn't want to return to homemaking as if nothing had happened.
2. Women are sometimes paid less for the same job. Sometimes they don't feel valued by their employers.
3. Sometimes they feel as though society doesn't take them seriously. Some people feel it is strange for a man to want those types of jobs.

T-226 Video notes

After you watch page T-203

A Pair work

In this activity, Ss examine what they have learned from the video.

- **Preview the activity** Go over the instructions. Read the questions. Model a discussion with a volunteer.
- **Do the activity** Have pairs do the activity. Help as needed.
- **Follow up** Have pairs share their discussions with the class. Make sure Ss support their opinions with reasons and examples.

B Writing

In this activity, Ss write about why they think jobs traditionally associated with genders might change or not in the future.

- **Preview the activity** Go over the instructions.
- **Do the activity** Have Ss make an outline and then expand upon it to complete their writing.
- **Follow up** Have some Ss share their writing with the class.

Project

A Write the script

In this activity, Ss write their own video about gender roles.

- **Preview the activity** Tell Ss they will work in small groups to make a video about gender roles and changes to them. Ss will write a script and then act it out on camera. Explain that they will take turns speaking and operating the camera.
- **Brainstorm** Have Ss think of examples of gender roles that have changed. Then have Ss make notes describing the effects of these roles on people, how the roles have changed, and the effects of such changes. Ss can focus on the people affected (well-known people or personal friends) and/or the resulting changes. Encourage Ss to do research.

  Sample idea:
  Women's sports
  - *Gender role:* Women were once considered too weak to play many sports.
  - *How it affected people:* Certain sports didn't allow women players.
  - *How it changed and was affected by change:* As more and more people began to empathize with the women's rights movement, more opportunities were created for women. In the United States in 1972, an act was passed ensuring equal access to athletics for women in educational institutions. More women then became able to play the sports they wanted.
  - *People affected:* Tennis players like Martina Navratilova and Billie Jean King began to gain respect as athletes.

- **Outline** Have Ss make an outline of their script. They can use their own ideas or the following structure:
  - Introduce and describe the gender role.
  - Talk about the effects of the role.
  - Discuss the changes to the role and the effects of that change.
  - Give examples of people affected.
  - Talk about possible further changes in the future.
- **Write the script** Have Ss write their scripts about gender roles that have changed. Have them read through their work as they go and revise as needed.
- **Check the script** Have Ss rehearse their scripts. Help as needed.

B Make and share the video

In this activity, Ss make and share their own video about gender roles.

- **Plan the video** Remind Ss that they will take turns speaking and operating the camera. Alternatively, Ss can set up the camera so they appear on-screen together to act out a situation.
- **Make the video** Have Ss make their videos.
- **Share the video** Ss share their videos with the class.
- **Option** Have a group discussion about the videos. Which video has the most unusual approach to the topic? Which video is the most informative? Which video is the most interesting?

8 THE HISTORY OF ADVERTISING

Story summary

"The History of Advertising" talks about advertising's past and suggests a few advertising styles of the future. Where advertising began is unclear, but in considering advertising as a form of communication, some of the first known messages to the public were carved on tablets by Egyptians. From there, the printing press in the 1400s led to the invention of the newspaper, where the first classified ads appeared in 1631. The first magazine followed in 1709. Mail service became more efficient in the late 1800s, and companies began to send catalogs and postcards directly into homes. Radio came along in 1921, and radio ads came shortly thereafter. And as automobiles became more popular in the early 1900s, so did billboards along the roads. The first television commercial aired in 1941, providing one of the most effective forms of advertising ever created, and infomercials began broadcasting 30 years later. With cell phones, the Internet, and social media, one can see that more and more new technologies are bringing more ways to advertise. In the future, there may even be ads in our dreams, on contact lenses, or on the moon. As long as there are ways to sell and communicate, there will always be advertising.

Language summary

Grammar Placement of direct and indirect objects
Verbs in the subjunctive

Vocabulary Expressions to discuss shopping
Marketing strategies

Before you watch page T-204

A

In this activity, Ss list types of advertising media.

- **Preview the activity** Explain that Ss will watch a video about the history of advertising. Go over the instructions. Tell Ss they will list as many types of advertising as they can think of.
- **Do the activity** Have Ss do the activity. Help as needed.

B Pair work

In this activity, Ss compare their lists from part A and think of more ways to advertise.

- **Preview the activity** Go over the instructions.
- **Do the activity** Have pairs do the activity.
- **Follow up** Have pairs briefly summarize their lists on the board for the class. Note the types of media mentioned.

While you watch pages T-204–205

A

In this activity, Ss check the ways to advertise mentioned in the video.

- **Preview the activity** Go over the instructions. Tell Ss that they are to check which items from their lists in *Before you watch* part A are mentioned in the video. Explain that the second time they watch, they are to write the types of media they hear that were not on their lists.
- **Play the video** Have Ss check their lists as they watch. Play the video again, pausing if necessary for Ss to write any advertising types that they missed.
- **Check answers** Go over the answers with the class.

Possible answers

ancient Egyptian stone and wooden tablets, newspapers, magazines, mail, catalogs, radio, billboards, TV, infomercials, cell phones, the Internet, Facebook, Twitter, YouTube

B

In this activity, Ss choose the correct information to complete sentences about the video.

- **Preview the activity** Go over the instructions. Have Ss read the sentences and answer options.
- **Play the video** Have Ss choose the correct answers to complete the sentences. Play the video again, if necessary.
- **Check answers** Go over the answers with the class.

Answers

1. b 2. b 3. c 4. b 5. a 6. a 7. b 8. a

C

In this activity, Ss identify facts about different advertising media.

- **Preview the activity** Go over the instructions. Have Ss read the sentences.
- **Play the video** Have Ss choose the medium each statement is about as they watch the video.
- **Check answers** Go over the answers with the class.

Answers

1. mail	3. newspaper	5. television
2. television	4. newspaper	6. mail

T-228 Video notes

After you watch page T-205

A
In this activity, Ss list types of advertising they find enjoyable or annoying.
- **Preview the activity** Go over the instructions. Read the questions. Model an example.
- **Do the activity** Have Ss list the forms of advertising they find enjoyable and annoying. Help as needed.

B Pair work
In this activity, Ss compare their lists from part A.
- **Preview the activity** Go over the instructions.
- **Do the activity** Have pairs discuss their opinions from part A. Help as needed.
- **Follow up** Have pairs tell the class about their discussions.

C Group work
In this activity, Ss discuss questions about advertising in general.
- **Preview the activity** Go over the instructions. Elicit an example for each question from the class before putting Ss into groups.
- **Do the activity** Have groups talk about different aspects and the future of advertising. Help as needed.
- **Follow up** Have groups tell the class about their discussions.

Project

A Write the script
In this activity, Ss write their own video about advertising.
- **Preview the activity** Tell Ss they will work in pairs to make a video about advertising. Ss will write a script and then act it out on camera.
- **Brainstorm** Have Ss think of their own video about advertising. They may want to analyze and comment on current ads they like and/or dislike, or they can discuss what makes an effective advertising medium and give examples. Have Ss make notes about their topic and what they want to say about it.

Sample idea:

Ineffective and effective ads
- *Description:* Each person will show examples of ads he or she doesn't think are effective and some for similar products that are effective.

- **Outline** Have Ss make an outline of their script. They can use their own ideas or the following structure:
  - Introduce and describe the ad or medium.
  - Talk about what makes it effective or not.
  - Back up opinions with explanations, reasons, and examples.
- **Write the script** Have Ss write their scripts. Have them read through their work as they go and revise as needed.

Sample script:

S1: *(shows ad for a car)* I can't stand this ad! It is so fake! This car looks very cool driving across the desert, but most people who buy this brand of car will never do that! They will be sitting in traffic. I understand the ad is supposed to create a fantasy, but in my opinion, this doesn't suit the brand.

(shows ad for another car) Now this is an effective ad! This car is shown in a city setting, where a small car like this would be appropriate. It's not trying to pretend to be something it is not. This will appeal to the people who like this brand.

- **Check the script** Have Ss rehearse their scripts. Help as needed.

B Make and share the video
In this activity, Ss make and share their own video about advertising.
- **Plan the video** Remind Ss that they will take turns speaking and operating the camera. Alternatively, Ss can set up the camera so they appear on-screen together to act out a situation.
- **Make the video** Have Ss make their videos.
- **Share the video** Ss share their videos with the class.
- **Option** Have a group discussion about the videos. Which video is the best? Which one is the most informative? Which video gives the best analysis?

9 HUMANS AND ANIMALS

Story summary

"What Would We Do Without Animals?" reviews the long-standing relationship between humans and animals. Humans are inextricably linked to animals. People have domesticated them, used them for transportation and work, and as a source of food. The earliest humans depicted their gods as part human, part animal. Today, when people want to describe the essence of a person, they often talk in terms of animals: evil like a snake, courageous like a lion, busy as a bee, and sly as a fox, to name a few. Since the time of Aesop's fables, people have also tended to attribute human qualities to animals. This tradition continues today in our storybooks, cartoons, and movies.

Language summary

Grammar *Whenever* and *wherever* contrasted with *when* and *where*
Noun clauses with *whoever* and *whatever*

Before you watch page T-206

A Pair work

In this activity, Ss think of animal comparisons for human traits to preview the video.

- **Preview the activity** Explain that Ss will watch a video about animal comparisons to humans. Direct Ss' attention to the list of words. Review pronunciation and meaning as needed. Go over the instructions. Remind Ss they are giving their own opinions and that they are to think of adjectives and animals for the last three items.
- **Do the activity** Have pairs think of animals that have characteristics similar to the adjectives and complete the list.

B Group work

In this activity, Ss discuss the animal–human comparisons in part A.

- **Preview the activity** Have Ss read the instructions.
- **Do the activity** Have the pairs of Ss who worked together in part A join another pair and compare their answers and discuss their ideas. Help as needed.
- **Follow up** Have the groups share their opinions with the class. Note the most popular choices for each trait on the board.

While you watch pages T-206–207

A

In this activity, Ss choose the best summary of the information in the video at a certain point.

- **Preview the activity** Go over the instructions. Have Ss look at the pictures and read the statements. Remind Ss to choose the statement that is the main point from the video as represented by the picture.
- **Play the video** Have Ss choose the correct answers as they watch. Pause or replay the video as needed.

- **Check answers** Go over the answers with the class.

Answers			
1. b	2. a	3. c	4. b

B

In this activity, Ss choose the correct information to complete sentences about the video.

- **Preview the activity** Go over the instructions. Have Ss read the sentences and answer options.
- **Play the video** Have Ss choose the correct answers to complete the sentences. Play the video again, if necessary. Help as needed.
- **Check answers** Go over the answers with the class.

Answers				
1. c	2. c	3. b	4. c	5. c

- **Option** Have Ss complete the activity from memory, then play the video again to check the answers.

C

In this activity, Ss match animals to the human traits associated with them in the video.

- **Preview the activity** Go over the instructions. Tell Ss to match the animals in the left column to the traits associated with that animal in the right column.
- **Play the video** Have Ss do the activity from memory first. Then play the video again for Ss to check their answers.
- **Check answers** Go over the answers with the class.

Answers			
1. j	4. g	7. l	10. h
2. f	5. b	8. d	11. e
3. a	6. k	9. i	12. c

T-230 Video notes

After you watch page T-207

A

In this activity, Ss compare their own animal–human comparisons to those in the video.

- **Preview the activity** Go over the instructions. Read the question. Model a comparison with a volunteer.
- **Do the activity** Have Ss do the activity. Help as needed.

B Pair work

In this activity, Ss discuss their results from part A.

- **Preview the activity** Go over the instructions.
- **Do the activity** Have pairs discuss their ideas. Then have Ss share their choices with the class.

C Group work

In this activity, Ss discuss influences on animal–human comparisons.

- **Preview the activity** Go over the instructions.
- **Do the activity** Have groups discuss possible cultural, geographical, and literary influences on animal comparisons around the world. Help as needed. Then have Ss share their opinions with the class. Note the different influences on the board.

Project

A Write the script

In this activity, Ss write their own video about animals and humans.

- **Preview the activity** Tell Ss they will work in small groups to make a video about how we think of humans in animal terms and/or how we attribute human characteristics to animals. Ss will write a script and then act it out on camera. Explain that they will take turns speaking and operating the camera.
- **Brainstorm** Have Ss choose a topic for the video or they can brainstorm ideas about several topics first before choosing one. Possible topics might include animals attributed with human characteristics, an analysis of why certain traits are associated with specific animals, or a discussion using animal simile references to talk about people. Have Ss make notes about their ideas.

  Sample idea:
  Animals attributed with human characteristics
  - *Description:* The group presents different animals as seen in movies, books, comics, and cartoons and describe how their personalities relate to humans.
  - *Examples:* Human characteristics in animals in *The Lion King*, *101 Dalmatians*, and *Bambi*

- **Outline** Have Ss make an outline of their script. They can use their own ideas or the following structure:
  - Introduce and describe what the video is about.
  - Talk about the animals and how they have been related to humans.
  - Give examples to support the point.
  - Wrap up the video with a final message or review of the topic.

- **Write the script** Have Ss write their scripts. Have them read through their work and revise as needed.

  Sample script:
  S1: When we think of feminine cartoon characters, we usually see a cat or maybe a bunny. Look at this cartoon . . .
  S2: And male characters are often lions, bears, or dogs. For example, . . .

- **Check the script** Have Ss rehearse their scripts. Help as needed.

B Make and share the video

In this activity, Ss make and share their own video about animals and humans.

- **Plan the video** Remind Ss that they will take turns speaking and operating the camera. Alternatively, Ss can set up the camera so they appear on-screen together to act out a situation.
- **Make the video** Have Ss make their videos.
- **Share the video** Ss share their videos with the class.
- **Option** Have a group discussion about the videos. Which video is the most unusual? Which video is the most insightful? Which one is the most interesting?

10 TIPS FOR BETTER PRESENTATIONS

Story summary

In the video "Tips for Better Presentations," a college professor offers advice on how to give a better slideshow presentation. Tips are given in three main categories and are interspersed with good and bad examples. Tip 1: Engage the audience. The professor says to tell a story and speak conversationally to keep the presentation interesting. He adds that speakers should avoid reading from the screen the whole time and remember that they, not the slides, are the stars of the presentation. Tip 2: How to use text. The professor explains that less text is better and reminds students to make every word count.

He also points out that they should avoid paragraphs and use bullet points on slides to make reading easier. They should also use a large, dark font that can be read by all. Tip 3: Do not let your audience get ahead of you. The professor explains that points from the presentation should appear on the slides one at a time to prevent people from reading things that have not yet been talked about. Additionally, handouts should be given out at the end of the presentation and you should let people know they will be given. That way people won't read them while you are speaking or spend a lot of time taking notes.

Language summary

Grammar	Overview of passives	**Vocabulary**	Discourse markers
	Subject-verb agreement with quantifiers		Idiomatic expressions related to the use of language

Before you watch page T-208

A

In this activity, Ss take a quiz about good presentation skills to preview the topic of the video.

- **Preview the activity** Explain that Ss will watch a video about how to improve slideshow presentations. Elicit from the class what slideshows are and what they are used for. Then direct Ss' attention to the list of statements. Go over the instructions. Explain that Ss should answer to the best of their knowledge.
- **Do the activity** Have Ss do the activity.

B Pair work

In this activity, pairs discuss their responses to the quiz from part A.

- **Preview the activity** Go over the instructions.
- **Do the activity** Have pairs discuss the quiz.
- **Follow up** Don't check the answers yet. Explain that the quiz answers will be revealed in the video.

Answers					
1. F	2. F	3. T	4. F	5. T	6. F

While you watch pages T-208–209

A

In this activity, Ss match actions to the two characters in the video and check answers for *Before you watch* part A.

- **Preview the activity** Go over the instructions. Have Ss look at the pictures and read the list of actions. Explain

that Ss will identify who does each action by writing *M* if it is the man or *W* if it is the woman.
- **Play the video** Have Ss do the activity while they watch the video. Play the video again, if necessary.
- **Check answers** Go over the answers with the class. Then have Ss check their answers to *Before you watch* part A. Discuss why each answer is true or false.

Answers							
1. W	2. M	3. W	4. M	5. M	6. W	7. M	8. W

B

In this activity, Ss choose correct phrases to complete sentences about the video.

- **Preview the activity** Go over the instructions. Have Ss look at the activity items and answer options. Explain that Ss will complete each sentence with the phrase that best matches what they hear in the video.
- **Play the video** Have Ss do the activity while they watch the video. Play the video again, if necessary.
- **Check answers** Go over the answers with the class.

Answers							
1. b	2. f	3. e	4. d	5. a	6. h	7. c	8. g

C

In this activity, Ss complete sentences about the video with the correct expressions.

- **Preview the activity** Go over the instructions. Have Ss read the statements and answer options.
- **Play the video** Have Ss answer from memory first. Then play the video for them to check answers.
- **Check answers** Go over the answers with the class.

> **Answers**
> 1. Poor slideshows
> 2. reads exactly what is on the screen
> 3. looking only at the screen
> 4. put your entire speech on the screen
> 5. only the key words
> 6. your font is too small
> 7. taking their own notes

After you watch page T-209

A Pair work

In this activity, Ss apply information from the video to their own lives.

- **Preview the activity** Go over the instructions. Explain that Ss will talk about their own experiences with presentations. If they have never seen or done a presentation, they can use information from the video or their imagination.
- **Do the activity** Have Ss do the activity. Help as needed.

B Pair work

In this activity, pairs create a presentation about additional tips to improve presentation skills.

- **Preview the activity** Go over the instructions. Have pairs think of three additional tips. Model an example: *I think an additional tip could be to speak loud enough so people in the back can hear you.*
- **Do the activity** Have pairs do the activity. Help as needed.

C Group work

In this activity, groups practice giving presentations.

- **Preview the activity** Go over the instructions.
- **Do the activity** Have pairs take turns giving their presentations. The group members give constructive feedback. Then they choose one person or pair to speak for the group.
- **Follow up** Have a person or pair from each group give their presentation. Then have the class discuss the top five additional ideas and who the best presenters are.

Project

A Write the script

In this activity, Ss write their own slideshow presentation.

- **Preview the activity** Tell Ss they will work in pairs to make their own slideshow presentation. Explain that their presentation can be about any topic they choose, but they should pay special attention to follow the tips in the video. Ss will write a script and then give the presentation on camera.
- **Brainstorm** Review some possible topics that pairs may want to use in their video (e.g., a review of a well-known book, the history of a country or event, or a famous sporting event). Then review some possible ways they can approach the presentation. Will it be about a single topic? Will it compare or contrast two topics? Will it explain causes and effects regarding a topic? Will it talk about problems and solutions? Give pairs a few minutes to discuss their ideas.
- **Outline** Have Ss make an outline of their script. They can use their own ideas or the following structure:
    - S1 introduces the topic of super cars (very expensive, fast cars) and gives an overview of what will be talked about (e.g., the people who drive them, why they are popular, etc.).
    - S2 presents a slide talking about who drives super cars with three pieces of supporting information.
    - S1 or S2 repeats the presentation above for the remaining points.
    - S2 makes a concluding statement that reviews the presentation and offers an opinion or call for action.
    - Partners distribute presentation handouts.
- **Write the presentation and slide content** Have Ss write their presentations using their outlines. Have Ss read through their work and create slides as needed. Then have Ss review to be sure that their presentation follows the tips presented in the video.
- **Check the presentation and slides** Have Ss rehearse their scripts. Help as needed.

B Make and share the video

- **Plan the video** Remind Ss that they can take turns speaking and operating the camera. Alternatively, Ss can set up the camera so they appear on-screen together to act out a situation.
- **Make the video** Have Ss make their videos.
- **Share the video** Ss share their videos with the class.
- **Option** Have a group discussion about the videos. Did each video follow the tips for good presentations? Are there any ways pairs can improve their videos?

11 ROLE MODELS

Story summary

In the video, Rachel, a student, is campaigning to get more people to think of themselves as role models. She believes it is not only awe-inspiring people and celebrities who can be role models and feels anyone can be a role model. As part of her project, she is convincing people on the street to think of themselves as role models. The first person she speaks to is an unemployed construction worker who considers himself too hotheaded to be a role model. His wife reminds him that he is easygoing and that the neighborhood kids love him, so Rachel convinces him to become a Little League coach, since his role model was his high school baseball coach. The next person with whom Rachel speaks is a nurse who at first thinks only doctors can be role models. While speaking with her, Rachel points out that her positive attitude toward patients can help them have a positive attitude about a life-changing illness. Eventually, the woman agrees to consider herself as a role model. Finally, Rachel speaks with a computer game designer who thinks only legendary figures like Nelson Mandela can be role models, not someone like himself, who rarely interacts with people. With some convincing, Rachel is able to encourage him to think about his presence in the online community and take a stand against cyberbullying. At the end, Rachel notes that during her three-month project, she was able to get 387 people to commit to being role models.

Language summary

Grammar Compound adjectives
Superlative compound adjectives

Vocabulary Compound adjectives related to the body
Phrasal verbs

Before you watch page T-210

A

In this activity, Ss select the qualities they think role models should have.

- **Preview the activity** Explain that Ss will watch a video about role models. Direct Ss' attention to the list of traits and confirm they understand each term. Explain that Ss are to choose the traits they think a role model should have. Remind Ss that they are giving their own opinions.
- **Do the activity** Have Ss do the activity.

B Pair work

In this activity, pairs discuss their answers from part A and talk about the qualities they feel most role models share.

- **Preview the activity** Read the instructions.
- **Do the activity** Have pairs do the activity. Then have pairs share their top three qualities with the class.
- **Follow up** Have the class vote to choose the top five qualities of most role models.

While you watch pages T-210–211

A

In this activity, Ss identify true and false statements about the video and correct the false items.

- **Preview the activity** Go over the instructions. Have Ss look at the list of statements.
- **Play the video** Have Ss do the activity while they watch the video. Then have pairs correct the false statements. Play the video again, if necessary.
- **Check answers** Go over the answers with the class.

Answers

1. F; People are signing a pledge to think of themselves as role models.
2. T
3. F; Rachel believes anybody can make a good role model.
4. F; At first, Sierra thinks pediatricians make better role models than nurses.
5. T
6. F; Rachel thinks a role model only needs to affect a few people or even one person.

B

In this activity, Ss complete statements about the video with the correct names.

- **Preview the activity** Go over the instructions. Tell Ss they will complete each statement by choosing the correct name of the person. Have Ss read the statements.
- **Play the video** Have Ss do the activity as they watch the video. Play the video again, if necessary.
- **Check answers** Go over the answers with the class.

Answers

1. Sierra	3. Rachel	5. Rachel	7. Sierra
2. Edgar	4. Tim	6. Edgar	8. Tim

C

In this activity, Ss match quotes to the people who said them.

- **Preview the activity** Go over the instructions. Have Ss read the quotations.
- **Play the video** Have Ss answer from memory first. After Ss have completed the activity, play the video for them to check answers.
- **Check answers** Go over the answers with the class.

Answers
1. E   2. R   3. E   4. S   5. R   6. S   7. T   8. T

After you watch page T-211

A Pair work

In this activity, Ss list and discuss the qualities that make Rachel a good role model.

- **Preview the activity** Go over the instructions. Explain that Ss are to think of qualities that Rachel has that help her be a good role model.
- **Do the activity** Have Ss list the qualities they think make Rachel a role model and then compare their lists. Elicit the qualities from the class and note the most common answers on the board.

B

In this activity, Ss list the qualities of a good role model and say why they are important.

- **Preview the activity** Go over the instructions.
- **Do the activity** Have Ss think of five qualities that make a role model of theirs good and why each quality is important. Help as needed.
- **Follow up** Have Ss share their ideas with the class.

C Writing

In this activity, Ss write about their own role model.

- **Preview the activity** Go over the instructions.
- **Do the activity** Have Ss use their list from part B or other ideas to make a paragraph outline and then expand upon the outline to complete their writing.
- **Follow up** Have some Ss share their writing with the class.

Project

A Write the script

In this activity, Ss write their own video about a role model.

- **Preview the activity** Tell Ss they will work individually to make a video about a role model. Ss will write a script and then act it out on camera. Explain that they will take turns speaking and operating the camera with another individual when filming.
- **Brainstorm** Brainstorm ideas with the class about role models Ss can talk about (e.g., a world leader, a famous movie star, someone they know). Next, talk about how Ss can approach making the video. They might create a biography of the person's life, a description of why the person is their role model, or try to persuade others to choose the person to be their role model as well. They may use their writing from *After you watch* part C as a starting point.
- **Outline** Have Ss make outlines of their scripts. They can use their own ideas or the following structure:

   My role model
   - Introduce the person and give a short overview of why he/she is your role model (e.g., high school art teacher; fair, smart, funny, kind-hearted).
   - Explain why the qualities the person has are important and give examples of how the person embodies them (e.g., "He treated everyone fairly, so students liked him. . . .").
   - Explain how the person affected you (e.g., "I am a great art lover because he helped me appreciate art").
   - Summarize how you feel about the person.

- **Write the script** Have Ss write their scripts using their outlines. Have Ss read through their work and revise as needed.
- **Check the script** Have Ss rehearse their scripts. Help as needed.

B Make and share the video

In this activity, Ss make their own video about a role model.

- **Plan the video** Ss may want to have a classmate operate the camera for them.
- **Make the video** Have Ss make their videos.
- **Share the video** Ss share their videos with the class.
- **Option** Have a group discussion about the videos. Categorize the role models according to type and or qualities. What is the most popular type of role model in the class? What unusual types of role models are presented?

12 JOB INTERVIEW DOS AND DON'TS

Story summary

"Job Interview Dos and Don'ts" covers tips for successful job interviews. In the video, a job applicant named Steve demonstrates the incorrect and correct ways to interview. The video reviews interview basics including dressing appropriately, arriving on time so you can prepare, and staying calm in order to appear confident. It also covers the importance of not "winging it" and pretending to know something about the company. During the interview, the potential employer will know if you did your homework on the company. The video also advises job applicants to prepare themselves for certain standard questions that are likely to be asked during the interview, such as "Why do you feel this is the best job for you?" Steve does well at his interview and, based on his research of the company, his understanding of the job description, and demonstration of initiative by asking intelligent questions, the hiring manager feels he is the right person for the job.

Language summary

Grammar Subject-verb inversion in conditional sentences
Adverb clauses of condition

Vocabulary Prepositions following *work*
Expressions related to success in the workplace

Before you watch page T-212

A

In this activity, Ss list some things people should or shouldn't do in a job interview.

- **Preview the activity** Explain that Ss will watch a video about tips for successful job interviews. Explain that they are to give their best ideas as to things people should and shouldn't do in order to do well in an interview.
- **Do the activity** Have Ss do the activity.

B Pair work

In this activity, pairs discuss their ideas from part A.

- **Preview the activity** Go over the instructions.
- **Do the activity** Have pairs discuss their ideas and list at least two additional tips for doing well in interviews.
- **Follow up** Hold a class discussion about interview tips using Ss' answers from parts A and B as a starting point. Make notes on the board.

While you watch pages T-212–213

A

In this activity, Ss label pictures with the information given at certain points in the video.

- **Preview the activity** Go over the instructions. Have Ss look at the pictures. Explain that Ss will write brief labels for each image.
- **Play the video** Have Ss do the activity while they watch the video. Pause the video as needed to give Ss time to write. Play the video again, if necessary.
- **Check answers** Go over the answers with the class.

Possible answers

1. Don't dress casually. Do wear business attire.
2. Don't exhibit nervous behavior. Do keep calm and still.
3. Don't wing it. Do your homework.
4. Don't say you want the job for the money.

B

In this activity, Ss choose the correct information to complete sentences about the video.

- **Preview the activity** Go over the instructions. Have Ss look at the statements and answer choices. Explain that Ss will complete the sentences with the correct phrases.
- **Play the video** Have Ss do the activity while they watch the video. Play the video again, if necessary.
- **Check answers** Go over the answers with the class.

Answers
1. b   2. b   3. a   4. c   5. b

C

In this activity, Ss take notes to answer questions about the video in their own words.

- **Preview the activity** Go over the instructions. Have Ss read the questions.
- **Play the video** Have Ss answer from memory first. After Ss have completed the activity, play the video for them to check answers. Have Ss compare their answers with a partner.
- **Check answers** Go over the answers with the class.

> **Possible answers**
>
> 1. try to have good posture, keep your hands away from your face and hair, maintain good eye contact
> 2. research the company ahead of time, understand the job description, ask intelligent questions to show interest
> 3. Supposing I hire you, why do you feel this is the best job for you?

After you watch page T-213

A Pair work

In this activity, pairs note the three job interview suggestions they think are most important.

- **Preview the activity** Go over the instructions.
- **Do the activity** Have Ss do the activity. Help as needed.
- **Follow up** Note the top five tips mentioned by Ss on the board. Discuss why Ss feel they are important.

B Pair work

In this activity, pairs prepare for a role play about job interviews.

- **Preview the activity** Go over the instructions. Keep Ss in their pairs. Have pairs prepare questions for a role play. They should choose a job and think of details about a fictional or real company, including at least one standard question.
- **Do the activity** Have pairs do the activity. Help as needed.

C Pair work

In this activity, pairs role-play a job interview.

- **Preview the activity** Go over the instructions. Keep Ss in the same pairs as part B.
- **Do the activity** Have pairs take turns role-playing the parts.
- **Follow up** Have pairs perform their role plays for the class. The class offers helpful feedback for the interviewees.

Project

A Write the script

In this activity, Ss write a script for a mock job interview.

- **Preview the activity** Tell Ss they will work in pairs to make a video role-playing a job interview. Explain that pairs can choose the job and the company (real or fictitious). Pairs should choose a job they are interested in, write a script, and then act it out on camera. They may use their work from *After you watch*.
- **Brainstorm** Review possible jobs and standard interview questions as a class. Give pairs a few minutes to discuss their ideas for jobs, companies, and strategies for the interview: Will each partner play each role once, or will they do the role play only one time? Will both partners do their best, or will one model bad behavior? Will the interview consist of acting only, or will comments be made to the viewer?
- **Outline** Have pairs make an outline of their script. They can use their own ideas or one of the following:

  Idea 1: The standard job interview
  - The players shake hands and introduce themselves.
  - The players ask and respond to the following questions:
    Question 1: Tell me about yourself.
    Question 2: Why are you interested in this job?
    Question 3: How are you the right person for this job?
  - Players shake hands and exit.

  Idea 2: Interview with narration
  - Two Ss role-play an interview, and a third student acts as the narrator describing how the person being interviewed is doing (e.g., "Had Julia not researched the company, she might not have gotten the job offer.").

- **Write the script** Have Ss write their scripts using their outlines. Have Ss read through their work and revise as needed. Have Ss check that at least one of their job interview styles meets the key tips presented in the video.
- **Check the script** Have Ss rehearse their scripts. Help as needed.

B Make and share the video

In this activity, Ss make and share their own video about a mock job interview.

- **Plan the video** Have Ss think about how they will handle using the camera and where they will shoot the video. An additional student may be brought in to film the role plays.
- **Make the video** Have Ss make their videos.
- **Share the video** Ss share their videos with the class.
- **Option** Have a group discussion about the videos. Did each video follow the tips for good interviews? If both partners played the same role, ask the class: Which partner would you give the job to? Why?

Video SCRIPTS

Unit 1 Video

DO OPPOSITES ATTRACT?

Narrator: When it comes to friendship and love, they say opposites attract. You probably recall seeing this a million times in the movies and on TV: The good girl who keeps falling for the rebel. Or the sloppy guy who always seems to end up with the neat roommate. The shy young woman who tends to be drawn to the outgoing boyfriend. Or the laid-back artist who prefers dating the type-A businesswoman.

It makes for good movies. But in real life, do opposites really enjoy being together? And even more important, do they really bring the best out in each other and make for harmonious friendships, relationships, and marriages? The answer is . . . no! Or usually not, according to the experts.

Sometimes opposites really do attract. Social scientists say that we sometimes admire people who complement us, who have skills or traits that we lack, someone who can help us get through life more easily. But more often, in friendships and in love relationships, we look for someone who is just like us. We need to date people who share our values, our outlook on life, and our experiences.

On online dating sites, for example, people often say they expect to date someone who is their opposite. But studies show that the people they decide to go out with usually have personalities that are very similar to their own.

But what if you begin dating someone and then realize they're really opposite from you? Should you give it up? Or can that relationship work? Social scientists might suggest rethinking that relationship, because all those differences that attracted you at first will likely cause you to clash and drift apart later on.

But before you consider saying goodbye to your boyfriend or girlfriend, this may cheer you up: When it comes to opposites, there's a big difference between attitudes and personality.

People can have opposite attitudes about many things – from big things, like religion or politics, to little things, like movies and wall colors – and still continue to have a great relationship.

But people who have opposite personalities? Well, that's a little more difficult, because they're more likely to clash. It's much harder for opposite personalities to empathize with one another, to reconnect after arguments, and to handle all the little compromises that relationships require.

So in the end, the good girl should probably do without her rebel boyfriend and start looking for a nice guy. The laid-back artist should try to run into someone who shares his relaxed energy. And that shy young woman? She may want to be on the lookout for an equally shy young man.

Unit 2 Video

ALL ABOUT FASHION

Narrator: Since the earliest human beings first covered their bodies with woven cloth, fashion has been a big part of the human experience. Clothing has many uses, of course. It's functional: It can protect us or keep us warm. Sometimes our jobs require us to dress a certain way. But what most often determines the way people dress today is self-expression. Our clothing tends to tell the world exactly who we think we are. And our self-expression has seemed to take some pretty interesting turns over the last 3,000 years.

What's fashionable is often determined by the people we look up to: royalty, the wealthy, celebrities, and musicians. For instance, men were encouraged to wear large, powdered wigs after France's King Louis XIV began wearing wigs to cover his bald spot. And the crazy, over-the-top looks of the early seventeenth century were inspired by the extravagant fashions of Queen Elizabeth herself. But in the 1960s, people decided they could create their own styles. And ever since, what's been one of the biggest influences on fashion is youth culture.

So, how are fashions created? Who decides what is classic and what is out of style? Sometimes, what's behind a new fashion trend is comfort. But sometimes it's just the opposite. There are a lot of people who don't mind being uncomfortable – as long as they look good.

Sometimes a fashion starts as a necessity. In the fourteenth century, people started wearing very tall shoes to try to avoid stepping in the mud and animal waste that covered the streets. Some shoes were as high as 30 inches! You know what these shoes eventually turned into? High heels! That heavy eye makeup the Egyptians wore? It helped block the sun's glare and allowed people to see more clearly.

Sometimes fashions have been about making things bigger. Or smaller. Yikes! Sometimes fashion discourages people from showing skin. Other times, it's all about revealing the body.

Often, what's trendy is something that seems to rebel against the established look. Sloppy looks will follow an elegant trend. Flashy might follow conservative. And when frumpy has been chic for a while, keep an eye out for something more formal or dignified to come along. It's no wonder that styles that were cool 30 years ago often come back into fashion as retro looks.

So, what will be stylish tomorrow? Will it be a funky, futuristic look like in the movies? Or more old fashions that have been recycled? Or a quirky combination of the two? What's for sure is that as long as we're permitted to choose what we wear, we will continue to express ourselves through clothing.

Unit 3 Video

PAST AND FUTURE PREDICTIONS

Reporter: Thinking about the future, we often wonder what new technology the next 100 years will bring. But what did the public 100 years ago think the world would be like today? And did any of their predictions come true?

Some of their assumptions were remarkably accurate. For instance, people in 1900 were crazy about photography. They imagined that in the twenty-first century, we'd be able to take a picture on one side of the world, sending the same picture to the other side of the world in less than one hour. Try less than one second! They believed that telephones would be wireless, letting us talk on the phone anywhere. And that using moving pictures, we'd be able to communicate with people all over the world. They thought we would tour the country driving houses on wheels. And that, fed up with doing our own cleaning, we would clean our homes automatically using electric scrubbers.

Other predictions didn't quite work out. They thought that a college education would be free for everyone. Aware of the danger posed by mosquitoes, they believed we would have killed them all. And believing in the power of modern medicine, they were sure that we would have put an end to cancer.

Some predictions sort of came true. They were curious about air travel back then, and lots of people thought we'd have flying cars by now. And while that prediction hasn't come true, there certainly are many people commuting to work in the morning by airplane these days. They thought store purchases would arrive quickly, traveling through tubes connected to every home. Today we get our purchases fast all right, but they usually come on a truck. And they thought students might learn by wires connecting their brains to machines. Well, there's no electricity flowing into the heads of our students, but our classrooms today are certainly "wired."

So what about the future? What do people familiar with how much has changed in the last 100 years think the world will be like in 2100?

Joshua Aquino: One hundred years from now? I think we'll all be just hanging out, letting robots do all the work.

Bao Lam: I imagine we won't get sick anymore, having figured out how to cure all diseases.

Yasmin Fernandes: Before you go to sleep, you tell a computer what you want to dream about that night. And while you're sleeping, it guides your dreams.

Mike Parker: No more cars. I'm sick of cars. We'll all be completely reliant on public transportation.

Patricia Kowalski: Cars will drive themselves.

Shane Smith: Two words: flying cars.

Reporter: It always seems to come back to flying cars, doesn't it? But who knows? Maybe this time, that prediction will come true. For *Channel 4 News*, I'm Gene Mackey.

Unit 4 Video

SUPERSTITIONS AROUND THE WORLD

Narrator: Everybody has their own idea about what brings them luck. Some believe a rabbit's foot can ward off evil. Others feel crossing their fingers improves their luck. Many agree that putting a *maneki-neko* in the window brings good luck. Some people say that finding a four-leaf clover is a good omen. Every culture has its own idea of what is lucky. But where do these ideas come from?

In many countries, it's believed that the number 13 is very unlucky. Believe it or not, people are so spooked by it that many tall buildings often skip the thirteenth floor. But why? What's so bad about the number 13? Historians explain that fear of the number 13 may come from a story in Norse mythology. It is claimed that Loki, the god of evil, was the thirteenth guest at a banquet of the gods when he caused a tragedy. Or it may come from the story of the Last Supper, where the Bible reports that Judas Iscariot, the man who betrayed Jesus, was the thirteenth guest. Or it may have come from ancient Persians, who believed that each of the 12 signs of the zodiac would rule the world for a period of one thousand years and that the sky would collapse in the thirteenth period.

Of course, 13 isn't the only unlucky number in the world. In some countries in Asia, it is assumed that the number 4 is very unlucky because the word for four in Chinese sounds very much like the word for death. A lot of superstitions have to do with death – or rather with avoiding it. In Japan, it's considered very unlucky to leave your chopsticks standing straight up in a bowl of rice because this is a traditional part of a Japanese funeral.

Some superstitions have practical origins. If you're on a boat in Hawaii, and your captain asks you to dump your bananas overboard as you're leaving shore so as not to bring bad luck, don't laugh. This superstition is assumed to have developed as a way to protect against the rats, spiders, and snakes that stow away in the bananas and that could infest the ship.

Perhaps you're one of those people who finds all this talk of superstition dubious and far-fetched. You walk under ladders without fear. You break mirrors and don't worry. You feel that you can live a life free from superstition. Well, all I can say is . . . good luck!

Unit 5 Video

MEET THE DIRECTOR

Director: The name of my movie is *Rot*. And essentially it's the story of a man who is dying of this flesh-eating disease, who, uh, before he dies, goes out to this cabin to be alone and to reflect on his life and his . . . his past mistakes and his regrets.

The idea of the movie was just to . . . to make the most moving, engrossing story I could. I wanted it to be touching. I wanted people to really connect with the story and the characters. And basically, it's a story of lost love – very universal themes that, uh, that I feel have been done before, but I wanted to do them in a more original way that they weren't as formulaic and as clichéd as stuff that's already been done, so, you know, I wanted to kind of give a fresh take on the same material.

It started more as just ideas that I've had. Uh, some of them go back over a year ago – just like a small, little idea that I thought was good, but not great, to actually pursue. But I knew it was a decent idea, so I held on to it, and then other ideas came. And finally, one day it just connected, you know, all the ideas.

The idea of a flesh-eating disease came about, and I thought that was a great metaphor for just what's going on with him, you know, through this . . . this really dark time in his life. And when I started telling people about it, they thought that it was such a good idea that I really had no choice but to make the movie, because everyone knew that it was . . . it was a really powerful idea, really moving.

I've just always . . . I've always wanted to direct, and this was the idea that I felt was the best and actually worth doing. I started scouting locations, talking to people, trying to raise money – doing all these things as I was still writing the movie, so I was still in the process of writing it. So I would give it to people, and at this point it probably wasn't that good because I was just, like . . . the first draft, and . . . like, alright, here, you know, here's the idea. And slowly it would form and become more of a tighter movie, more compact, and . . . and much better.

Obviously studios aren't going to give me money to go make a movie. An up-and-coming director – it's just not going to happen.

The first part of *Rot* I, uh, funded myself with all my money. And unfortunately, when we got back in to complete it, I didn't have any more money, so I had to turn to crowdfunding to raise the rest of it. And I thought that it was just going to be family and friends. But surprisingly, a lot of people did donate to the movie, that just came across it and . . . and just thought it looked cool. They liked the idea, and they believed in it. And that's the only reason that they donated their money.

So many people did believe in the idea that it was easy getting help from so many different people. Everyone just kind of jumped on board and really connected with the idea. And people really believed in it, and they believed in me.

It used to be such an expensive proposition to make a movie that it was just impossible for . . . for up-and-coming filmmakers like myself. But now, uh, through crowdfunding, it's really, uh, it's really made it easier for people that really have a strong idea to get in there and raise money, uh, and get people to believe in the project.

I want to put the movie in as many film festivals as possible. I want to use it as a calling card almost, so from there I can get my next movie made. You know, I want as many people to see this movie as possible. Now, obviously, I know that might not be the case. It might take some time to get it going. There's so many filmmakers out there right now that it's, it's really hard to get your movie noticed. But I feel that with the right idea and the right story, there's no reason why you can't do it.

Unit 6 Video

HILLARY REYNOLDS BAND

Hillary: Well, we are the Hillary Reynolds Band, and we are Boston based. We're from all different parts of the country and met in Berkelee College of Music. Uh, and we've been making music together now for a couple of years.

Trevor: We're often asked to describe our music, uh, you know, in a word or a couple of words. And I suppose the easiest way to describe it would be either indie-folk or folk-pop. And what we try to do is combine catchy pop melodies, hooks, that sort of thing, with acoustic folky instruments. We try to create soothing, acoustic textures on which to put pop melodies and pop songwriting. So we have all sorts of acoustic instruments: I play the cello, Jeff plays ukulele, Hillary will play the mandolin, Chris plays acoustic upright bass. Um, so we try to use those kinds of instruments and those kinds of sounds and textures to get across pop songwriting.

Hillary: Most signed artists have a whole team of people that are dedicated to making the "machine" work. And we don't have that luxury at this point. And so we'll book our own tour; we'll book our own studio time; we'll write our own songs; we'll arrange them ourselves; and upcoming for our . . . our next album, we'll be producing as well.

Our process for writing songs is very diverse. And sometimes I will approach the band with a full song that's just needing some arrangements and needs a top and tail. Uh, there are other times where we will collaborate a hundred percent together, and we'll start off with nothing and then leave a rehearsal, leave a session with everything. Uh, and, so, between the two, there's a lot of space for variation. And that is what makes our songwriting so complex and so . . . so great.

Trevor: You know, we sort of play cover songs as a way to get people's attention, and as a way to . . . people are interested because they hear music they know. And then once they're listening to us and what we have to offer, it . . . they're in a better space to hear our original songs. And I think the more we play covers, the more they are willing to give our original songs a chance.

Jeff: In the past, we would make a lot of cold calls because we wouldn't have a whole lot of contacts around the country with whom to book engagements and all these things. So these days, it's the case that people will contact us instead, because we have then made a name for ourselves, having been around for so long. The more, um, gigs you play and the bigger your résumé is, the easier it then becomes to get more high-profile gigs and work your way up that ladder.

Hillary: Our fans reach out to us through all of the mediums of social media and all those platforms. And it's a really overwhelmingly awesome feeling to get a message from somebody who's reaching out, telling accounts of how a song has impacted them, helped them get through a tough time, or, you know, made them feel good. And we welcome all of that.

Trevor: Those are the best kinds of feedback.

Hillary: Those are the best. Yeah.

Trevor: Uh, it takes a lot of hard work to be successful in the music business. And the harder you work, the better your chances of becoming successful at what you love to do. And passion is very important. You have to love it. If you love it, it's easy to work hard.

Well, in terms of what we want for ourselves going forward . . . In the past, people would define success, or bands would define success, by signing with a major label, becoming really famous, mainstream radio. But we're really happy if we can make music for our lives and make music as friends and play our music for people. Um, so, I think, you know, how we want to come across is just as a group of friends making music together and pouring our lives and pouring our hearts into songs. And, hopefully, that comes across to the listeners and, hopefully, people can listen to our music and feel like they know us as people.

Unit 7 Video

CHANGING GENDER ROLES

Narrator: Which of these men would you say are more manly? And which of these women look as if they are more feminine? Your answer may reveal your opinion of the gender roles that define proper behavior and occupations for men and women.

For many centuries, gender roles were pretty simple and somewhat similar. In everyday life, men and women shared the work on the farm and in businesses that were run from the home.

Then, the Industrial Revolution helped bring about a pretty big change. There were new factories that needed workers, and the workplace became separate from the home. Men left the home to take jobs. Before long, people behaved as though it were absolutely natural for men to work and for women to stay home with the kids.

But then, in the twentieth century, some 200 years after the Industrial Revolution, gender roles went through another big change. When men went off to fight in World War I and World War II, women filled in at factories, offices, and stores. Many women loved these new opportunities. They felt as if they had been freed from the home and didn't want to return to homemaking when the war was over, acting as though nothing had changed. Many sought education in fields dominated by men.

Soon, they were becoming doctors, business leaders, and even heads of state. Some men who welcomed this change decided they wanted to be nurses, teachers, secretaries, and receptionists. More men started staying home with the children.

But there were people who resisted this change. Even today, some still look down on women with children who work outside the home. In many fields, women who perform the same job as men are paid less. They feel as though their employers don't value them as much. Men whose jobs are considered feminine often feel as if society doesn't take them seriously. More men hold jobs as nurses today than ever before, but some people who can't cope with these changes behave as though this is a strange job for a man to want.

And what happens next? No one knows. Perhaps children who are growing up today will be able to choose to be anything they want. Maybe there will be equal numbers of men and women who are presidents and teachers, doctors and nurses, police officers and hairstylists.

Or maybe everything will just reverse. All the roles women once held will belong to men. Women will do the things that men used to do. Whatever happens, one thing is certain: Everything is bound to change all over again.

Unit 8 Video

THE HISTORY OF ADVERTISING

Narrator: Advertising, it seems, is everywhere. Almost anywhere we go and everywhere we look, we're surrounded by ads offering us deals, suggesting products to us, and insisting we give them our attention. By some estimates, with online ads, we may see thousands of ads each day! But when did this all begin? And how did it get so crazy?

The history of advertising is really the history of communication. Every time a new technology is invented that allows people to communicate with each other, advertisers use it to sell more stuff to their customers.

It all began thousands of years ago; we don't really know when. We do know that around 2000 BCE, Egyptians were announcing messages to the public by carving on stone and wooden tablets. Heh, making a typo back then could really ruin a person's day!

Advertising as we know it today started with the invention of the printing press in the 1400s. That led to the rise of newspapers and right along with it – drumroll, please – newspaper advertisements!

The first classified ads appeared in 1631, and the world's first magazine, the *Tatler*, was published in England in 1709. Ever since, newspaper and magazine ads have recommended everything from coats to carriages to hair care products to their readers.

Mail services have been delivering letters to people for thousands of years. But by the late 1800s, modern-day efficiency meant that it cost a sender a lot less to mail something. Companies like Montgomery Ward and Sears & Roebuck began sending postcards and catalogs as advertisements directly to customers – and direct marketing was born. Now you know who to say thanks to for that mailbox full of junk mail!

The radio came along in 1921, and it wasn't long until radio hosts were mentioning products on the air.

The automobile became widespread in the early twentieth century, and soon drivers touring the countryside were greeted by billboards telling them where to buy gas for the car.

The television was invented in 1927, and the first television commercial debuted in 1941, entertaining viewers and providing advertisers with one of the most effective forms of advertising ever created. And it was only another 30 years before that other great invention was born: the infomercial.

Then cell phones became popular in the 80s; the World Wide Web, or the Internet, in the 90s; and Facebook, Twitter, and YouTube in the twenty-first century. With each new technology, there were new kinds of ads demanding that we pay attention.

And tomorrow? Who knows? Perhaps advertisers will propose that advertisements be broadcast in our dreams, or get messages to us in our contact lenses, or show us ads on places like the moon. One thing is for sure – as long as there are things to sell and ways to communicate, advertisers will find ways to advertise.

Unit 9 Video

HUMANS AND ANIMALS

Narrator: Since the beginning of civilization, wherever you found humans, you'd find animals, as well. We are inextricably linked to animals. When we have wanted companions, we have domesticated animals like dogs and cats. When we have needed transportation, horses and donkeys, elephants and camels, and even dogs have taken us wherever we wanted to go. When we have needed help in the fields, our cattle and oxen have pulled whatever we needed them to pull. To help us survive, animals have given us milk, eggs, and meat when we needed them.

Whatever it is that draws us to animals, the connection is a deep one. Whenever the earliest humans depicted their gods, it was usually as an animal or a creature part human, part animal. They saw animals when they looked to the skies, where they believed their gods lived. And they saw animals when they looked at other human beings.

Today, thousands of years later, whenever we want to describe the essence of a person, we usually compare them to animals. The descriptions may change from culture to culture, but in English, when we think of an evil person, we think of a snake. Whoever is courageous gets named a lion. A vain person may be called a peacock, and a scared person we liken to a chicken.

Over the years, we've developed quite a lot of ways to describe people using animals. We talk about people who are as wise as an owl. An industrious person is as busy as a bee. Whoever is kind is referred to as gentle as a lamb. When someone looks suspicious, we may say that they're as sly as a fox. Blind as a bat is what we say about whoever has terrible eyesight. We know people who are hairy as a gorilla or as hungry as a horse. Whenever we meet a really fun-loving child, we call them playful as a kitten. When we're frustrated with the pace someone is moving at, we'll call them as slow as a snail.

And while we frequently see animal behavior in our fellow human beings, we see human behavior in animals almost constantly. Since the time of Aesop's fables in the sixth century BCE, we have been telling stories that attribute human qualities to animals.

Today, humanlike animals fill our storybooks, our cartoons, our movies, and our stores. Whatever would we do without the animal world?

Unit 10 Video

TIPS FOR BETTER PRESENTATIONS

Prof. Lundgren: Over the years, a lot of presentations in my classroom have been aided by slideshows. Unfortunately, plenty of time has been spent watching poor slideshows as well. Here is some of the best advice you'll ever get on how to create good slides and give better presentations. Audiences are filled with dread every time someone uses a slideshow because plenty of presentations are incredibly boring.

Tyler: To begin, I'll talk about how the universe was formed 13 billion years ago. Next, I'm going to talk about how our solar system was being developed when the universe was cooling 9 billion years later. In conclusion, I'll talk about how the sun will be transformed into a red giant.

Prof. Lundgren: To keep it interesting, some people try to tell a story.

Laura: It's believed that 13.7 billion years ago, our universe was started with the Big Bang.

Prof. Lundgren: Don't read your slides. No one wants to hear a presentation read word for word.

Tyler: Some scientists believe that all matter is going to be pulled back together in the Big Crunch.

Prof. Lundgren: Instead, talk about the subject as if you were having a conversation.

Laura: Fractions of a second later, the universe was being pushed apart by superforces.

Prof. Lundgren: Most people make the mistake of looking at the screen the whole time.

Tyler: In addition, a majority of scientists believe galaxies are still being propelled apart, perhaps by a force called dark energy.

Prof. Lundgren: Remember: You're the star of your presentation, not your slides. You're succeeding if everyone wants to watch you, not your slides.

Laura: 4.6 billion years ago, the sun and our solar system were born from something called a molecular cloud.

Prof. Lundgren: When it comes to text, less is more. Don't use paragraphs, and definitely don't put everything you want to say on the screen.

Tyler: The universe is filled with billions of galaxies. Each galaxy may be made up of millions to trillions of stars.

Prof. Lundgren: Instead, keep it light. Each slide needs only a few words, and every word counts. Remember: Bullet points are read more easily than paragraphs.

Laura: 3.6 billion years ago, the earliest forms of life were developing.

Prof. Lundgren: Your text must be read by everyone in the room. If your font is too small, it won't be recognized by anyone who sits at the back.

Tyler: Our own galaxy, the Milky Way, was shaped into a large spiral.

Prof. Lundgren: Dark text on a light background is the best.

Laura: Likewise, we often wonder, could life have formed on any other planets?

Prof. Lundgren: Points to be covered should be posted one at a time. Otherwise, your later points will be read by the audience while you're still talking about the earlier ones, and they'll get ahead of you.

In conclusion, if you have a handout, it should be handed out at the end so your audience won't read ahead while you're talking. If you let your audience know at the start that you'll hand out the presentation at the end, anyone who wants to take notes won't feel they have to write during the whole presentation.

Laura: To sum it up, I just wanted to say thanks for listening.

Prof. Lundgren: And that's it. Now, I expect to be presented with some really good slideshows this semester. See you in class.

Unit 11 Video

ROLE MODELS

Rachel: In 2012, for a class project, I started a campaign to create more role models in the world. I spent every Saturday asking people to think of themselves as a role model.

* * *

Rachel: Hi there!

Sharon: Hi.

Edgar: Hi. What's going on?

Rachel: I'm talking to people about role models. Do you have a role model?

Edgar: Definitely. My high school baseball coach. He was great!

Rachel: What was he like?

Edgar: A much-loved guy. He was the hard-driving type, for sure, but also the most kind-hearted man you'd ever want to meet. He made you want to work harder to live up to his expectations, you know.

Rachel: And are you anybody's role model?

Edgar: Me? No. Definitely not. No. No, I'm not the role model type. Too hot-headed, you know.

Rachel: See, I think anybody can be the role model type. It's not about being the most awe-inspiring person or even a near-perfect person. It's just about committing to act in ways that someone else can look to follow.

Edgar: Huh, I'm an unemployed construction worker. Who's going to want to take after me?

Sharon: Oh, come on. You're too self-critical. He is a very warm-hearted guy. All the kids in the neighborhood love him. He is the most easygoing person when it comes to kids.

Edgar: What is this? You're siding with her?

Sharon: I'm just saying . . . Maybe you should be a little league baseball coach this year. It'll help you get through the time you're not working.

Rachel: There you go!

Edgar: A little league baseball coach is a role model?

Rachel: Sure! You just said your high school coach was your role model. What do you say?

Edgar: Sure. I'll do it.

Rachel: That's great. Would you like to sign our pledge sheet?

* * *

Sierra: Me? A role model? I don't think so.

Rachel: Anybody can be a role model to somebody. You don't have to be some highly acclaimed leader or a well-known celebrity. What do you do?

Sierra: I'm a nurse.

Rachel: What a great job! So, who could you be a role model to? Maybe your patients?

Sierra: But I'm not, like, a surgeon or a pediatrician. I just check on patients and give them medication. I help them get around.

Rachel: But I'll bet the way you interact with them could have far-reaching effects on their lives. You look after a lot of sick people, right?

Sierra: Every day.

Rachel: And how do you react? Do you get all sad-faced around them?

Sierra: No. I try to always be the most positive-thinking person in the room. I feel like you can't get better if you're always feeling down.

Rachel: That's a great thing to model! Helping people choose to have a positive attitude about a life-changing illness.

Sierra: That's very thought provoking.

Rachel: So, can I count on you to keep thinking of yourself as a role model?

Sierra: OK.

* * *

Tim: Look, when you say "role model," I think of someone who's widely respected, like Nelson Mandela. He's this soft-spoken leader who confronted injustice and got an entire nation to face up to their history and be more open-minded. That's a role model.

Rachel: So he's a role model for everyone in the world. I'm just asking you to be a role model for one person. Or 10. Or 50.

Tim: Look, I'm not against it, but I'm a game designer. I sit in front of a screen all day. The closest I get to injustice is cyberbullying.

Rachel: There you go!

Tim: What?

Rachel: Maybe you could create a game that would help stop cyberbullying or teach kids how to treat each other better online. I don't know.

Tim: Yeah. You might be onto something. I sort of like that – sort of an online role model for gamers. But don't you actually have to meet people to be a role model?

Rachel: Did you ever meet Nelson Mandela?

Tim: Good point. OK, I'll do it.

Rachel: Great! Why don't you sign our pledge.

Tim: Alright.

Rachel: In three months, I got 387 people to commit to being a role model for someone else. Who will you be a role model for?

Unit 12 Video

JOB INTERVIEW DOS AND DON'TS

Narrator: Meet Steve, a recent college graduate who just landed his first job. Steve got a great education, but had he not learned to interview well, he might still be looking for work. Here are the job interview dos and don'ts that helped Steve get his first offer.

The way you dress for the interview says a lot about how seriously you take the job. Assuming you're not interviewing to play soccer or to be a lifeguard, business attire is always the best choice.

Had Steve come late for his interview, he might never have gotten the job.

Steve: Hi. Uh, sorry, uh, I have a meeting with Ms. Bayliss. I'm really sorry.

Narrator: Arriving early lets you stay calm and gives you time to prepare should you want to go over your notes.

Steve: Hi, I'm Stephen Jones. I'm a little early.

Receptionist: Great. Ms. Bayliss will be with you shortly.

Narrator: Job interviews are stressful. And when we're nervous, our bodies do some pretty funny things, whether or not we're aware of it.

Had Steve not been able to be still and calm, he wouldn't have seemed so confident. In the interview, try to have good posture, keep your hands away from your face and hair, and maintain good eye contact. It will help you seem confident, whether or not you actually feel that way.

Ms. Bayliss: So, Mr. Jones, we should talk about you, assuming you know something about us and what this job entails.

Steve: Uh, well, um, I know your company is Acme Design, so obviously you design "acmes," right? And provided I'm not mistaken, you're looking for a sales guy?

Ms. Bayliss: Marketing, actually. There's a difference.

Narrator: Always research the company ahead of time.

Steve: I know Acme Design is a leader in creating custom software for insurance agencies.

Narrator: Understand the job description, provided there is one.

Steve: You're hiring for an entry-level position to assist the marketing director.

Narrator: And ask intelligent questions that show your interest in the company.

Steve: I notice you don't currently market your products to companies outside your region. I'd be very interested to work on that, assuming that's a direction in which you'd like to go.

Narrator: Had Steve not shown so much initiative, he might not have been the boss's first choice. The interviewer will likely ask you a few standard questions like . . .

Ms. Bayliss: Supposing I hire you, why do you feel this is the best job for you?

Steve: Well . . . Um . . . Let's see . . . Well, I'm unemployed. So I'm looking for a job that offers a high salary and great benefits.

I'm really interested in marketing in the software industry, and Acme seems like a company with a lot of opportunity for advancement, provided you think I'm the right person for the job.

Narrator: Following these tips won't guarantee you the job. But provided that you're qualified, they will give you the best chance for getting the job you want – just like Steve.

Student's Book Credits

Illustration credits

Jo Goodberry: 12, 103
Paul Hostetler: 22, 23, 64, 101
Kim Johnson: 3, 26, 36, 65
Dan McGeehan: 41, 56, 84
Rob Schuster: 72, 87
Koren Shadmi: 9, 17, 53, 83
James Yamasaki: 28, 86

Photography credits

Back cover: (*clockwise from top center*) ©Leszek Bogdewicz/Shutterstock, ©Wavebreak Media/Thinkstock, ©Blend Images/Alamy, ©limpido/Shutterstock; **2** ©George Doyle/Thinkstock; **5** ©Davide Mazzoran/Thinkstock; **6** (*left to right*) ©Corbis/SupersStock, ©Jeff Greenberg/Alamy, ©Blend Images/Alamy; **8** ©Corbis/SuperStock; **10** (*top to bottom*) ©Coprid/Shutterstock, ©Neamov/Shutterstock, ©Barghest/Shutterstock, ©robert_s/Shutterstock, ©mama_mia/Shutterstock; **11** ©Ira Berger/Alamy; **13** ©alexnika/Thinkstock; **14** ©Fuse/Thinkstock; **15** ©Cultura Limited/SuperStock; **16** (*clockwise from top left*) ©Dimitrios Kambouris/Getty Images, ©Alberto E. Rodriguez/Getty Images, ©Jeffrey Mayer/WireImage/Getty Images, ©Vittorio Zunino Celotto/Getty Images; **18** (*left to right*) ©Krzysztof Gawor/Getty Images, ©Science Photo Library – SCIEPRO/Getty Images, ©Eric Isselée/Thinkstock; **19** ©EVERETT KENNEDY BROWN/epa/Corbis; **20** ©Beyond/SuperStock; **21** ©Gilles Podevins/Science Photo Library/Corbis; **24** ©Europics/Newscom; **25** ©Newspix/Getty Images; **27** (*clockwise from top left*) ©Christin Gilbert/agefotostock/SuperStock, ©al_ter/Thinkstock, ©Franck Boston/Thinkstock, ©GregC/Thinkstock, ©Nathan Allred/Thinkstock, ©Comstock/Thinkstock; **29** ©Photimageon/Alamy; **31** (*top to bottom*) ©Stockbyte/Thinkstock, ©Mykola Velychko/Thinkstock, ©Jupiterimages/Thinkstock, ©Valeriy Lebedev/Thinkstock; **32** (*clockwise from top left*) ©Jupiterimages/Thinkstock, ©Maksim Kabakou/Thinkstock, ©Elnur Amikishiyev/Thinkstock, ©Paul Poplis/Getty Images, ©guy harrop/Alamy; **33** ©Eric Staller/Splash News/Newscom; **34** ©GERARD CERLES/Getty Images; **35** ©MANAN VATSYAYANA/Getty Images; **38** ©I love images/SuperStock; **39** ©AF archive/Alamy; **42** ©Digital Vision/Thinkstock; **43** (*top to bottom*) ©courtesy of One Day on Earth, ©courtesy of One Day on Earth, ©courtesy of One Day on Earth; **44** ©OJO Images/SuperStock; **45** ©RichardBaker/Alamy; **46** ©Fernando Garcia-Murga/AgeFotostock; **47** (*left to right*) ©Fox Photos/Getty Images, ©Dave J Hogan/Getty Images; **48** (*left to right*) ©Kevin Winter/Getty Images, ©John Shearer/Getty Images, ©Chris McGrath/Getty Images; **49** ©Stanislav Tiplyashin/Thinkstock; **50** ©Jack Hollingsworth/Thinkstock; **51** ©Red Box Films/ZUMA Press/Newscom; **52** ©CBS/Getty Images; **54** ©Exactostock/SuperStock; **57** ©Wavebreakmedia Ltd/Thinkstock; **58** (*left to right*) ©Jose Luis Pelaez Inc/Blend Images/Alamy, ©Image Source/Alamy, ©David Litschel/Alamy; **59** ©Sergey Mikhailov/Thinkstock; **62** (*clockwise from top left*) ©Iryna Rasko/Shutterstock, ©Nastco/Thinkstock, ©Jupiterimages/Thinkstock, ©Ilya Shapovalov/Shutterstock; **63** ©james turner/Alamy; **66** (*left to right*) ©Art Directors & TRIP/Alamy, ©Raine Vara/Alamy, ©Raymond Boyd/Getty Images; **67** ©John Wynn/Thinkstock; **69** ©Photos 12/Alamy; **70** (*clockwise from top left*) ©Presselect/Alamy, ©Jean-Louis Atlan/Corbis, ©Rick Friedman/Corbis, ©Paris Match/Getty Images; **71** ©Photo by Adam Scull/Newscom; **73** ©Image Source/Getty Images; **74** ©Brad Perks Lightscapes/Alamy; **75** ©Getty Images/Agefotostock; **76** ©David De Lossy/Thinkstock; **77** ©STAN HONDA/Getty Images; **78** (*left to right*) ©Purestock/Thinkstock, ©Flirt/SuperStock, ©iStock/Thinkstock; **79** (*left to right*) ©iStock Collection/Thinkstock, ©Mitchell Kranz/Shutterstock, ©Fuse/Thinkstock; **80** (*left to right*) ©Tim Mosenfelder/Getty Image News/Getty Images, ©AFP/Getty Images; **82** ©Khakimullin Aleksandr/Shutterstock; **85** ©Tom Briglia/Getty Images; **88** (*left to right*) ©Elliot & Fry/Getty Images, ©Nick Harvey/WireImage/Getty Images, ©Michael Tran/FilmMagic/Getty Images; **90** (*clockwise from top left*) ©Christian Alminana/WireImage/Getty Images, ©L. Busacca/WireImage/Getty Images, ©Valerie Macon/Getty Images, ©Michael Kovac/WireImage/Getty Images, ©John Parra/WireImage/Getty Images; **91** ©Ian Gavan/Getty Images; **92** (*top to bottom*) ©iStock Collection/Thinkstock, ©iStock Collection/Thinkstock, ©iStock Collection/Thinkstock, ©Blend Images/Shutterstock, ©Siri Stafford/Thinkstock, ©gulfimages/SuperStock; **93** ©Jacek Sopotnicki/Thinkstock; **94** ©itanistock/Alamy; **95** ©VMAA/ZOB WENN Photos/Newscom; **96** (*clockwise from top right*) ©Bryan Smith/ZUMAPRESS/Newscom, ©YOSHIKAZU TSUNO/AFP/Getty Images/Newscom, ©Andrew Hasson/Photoshot/Getty Images; **100** ©Comstock Images/Thinkstock; **102** ©mediaphotos/Thinkstock; **105** (*left to right*) ©Jacob Wackerhausen/Thinkstock, ©Suprijono Suharjoto/Thinkstock, ©Chace & Smith Photography/Fuse Collection/Thinkstock; **131** ©mangostock/Thinkstock; **133** ©Mark A Schneider/Getty Images; **135** ©Blend Images/SuperStock; **136** ©George Doyle/Thinkstock; **138** ©William Curch – Summit42.com/Getty Images; **140** ©Agefotostock/SuperStock

Text credits

The authors and publishers acknowledge the following sources of copyright material and are grateful for the permissions granted. While every effort has been made, it has not always been possible to identify the sources of all the material used, or to trace all copyright holders. If any omissions are brought to our notice, we will be happy to include the appropriate acknowledgments on reprinting.

9 Adapted from "How Social Media 'Friends' Translate Into Real-Life Friendships" by Terri Thornton, *Mediashift*, July 13, 2011. Reproduced with permission of Mediashift, PBS; **16** Adapted from "Judging Faces Comes Naturally" by Jules Crittenden, *Boston Herald*, September 7, 1997. Reproduced with permission of the Boston Herald; **17** Adapted from "Overcoming a Bad First Impression" by Susan Fee, Professional Clinical Counselor, www.susanfee.com. Reproduced with permission of Susan Fee; **25** Adapted from "Family: I Unplugged My Kids" by Melissa McClements, *The Guardian*, January 1, 2011. Copyright © Guardian News & Media Ltd 2011; **35** Adapted from "Do Good-luck Charms Really Work in Competitions?" by Alex Hutchinson, *The Globe and Mail*, October 18, 2010. Reproduced with permission of Alex Hutchinson; **43** Adapted from "'One Day On Earth' Debuts Worldwide, Offers Time Capsule Of Our Lives" by Mark Johanson, *International Business Times*, April 21, 2012. Reproduced with permission of International Business Times; **51** Adapted from "Sixto Rodriguez: On the Trail of the Dylan of Detroit" by David Gritten, *The Telegraph*, June 14, 2012. Copyright © Telegraph Media Group Limited 2012; **61** Adapted from "Living the Simple Life – and Loving It" by Julia Duin, *The Washington Times*, January 5, 1996. Copyright © 1996 The Washington Times LLC. This reprint does not constitute or imply any endorsement or sponsorship of any product, service, company or organization. License # 37237; **69** Adapted from "Word-of-Mouth Marketing: We All Want to Keep Up with the Joneses" by Martin Lindstrom, www.martinlindstrom.com, September 21, 2011. Reproduced with permission of Martin Lindstrom; **77** From "A Summer Job That Promises Nature Walks for Pay" by Cara Buckley, *The New York Times*, August 13, 2008. Copyright © 2008 The New York Times. All rights reserved. Used by permission and protected by the Copyright Laws of the United States. The printing, copying, redistribution, or retransmission of this Content without express written permission is prohibited; **80** Adapted from *Schaum's Quick Guide to Great Presentation Skills* by Melody Templeton and Suzanne Sparks Fitzgerald, published by McGraw-Hill, 1999. Copyright © 1999 by the McGraw-Hill Companies, Inc.; **87** Adapted from "Slang Abroad" by Ben Falk, *The Daily Colonial*, April 1, 2006. Reproduced with permission; **95** Adapted from "Leading Questions" by Alison Benjamin, *The Guardian*, March 28, 2007. Copyright © Guardian News & Media Ltd 2007; **103** Adapted from *Job Savvy: How to Be a Success at Work Fifth Edition* by LaVerne L. Ludden, published by JIST Publishing, 2012. Reproduced with permission of JIST Publishing.

Answers

Page 32, Exercise 1B: Story 2 is false.
Page 34, Exercise 5B: They are all hoaxes.
Page 84, Exercise 2A: before, Are you OK?, See you later, excellent, great, tonight

Video Activity Worksheets Credits

Video credits
Video screen grabs courtesy of Steadman Productions, Boston, MA: 198, 201, 208, 210, 211, 212

Photography credits
190 (*left to right*) ©YuriyZhuravov/Shutterstock, Inc., ©pav197lin/Shutterstock, Inc., ©Inna Astakhova/Shutterstock, Inc., ©Hasloo Group Production Studio/Shutterstock, Inc.; **191** ©altafulla/Shutterstock, Inc.; **192** (*top left to right*) ©Africa Studio/Shutterstock, Inc., ©S_L/Shutterstock, Inc., ©gpointstudio/Shutterstock, Inc., ©3355m/Shutterstock, Inc., (*bottom left to right*) ©elvistudio/Shutterstock, Inc., ©Geo Martinez/Shutterstock, Inc., ©AlexAnnaButs/Shutterstock, Inc., ©Elisanth/Shutterstock, Inc.; **193** ©PHOTOCREO Michal Bednarek/Shutterstock, Inc.; **195** ©Jean Marc Cote/Wikipedia Commons; **197** ©Everett Collection/Shutterstock, Inc.; **202** (*top to bottom*) ©Adriaen van Ostade/Wikipedia Commons, ©Library of Congress/Wikipedia Commons, ©Unknown/Wikipedia Commons, ©Williams/Wikipedia Commons, ©benjikat/Shutterstock, Inc.; **203** ©Hotelfoxtrot/Shutterstock, Inc.; **205** (*top left to right*) ©eFOOTAGE.com, ©Oleg Znamenskiy/Shutterstock, Inc., ©James Steidl/Shutterstock, Inc., (*bottom*) ©Boguc/Shutterstock, Inc.; **206** (*top to bottom*) ©alex83/Shutterstock, Inc., ©iofoto/Shutterstock, Inc., ©Vishnevskiy Vasily/Shutterstock, Inc., ©OlegD/Shutterstock, Inc., ©Matthew Cole/Shutterstock, Inc.; **207** ©Mykhaylo Palinchak/Shutterstock, Inc.

Teacher's Edition Credits

Photography credits

xv ©Leszek Bogdewicz/Shutterstock; **xvii** ©Goodluz/Shutterstock, (*insert*) ©Noel Powell/Shutterstock; **xx** (*left*) ©Pananche Productions/Oxford Scientific Video/Getty Images, (*right*) ©Holger Mette/Shutterstock, (*center*) ©Boguc/Shutterstock; **xxii** ©Blend Images/Alamy